girls — on boredom, rebellion, and being in-between

HANNIBAL

MOMU — FASHION MUSEUM ANTWERP

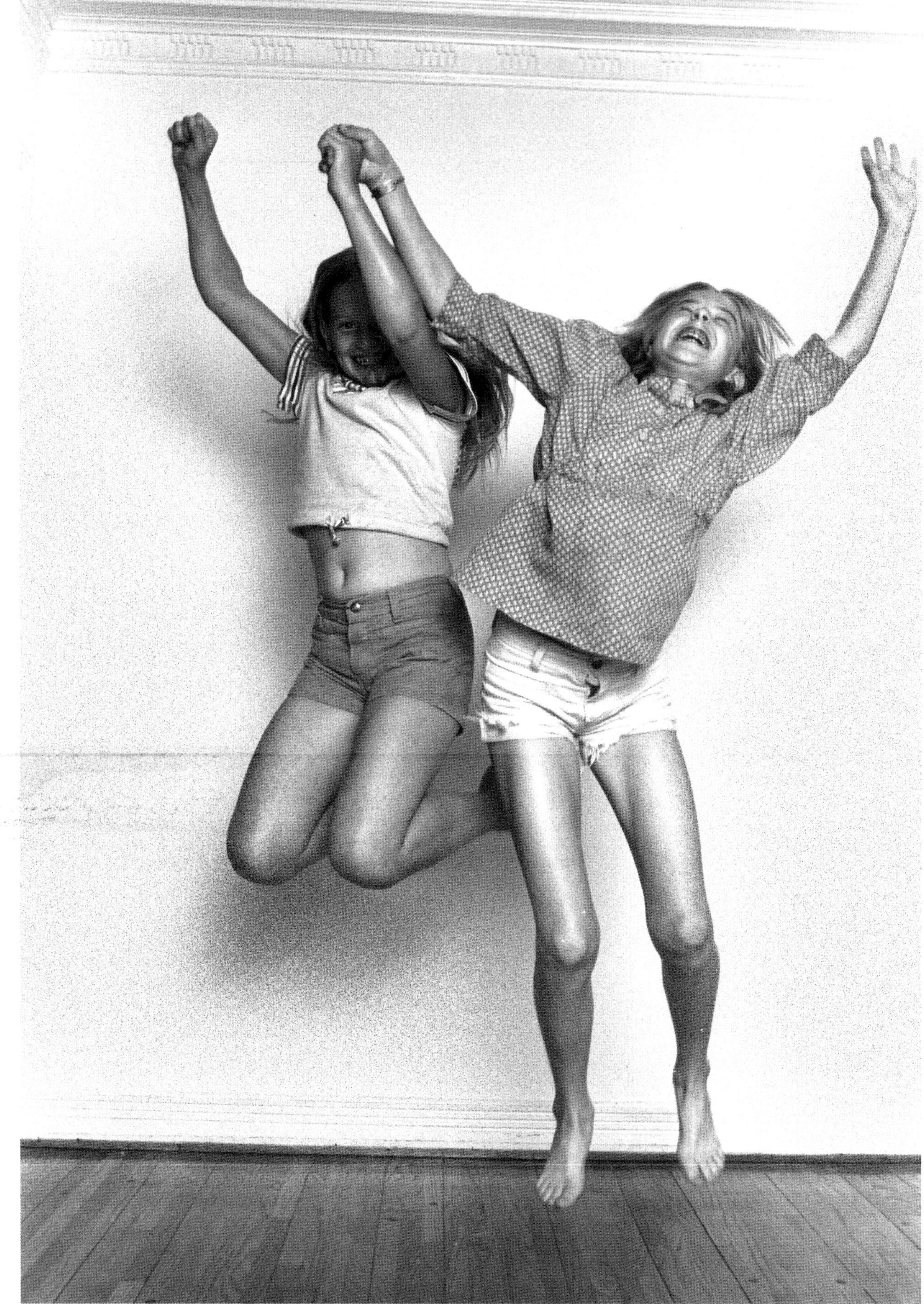

contents

Jim Britt
Sisters, 1976

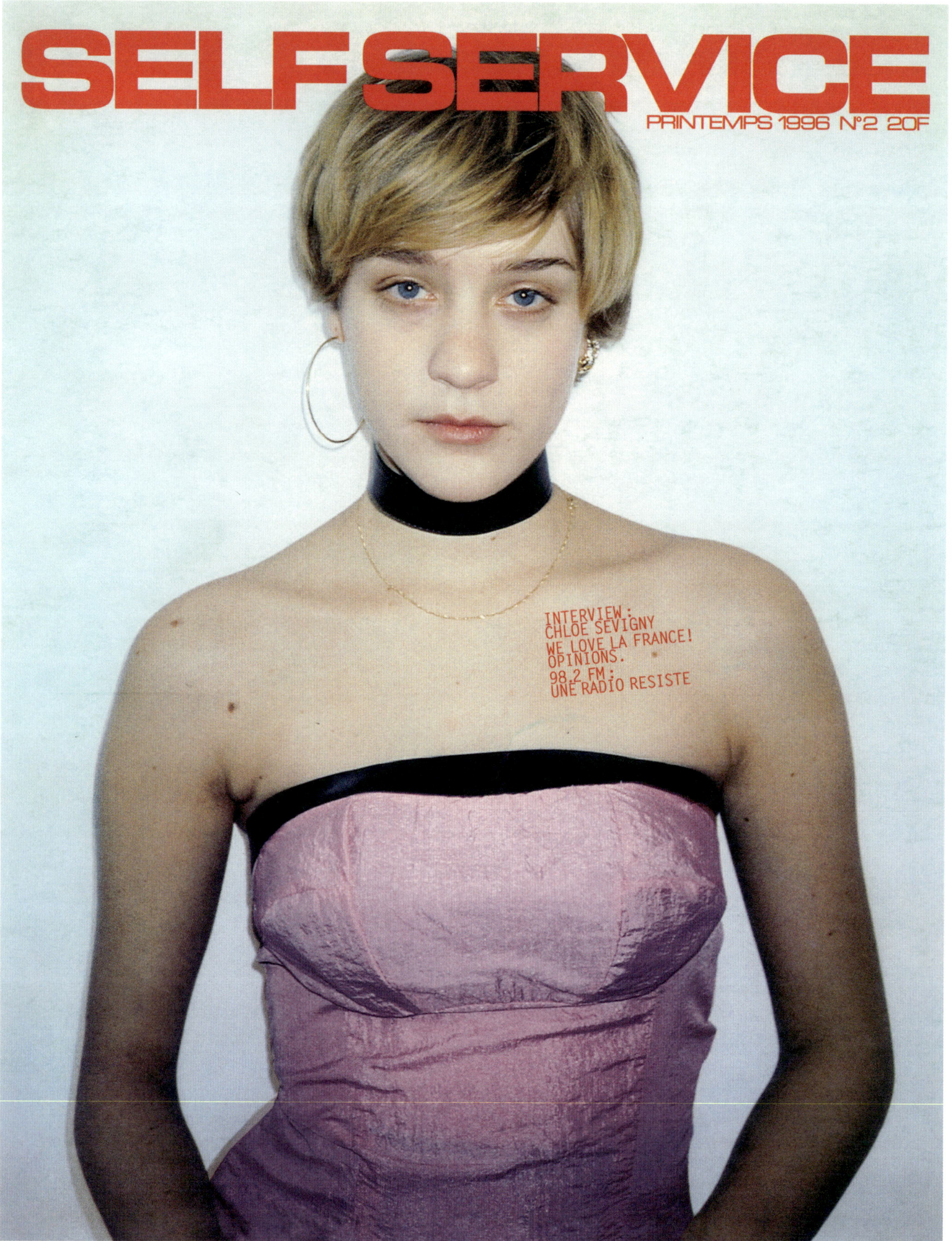
SELF SERVICE
PRINTEMPS 1996 N°2 20F
INTERVIEW :
CHLOE SEVIGNY
WE LOVE LA FRANCE!
OPINIONS.
98.2 FM :
UNE RADIO RESISTE

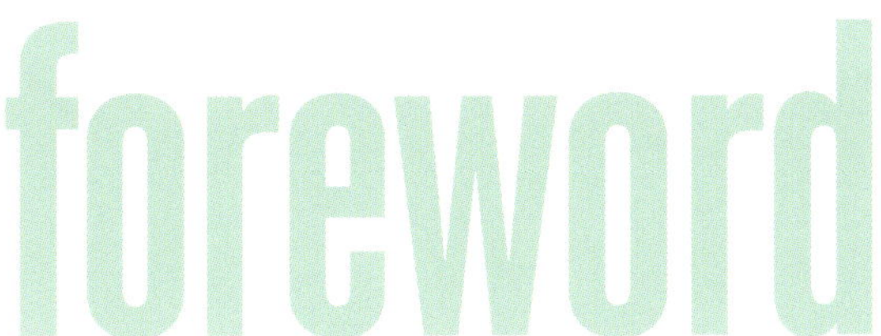

foreword

Kaat Debo

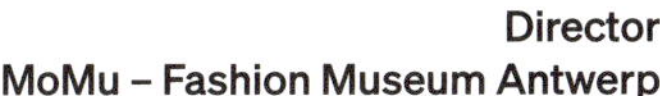

Director
MoMu – Fashion Museum Antwerp

A few times a year I meet up with girlfriends whom I've known since kindergarten. We all take turns hosting our get-togethers. On one occasion, the teenage son of one of my friends happened to walk in on us, teasingly greeting us as 'the 40-year-old girls'. My girlfriends and I found this hilarious, albeit a bit confrontational. Did he say this because he always hears us giggling and acting silly, or was he mocking us because these days he also hears us gripe about all the things that make us visibly older? I am now on the verge of celebrating my 50th birthday and my friend's teenage son is a grown man. I sometimes wonder if he would still call us girls today. Because when do you stop being a girl? And do you decide this yourself or do others make this decision for you? Is it age-related, a phase, or rather an attitude, a feeling or an aura you radiate? And which expectations, prejudices or fantasies does this imply?

In the autumn of 2025, MoMu – Fashion Museum Antwerp is hosting *GIRLS*, an exhibition on what it means to be a girl. As the mother of two teenage daughters, this exhibition is probably closest to my own personal reality. Watching a teenage daughter grow up, search, struggle... can be an incredibly beautiful experience, but also a frustrating, challenging and vulnerable time, both for the teenager and the parent. Research on teenagers in Flanders shows that girls experience more pressure on several levels: more parental control despite being less deviant, more academic pressure despite the fact that they perform better at school, more time pressure and more pressure from social media. On top of that, they are more likely to feel victimised, which means that, in studies, they have lower mental well-being scores than their male peers (Prof. Dr. Lieve Bradt, JOP-Youth Research Platform).

GIRLS is about the complexity, beauty and struggle of growing up and finding your place in the world and how artists, fashion designers, photographers, costume designers and filmmakers think about girlhood. In her essay for this book, Morna Laing describes girlhood and the figure of the girl 'as culturally mediated categories, subject to ongoing definition... [a] multi-layered code who holds spectacular currency in the fashion media'. Throughout history, notions such as the child, the teenager and the girl have been redefined time and again, in ever-changing social contexts: as objects of feminist discourse and even as desirable subjects in a capitalist consumer culture.

Chloë Sevigny photographed by Mark Borthwick,
***Self Service*, issue No. 2, Spring 1996**

Today's fashion is an interesting platform in which the complexity and ambiguity of these concepts is represented. After all, teenagers had already become a distinct category by the time of the Youthquake movement of the 1960s, playing an increasingly central role in marketing strategies. Or as Elisa De Wyngaert points out in this book, teenagers, and especially girls, were recognised as an influential consumer group from this point onwards. While teenagers and the portrayal of girls are central to the marketing of fashion brands, teenagers have rarely, if ever, had an active say in this.

It was the explicit wish of curator Elisa De Wyngaert that this exhibition would be inclusive of LGBTQIA+ youth and that it would be created in conversation with today's teenagers. We therefore organised several focus groups in 2024 with girls between the ages of 9 and 19, overseen by Shanti Ofori and Jana Tricot. The results of this process served as a starting point for the video installation that director Leonardo Van Dijl created for the exhibition.

This exhibition and publication would not have been possible without the commitment and hard work of many hands and minds. I wish to thank the authors, lenders, artists and designers for their indispensable collaboration on this project. In particular, I would like to mention Jen-Fang Shueh (Jenny Fax), Chopova Lowena, Sofia Coppola and Sofia Lai for the in-situ installations they created together with MoMu. I would also like to thank Elisa De Wyngaert, the curator of the exhibition and accompanying book, who challenged herself to explore the many layers of this cross-disciplinary subject. Claire Marie Healy curated the selection of films in the exhibition with great insight. For the design of the exhibition and book, we were able to rely on the amazing expertise of Janina Pedan and Paul Boudens respectively. Finally, I would like to express my sincere thanks to the entire MoMu team and the team at Hannibal Books.

Edgard Tytgat
***The Last Doll*, 1923**
Oil on canvas

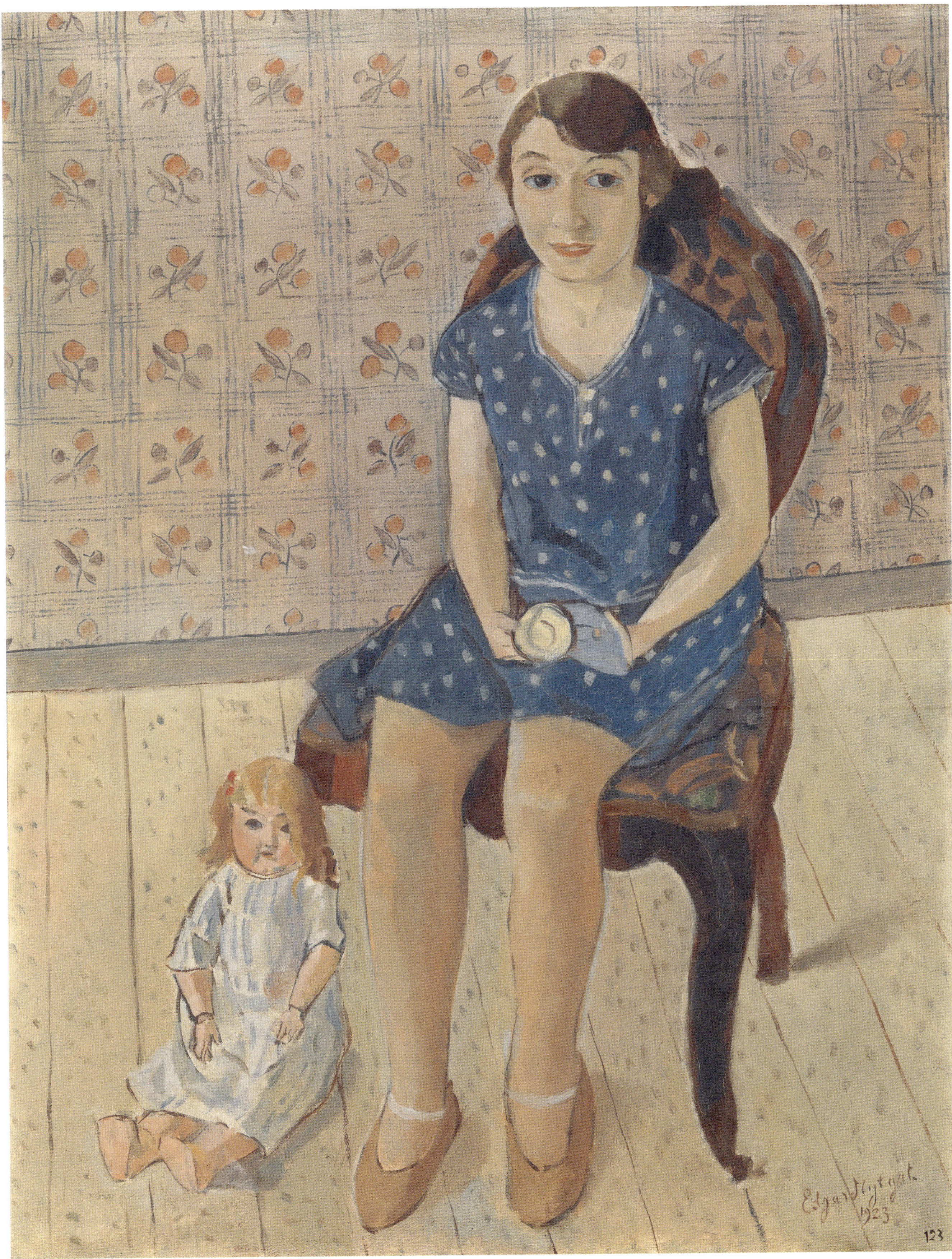
Edgard Tytgat
1923
123

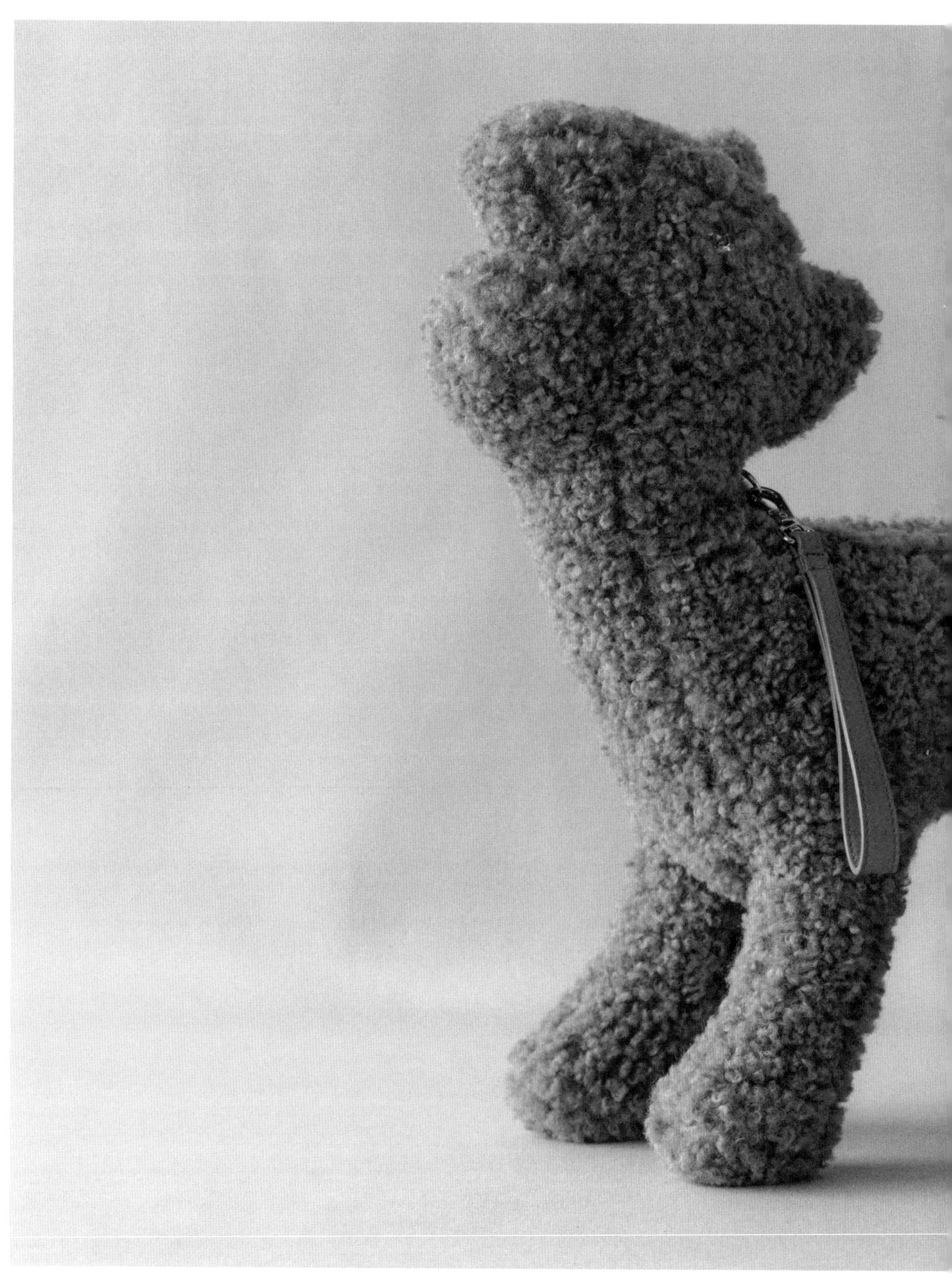

Simone Rocha Autumn-Winter 2024–2025
‘Teddy Creature Bag’ (left),
puppy handbag with zipper, c. 1936 (right)

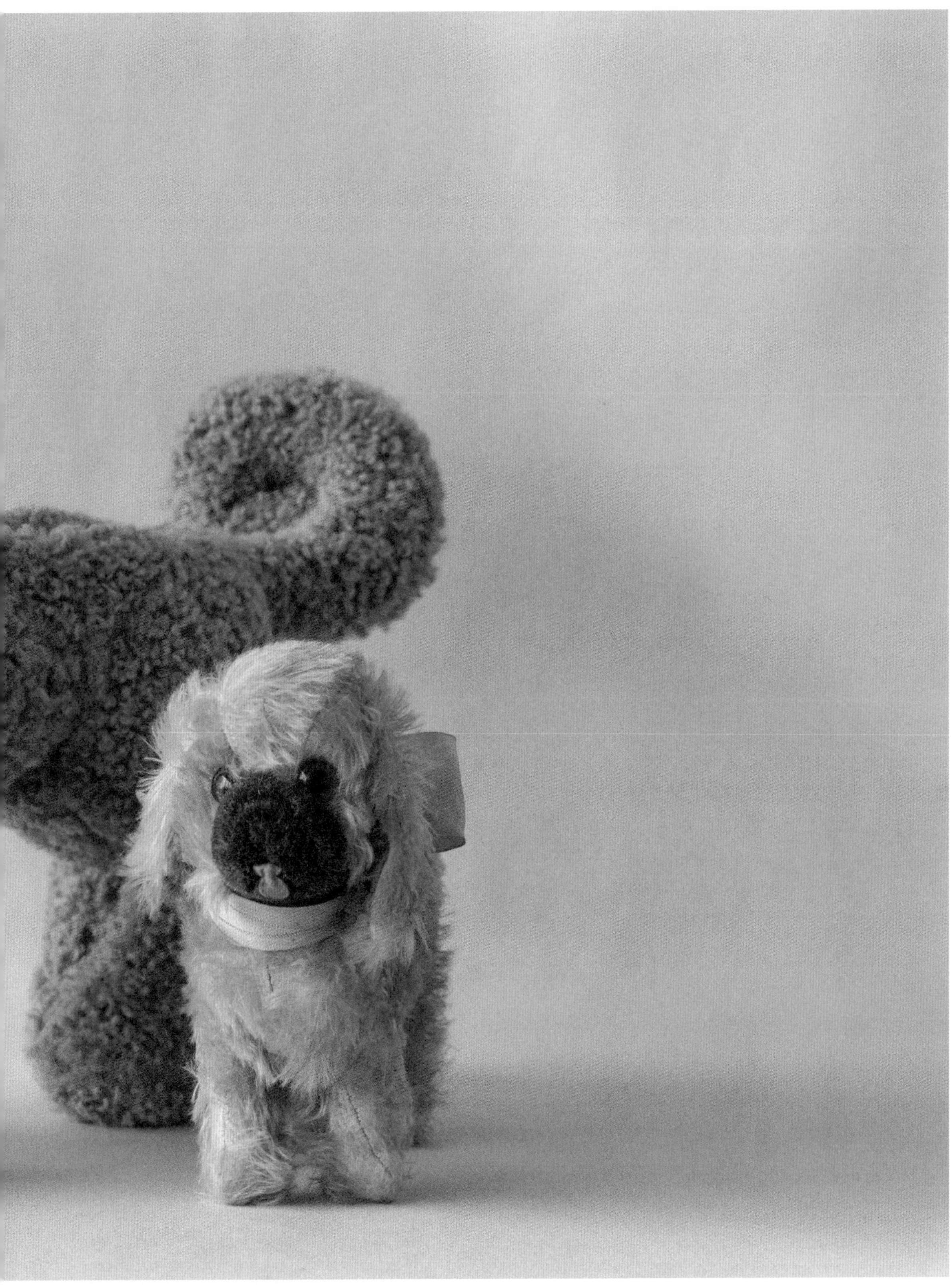

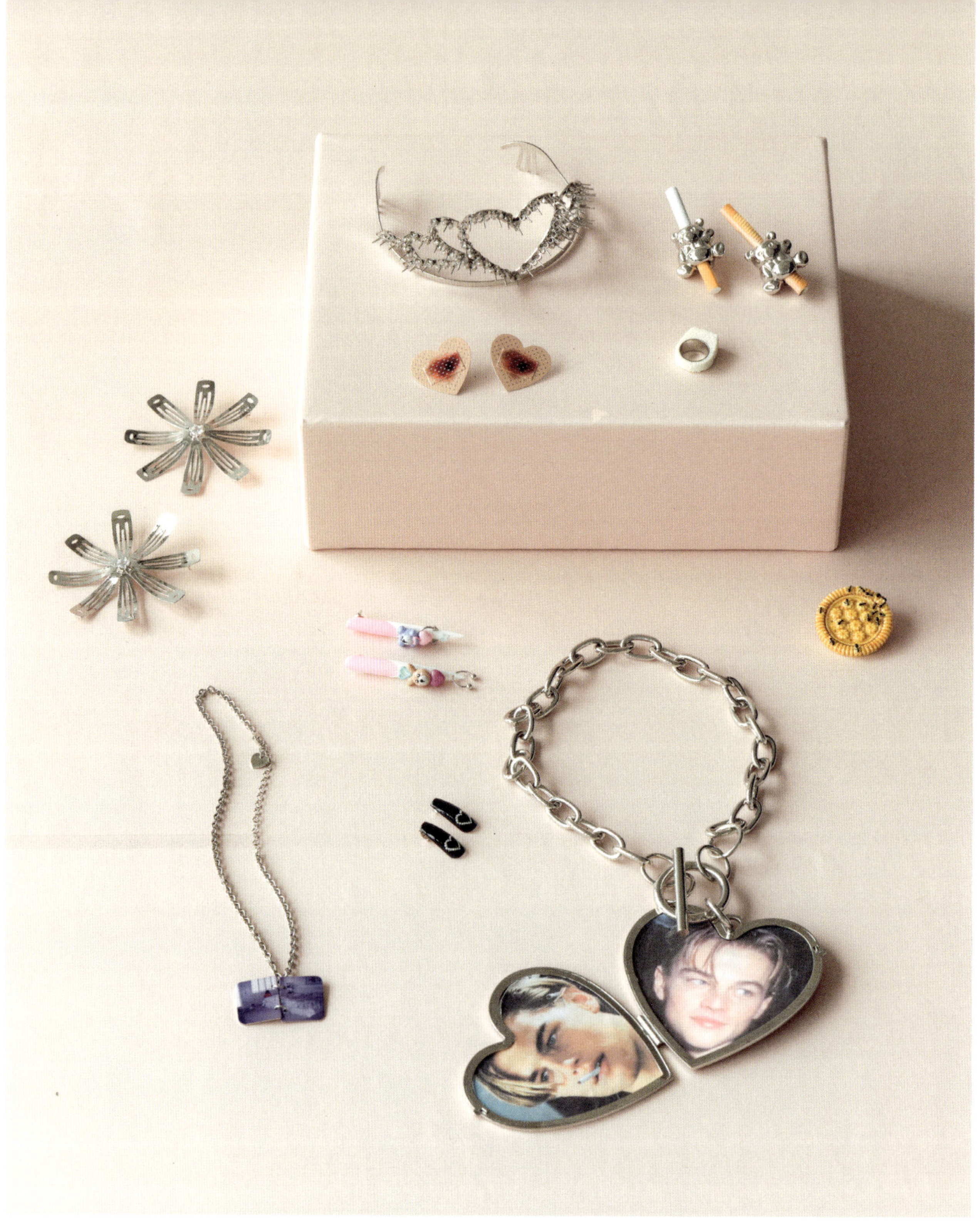

D’heygere for *I’m Sorry* by Petra Collins, Cookie Earring, Diary Necklace,
Black Heart Nail Earrings, Heart Bandage Earrings, Flower Hair Clip Earrings, 2025
D’heygere Autumn-Winter 2023–2024, Canister Bear Earrings
D’heygere for Vaquera Autumn-Winter 2025–2026, XL Heart Locket Necklace
D’heygere Spring-Summer 2024, Sugar Ring
D’heygere Autumn-Winter 2025–2026, Stud Tiara
D’heygere in collaboration with Nails by Mei Autumn-Winter 2025–2026, Kawaii Stiletto Nail Earrings

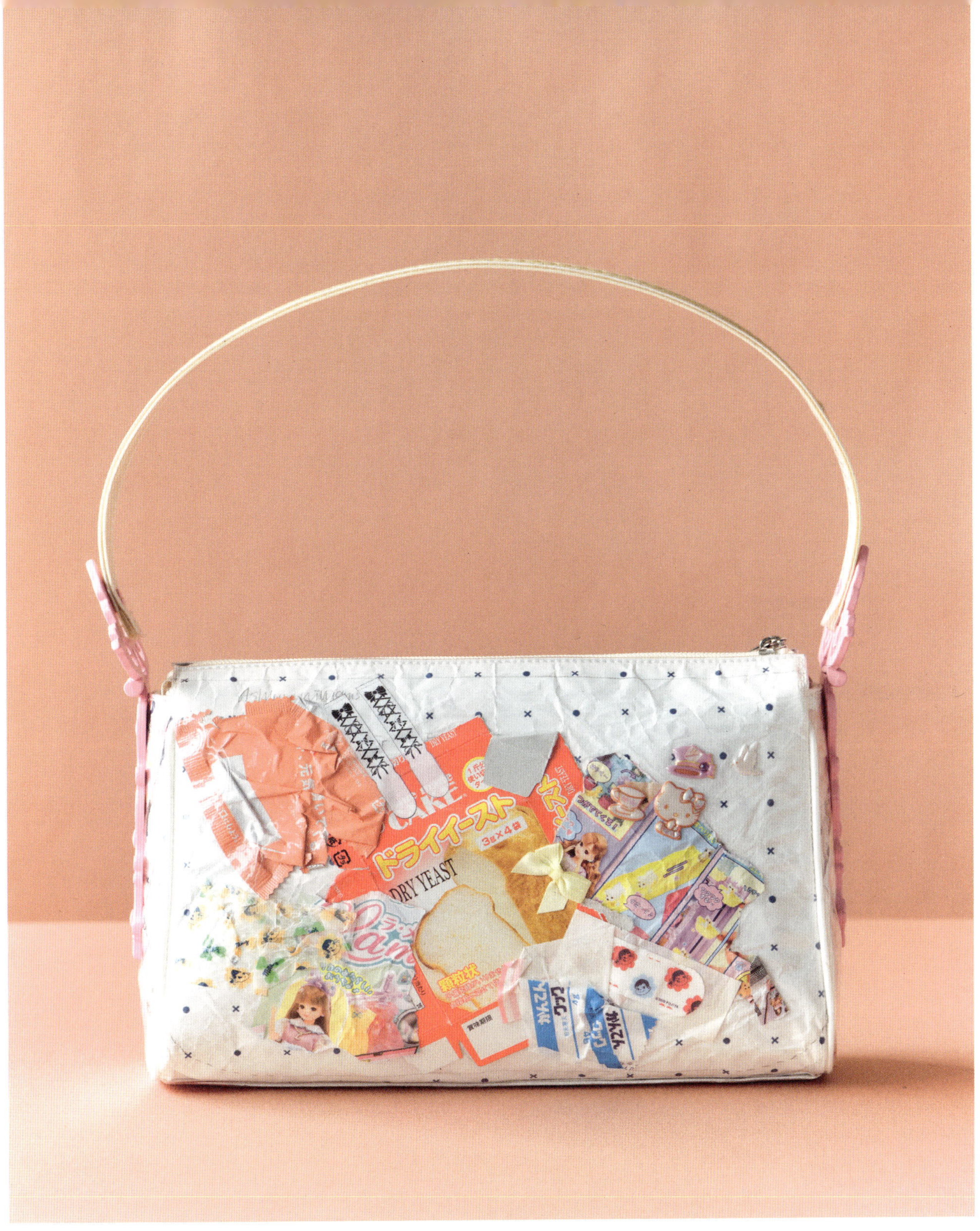

Ashley Williams
Spring-Summer 2025
'Clutter Bag'

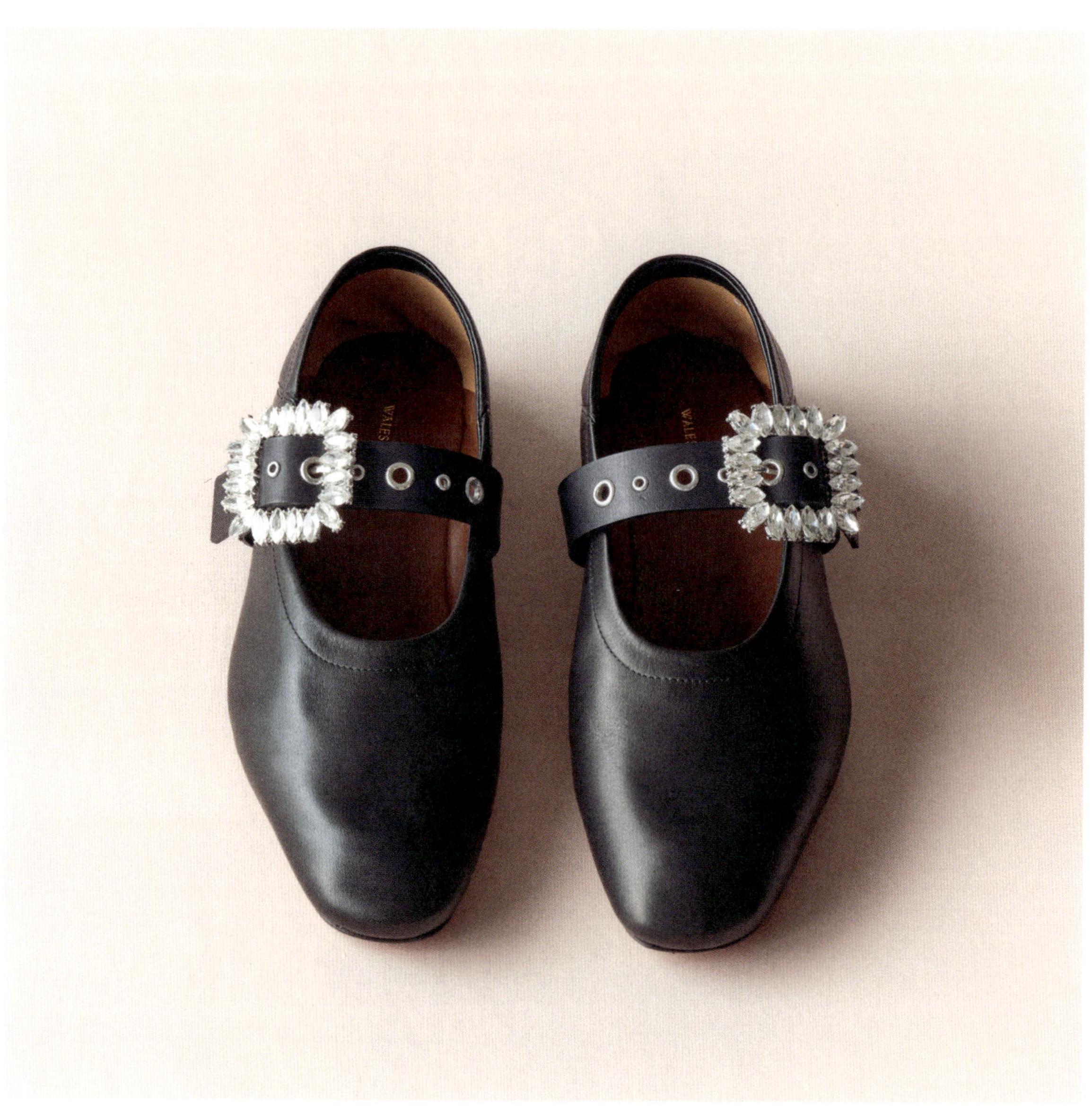

Wales Bonner
Autumn-Winter 2023–2024
Mary Janes

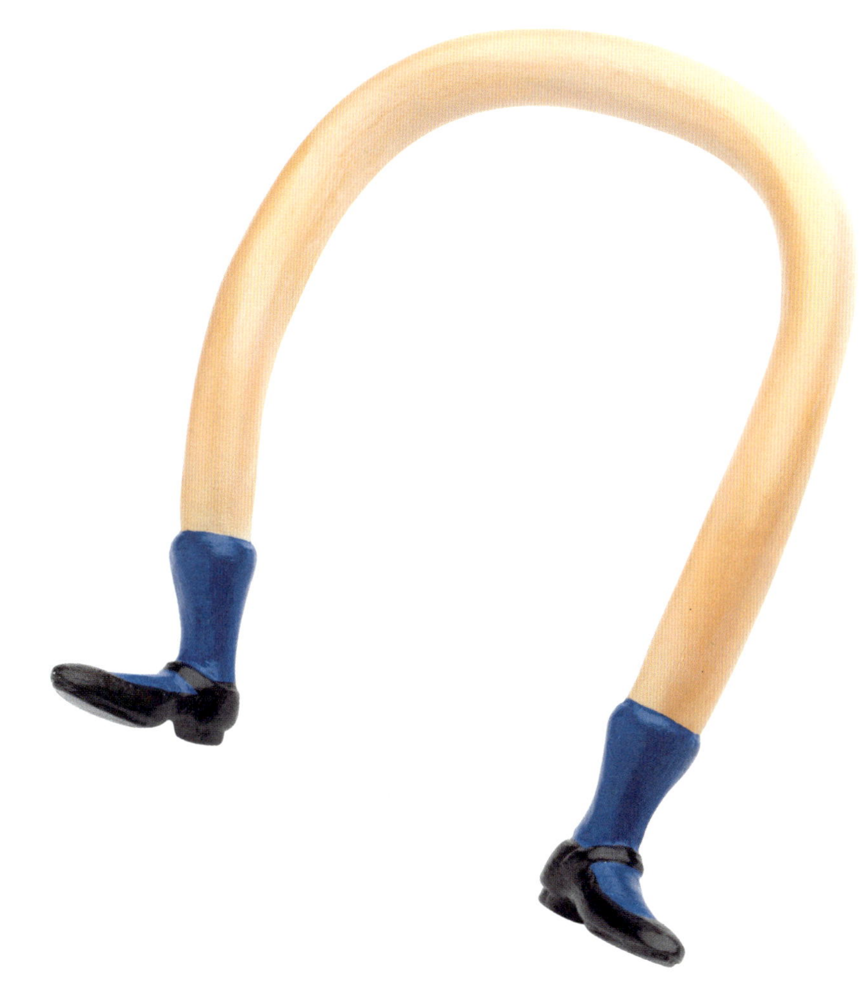

Meret Oppenheim
Untitled, 1936 design (2003 execution)
Porcelain and paint

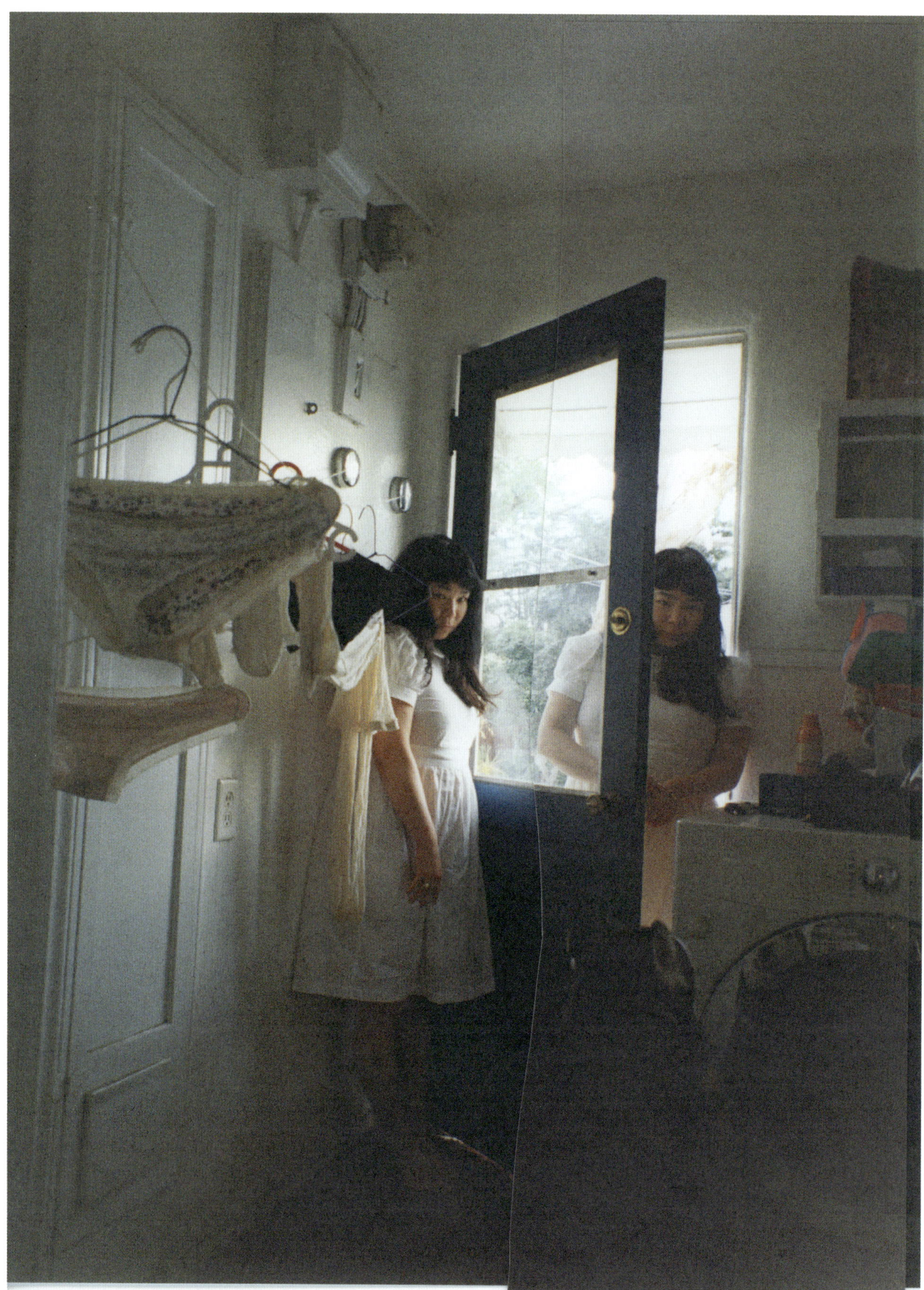

Elisa De Wyngaert

in-between: the lingering years of girlhood

Growing up, my neighbour kept pigeons. Each year, their cooing became the first whisper of spring, the arrival of bare-legs season and the joy of escaping the smelly high-school toilets. Pigeon calls still stir anxious teenage flutters in me. There's something about the intensity with which you experience life at that age, and although we couldn't capture life in the 1990s as teens do today, I still remember those years like a film — scene by scene.

'I'm not alone: psychologists say our sharpest memories are formed at fifteen.'

In Western art's canonised history, the *girlhood years* have been framed as a fleeting phase: tender, naive, in transition. A phase marked by sweetness and passivity. As an eternal muse, the 'young girl' in art history was an anonymous girl, a daughter *of*, a silent subject playing the piano, holding a kitten, covered in symbols and paraphernalia hinting at her virtue and innocence. She's not bothering anyone, she's just there. Art that truly centred girlhood, biographical history and femininity as serious subjects had long been dismissed as sentimental or lacking intellectual rigour — a trivialisation that, as this essay will explore, overlooks the emotional, psychological and political depth of these artists and their enduring resonance. Through the eyes of the artists, designers, photographers and filmmakers in this exhibition, girlhood is not a theme, not captured through a voyeuristic gaze, but a way of seeing — of remembering and imagining. As Siri Hustvedt wrote so eloquently, 'Femininity and childhood have been continually linked in Western culture as conditions of shrunken intellect and dependence. And yet, the dependent child lives on in the adult, in every adult, in memory that is more feeling than autobiographical image.'[1]

'You don't just leave girlhood — you drag it with you.'

Fumiko Imano
Laundrette/LA/USA, 2019

Louise Bourgeois (1911–2010, France/USA) often said her childhood never lost its magic, mystery or drama and that all her subjects found their inspiration in that time.[2] She became an internationally celebrated artist whose allegiance to her child self continues to resonate with younger generations of artists across disciplines. Still, for a long time she struggled to be recognised in a male-dominated art world, and although she might not have explicitly identified as a feminist artist, she brought the subjects of memory, femininity and sexuality, the female psyche, motherhood and domestic life into her art in an unprecedented way.

The Easton Foundation holds the extensive archive of writings the artist kept over many decades. Her earliest diaries reveal an intelligent young girl with a restless mind, attuned to social tensions and her own fluctuating emotional states. On 14 December 1923, the almost-twelve-year-old Louise Bourgeois wrote:

> **'I despair but can't find**
> **the strength to think things through**
> **and yet I have quite a lot of things to think about**
> **The people who will read**
> **this diary will certainly think**
> **that this child is too nervous**
> **she has nothing else to do**
> **but sleep play eat, but**
> **not at all I have things to think about**
> **to reflect upon mysteries to dig up**
> **all these worries are not**
> **important to you**
> **but for me it isn't the same.'**[3]

She articulates a sentiment that resonates across generations of adolescents: the intensity of one's emotions is deeply felt yet is often dismissed by others. No longer a child, but not yet an adult, a teenager occupies an 'in-between' marked by both emotional depth and social invisibility.

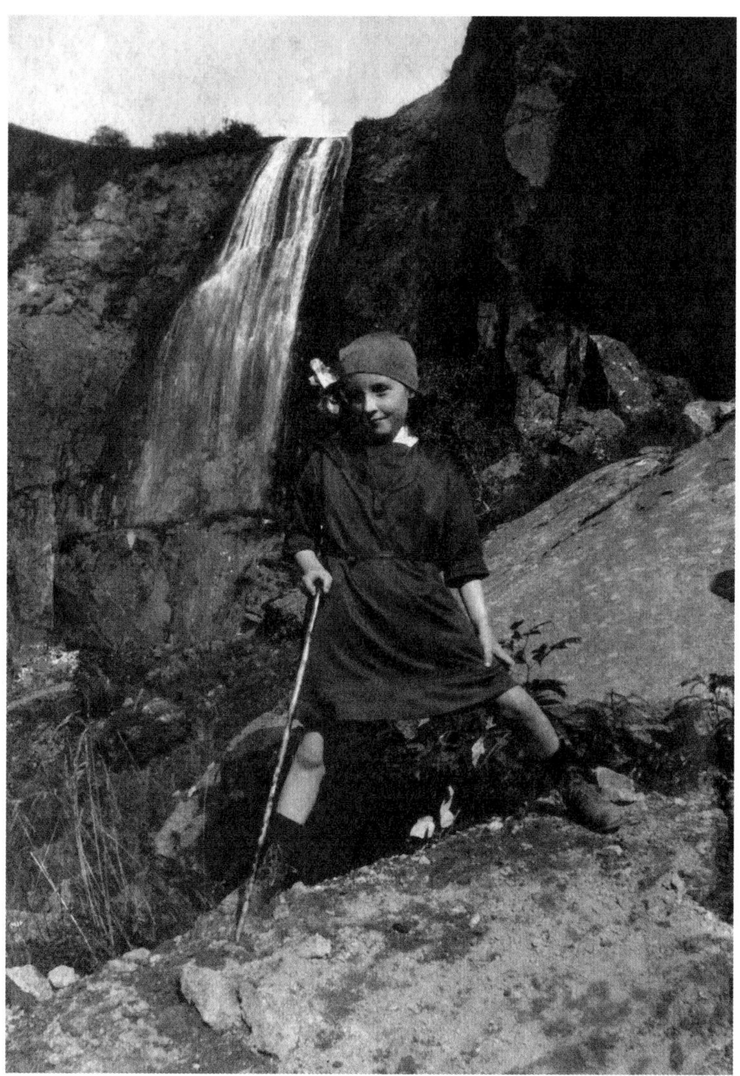

Louise Bourgeois at La Grande Cascade du Mont-Dore, Auvergne, France, 1920

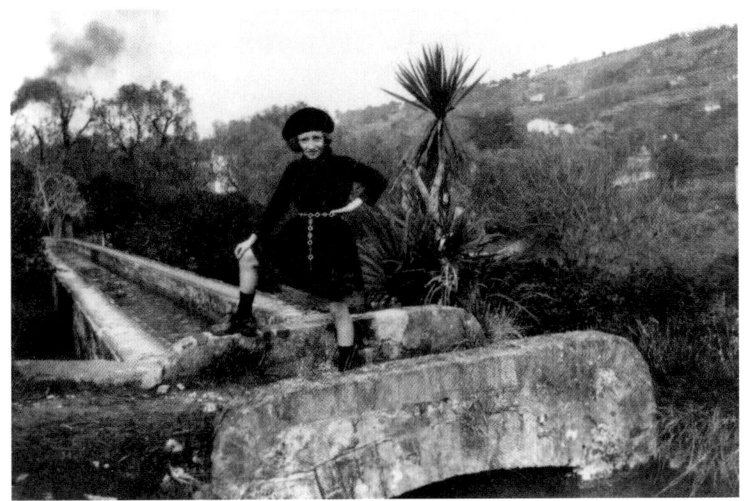

Louise Bourgeois,
Le Cannet, France, 1922

Louise Bourgeois used her art and writings to work through difficult memories that stemmed from familial trauma and emotional instability, moving fluidly between tenderness, humour and rage.

The 1992 performance *She Lost It* at The Fabric Workshop in Philadelphia, for example, centred around a previously unpublished text Bourgeois wrote in 1947.[4] Performed when Bourgeois was 80 years old, it conveyed a dark allegory of patriarchy and power disguised as a children's story:

> **'A man and a woman lived together. On one evening he did not come back from work. And she waited. She kept on waiting and she grew littler and littler. Later, a neighbor stopped by out of friendship and there he found her, in the armchair, the size of a pea.'[5]**

The tiny pea is an eerily precise metaphor for Bourgeois's lifelong fear of separation, abandonment and betrayal. When girls are not encouraged to grow up but to grow down, to become 'littler and littler', they carry that shrinking into adulthood. Women, then, remain lesser than their husbands and, like girls, held in a state of dependence. The story echoes the dominant nature of heterosexual relationships: how Bourgeois's mother tolerated the behaviour of her philandering father, and her own experience of balancing motherhood with her artistic ambitions. The 'parable', a term Bourgeois applied to her short, poetic stories, was silk-screened onto a 54 metre-long strip of gauze that guided visitors through the exhibition space. During the performance, it was also revealed through the act of unwrapping and wrapping the performers. Red embroidery spelt out different phrases across the performers' garments: 'HIDE AND SEEK', 'FEAR MAKES THE WORLD GO ROUND', 'THE DAY THE BIRD WAS ATTRACTED, IT FOULED ITS NEST', 'THE COLD OF ANXIETY IS VERY REAL',

DÉCEMBRE

MARDI 11

je pars comme d'habitude en
classe mais le train a 3 quarts
d'heure de retard nous allons
de Sceaux ceinture à Denfert à
pied car deux autres trains se sont
rencontré Le cerbère ne me dit
rien car il n'est pas là
Le reste de la journée se passe
bien
Le soir je mange au magasin
pour me coucher en rentrant
car je suis très fatigué

ST DAMASE

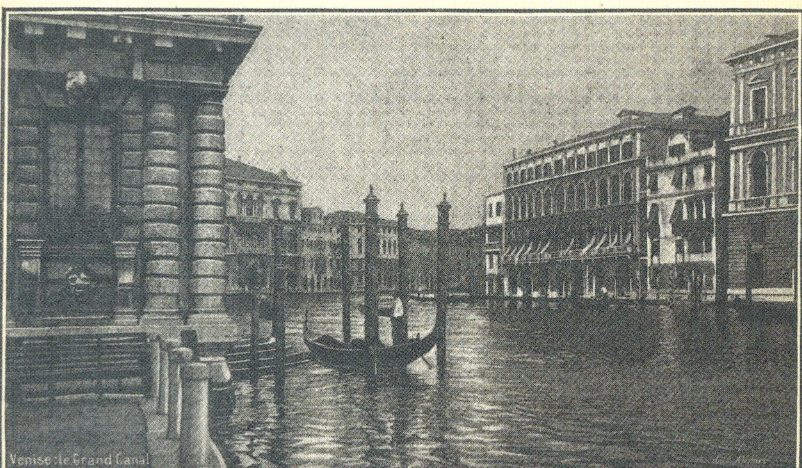
Venise : le Grand Canal

MERCREDI 12

je me lève bien puisque j'ai
bien dormi toute la nuit en
et longtemps
j'ai mon carnet je suis 13ème
et il me manque 4 notes
moi je suis contente de moi
voila!

STE CONSTANCE

— 276 —

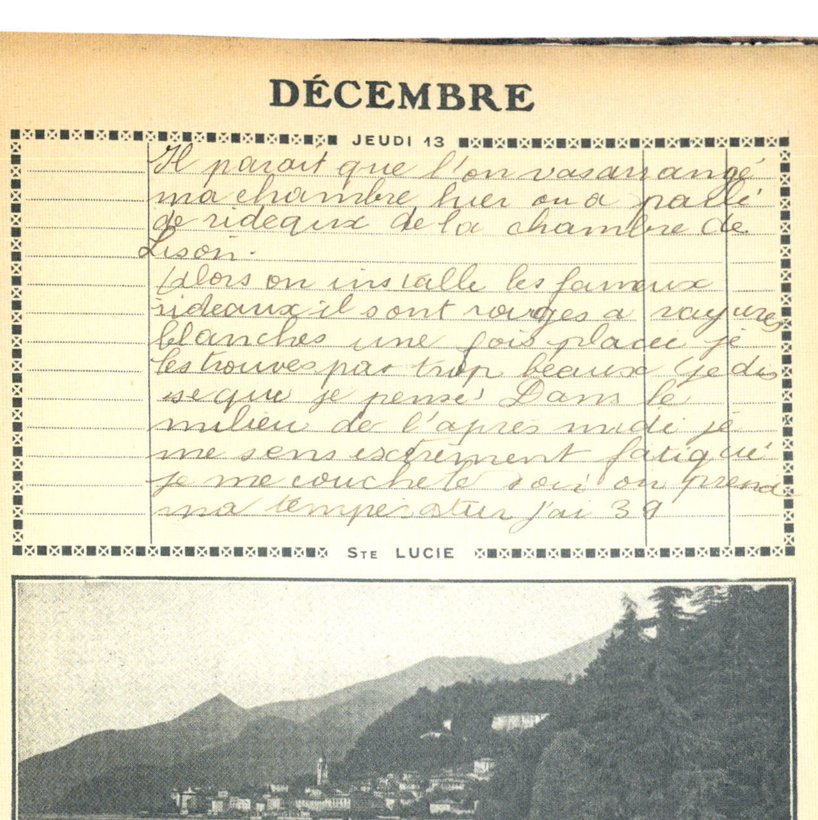

DÉCEMBRE

JEUDI 13

Il parait que l'on vas arrangé
ma chambre hier on a parlé
de rideaux de la chambre de
Lison.
Alors on installe les fameux
rideaux il sont rouges à rayures
blanches une fois placée je
les trouves pas trop beaux je di
se que je pensé Dans le
milieu de l'apres midi je
me sens escrément fatigué
je me couche le soir on prend
ma temperatur j'ai 39

STE LUCIE

Bellaggio (lac de Côme)

VENDREDI 14

je me desespere mais j'ai pas
le courage de reflerchir et cepen
dant j'en ait des choses à penser
Les personnes qui liront ce
journal penseront certainement
cetté enfant se monte la tête
elle n'a rien à faire qu'a
Dormir jouer manger. mais
pas du tout j'ai des choses à pen
sé à reflechir des mysteres à appro
fondir tous ces soucis ne sont
pas grands pour vous.
mais pour moi ce n'est pas
pareil

ST NICAISE

— 277 —

Louise Bourgeois
Diary entries, 11–14 December 1923

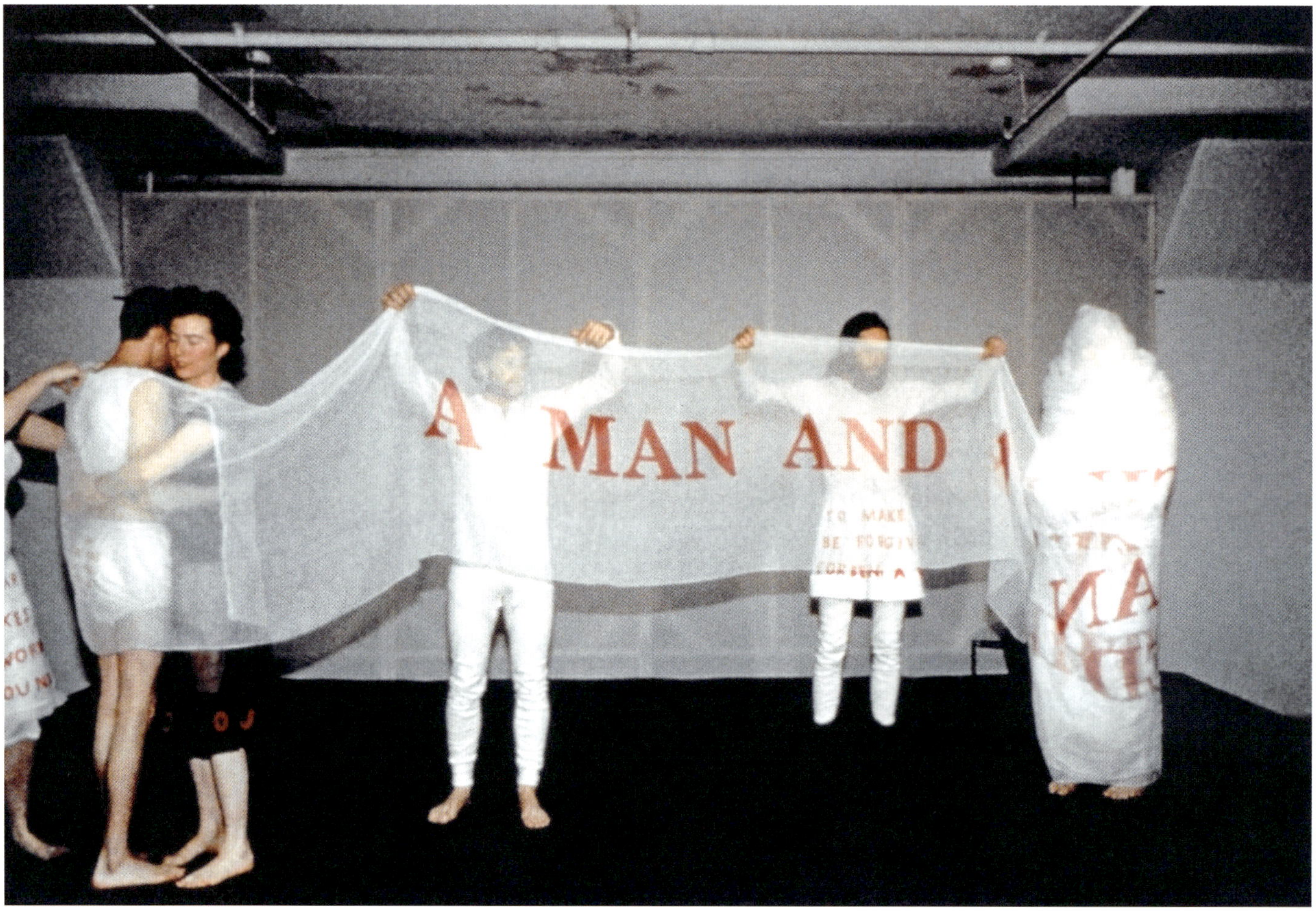

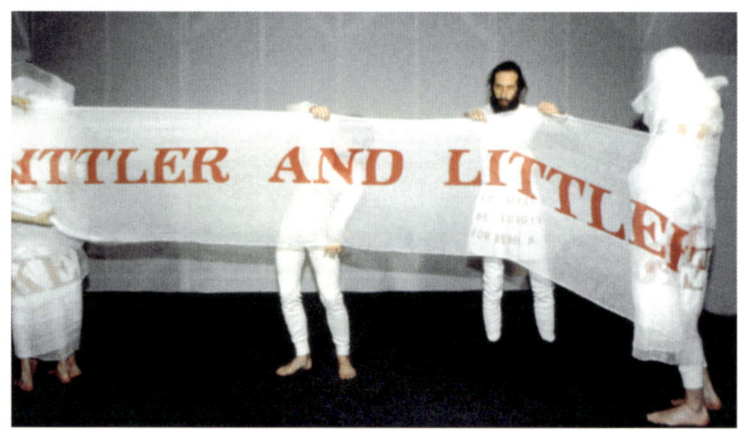

She Lost It, performance by Louise Bourgeois
at The Fabric Workshop, Philadelphia, PA, 5 December 1992

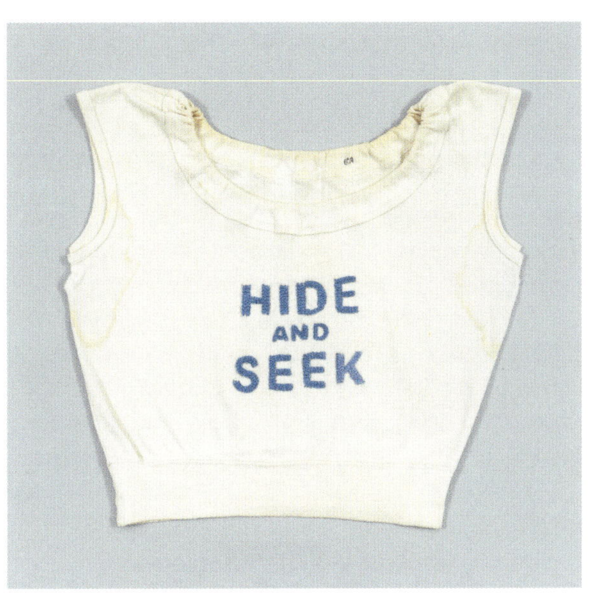

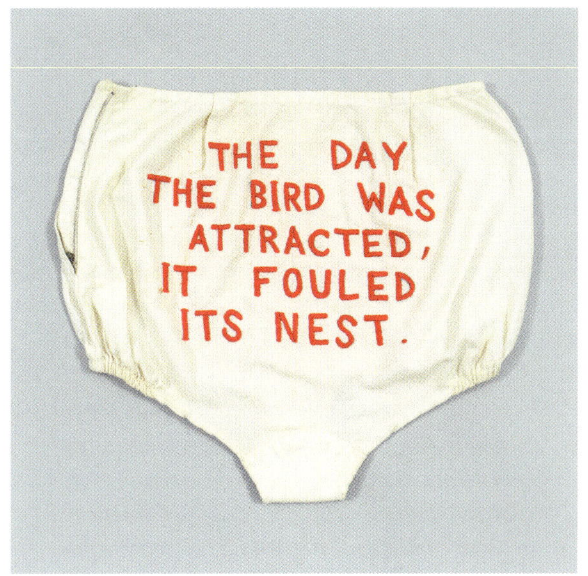

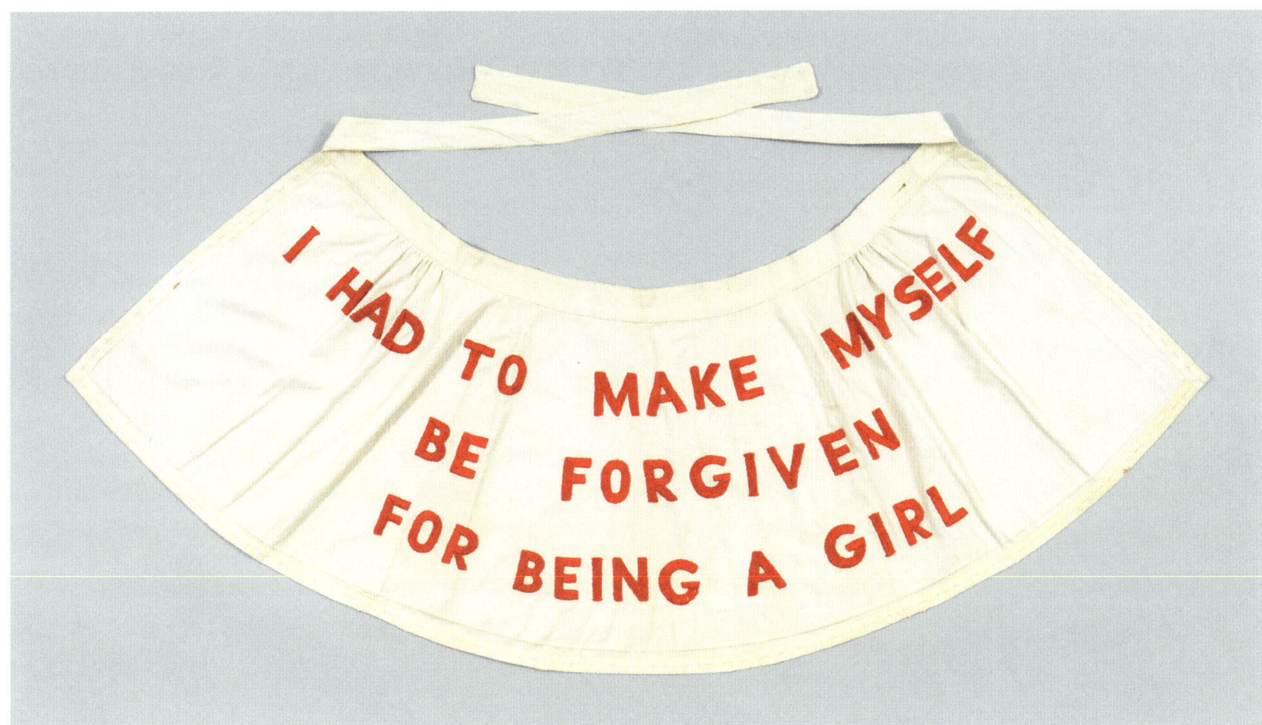

Garments from Louise Bourgeois's performance *She Lost It*, 1992
Embroidered fabric

and 'I HAD TO MAKE MYSELF FORGIVEN FOR BEING A GIRL', each conveying personal psychological weight.

Born in 1911, as the second daughter in her family, she grew up with the intense belief that she needed to *make herself forgiven for being a girl*:

> **'A daughter is a disappointment. If you bring a daughter into this world, you have to be forgiven, the way my mother was forgiven because I was the spitting image of my father. That was my first piece of luck. It may be why he treated me like the son he always wanted. I was gifted enough to satisfy my father. That was my second piece of luck.'[6]**

This experience of gender disappointment was embroidered on a white cotton apron: a garment symbolic of both domestic labour and protection. Bourgeois grew up in the early 20th century, a time when designer fashion not only gained prominence but also when children's fashion became distinctly gendered. Around the ages of 4 to 6, boys transitioned from dresses to short trousers before moving to long trousers in adolescence. Girls' clothing, however, remained decorative and restrictive, mirroring an education system that primarily prepared them for their roles as wives and mothers. As Simone de Beauvoir asserted in *The Second Sex* (1949), those societal expectations — reflected, among other things, in clothing — only serve to constrain girls' autonomy:

> **'One is not born, but rather becomes, a woman.'[7]**

Thirteen months after Louise Bourgeois was born, her mother gave birth to a son, but by then she had already become the focal point of her father's attention. As Juliet Mitchell wrote, 'her personal story of the relationship with her mother and father, for whom she felt she had to be both the family's prettiest girl and cleverest boy, was extreme'.[8] Moving to New York in 1938 with her husband, Robert Goldwater, Bourgeois felt like a runaway girl.

In the 1970s, important voices emerged that advocated for art that reflected women's lived experiences and challenged dominant power structures. Notably, art critic and curator Lucy Lippard (b. 1937, USA) was a crucial advocate for this shift, calling for non-elitist art that broke down barriers between artists and audiences. This shift in the art world resonated across disciplines. In the 1990s, in film, directors such as Sofia Coppola (b. 1971, USA) pioneered work driven by a desire to capture the intensity, vulnerability and sexuality of this formative time. A similar shift took place in fashion, albeit more slowly.

Fashion, like all creative industries, has long been male-dominated, but women and certainly teenage girls have always inspired it. The 'teenager' only emerged as a distinct social and sartorial category in the mid-1950s. It was then that retailers and clothing manufacturers began to recognise teenage girls as an influential consumer group, introducing dedicated shopping spaces and teen-appropriate sizing. The relationship between teenagers and ready-to-wear adult fashion intensified in the 1990s as teenage models were increasingly hired to represent adult women in campaigns and on the runway.

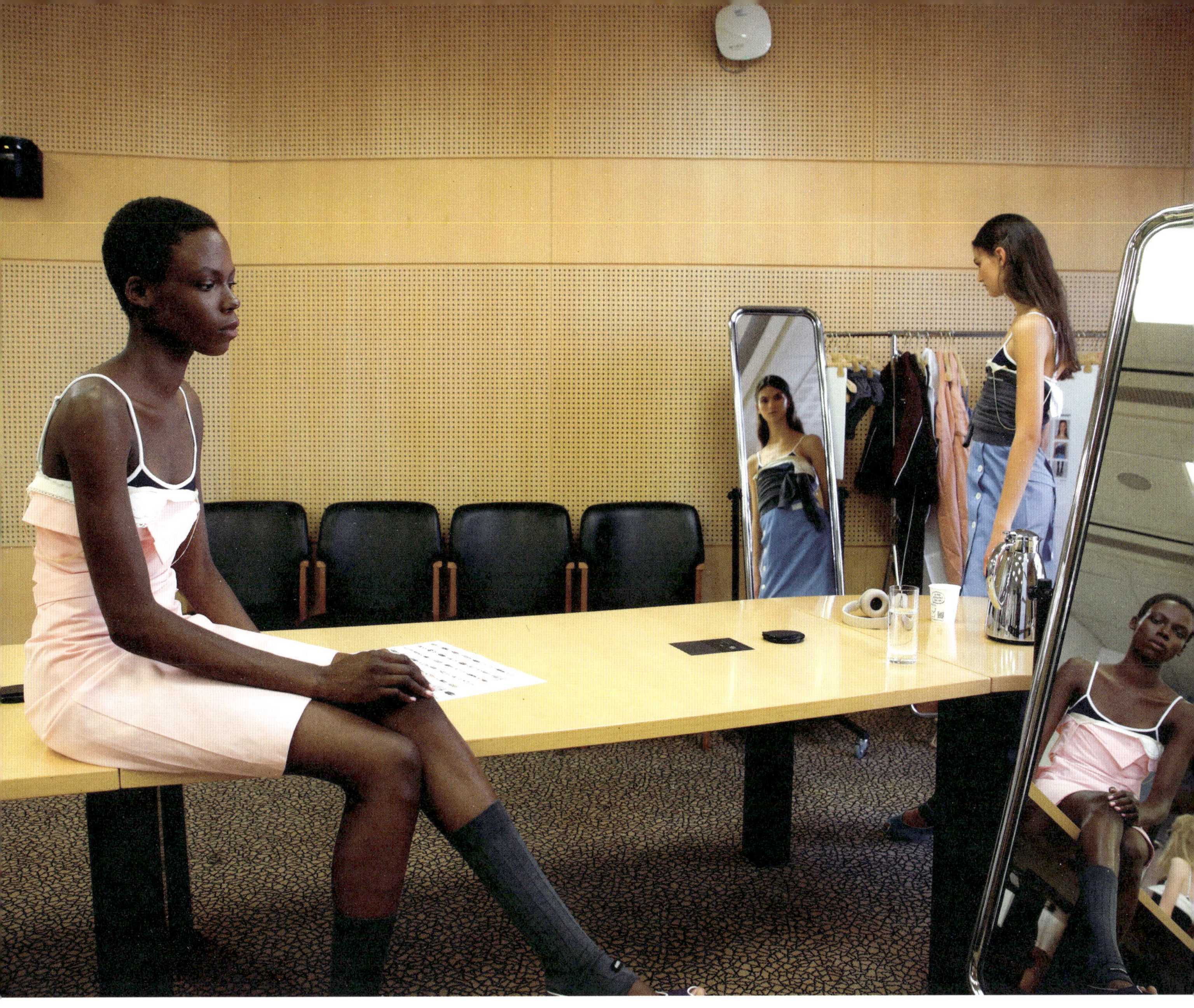

Miu Miu
Spring-Summer 2025
Backstage photography by Michella Bredahl, styling by Lotta Volkova

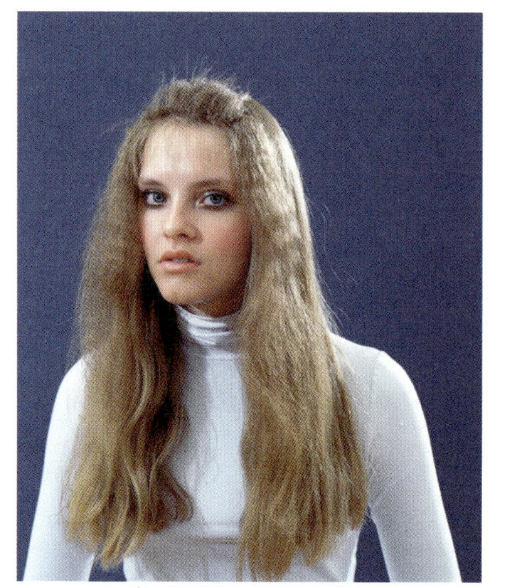

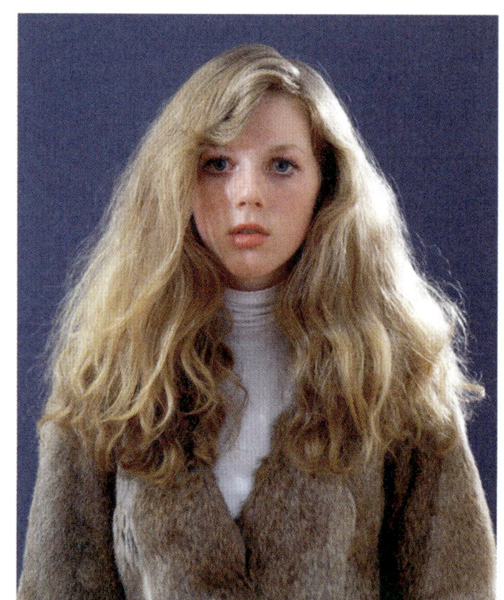

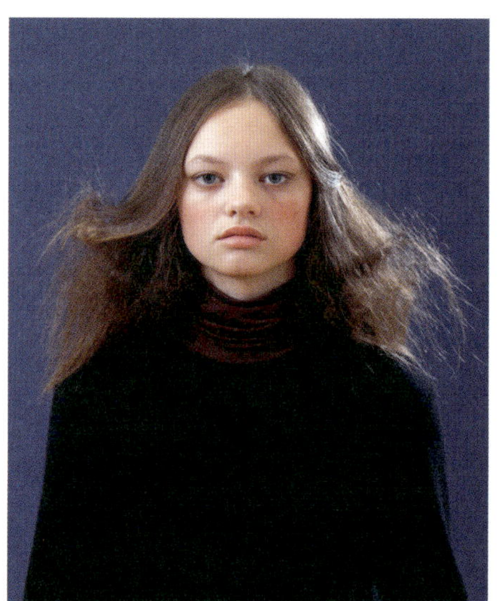

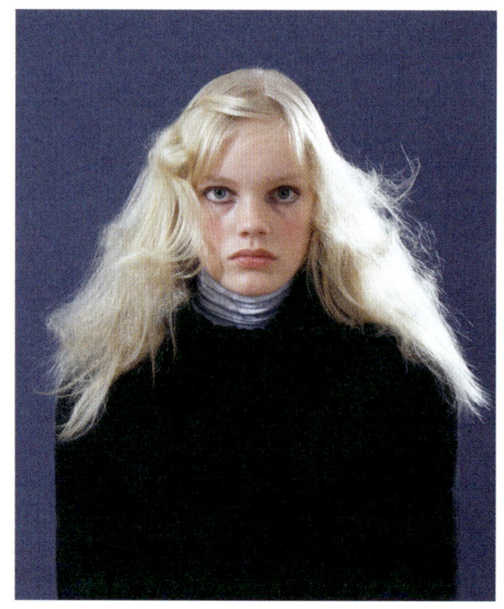

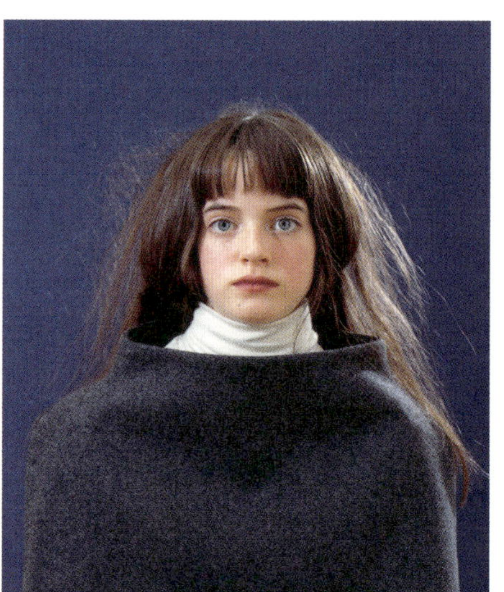

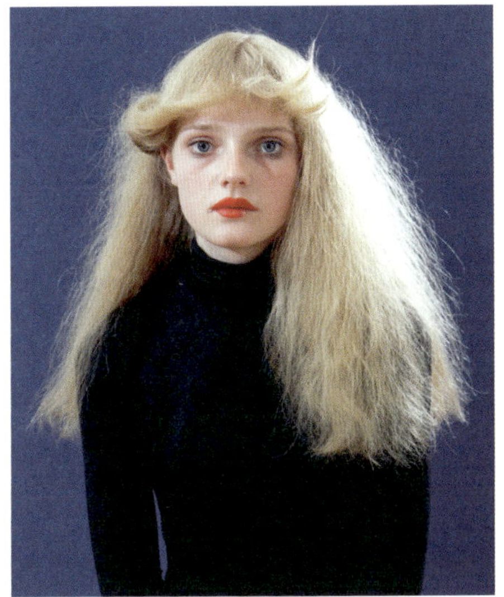
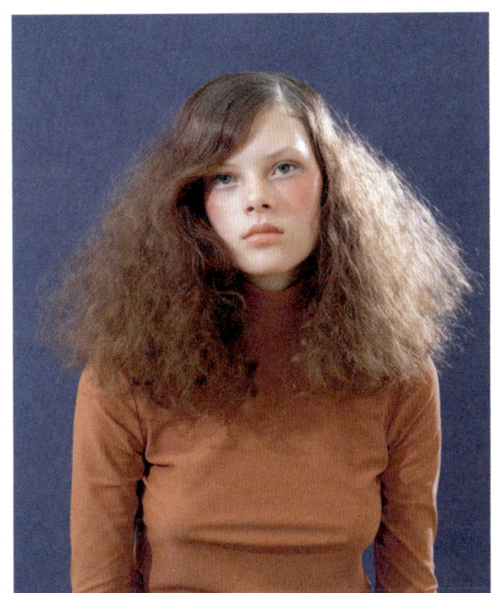
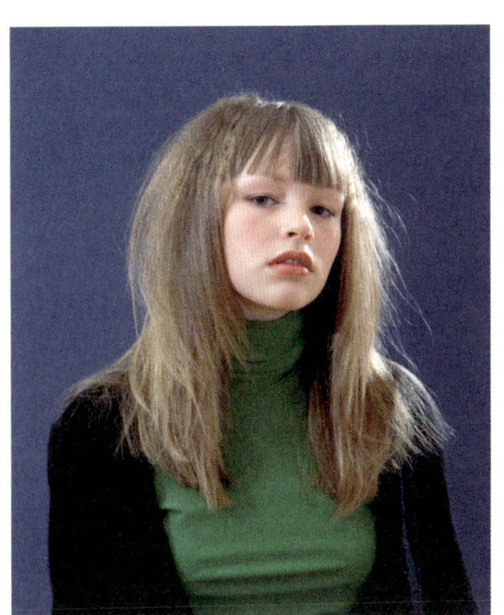
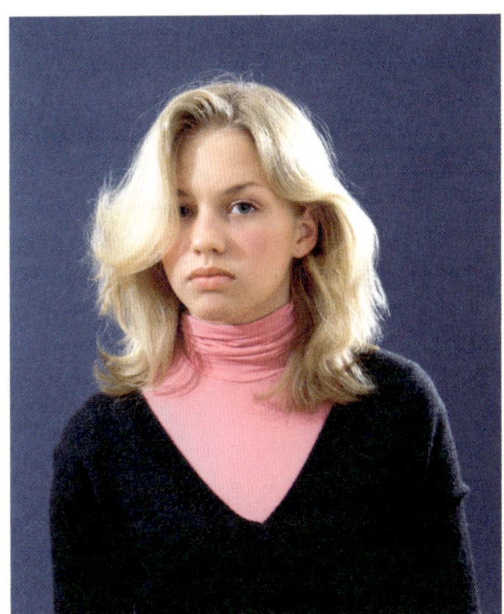

Class of 1998 photographed by Anuschka Blommers & Niels Schumm wearing Veronique Branquinho Autumn-Winter 1998 for *Self Service* No. 8

Veronique Branquinho
Invitation to the Spring-Summer 2000 show

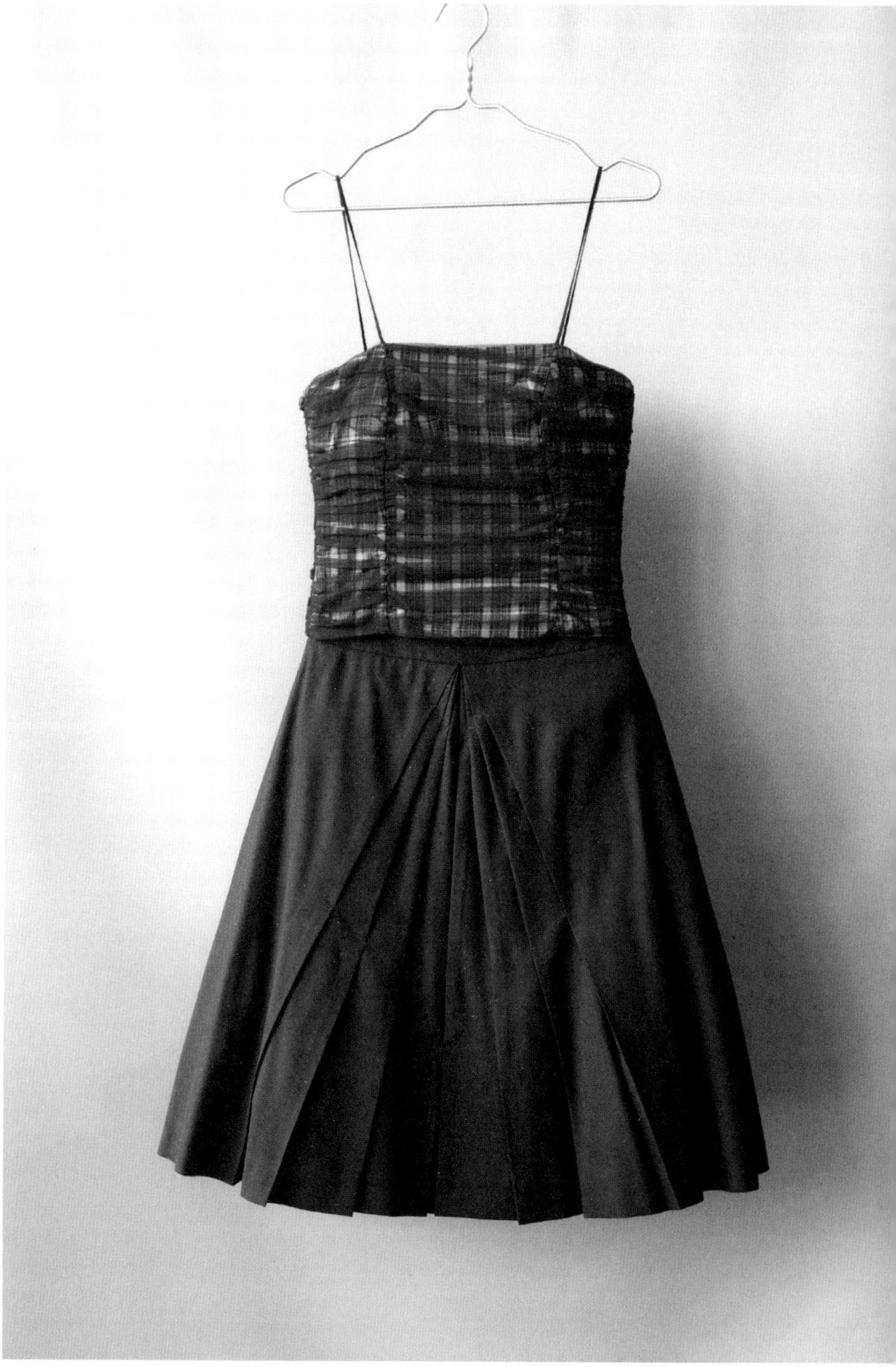

Veronique Branquinho
Spring-Summer 2000

At the same time, the 'girly' aesthetic of the era often reflected a hyper-feminised, fetishised and sexualised vision of girlhood, shaped and filtered through an objectifying gaze. In this heightened period, one could overlook the more nuanced work by designers such as **Miuccia Prada** (b. 1949, Italy) and **Veronique Branquinho** (b. 1973, Belgium), who proposed more ambiguous renderings of femininity and girlhood.

Miuccia Prada described her own girlhood as dull: her parents were strict and serious and she was bored. By the age of fifteen, she had rebelled:

> **'I was always frustrated because I had to dress so seriously. I was a proper young girl and I was dreaming of pink shoes, red shoes, pink dresses. Anything with colour. Exciting underwear. Everybody had this kind of dull underwear and wore boring striped dresses. I couldn't stand it...'[9]**

After taking over her family company, Prada, in the 1980s, she launched her youthful, playful, avant-garde sister brand, Miu Miu in 1993 ('Miu Miu' was her childhood nickname). Even today, Miu Miu still reflects her experimental, intuitive teenage nature. Early campaigns, such as Spring-Summer 1994, photographed by Corinne Day (1962–2010, UK), presented a radically different image of the girl-not-yet-woman, featuring Rosemary Ferguson in a hotel room, resting and on her own adventure. Day's photography in the 1990s captured raw, unfiltered moments offering a portrayal of adolescence that was far more authentic than anything in fashion previously. Veronique Branquinho, who launched her eponymous brand in 1998, was deeply influenced by the transitional phase between girlhood and womanhood. Similar to Prada, she used her own visceral teenage desire to break free from monotony as her fuel. Her Spring-Summer 2000 collection, for example, was about getting dressed for a 'prom', where a carefully chosen dress doesn't quite match the rest of the outfit: a gown paired with a hastily thrown-on trench coat, awkward jumper or short jacket. Her work continued to revolve around the one foot still in the world of the girl and one foot in the world of the woman. While nobody actually went to proms in Belgium at the time, Branquinho knew it from American television. Laura Palmer in *Twin Peaks*, the fashion in *Grease*, Sissy Spacek as Carrie in the eponymous film, Madonna's 'Like a Virgin', Cyndi Lauper's 'Girls Just Want to Have Fun' — all of it fascinated her.[10] In her collections, seeming innocence (modest flowing dresses, pleated skirts, crisp shirts and trustworthy tweed) met a sense of menace (see-through fabrics, blackened teeth and pale faces, mysterious beings disguised in hoods and capes).

In the 2010s and 2020s, a new generation of designers — including Simone Rocha, Molly Goddard, Chopova Lowena, Jenny Fax, Sandy Liang, Ashley Williams and the ever-relevant Miuccia Prada, alongside stylists such as Lotta Volkova at Miu Miu — introduced personal visions of femininity and girlhood. These designers' work is often labelled as 'girly' or 'coquette' for the sake of convenience, yet what they truly accomplish is a disruption and redefinition of traditional femininity. In their hands, girlhood resists mere softness — it is articulated through a language of contradiction and craft: at once volatile, perverse, fantastical, smocked and pearled. It moves beyond binary definitions. While this reclamation of femininity has faced suspicion (especially complicated by the rise of conservative powers hoping to push or lead women and girls back into the traditional roles in either matching modest or hyper-sexualised dress) their work marks a meaningful and inclusive reimagining: a girl's gaze — for all ages — in fashion.

For a generation of younger artists, memories and emotions from girlhood — such as loneliness, boredom, alienation or feeling 'othered' — serve as a foundation for their practice.

Born to Norwegian and Nigerian heritage, artist **Frida Orupabo** (b. 1986, Norway) began creating intriguing collages in her early twenties as a way of exploring the layered, intersectional experiences of Black girls and women.

> **'Being brought up in Norway in a predominantly white society, in a white family (except for my sister), I felt for a very long time I was unable to speak. The only thing I had was my eyes and my anger. Anger is a form of resistance. It sends out a message to your whole body that something is wrong — that what is being done towards you is not OK, even when you remain quiet as an oyster.'**[11]

Car Ride (2022) is striking in its restful silence — symbolic of the teenage twilight zone between dependency and autonomy. A young girl, in the back seat, is being taken along for a ride. The teddy bear on the roof, a treasured object, will perhaps be left behind, soon hidden from friends. While the girl drifts into daydreams, *quiet as an oyster*, it won't be long before she takes the wheel.

Arisa Yoshioka's (b. 2000, Mongolia) work also echoes the way girlhood unfolds as a continuous negotiation of where one belongs. Yoshioka spent the first half of her childhood in Mongolia, while the later years of her childhood unfolded in Japan. Being split between two cultures, her work weaves together melancholy, nostalgia and dreamlike recollections: each work tells us a story, but remains elusive. Is the white dress attached to her self-portrait a family heirloom or a symbol? Which girl is she during her gymnastics in Mongolia: the one shaped by discipline, the dreamer stretching toward escape, or someone else entirely? The truth for her lies in the haziness of memory; of being a girl caught between cultures.

Fumiko Imano's (b. 1974, Japan) girlhood was split into two parts of the world too. Her family relocated to Brazil when she was young and she became 'the only Japanese girl' at school, an outsider: 'alone sucking my thumb'.[12] At eight, the family moved back to Japan, where Imano felt even more alien and found it hard to adapt herself to the culture, and was bullied at school. She felt homesick for Brazil and found solace in 'flipping through old family photo albums'.[13] In the early 2000s, when she was studying fashion photography at Central Saint Martins and the London College of Fashion, she embarked on a decades-long series featuring her imaginary identical twin sister. Using a 35mm camera, scissors and glue, she inserted her imagined twin into the works. Imano and her twin have since lived out decades of adventures. Her work has offered her relief, escapism and success. The photos recall 1970s- and 1980s-style family albums, where her father used to say, 'Look at me!' — the twins also always look directly at the camera. Though Imano was saved by her twin, she wouldn't want her to exist in real life. It's in her imagination that the enduring magic of her eccentric, funny and flawed vision of girlhood lives on: always together, never alone. Always ordering room service.

For some fashion designers of that generation, memories of family life and belonging are entwined with vivid, tactile recollections of garments they were mesmerised by when growing up. **Jen-Fang Shueh** (b. 1979, Taiwan), the designer behind Jenny Fax, was raised in Taipei with two sisters, a brother and a mother she describes as 'a super busy working lady'.[14] Left to roam freely, she recalls how her mother pre-paid the local video store

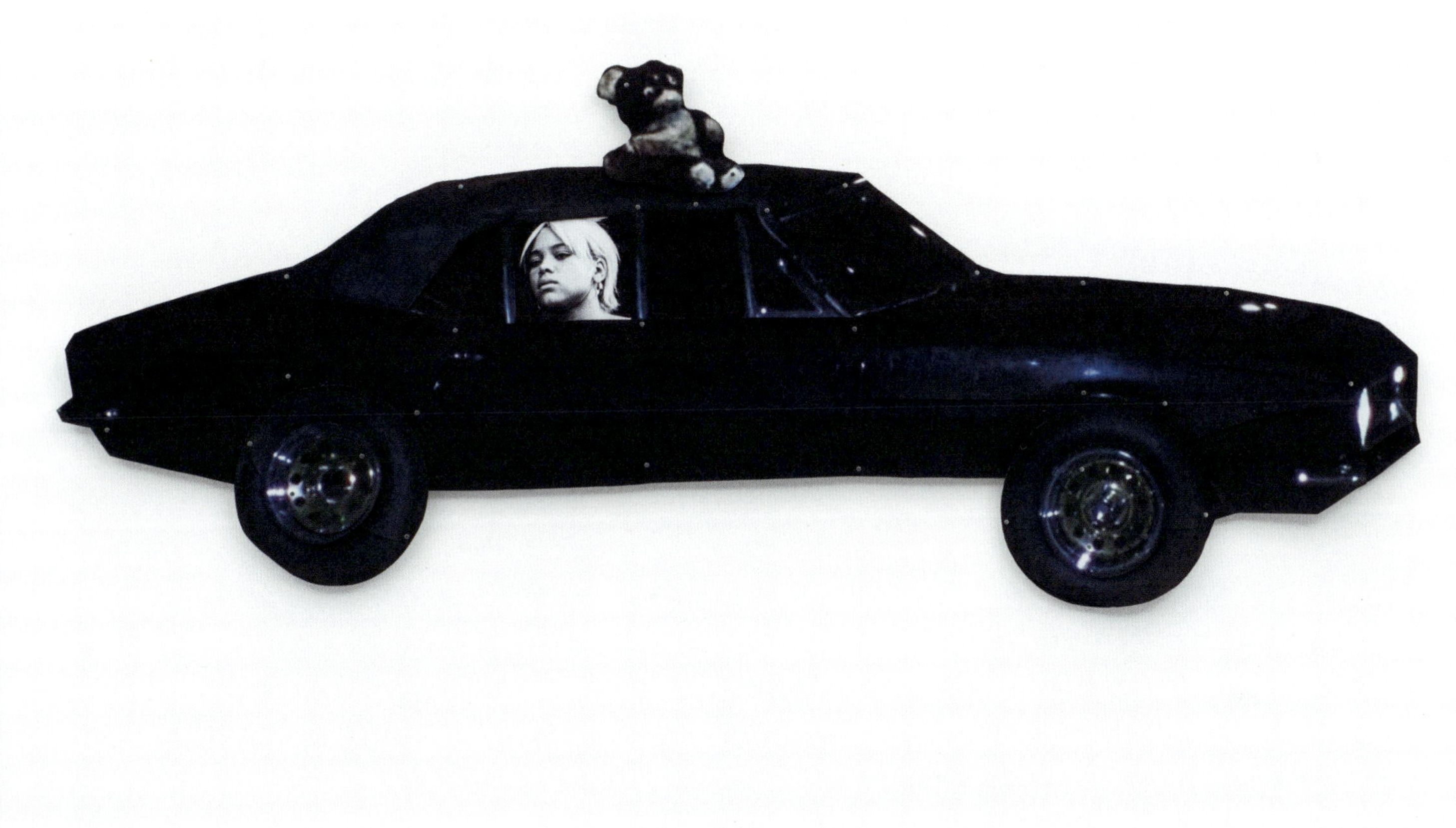

Frida Orupabo
Car Ride, 2022
Collage with paper pins on birch plywood panel

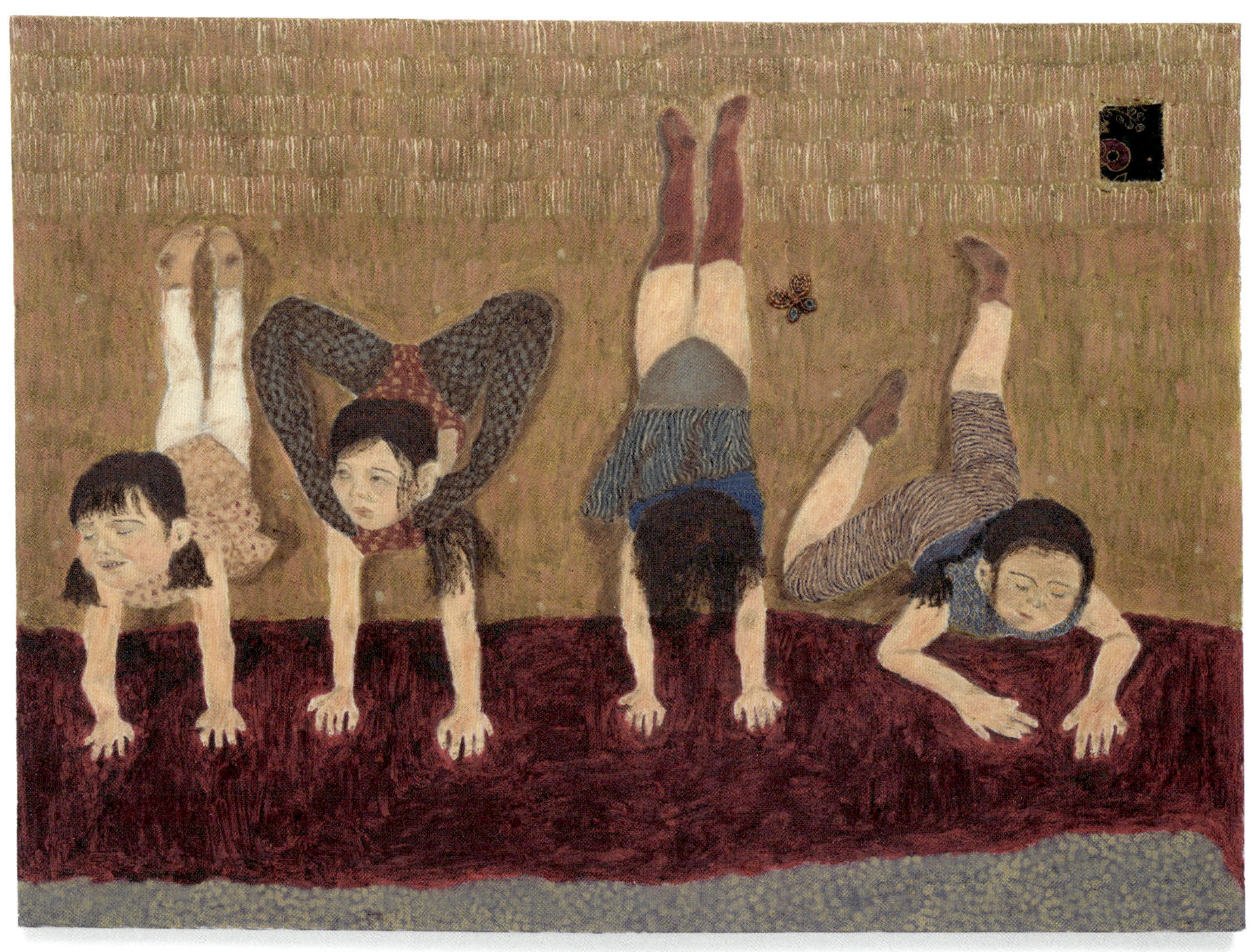

Arisa Yoshioka
Untitled 3, 2023
Oil and fabric on linen

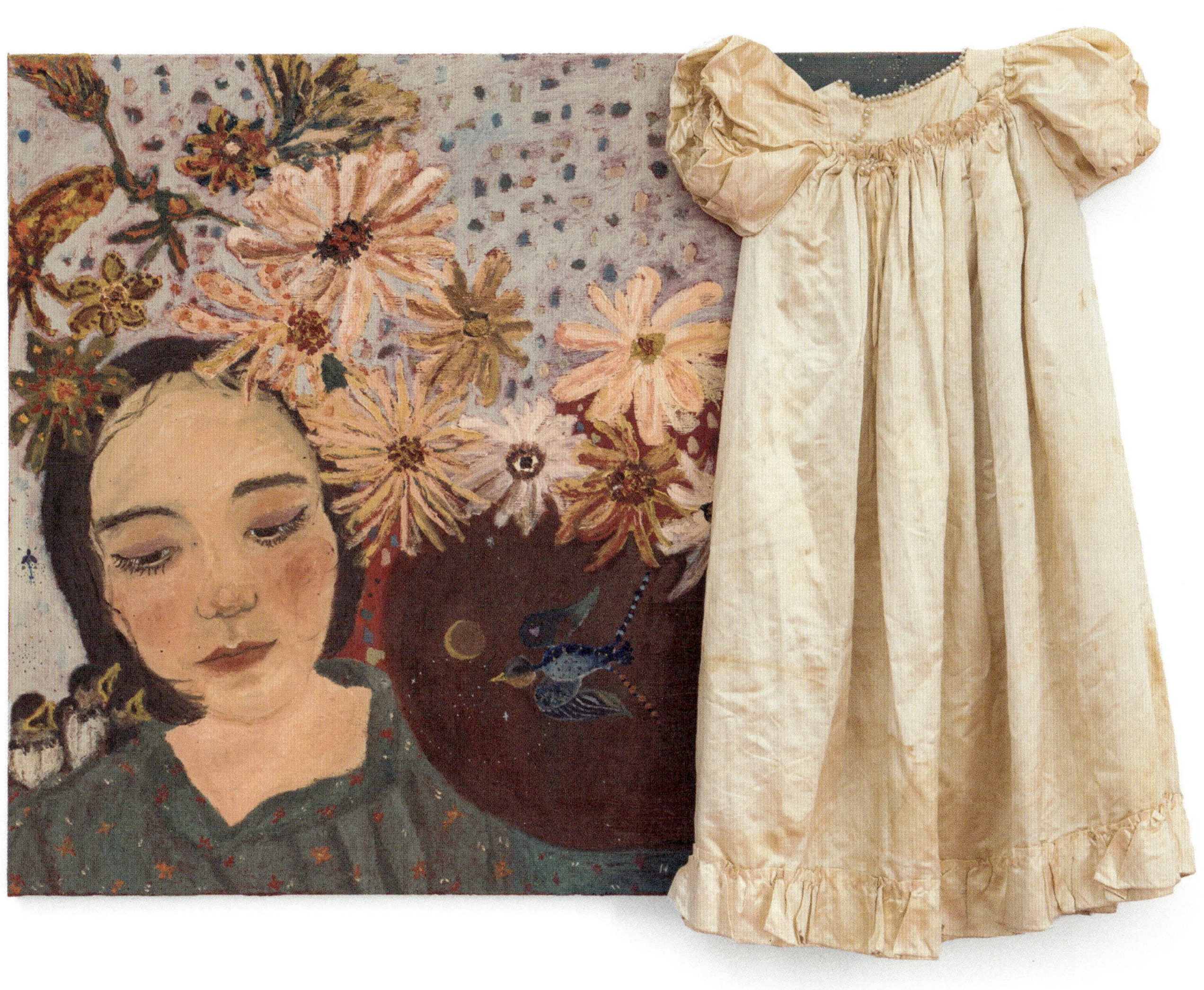

Arisa Yoshioka
Self-portrait, 2024
Oil on linen, vintage dress attached

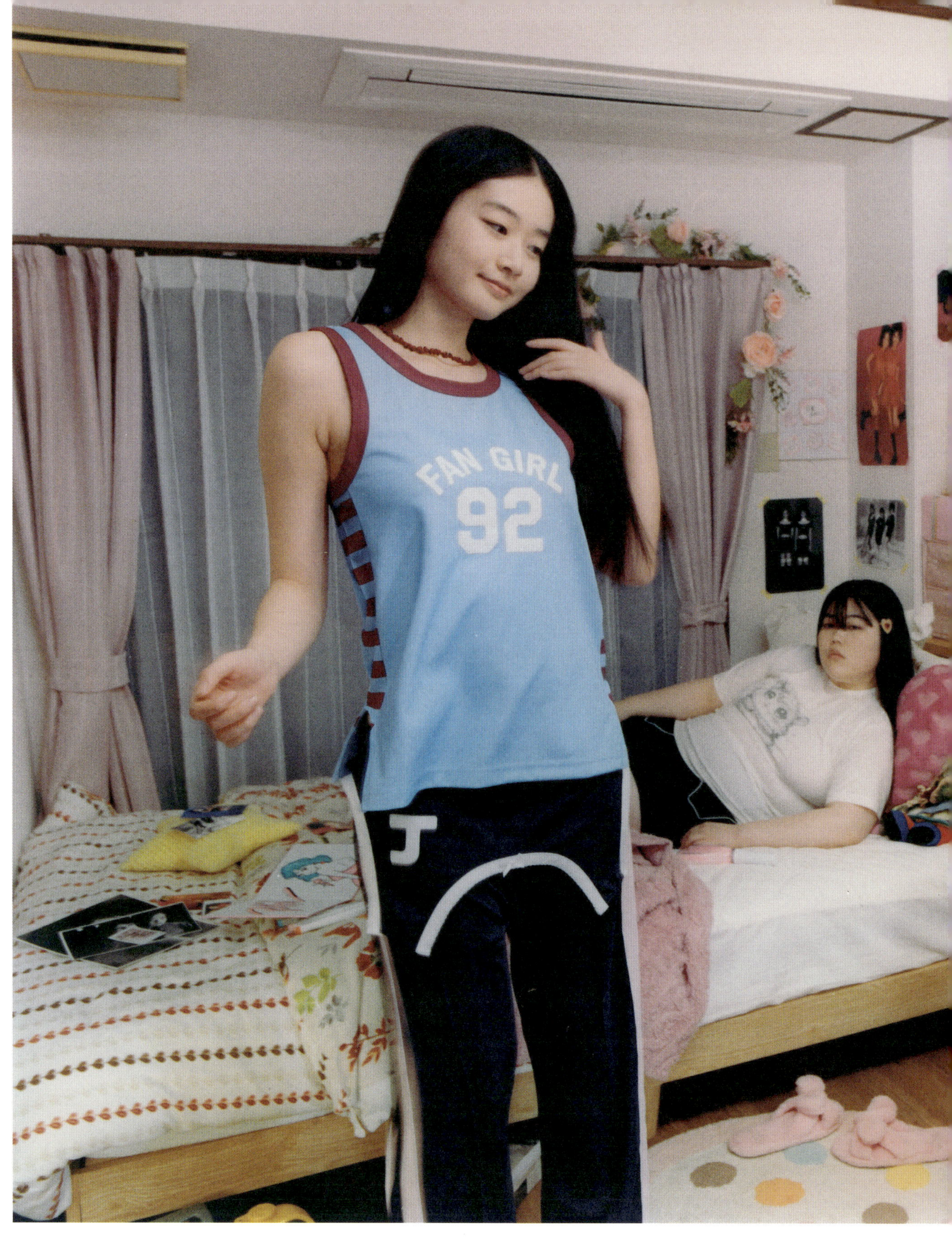
FAN GIRL
92

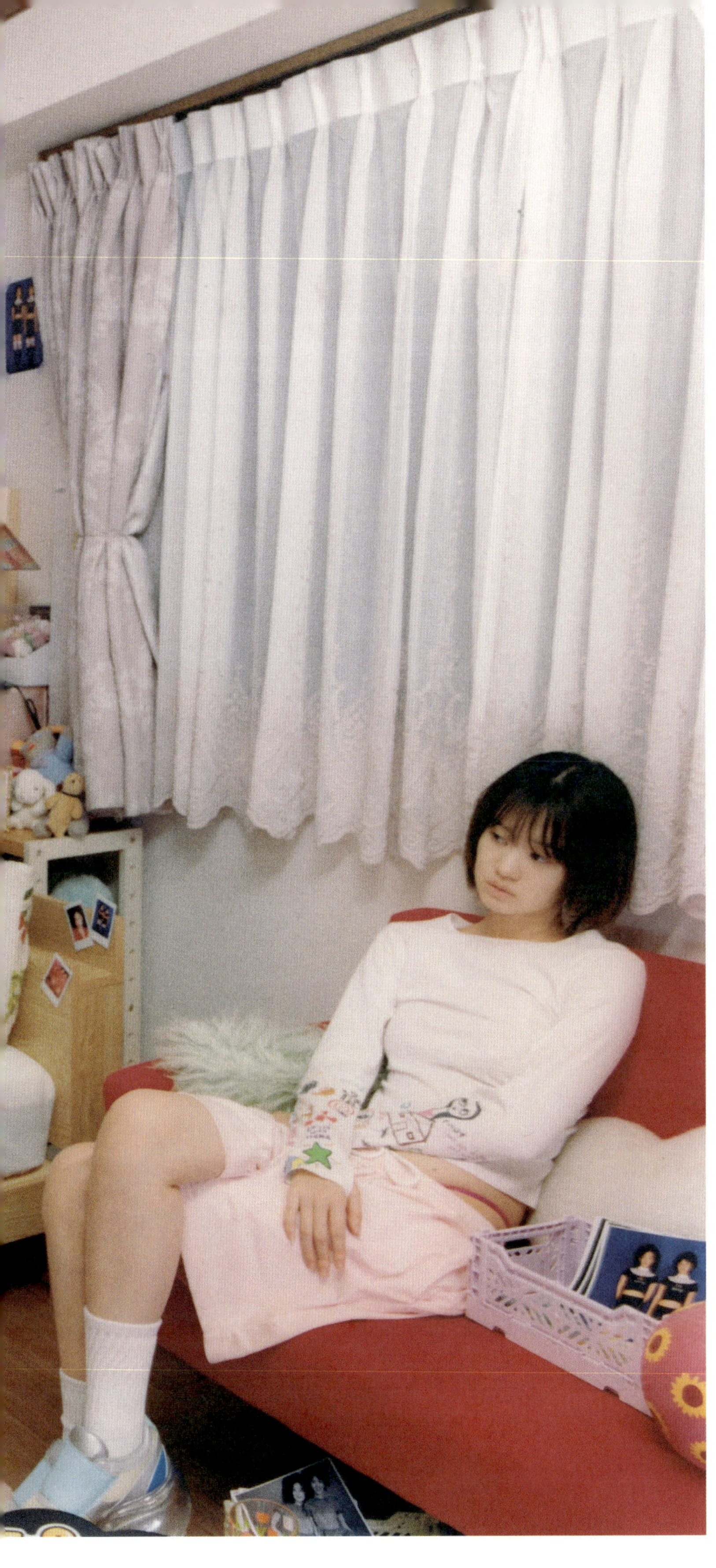

I'm Sorry by Petra Collins
in collaboration with Jenny Fax,
photographed by Fish Zhang, 2025

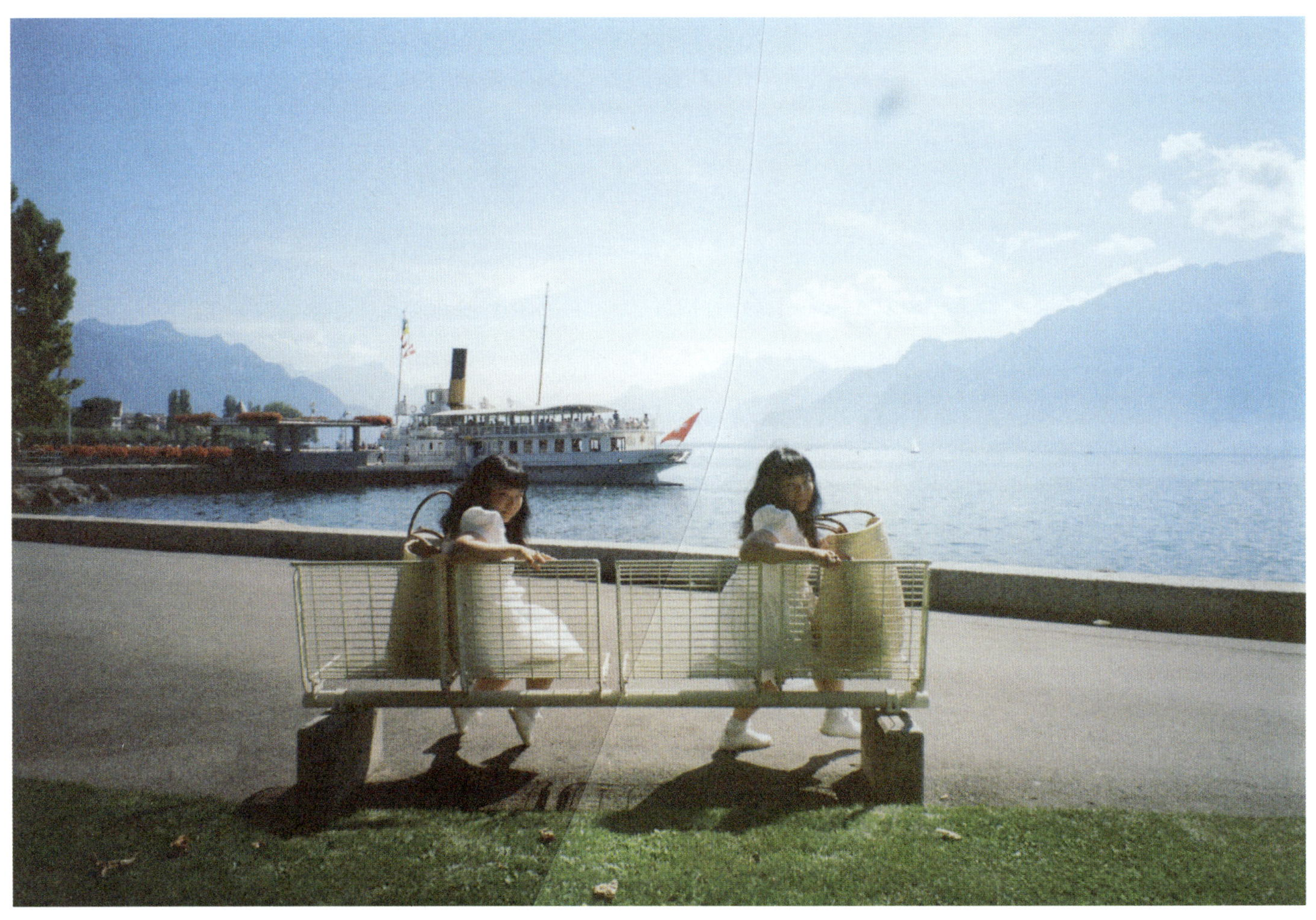

Fumiko Imano
Perdonnet/Vevey/Switzerland, 2018

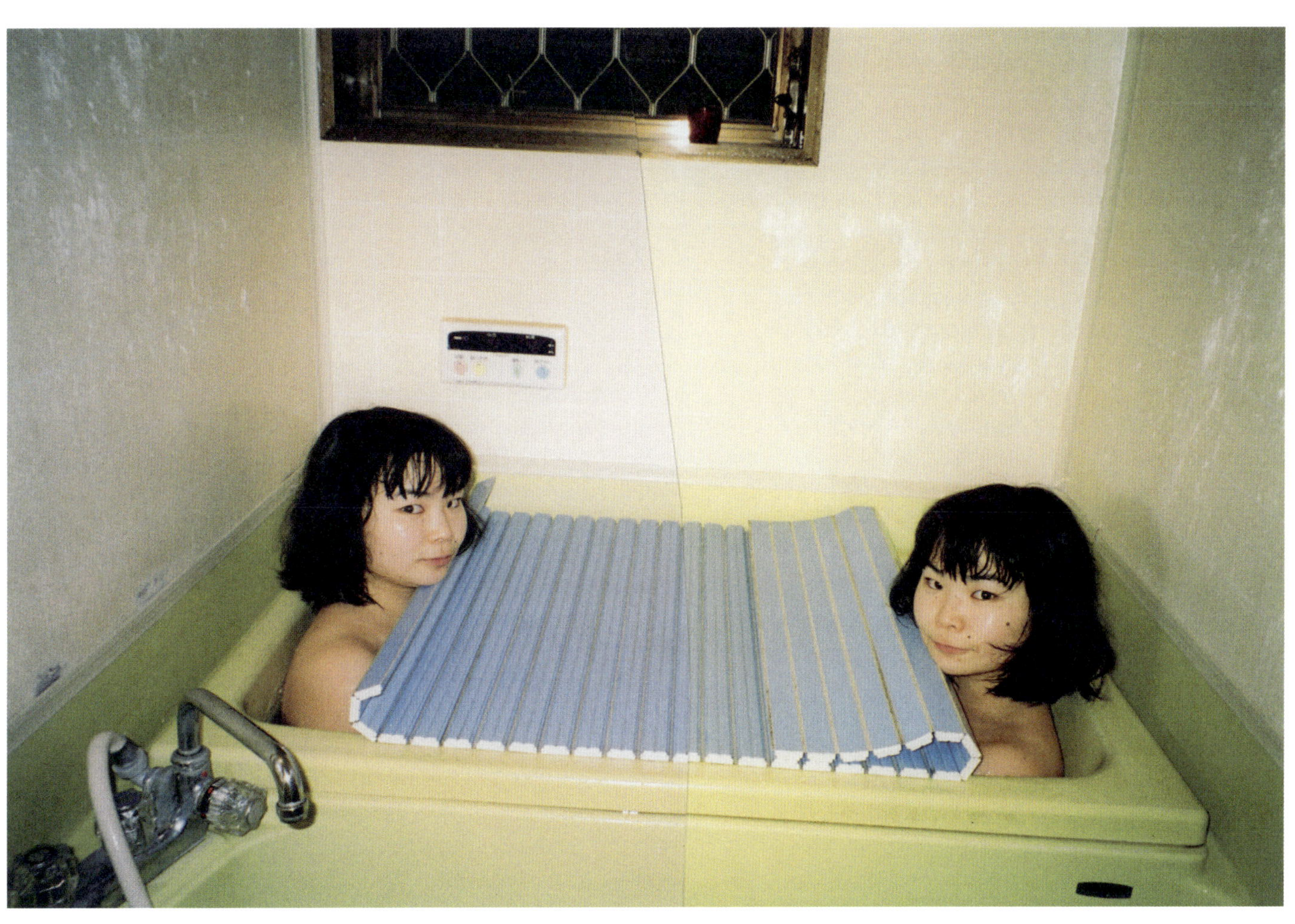

Fumiko Imano
Yellow bath/Hitachi/Japan, 2007

so that the children could rent one videotape a day, and they watched all the Hong Kong horror movies.

Some of her sharpest memories stem from childhood road trips across the Taiwanese countryside: the damp velvet seats of her father's Ford; the tension of witnessing her parents argue in the car; her mother walking home alone along the highway. Each collection oscillates between her childhood longing for princess dresses and something broken or destructible. Her work doesn't romanticise girlhood. Instead, it lays bare its layers: its silliness, its sadness, its magical, cinematic quality.

Simone Rocha (b. 1986, Ireland) grew up surrounded by textiles; her father, designer John Rocha, was born in Hong Kong. Simone was born and raised in Ireland, the birthplace of her mother, Odette Rocha, who describes her daughter as a storyteller who grew up interested in Irish myths, legends and folklore.[15] As a teenager, she was captivated by the darker, more rebellious edges of fashion, but when her peers dressed in pristine white frocks for their First Communion — and as a non-Catholic, she couldn't — it left a deep and lasting impression. It was a moment marked by envy and longing — a desire to be part of that sartorially intriguing ritual, an outsider looking in. Rocha's work in fashion celebrates womanhood and a personal, subversive femininity, while evoking her visceral memories of girlhood paraphernalia — the objects that surrounded her and the ones she longed for.

Contemporary art, like fashion, has played a crucial role in exploring and expressing gender in its many forms, a role that feels especially urgent in light of ongoing legislative and political efforts to deny trans girls and women their rights and restrict their gender identities based on binary notions of biological sex.

the in-between

In *Charlotte* (2023), **Nathanaëlle Herbelin** (b. 1989, Israel) captures a moment of intimate gender exploration, portraying her neighbour Charles — seen through their facing windows. Still living with his mother, uncertain whether to feel like a boy or a girl, Charles/Charlotte is caught in 'the in-between'. The painting conveys both trust and distance: Herbelin — like us — is looking in. There is tenderness, but also isolation in this moment of self-discovery. It echoes ideas articulated by Judith Butler in *Gender Trouble* (1990), where they argue that gender is not fixed at birth but continually formed — a process shaped by culture, choice and resistance. Girlhood is not a given but something constructed and redefined over time. Against that backdrop of deeply politicised gender discourses, Herbelin's painting offers not just observation, but solidarity. The window becomes a soft boundary — a gesture of care that both protects and reflects the courage of becoming.

Simone Rocha
Spring-Summer 2022

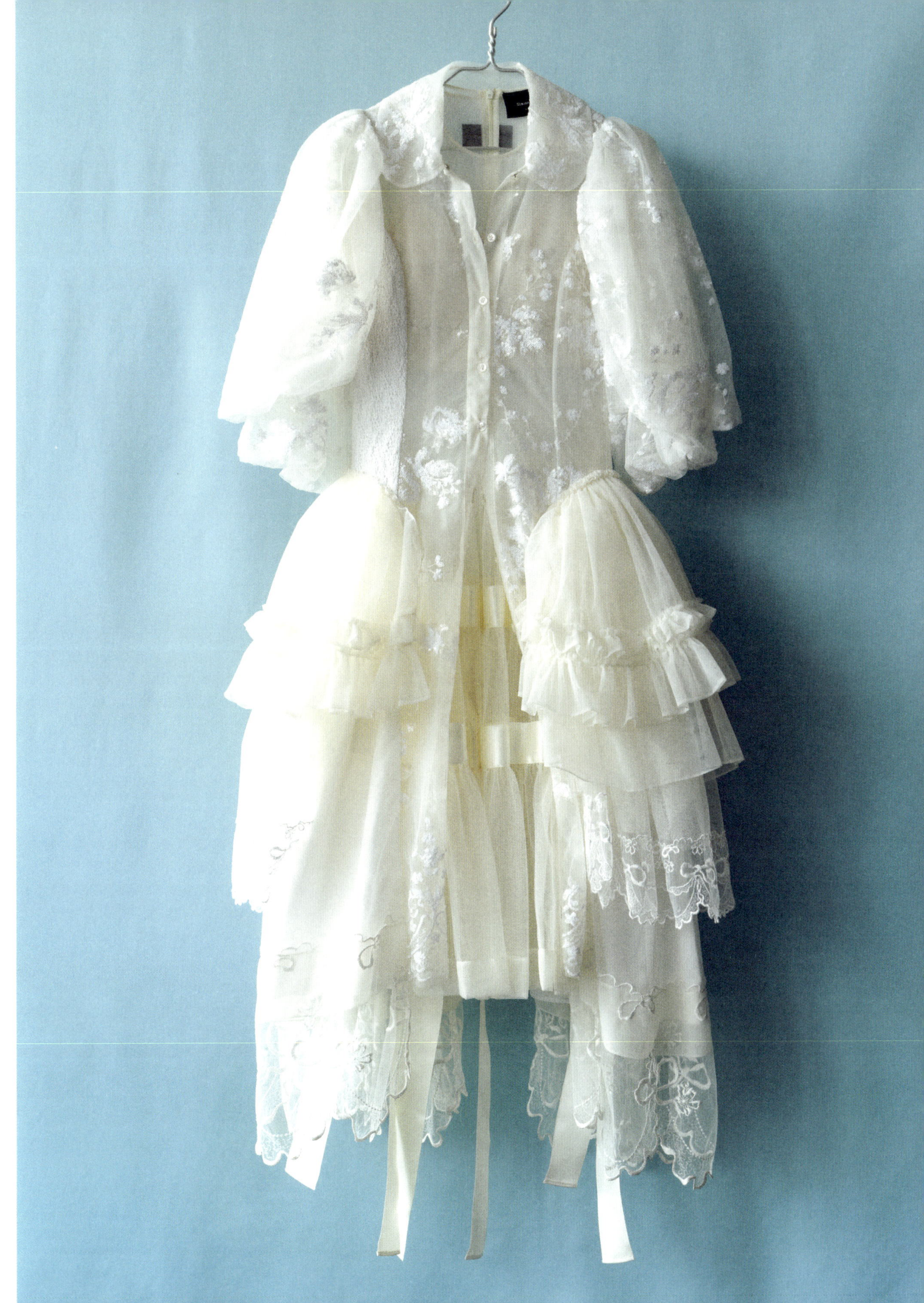

before it slips away

Photographing the unselfconscious magic of teenage girls is most resonant when the subjects have agency in the creation of the work. In 1976, photographer **Jim Britt** captured the candid, awkward charm of his daughters Melendy (Mimi) and Jody, just a year apart and almost twin-like. Over a decade later, one of their photos was used as the Autumn-Winter 1988–89 campaign for Comme des Garçons.

That same sense of comfort and trust is captured in *This is Me, This is You* (1997–2000) by **Roni Horn** (b. 1955, USA). Created over the space of two years, the work offers a dynamic portrait of her niece Georgia, who invited the artist to photograph her. Horn was just following her lead:

> **'Maybe she was eating, or maybe she was just waking up, or she was taking a bath, or she was out swimming in the ocean, or whatever she was doing. And if I was there and I took some snapshots, wanted to get eye contact, and that it was an automatic camera so you would hear two shots. That's all I needed.'**[16]

The 48 portraits were taken with a point-and-shoot camera, paired with another 48, shot just seconds apart — almost identical, yet revealing a play between self-awareness and the moment immediately after. Georgia enjoyed dressing up, and Horn noticed that she would sometimes change her clothes three to four times a day — not because she was being photographed, but because she liked to explore her options. The work shows just how transformative two years can be: how one evolves in adolescence, and how, if you blink, you might miss the glory of it all.

In *Isabetta* (1934–35) and *Memories* (1981), a young girl meets our gaze with piercing blue eyes. The girl is **Alice Neel**'s (1900–1984, USA) daughter, Isabetta, her second child and only surviving daughter with the Cuban artist Carlos Enríquez. Their first child, Santillana, died of diphtheria around her first birthday in 1927. As her due date with Isabetta approached, Neel was plagued by depression and anxiety. When Isabetta was born, Neel struggled to reconcile the societal expectations of motherhood with her own urgent desire to pursue a life as an artist. She later said, 'I always had this awful dichotomy. I loved Isabetta, of course I did. But I wanted to paint.'[17] Carlos, hoping to give Alice a break, took Isabetta to Havana. The plan was for Neel to join them there before moving to Paris as a family. Instead, Carlos left for Paris alone, leaving Isabetta with his sisters in Cuba. Neel suffered a breakdown and was institutionalised in Philadelphia. Upon her release, she seemed to accept what the therapists had been telling her: that being a mother and an artist are irreconcilable.[18]

Mother and daughter would not see each other again for four years. When they did meet again, Neel painted her in the summer of 1934. Isabetta had barely been walking when Alice had last seen her, now she was five years old. Isabetta, raised in Cuba, only saw her mother a handful of times throughout her life. Painted as a memory of this reunion, *Memories* (1981) is a late recalling of how her baby had become a girl. In *Baby on the Fire Escape: Creativity, Motherhood, and the Mind-Baby Problem* Julie Phillips wrote: 'Children in her paintings often look fragile, astonished, curious, restless, but this is a portrait of an independent, almost invulnerable child — a daughter who doesn't need her mother.'[19]

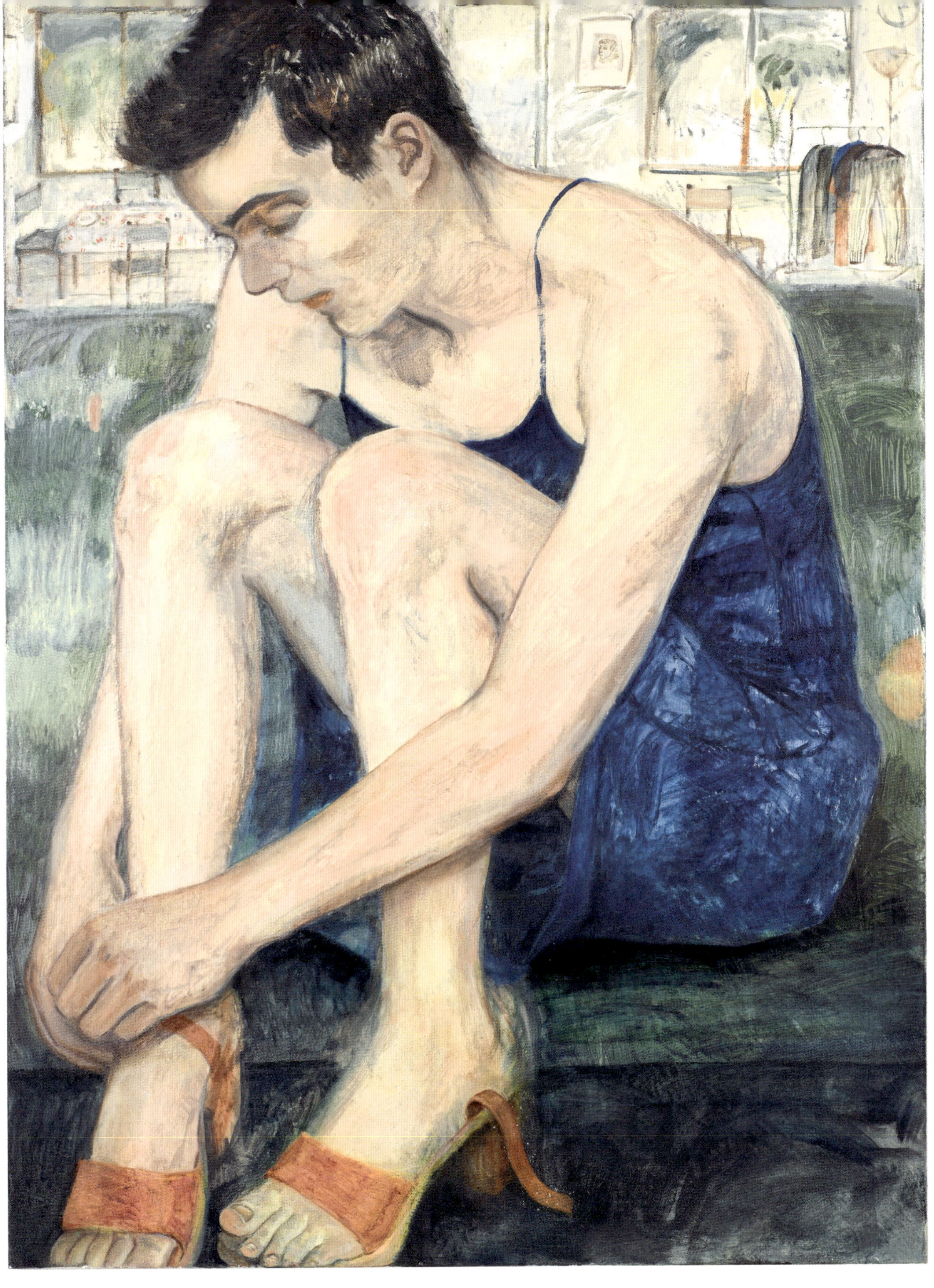

Nathanaëlle Herbelin
Charlotte, 2023
Oil on canvas

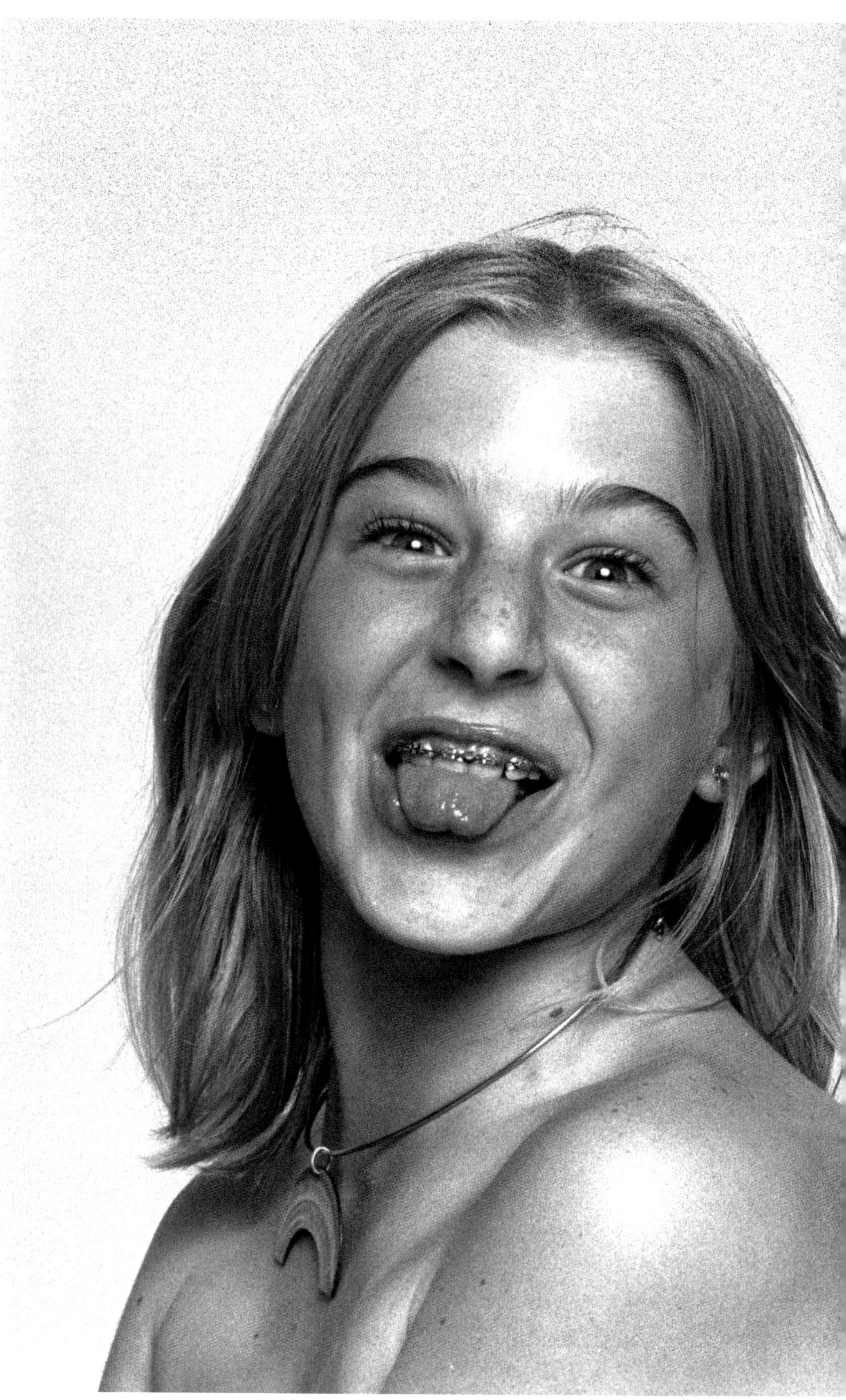

Jim Britt
Sisters, 1976

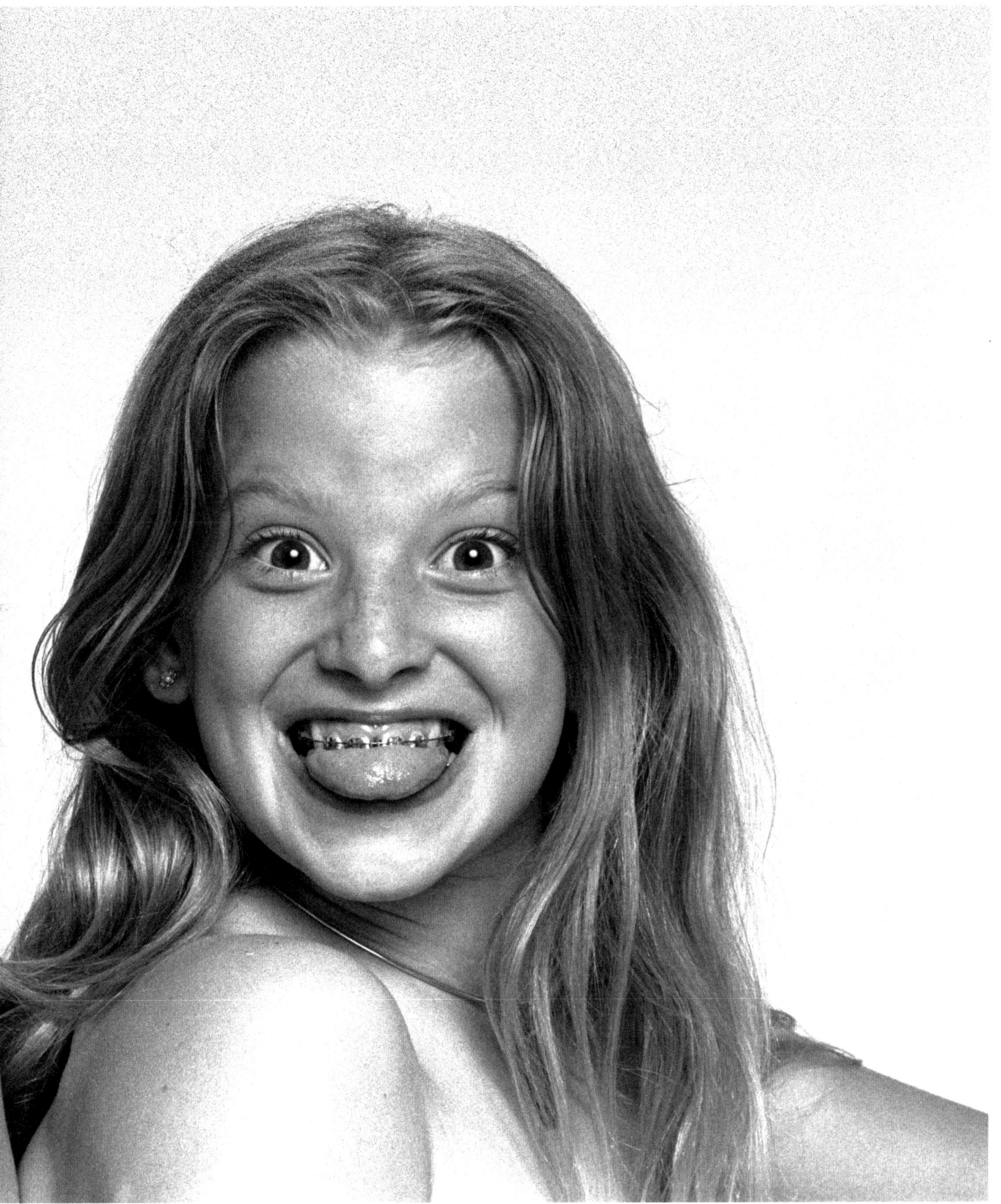

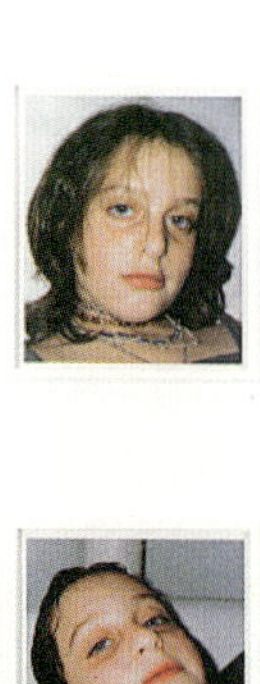
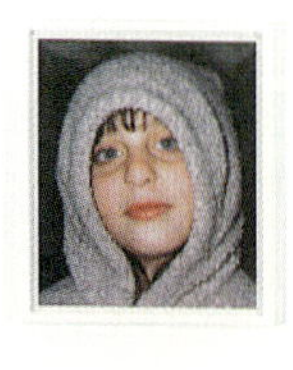
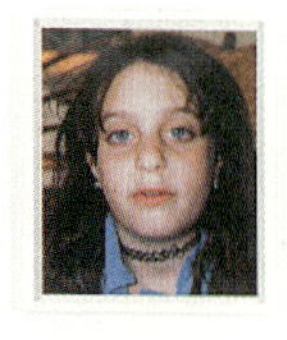
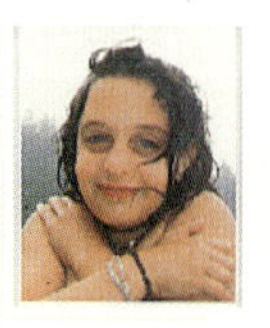
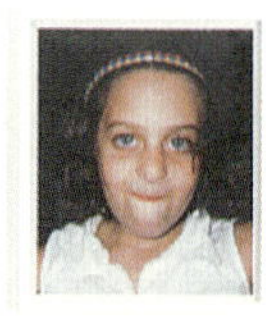
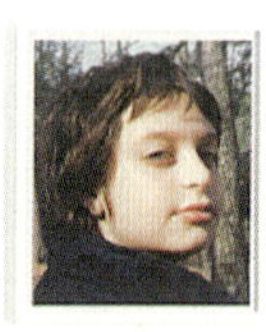
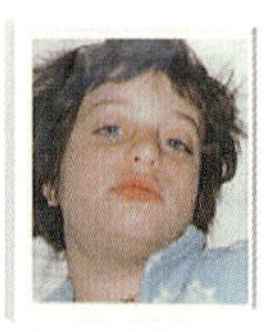
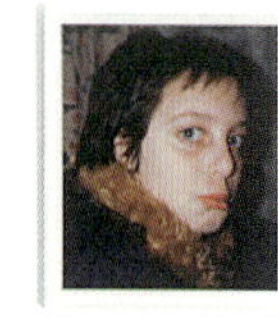
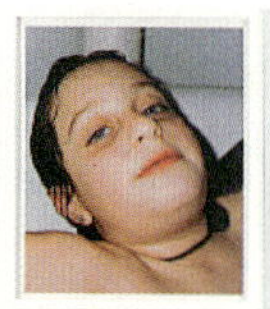
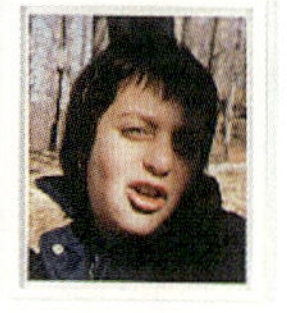
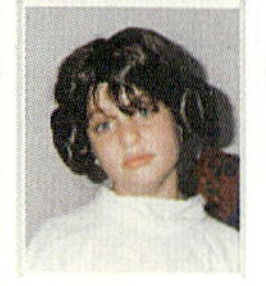
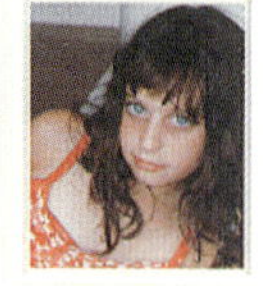
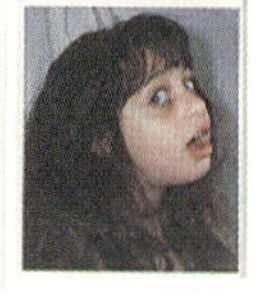
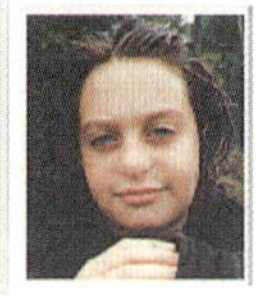
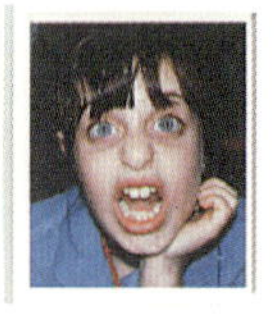
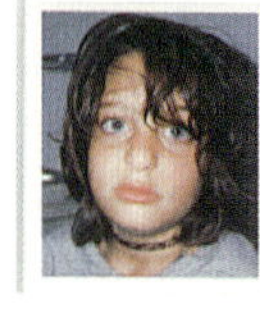
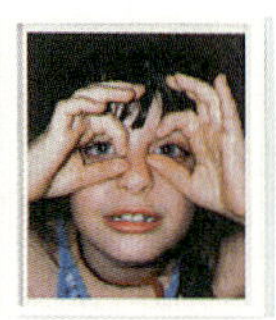
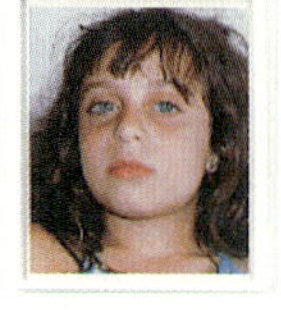
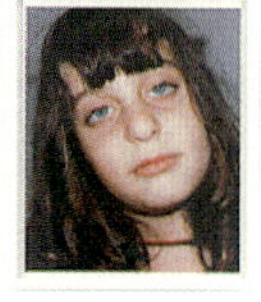
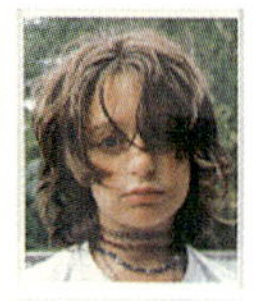
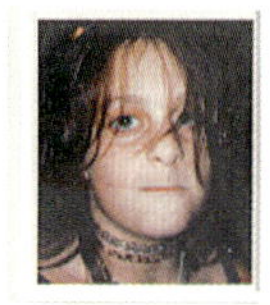
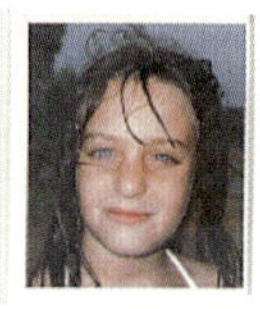
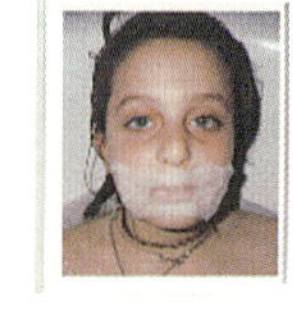
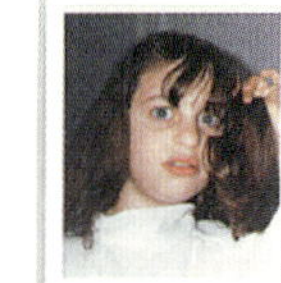
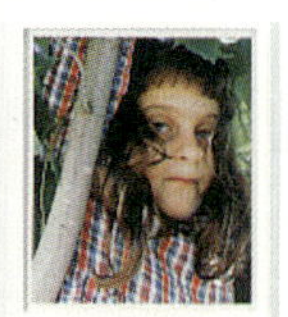
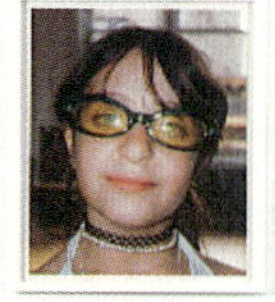
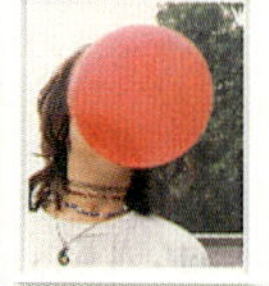
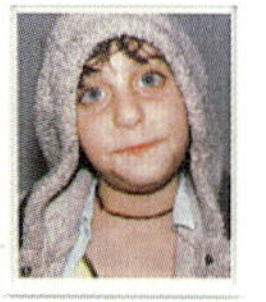
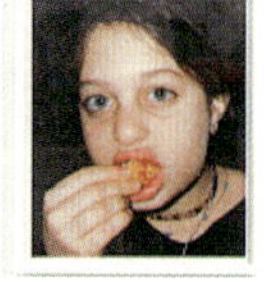
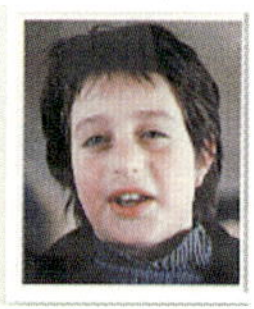
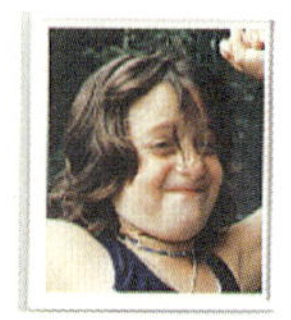
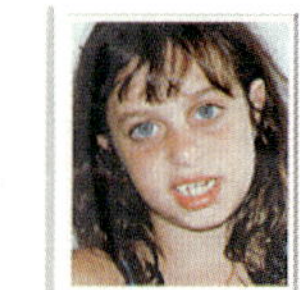
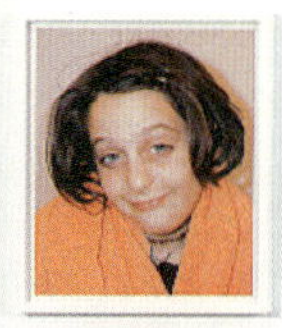
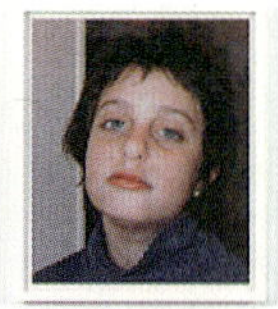
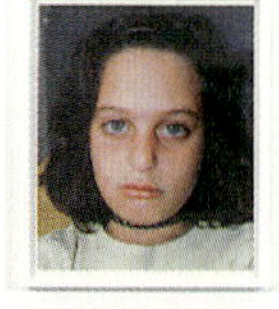
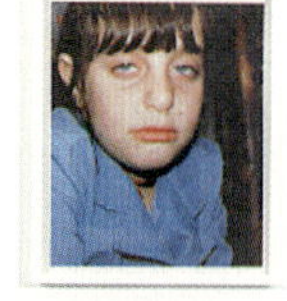
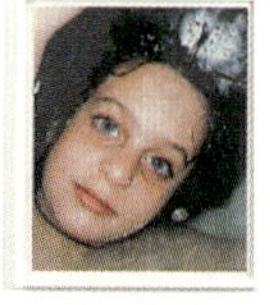
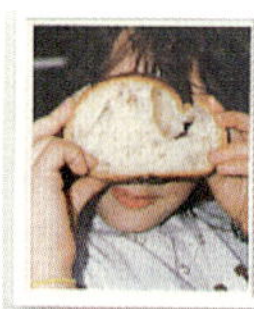
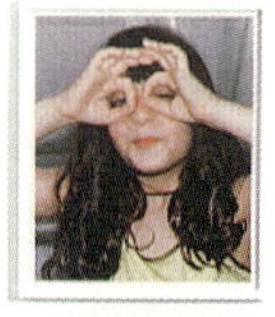
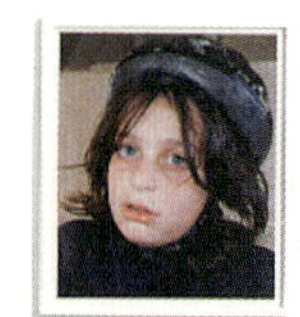
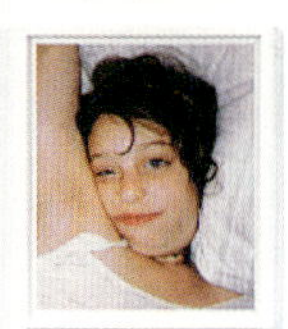
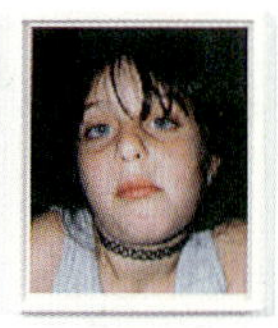
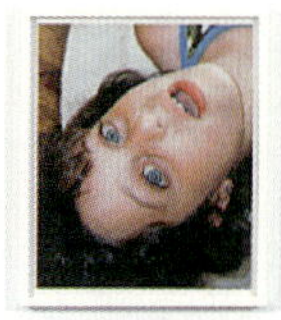
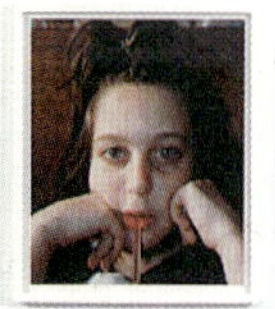
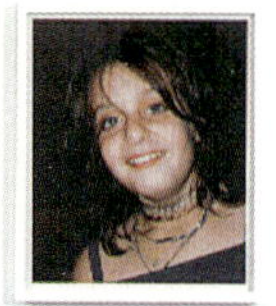
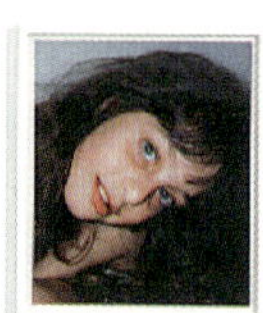
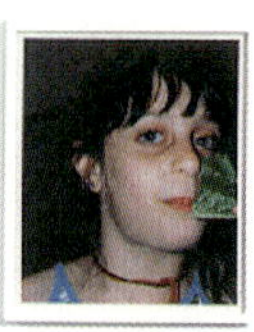
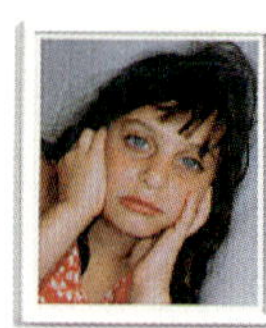

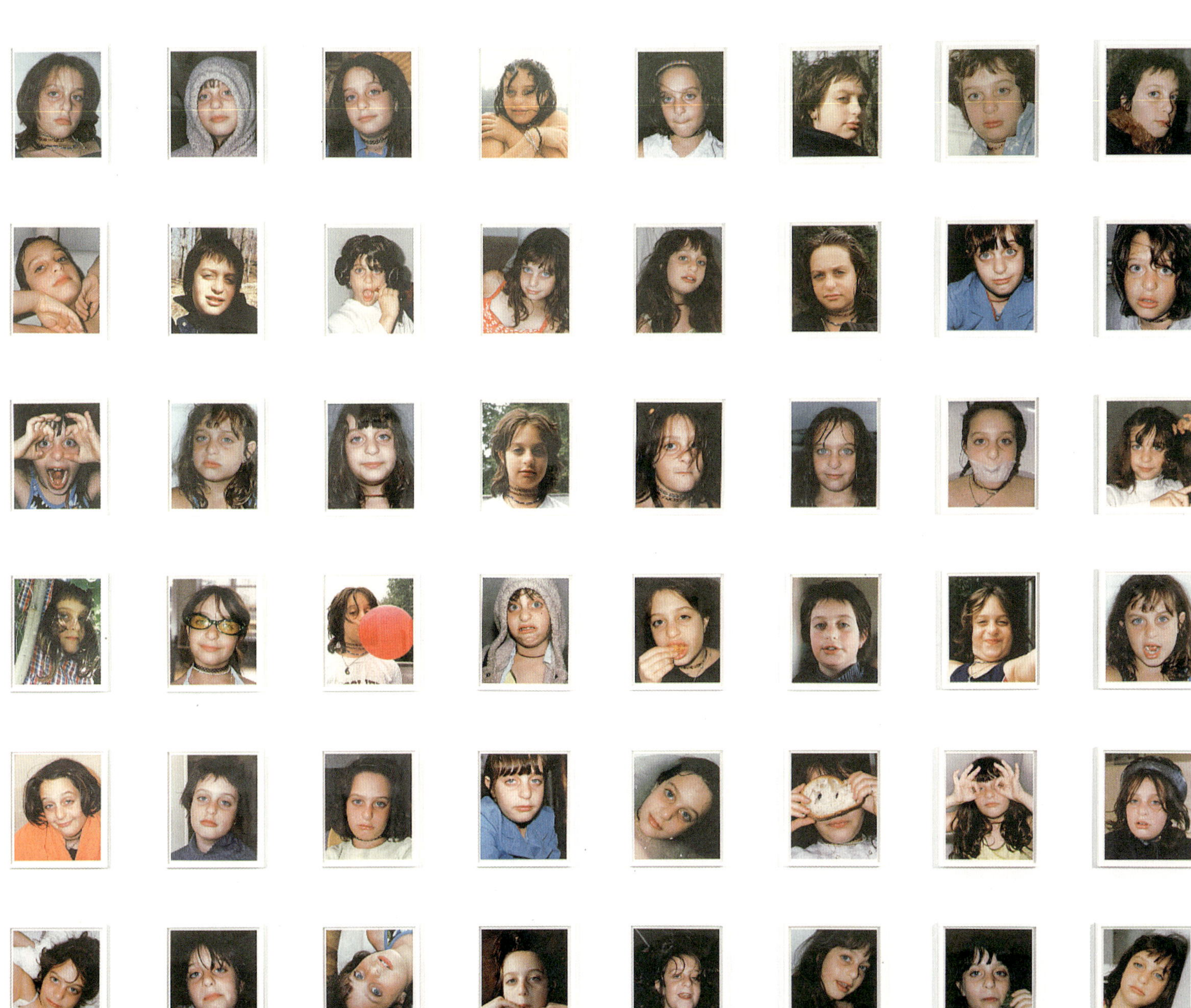

Roni Horn
This is Me, This is You (edition 2/6), 1997–2000
96 mounted and framed c-prints

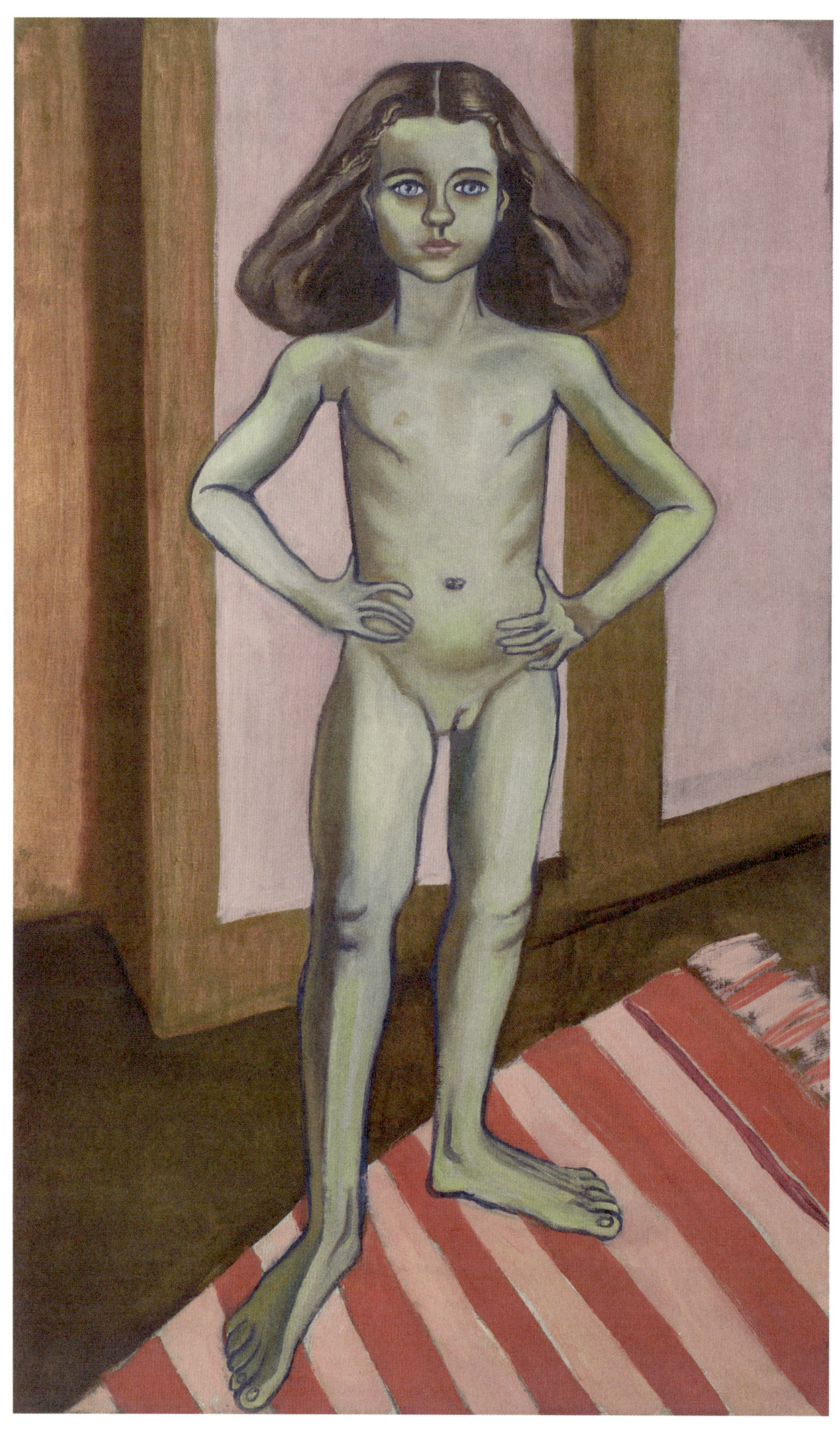

Alice Neel
Isabetta, 1934–1935
Oil on canvas

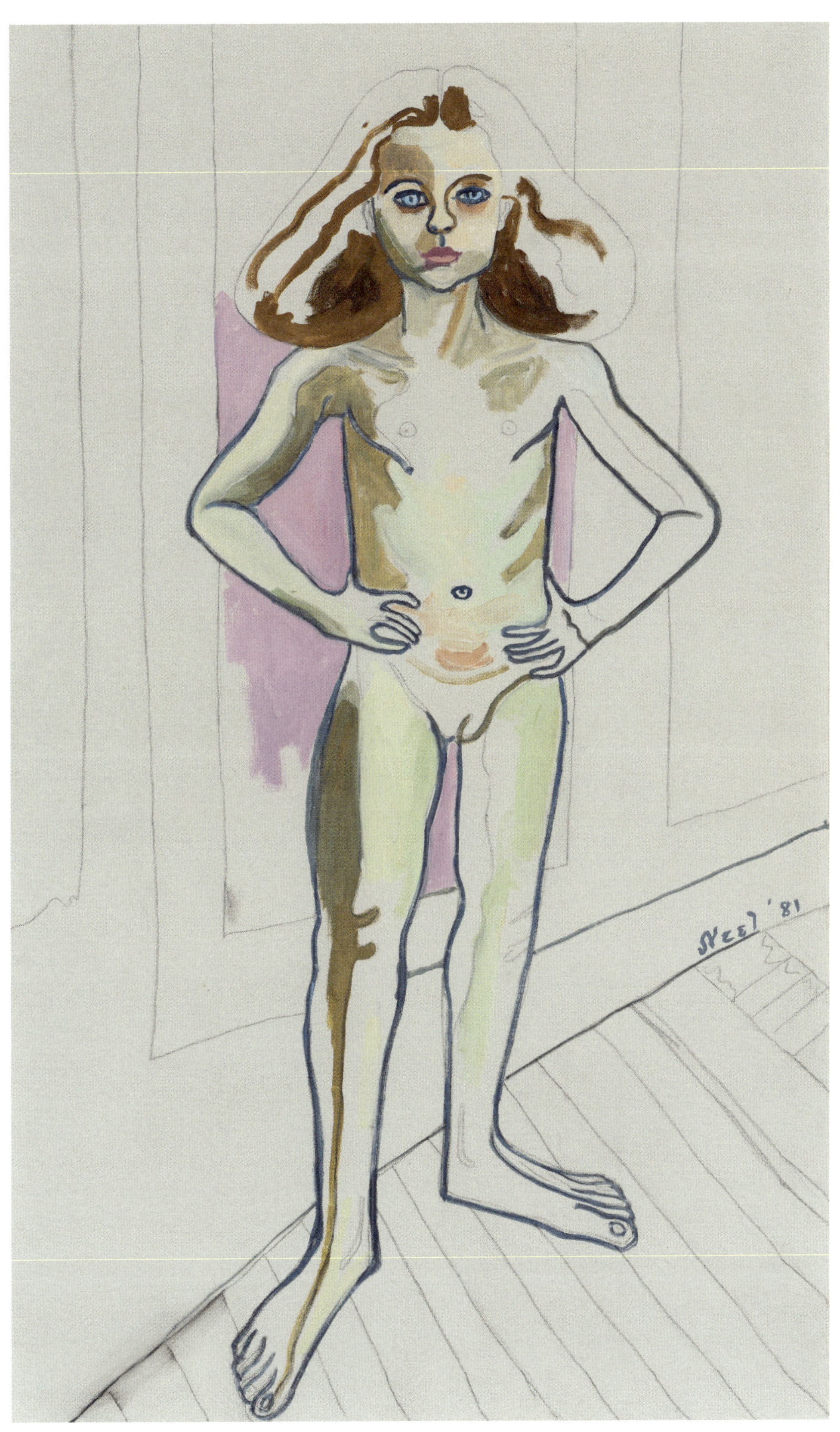

Alice Neel
Memories, 1981
Oil on canvas

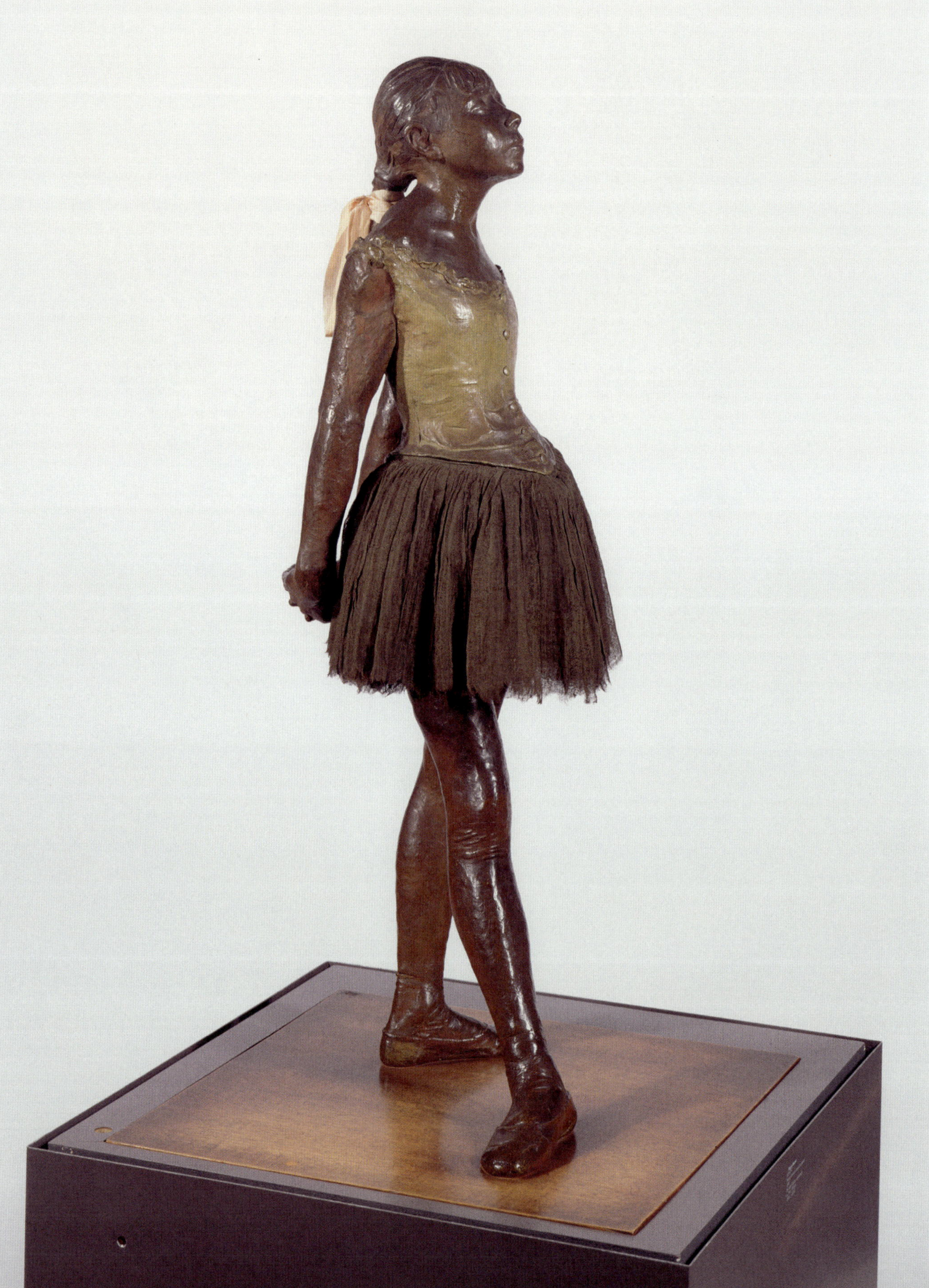

Isabetta died of suicide in 1982 at the age of fifty-four; Neel, who hadn't seen her daughter for over thirty years, died in 1984. A socially engaged artist, Neel's legacy lies in her special ability to reveal the psychological depth of those that had been overlooked by traditional portraiture — women, people of colour, children, artists and the marginalised.

The memories of those fleeting girlhood years linger in objects and outgrown garments. In **Robert Gober**'s (b. 1954, USA) *Untitled* (1992), a child's shoe sprouts human hair from its insole.

> **'I saw this shoe in the middle of East 10th Street early one morning. It had a poignancy as if a little girl had lost it and was still walking around the city with one shoe. I'm sure the reality is that it was in the garbage and the garbage was ransacked or sloppily loaded into the garbage truck and that the shoe was abandoned because it was unwanted or outgrown.'**[20]

There's something quietly unsettling about seeing just one child's shoe — something is missing, something's not right. Beginning in 1986, Robert Gober expanded his practice to include wax sculptures of human body parts, using them to explore themes of gender, sexuality and vulnerability. The Mary Jane is a shoe historically tied to white, middle-class girlhood: neat, obedient, polite. Here, it becomes intimate and abject: childhood innocence disrupted.

The Little Fourteen-Year-Old Dancer (1880–81) by **Edgar Degas** (1834–1917, France) carries a similar disquiet. The sculpture, two-thirds life-size, portrays Marie van Goethem, a young ballet student born in Brussels and raised in poverty. The original sculpture was made of wax and dressed in a real tutu, with a silk ribbon braided through human hair. Shown in a glass case, its stark realism unsettled contemporary viewers — some called it uncanny, like a specimen on display in a natural history museum.[21] Degas's work disrupted the idealised image of girlhood. His dancer is not mythic — she's real. Degas depicted the reality of the *petits rats* at the Paris Opéra as working-class girls. Marie posed for Degas to supplement her income. Over time, she faded from history.[22]

There is an alluring connection between girlhood and the ancient process of wax modelling. In 1999, **Iris Häussler** (b. 1962, Germany) also turned to the material, sourcing her own family's laundry to create sealed sculptures with shirts, undergarments, childhood dresses. The works relate to our most intimate sensory associations — sense and touch. In *She 06* (2006), a pristine white sailor's dress floats in wax. Häussler never wore it but it was always in her wardrobe.[23] The dress is a vision of girlhood as something imagined: a thing a parent buys when the child is still an abstract concept. Waxing recalls mummification — a preservation of memory — but it can melt and crack. It demands constant care. We may try to hold the past, but memory is unstable.

Edgar Degas
***The Little Fourteen-Year-Old Dancer*, 1880–1881**
(cast c. 1922)

In this exhibition and publication, girlhood emerges as an ambiguous language: delicate, subversive, volatile, unresolved; satin with frayed edges, wax cracking, photos manipulated, personal memories as generators for metaphorical associations. The artists reveal how the freedom to roam, the intense boredom or loneliness, feeling strange or 'othered' can render the girlhood years an endless chapter — one we long to escape or rebel against. But that — even as we age — we keep one foot, or at least a little toe, in the trenches of those years.

Will there be an exhibition about boys? Perhaps even one at MoMu. There should be. There likely will be. But the hypothetical questions — why focus on 'girls' and not 'boys'? Why so binary? — linger in my mind, more than they should. They wake me at night, a jolt of terror. Will people be upset? And then I remind myself: girls deserve this space.

So let this be about the girls. For the trans kids. For those who lift them up — the friends, the siblings, the parents, the teachers, the mentors, the charities, the ones who listen. There is no future without teenagers. Yet, for too many, that future is rough and uncertain. In the worst places to be a young girl, gender inequality, poverty, conflict and deep-rooted discrimination steal opportunities before they begin. This project is for them, too. A reminder that through art, fashion and culture, representation and storytelling are essential in shaping visibility, empowering agency and catalysing societal transformation.

notes

1 Hustvedt, S., *Mothers, Fathers and Others* (London: Hodder & Stoughton, 2021), 203.
2 Bourgeois, L., *Album* (New York: Peter Blum Edition, 1994), n.p. Reprinted in Bernadac, M.-L., and Obrist, H.U. (eds.), *Louise Bourgeois: Destruction of the Father/ Reconstruction of the Father: Writings and Interviews 1923–1997* (London: Violette Editions, 1998), 277.
3 Bourgeois, L., diary entry, 14 December 1923, Louise Bourgeois Archive/ The Easton Foundation, New York (hereinafter cited as TEF).
4 https://fabricworkshopandmuseum.org/artist/louise-bourgeois/ (accessed 5 May 2025). Philadelphia 1992: opening of the 15th Anniversary 'Annual Benefit of Fabric Workshop' with a new installation and a performance of *She Lost It* by Louise Bourgeois in collaboration with The Fabric Workshop.
5 Bourgeois, L., diary entry, 24 November 1947 (TEF).
6 As quoted in 'Art, no less than wisdom, waits on life', in Gorovoy, J., Herkenhoff, P., and Tabatabai Asbaghi, P., *Louise Bourgeois: Blue Days and Pink Days* (Milan: Fondazione Prada, 1997), 25.
7 De Beauvoir, S., *The Second Sex* (trans. H.M. Parshley), (New York: Vintage Books, 1989), 267.
8 Mitchell, J., 'Louise Bourgeois and Sigmund Freud: *Passage Dangereux*, the Girl in Psychoanalysis and Art', in Larratt-Smith, P., *Louise Bourgeois. Freud's Daughter* (New Haven and London: Yale University Press, 2021), 136.
9 Specter, M., 'Miuccia Prada: The Designer', *The New Yorker*, 7 March 2004. https://www.newyorker.com/magazine/2004/03/15/miuccia-prada-the-designer.
10 Interview with Veronique Branquinho by Elisa De Wyngaert via email on 20/04/2025.
11 Blomkamp, S., 'Frida Orupabo: Quiet Like an Oyster', *Oath Magazine*, January 2023. https://www.stevenson.info/sites/default/files/Frida%20Orubapo%20Quiet%20as%20an%20Oyster_SCB_final.pdf.
12 Interview with Elisa De Wyngaert via email on 11/04/2025.
13 Ibidem.
14 Cheng, C., 'Jenny Fax', *COEVAL Magazine*, 22 November 2019, https://www.coeval-magazine.com/coeval/jenny-fax.
15 Burley, I. (ed.), *Simone Rocha* (New York: Rizzoli, 2024), 194.
16 Whitney Museum of American Art, 'Roni Horn: This Is Me, This Is You', video interview, 16 April 2013. https://whitney.org/media/407.
17 Phillips, J., *Baby on the Fire Escape: Creativity, Motherhood, and the Mind-Baby Problem* (New York: W. W. Norton, 2022), 34. This story is told in more detail in this group biography by Julie Philips.
18 Ibid., 36.
19 Ibid., 41.
20 This reflection appears on the Matthew Marks Gallery website, accompanying his 1992 sculpture *Untitled*: https://matthewmarks.com/online/gober-1976-2019/untitled-1992.
21 Laurens, C., *Little Dancer Aged Fourteen: The True Story Behind Degas's Masterpiece* (trans. W. Wood), (New York: Other Press, 2018), 66.
22 The bronze editions made after Degas's death in 1917 aimed to preserve the wax statue's original characteristics. The glass case, the only element Degas insisted on, emphasised the Dancer's status as a work of art. Twenty-nine known bronzes were produced, mostly between 1922 and 1937.
23 Telephone call with Iris Häussler on 23/10/2024.

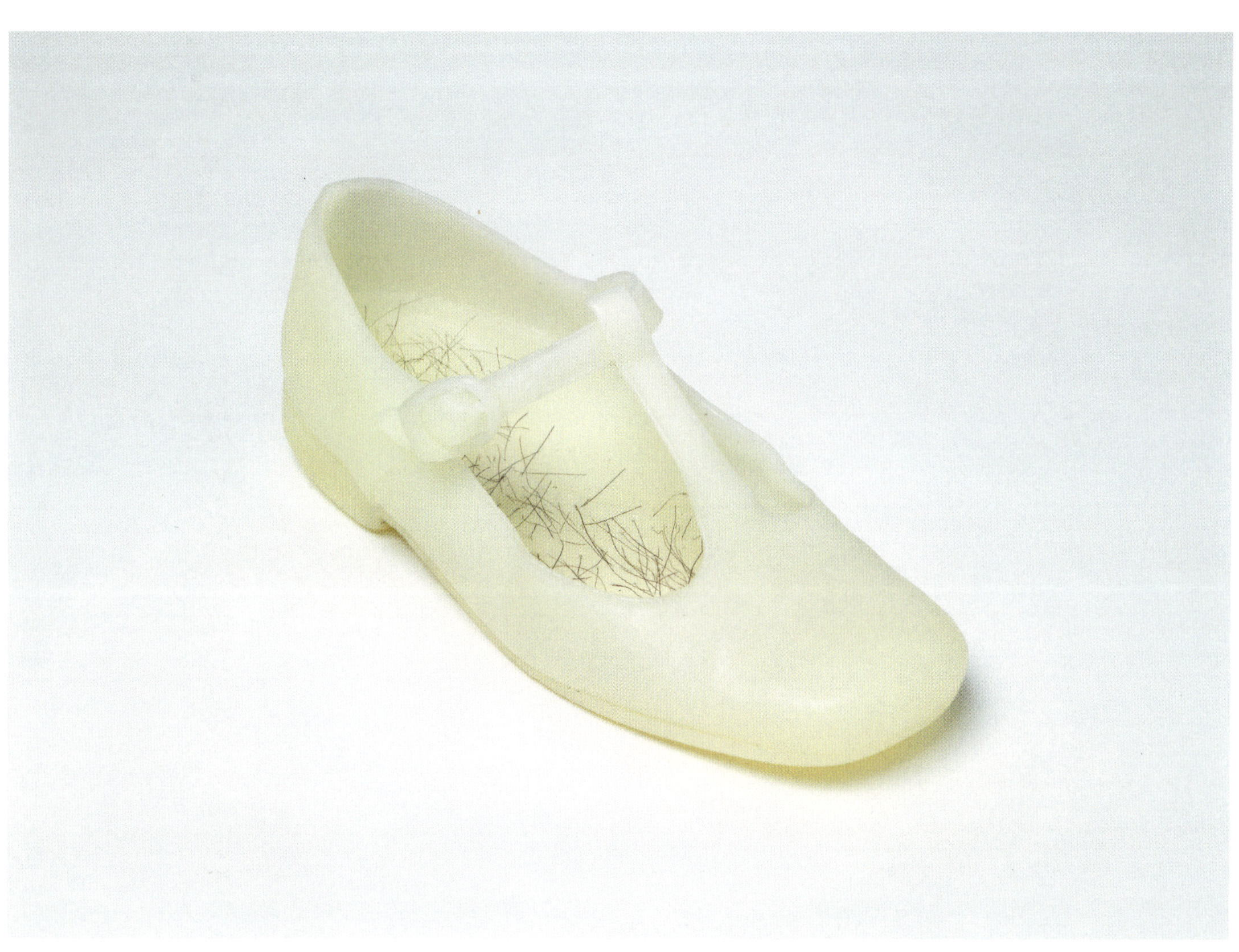

Robert Gober
Untitled, 1992
Wax and human hair

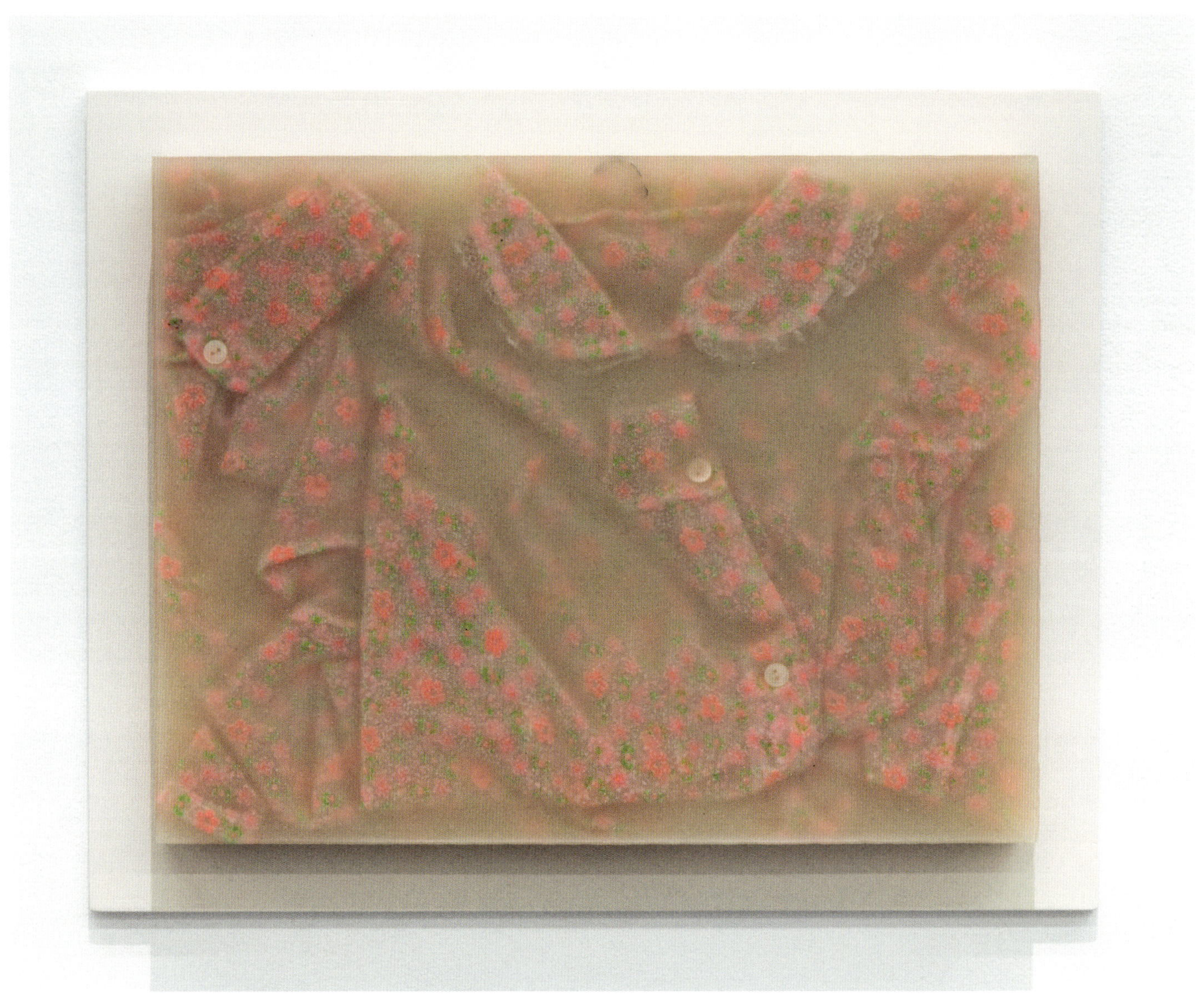

Iris Häussler
Tochter der Schwester Der Mutter (Niece), 1999
Fabric and wax

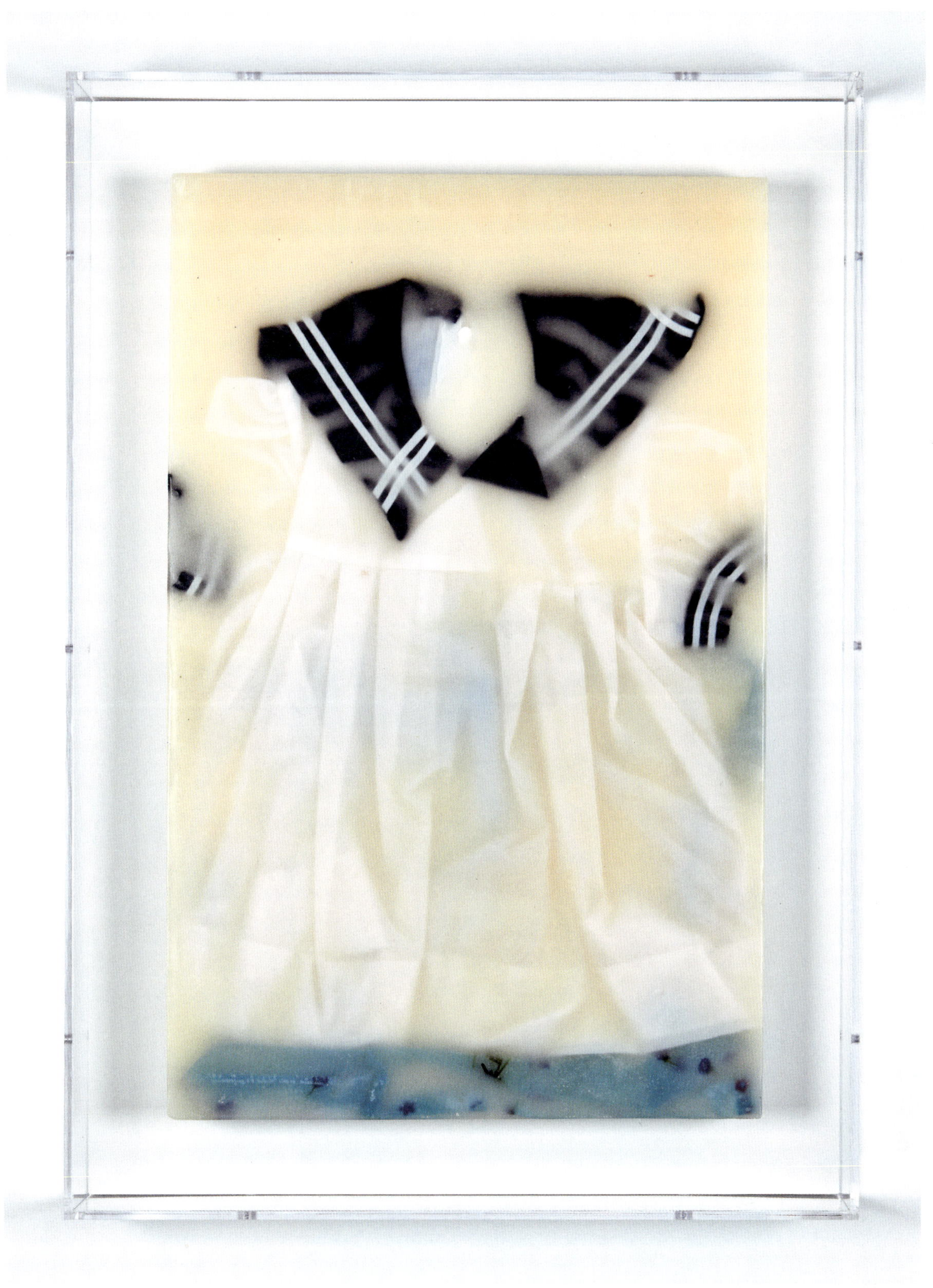

Iris Häussler
She 06, 2006
Fabric and wax

pp. 52–53

Jenny Watson
Home Made Dress / Secret, 2023
A4 coloured paper

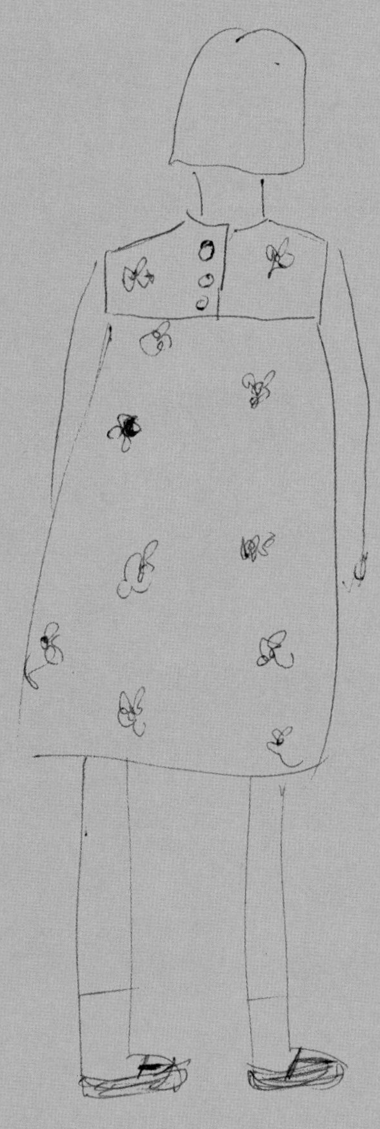

Home made dress

2023

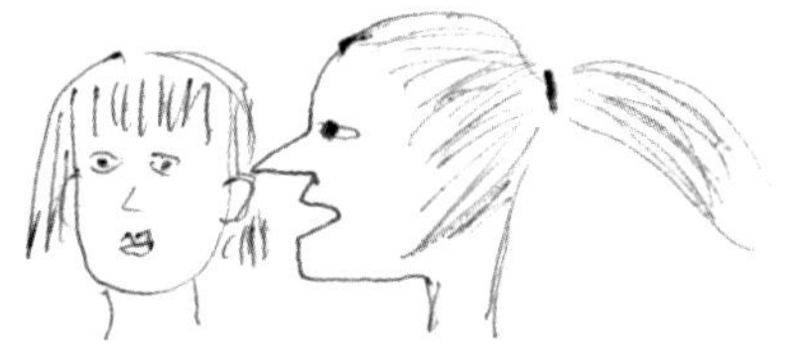

Secret

Jw 2003

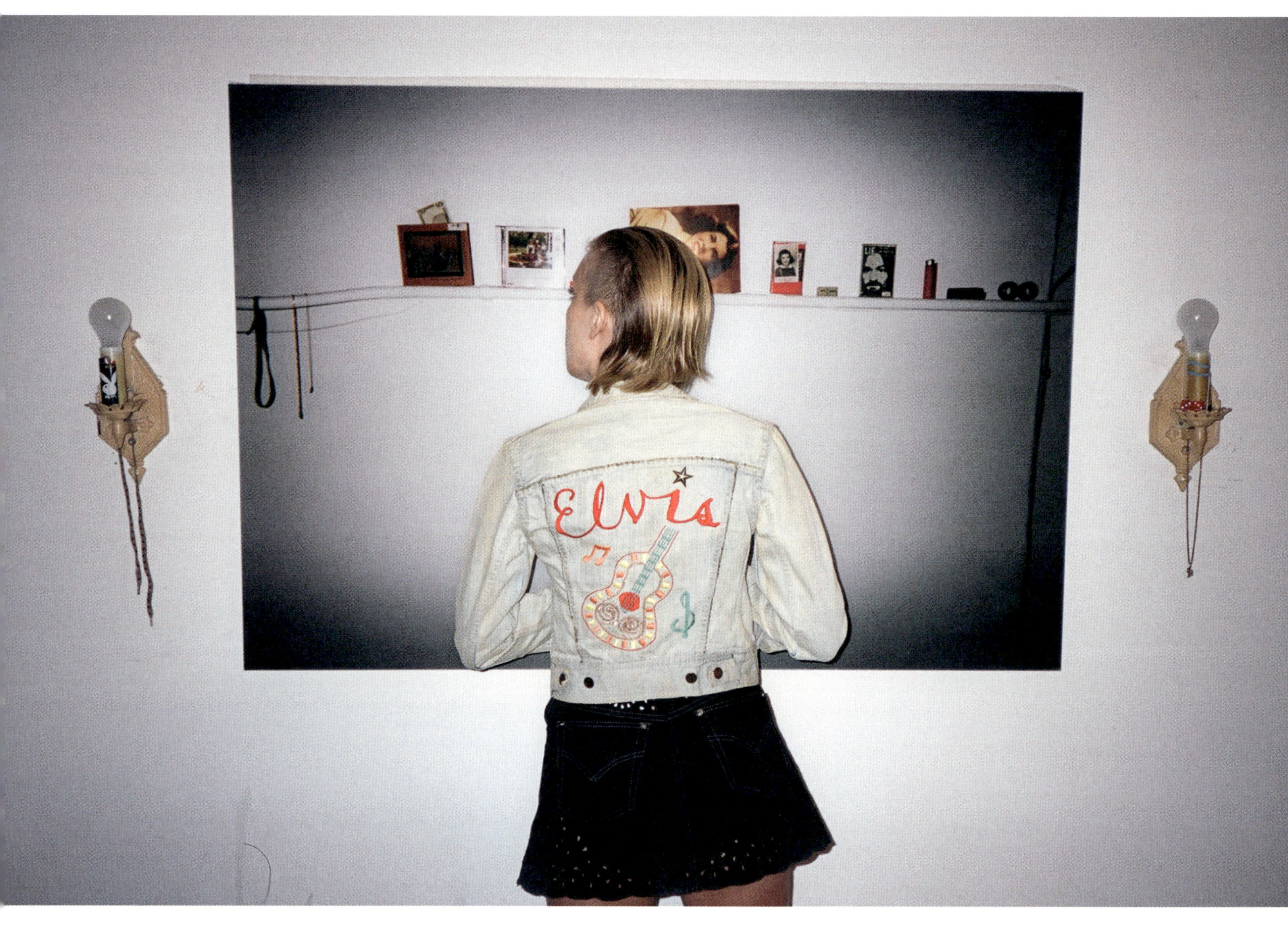

Chloë Sevigny wearing the 'Elvis jacket' from the movie *Out of the Blue* (1980), photographed by William Strobeck in 2012

Claire Marie Healy

girlhood & clothing & film

I can't stop thinking about putting on Linda Manz's denim jacket. Worn by the actress in Dennis Hopper's 1980 film *Out of the Blue*, it is embroidered on the back with a guitar, musical notes and the name 'Elvis' in cursive script; close-up, you notice pink and silver sequins that swirl and glint at the seams. Such details catch me like a ladder in tights.

The embroidery gets plenty of airtime in the film, in part because the teen-girl character who wears it is always storming away from us like a hurricane (one time, she cleanly knocks over a cheerleader as she goes). 15-year-old Cebe, played by the 17-year-old Manz, is a self-proclaimed punk-rock acolyte ('Subvert normality!') with an incarcerated father and heroin-addicted mother. She's harsh, foul-mouthed, a square (peg) in an inescapable round hole. Why do I find her well-worn jacket so tender? The jacket moves us, as she moves in it, because this particular teenage girl is defined by her obvious anger, but also her secret plea to be protected.

With its naive, childlike design worn in the service of rebellion, Cebe's denim jacket retains traces of both childhood and adulthood: the inherent in-betweenness of girls who experience too much of life, too soon. ('I'll always be that character', Linda Manz would say in her womanhood. 'I'm just a tough little rebel, I guess. A survivor'.) It is also charged in a manner unique to garments that were always intended for the screen. This is a jacket that only ever really existed in a movie, as worn by an actress who, for most audiences, only lives on in their minds as a teenage girl. Manz pretty much stopped acting after *Out of the Blue*, but when she performed one last time in her adulthood (in Harmony Korine's *Gummo*, 1997), she sold the jacket to a fellow forever-girl: Chloë Sevigny. One of her most-prized possessions, the actress wears it, striking her own punk-rock pose, in a much-Tumblrd photo taken by William Strobeck in 2012.

I love this passing of the torch between Manz and Sevigny, two actresses so strongly associated with girlhood. That's the funny thing about certain items of fashion in film: their potential for an afterlife. The critic Maya Cade, of Black Film Archive, has spoken about 'screencap culture' as a way of reframing how we engage with film as a connection point; the teen-girl fashion we might remember from coming-of-age movies often provides that connection.[1] Such is the power of certain on-screen looks – you don't always have to have seen the film.

In the best examples of girls' fashion on film, they are little acts of disruption in cinema's patriarchal gaze. Anna Backman Rogers, picking up the thread from Teresa de Lauretis's theory of cinema's operation as a technology of gender, says that 'a feminist film must address the spectator as female and reveal to her "the terms of production of woman as text, as image"'.[2] Following this concept, it is clear that in a coming-of-age film about the experience of girlhood — in which an adolescent will be shown coming into her identity — the way a filmmaker demonstrates how the girl creates herself, through the tools of appearance available to her, is of vital importance. In this context, scenes of girls getting dressed, looking in the mirror, customising items, dancing, and going out — the girls' drive towards 'looked-at-ness' — are all gestures with potential for both personal resonance and wider feminist ones. But the way clothing in cinema contributes to the visual grammar of girlhood has not been something generally deemed worthy of critical enquiry.

Reinstating the importance of fashion in coming-of-age films — not as the superficial ornamentation of the girlish, but as objects accounting for the interiority and personality of girls — is also one way of giving the credit that is overdue to costume and production designers throughout time. In a world in which the fashion and film industries are more entangled than ever, these are the figures who do so much to create those memorable images which in turn give expression to our shared girlhoods.

Such points of connection have been the red thread — the school playground cat's cradle — of my Girlhood Studies project, which I began formally in 2019 but which I have been working through, in one way or another, since my early twenties. Movies, clothing and the real self-expression of girls have always struck me as enmeshed: more, they seem to me to be layered one over the other, strengthening. Cebe's denim jacket; Jacy's hair slide; Sili's yellow sunglasses; Christiane F.'s silver satin bomber; Lux Lisbon's felt-tipped knickers; Manuela's school blouse; Vic's bodycon dress; Dorothy's red slippers.[3] I want to handle such garments with greater reverence, to attend to their details; ask how watching them on-screen helps us speak with our own girlhoods.

But I'm getting ahead of myself. Let's go back to where it is said this all began: with the cultural tectonic shifts that produced a 'youthquake'. The term was coined by *Vogue* editor-in-chief Diana Vreeland in 1965, and marked a moment in which media representations of the girl, and teenage girls themselves, first fell into Mary-Jane lockstep.

That beatnik girls wear 'pants' in the 1950s and miniskirts in the 1960s is a fact so regularly satirised that these days we fail to recognise its importance: the impact of such shifts in uniform, underlining as they did the notion that youth and femininity were symbolic of new freedoms, cannot be underestimated. These are decades during which the image of the girl (childlike, playful and, problematically, boyishly thin) retooled the engines on which the fashion industry ran forever: the miniskirt literally excluded older women in a moment where, for the first time, 'youthfulness became the new feminine ideal... and the central market became the working girl.'[4]

Cinema helps us get to the youthquake; in fact, it provides the first tremors. Well before crop-haired Sevigny starred in *Kids* (1995) — blue ringer tee with white trim, glazed look — there was fellow gamine Jean Seberg in Otto Preminger's *Bonjour Tristesse*. The 1958 film was based on Françoise Sagan's sensational 1954 novel. Just 17 years old herself when she wrote it, the author is the original of her protagonist, the rebellious and world-weary Cécile. The book, deemed 'immoral' on its release, paved the way for the adolescent boom in France and elsewhere; and the film, and its styling of Cécile courtesy of costume coordinator Hope Bryce,

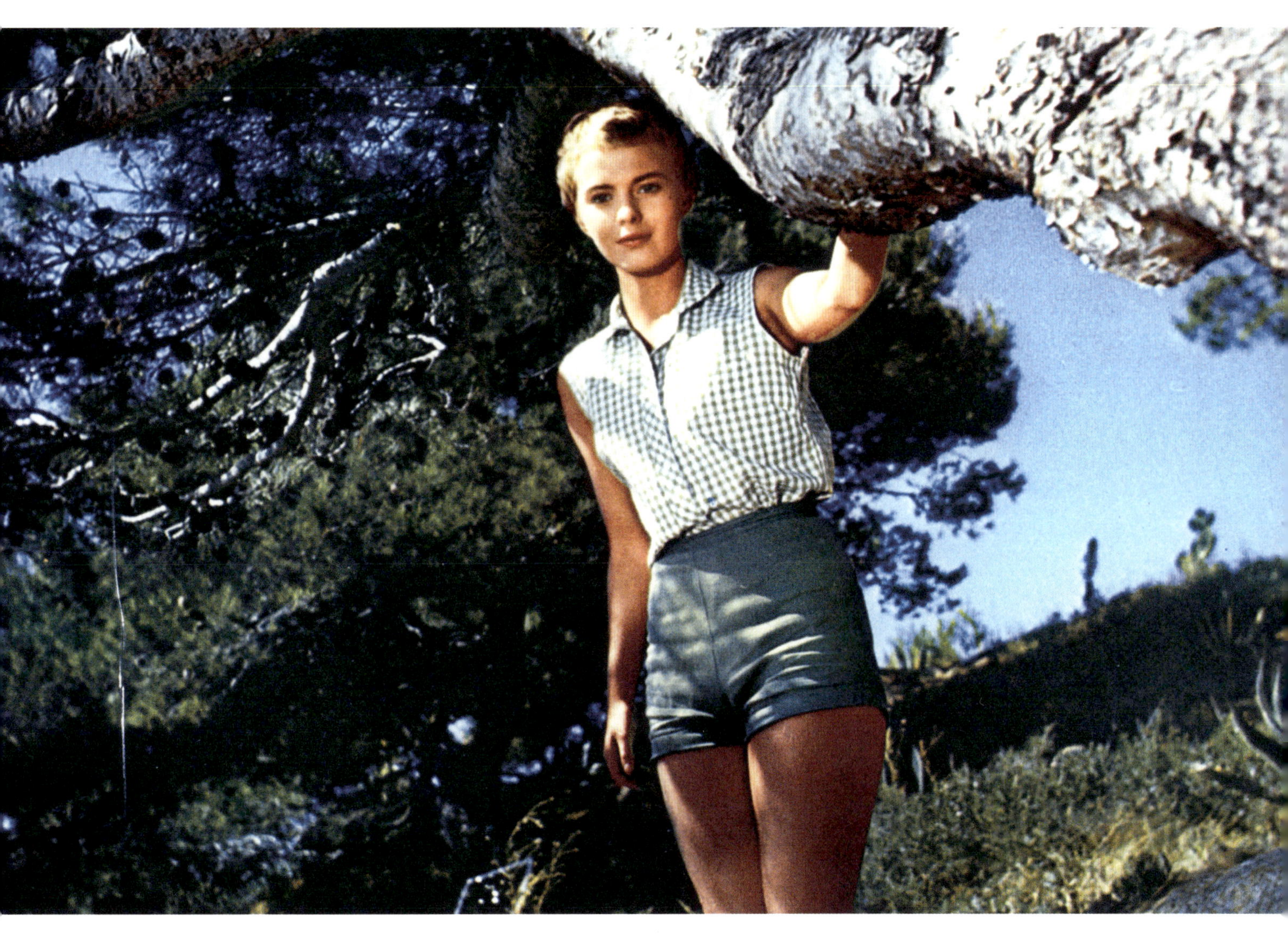

Jean Seberg in *Bonjour Tristesse*,
directed by Otto Preminger,
based on the novel by Françoise Sagan, 1958

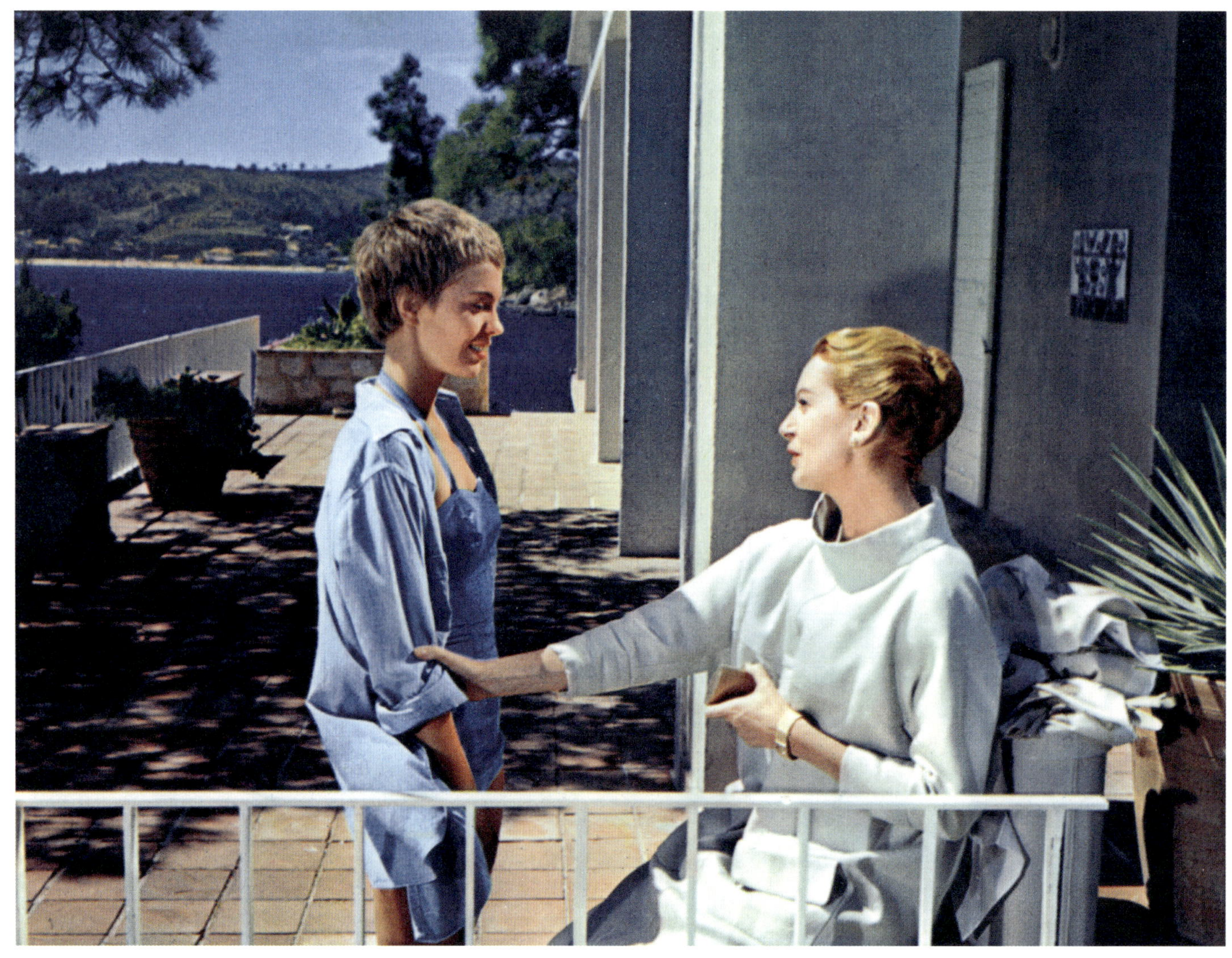

Jean Seberg and Deborah Kerr
in *Bonjour Tristesse*, directed by Otto Preminger,
based on the novel by Françoise Sagan, 1958

is one of that movement's first images of girlhood as its own, irrepressible category — a state of mind both immature and mature, tomboyish and feminine; vulnerable and dangerous.

While it begins in monochrome in Paris, the moment we are dropped into *Bonjour Tristesse*'s Technicolor, CinemaScope action on the French Riviera, it is like the new girl of the 1960s has truly arrived. Seberg, as Cécile, is the spoilt, playful daughter of a rich playboy in the story, whose aping of her father's habits lends her the cynical edge of the modern teenager; in order to preserve her own freedoms, she goes toe-to-toe with his elegant fiancée Anne, with tragic consequences. In its plotting, the ley lines of *Bonjour Tristesse* are precisely placed for a direct comparison of a new image of youth culture with the older generation.[5] 'Seventeen now isn't what it was when you were seventeen', says Cécile to Anne. Later, in an emotionally heightened state, she says she just wishes 'she were a lot older... or a lot younger'. Cécile's uniform reflects an adolescent in-between-ness: chambray shirts tied in a variety of knots and ties, hotpants in green, white, red – she's always somewhere between dressed and not-dressed. Her most frequently worn swimming costume is of the palest yellow, like something that has been left out in the sun too long; and though the memorable gowns in the film might be designed by Givenchy, Cécile looks more herself — that is, sent from the future — at the beach (Anne is correct when she tells the teenager she will look older if she wears age-appropriate gowns, because then she won't look like she's cosplaying at womanhood).

As important as Cécile's clothes is how she moves in them: she is constantly running through forests and jumping over rocks. In my favourite moment, she drags on a cigarette — face scrunched, in the shortest shorts and a striped boatneck top — while the older woman looks on. This is a movie about holding on to and rejecting daughterhood all at once — and it indicates the new look of the daughter.[6]

Sevigny may recall Seberg, but the figure of the ingénue they both represent is as old as the history of cinema itself — and shows us how long certain ideas of girlhood have been in circulation. In life, as in fiction, an ingénue is the 'artless, innocent girl or young woman; also, the representation of such a character on the stage, or the actress who plays the part'. Waif-like and wide-eyed, 1920s silent movie actresses, such as Lillian Gish and Mary Pickford, played such child–woman characters well into their thirties; coming-of-age dramas in cinema and TV are cast in much the same way now. As Kevin Brownlow wrote of Pickford in 1969, 'The ideal American girl is *still* the Mary Pickford character: extremely attractive, warm-hearted, generous, funny — but independent and fiery-tempered when the occasion demands'.[7] Thus, while it is true we don't see stories explicitly *about* female adolescence in the movies until the 'birth of the teenager' in the 1950s and into the 1960s, when it comes to ideas of the girl on screen, she can be identified not only in the very earliest films of Hollywood, but in the industry's very psychology.

Critic Molly Haskell has written about this girlhood–womanhood binary as the essential contradiction of cinema's treatment of women. She also noted of those breathless little girls of early Hollywood: 'Through the myths of subjection and sacrifice that were its fictional currency and the machinations of its moguls in the front offices, the film industry manoeuvred to keep women in their place; and yet these very myths and this machinery catapulted women into spheres of power beyond the wildest dreams of most of their sex.'[8]

Indeed, women's presence behind as well as in front of the camera since those early years — as screenwriters, editors, critics, and production and costume designers — is a fact of their prominence in film that is rarely acknowledged. Recently, this creative labour has been reassessed as forming contributions that have shaped film just as much as the usual roll call of 'Great Male' directors.

The Last Picture Show (1971), the successful adaptation of the Larry McMurtry, 1950s 'small town America'-set novel, was the product of the creative collaboration of then husband-and-wife team Peter Bogdanovich and Polly Platt. Only Bogdanovich, however, has ever been credited as director. During its filming, Bogdanovich began an affair with Cybill Shepherd, the girl-actress who, in the film, plays the coquettish teenager Jacy. As quoted in Karina Longworth's 2020 podcast, *You Must Remember This*, about the late production designer, Platt 'wanted the actors (to look) like real people' in *The Last Picture Show*: for instance, she had the idea that Jacy's hair should appear in pin curls as she applies cold cream in an early scene with her mother. (This was directly in contrast to the usual on-screen falsehoods of the era, in which young women were permanently made-up, even in their teenage bedrooms). Platt also placed a hair clip in Jacy's blonde bob as part of her styling of the character, a girl-coded item which seems to distil the character's wilful contradictions within it: Jacy's claims to maturity even while she employs protestations of girlish innocence to manipulate others. But despite Jacy's best efforts, and as a painful scene with an older man demonstrates, the camera can see the vulnerable girl behind the wilful seductress.

Platt's marriage would break down before filming was over. As the production designer put it simply, 'I was so detached, that I worked on Cybill's clothes just as hard as everyone else's, if not harder. I'm very proud of her costumes.'

Catherine Breillat, who decided she would become a filmmaker at the age of 12, has never been one to shy away from the brutal, embodied realities of girlhood(s). After making the confronting and brutalising *A Ma Soeur!* [Fat Girl] (2001), she even made another film (2002's *Sex is Comedy*), based on the process of filming the former project's scene of a girl losing her virginity. But in her first feature, *Une Vraie Jeune Fille* [A Real Young Girl] (1976), she took those Lolita-esque tropes of her male peers and blasted right through them. In this portrait of a young girl's uninhibited exploration of her burgeoning sexuality over the course of a summer, Breillat creates a kind of surface tension between hyper-babyish garments and the realities of Alice's changing desires (and changing body) underneath the fabric. In one scene, her protagonist — complete with an Alice band — gets undressed in front of the mirror, stripping past her bra and knickers in her childhood bedroom. Examining and touching her body, she changes into a ribboned, translucent gingham vest and knickerbockers set: a hyper-babyish set that she immediately and randomly vomits all over once she's in bed. The moment is like a bodily rejection of the audience's expectations: that is, of what usually happens when a young girl undresses in a bedroom in front of the camera. Still, there is nothing more perverse in *Une Vraie Jeune Fille* than any of the films of Breillat's male peers, from Truffaut to Fassbinder. That is because, when a man focuses on a girl's sexuality on screen, it's normal; when a woman gives expression to the same, it's considered obscene (*Une Vraie Jeune Fille* would not actually be seen in cinemas, due to its widespread censorship, until the year 2000).

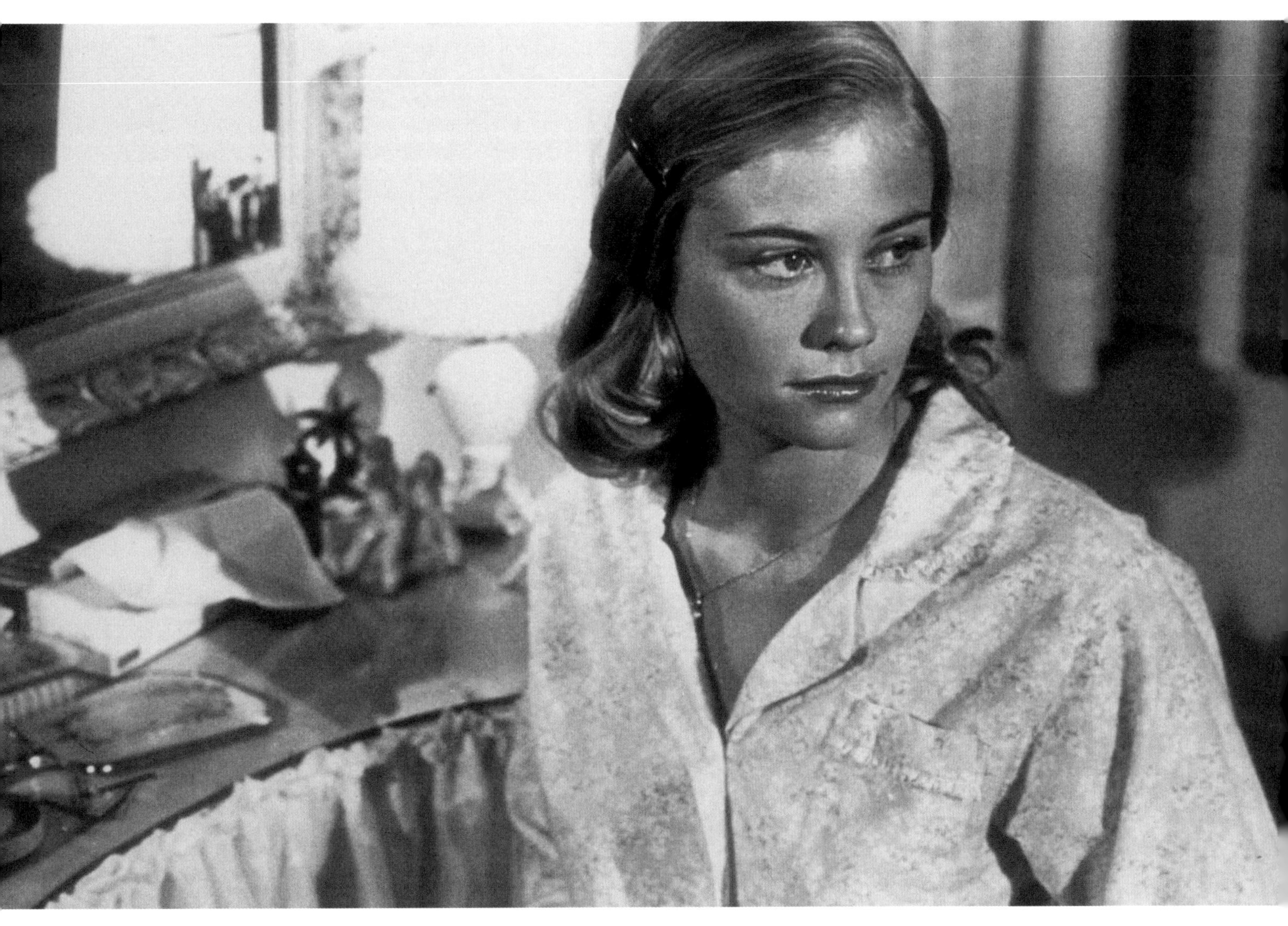

Cybill Shepherd in *The Last Picture Show*,
directed by Peter Bogdanovich and Polly Platt,
based on the novel by Larry McMurtry, 1971

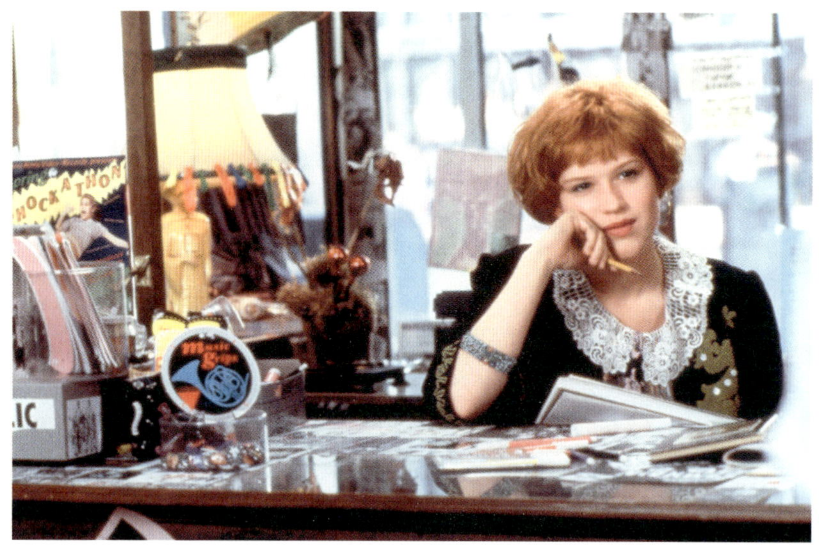

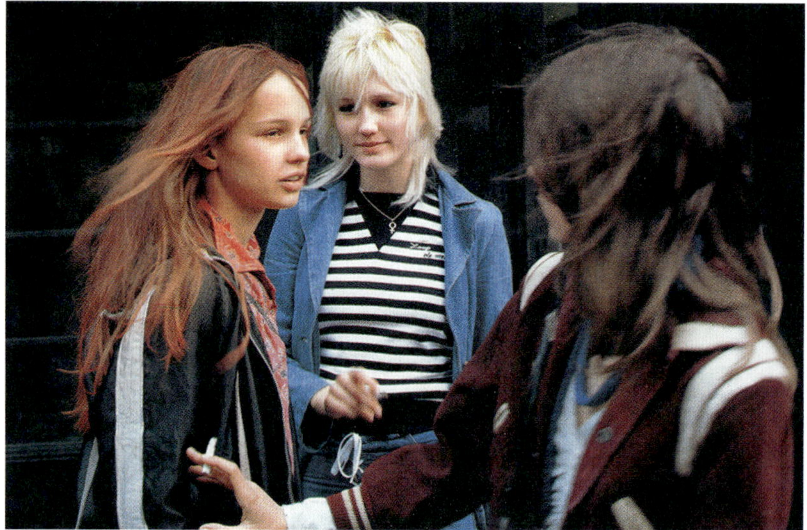

Molly Ringwald in *Pretty in Pink*,
written by John Hughes and directed
by Howard Deutch, 1986

Christiane F. – Wir Kinder vom Bahnhof Zoo,
directed by Uli Edel, based on the autobiography
by Christiane Felscherinow, 1981

Raf Simons (right)
Autumn-Winter 2018–2019
Christiane F. T-shirt

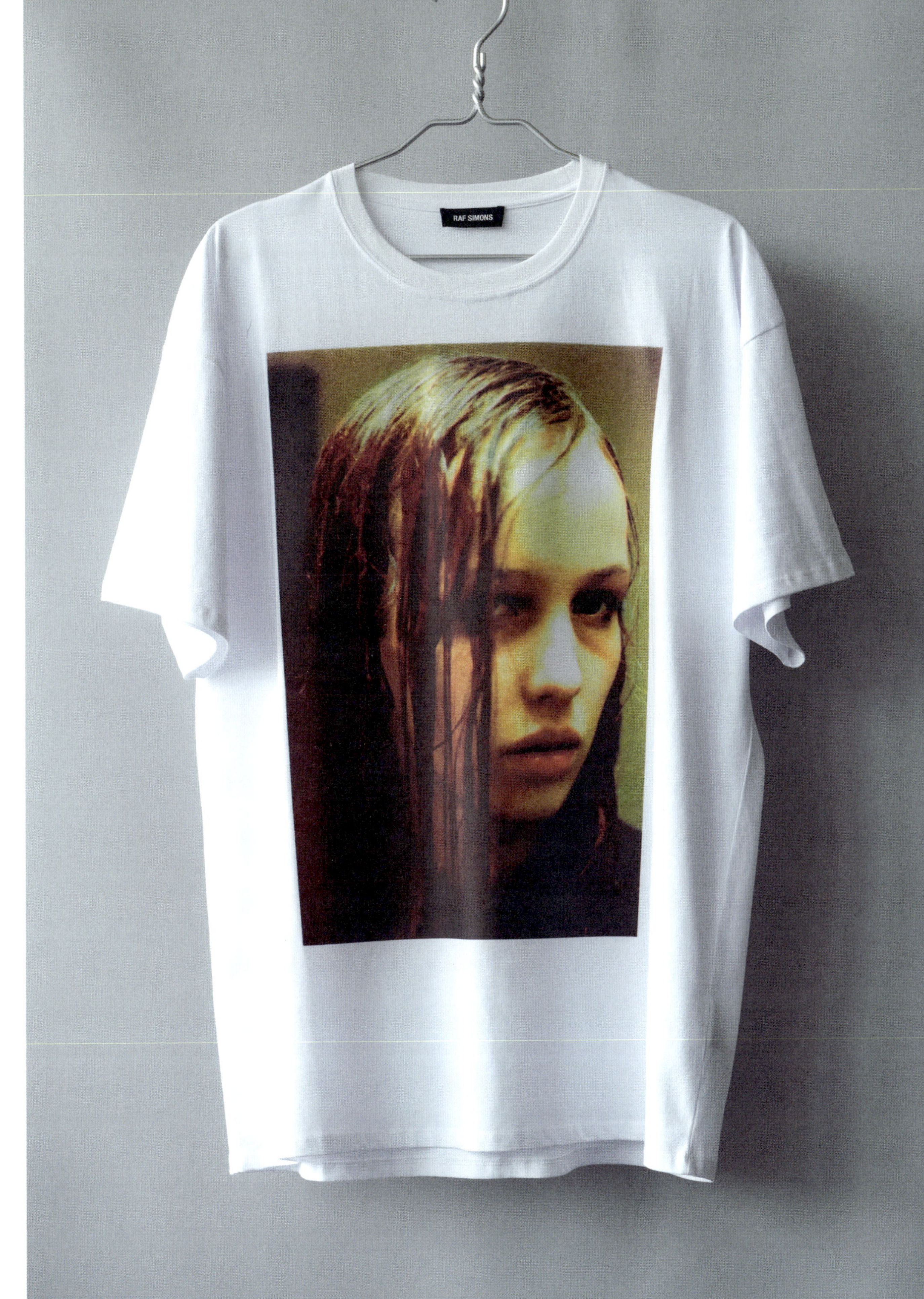
RAF SIMONS

From a girl undressing to girls getting dressed, the 1980s was a decade in which subculture entered the stylings of the on-screen teenage girl like never before. If *Out of The Blue* is an undeniable outlier (the film was, in the end, barely seen), its central character type — the outcast girl rebel — is multiplied across this decade: in *Times Square* (1980), *Fame* (1980) and *Ladies and Gentlemen, The Fabulous Stains* (1982), to name but a few. This is the decade of the teen-girl moral panic: Mary Ellen Mark's *LIFE* magazine report of Seattle's homeless teenage population (which eventually grew into the *Streetwise* documentary), or the smash 1978 addiction memoir of Christiane F. in Germany (*Christiane F. – Wir Kinder vom Bahnhof Zoo*) [Christiane F. – We Children from Zoo Station], became cultural phenomena that brought the image of disenfranchised, runaway girls into the mainstream conversation, as well as into cinema. Uli Edel's adaptation of Christiane F.'s story of heroin addiction, and the potent image of the waif-like, red-haired 13-year-old David Bowie fan it produced, was immediately folded into fashion parlance: Raf Simons even emblazoned stills from the movie on T-shirts and sweaters for his Autumn-Winter 2018–2019 collection. While many of *Christiane F.*'s scenes still shock, the most indelible image, for me, takes place in the first beats. As the girl's voiceover announces Christiane is going to 'Europe's coolest discotheque', we see her striped rainbow socks in silver kitten heels in close-up; we also see that she's carried the sandals to the club in a plastic bag, so she can change out of her Adidas Sambas on the pavement outside.

Elsewhere, in the multiplexes, such subcultural undercurrents went widescreen. Director John Hughes near single-handedly established the mode of the classic high school drama made for a vast audience. I see such films as co-creations, however, with his ingénue misfit, Molly Ringwald. In 1986's *Pretty in Pink* (written by Hughes as a tribute to Ringwald's own style, and directed by Howard Deutch), another potential gesture towards freedom for the girl is given delicious airtime: customisation. Andie is poorer than the other girls in school: she wears antique jewellery, granny knits and chalky makeup. In the film's opening sequence, we watch the protagonist putting together her outfit for school as the Psychedelic Furs' title track plays: we even hear her tell her father (Harry Dean Stanton) how much it cost ('$15 for the shoes, second-hand, and I made the rest'). Although the character's final Frankenstein prom dress has been much derided in popular culture, it too is reflective of a more authentic approach to teen-girl costume design: as costume designer Marilyn Vance has defended, the whole point is that Andie designed it herself. In the brainstorming montage, the character touches her hand thoughtfully to the cold-shoulder neckline of the black jersey she is already wearing, demonstrating to the viewer how the idea is forming in her mind. It doesn't matter if we like this dress or not. It matters that we bear witness to Andie taking out the scissors and creating this version of herself.

Such earnest marketing to teens soon creates its own pushback. In 1988's *Heathers* (director Michael Lehmann, costume design Rudy Dillon) the sardonic heroines are like the John Hughes' Brat Pack reflected in a funereal funhouse — the shoulder pads are bigger, the scrunchies more voluptuous, and the dialogue as cutting, comparatively, as a chainsaw. And in the memorable 'Get ready with me' opening sequence of *Clueless* (1995), Cher's voiceover in combination with the extravagant display of technology and wealth ('I actually have a *way* normal life for a teenage girl') is one example of that film's success at striking an overtly self-conscious and knowing tone that is still much imitated though rarely

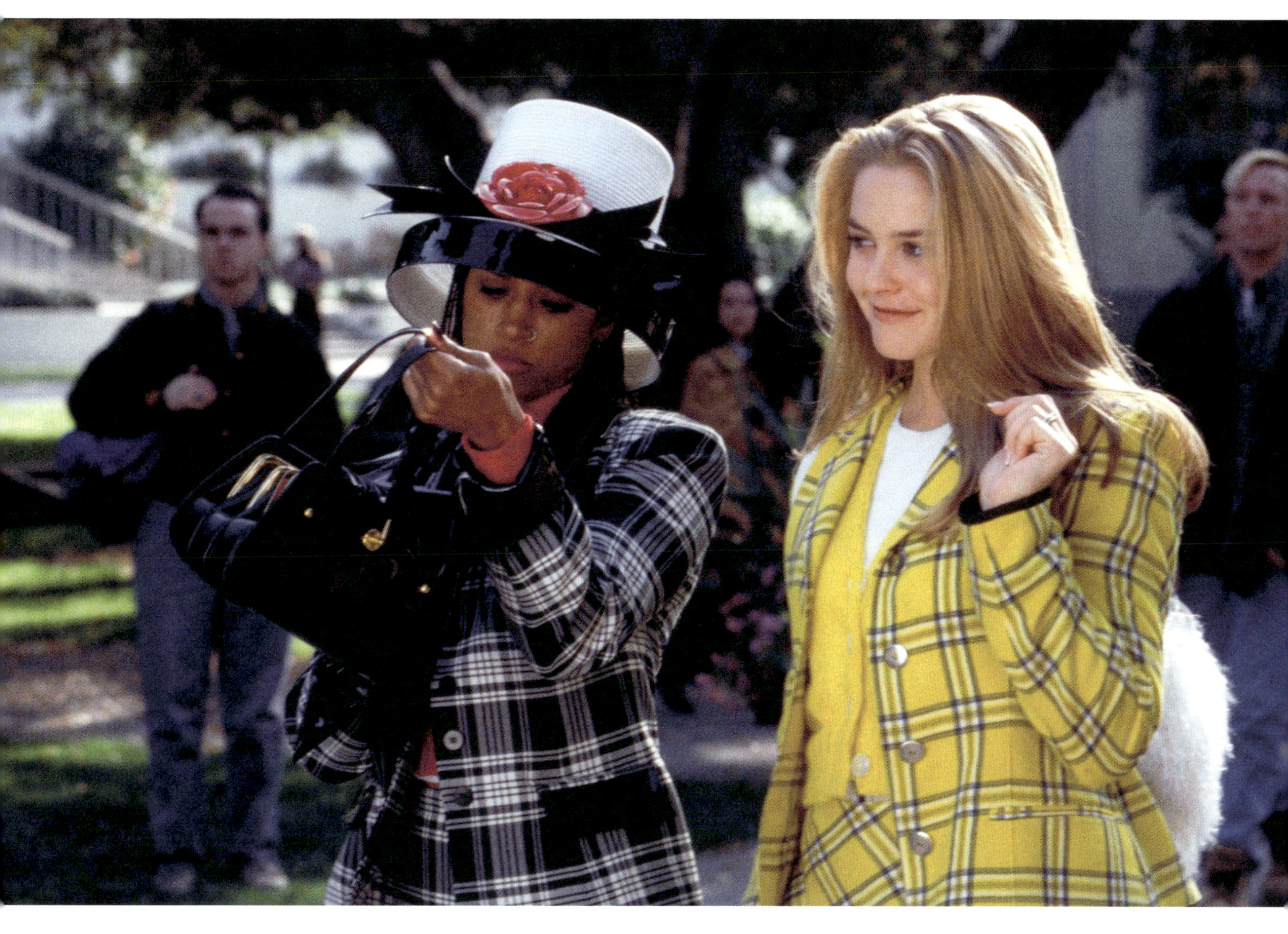

Stacey Dash and Alicia Silverstone in *Clueless*, directed by Amy Heckerling, 1995

matched. Both films cleverly ignored what girls were actually wearing in high schools in America at that time in favour of a heightened vision. Cher and Tai's yellow and black plaid back-to-school skirt suits with knee socks, for instance, was the result of costume designer Mona May combining the Kurt Cobain-inspired grunge trend with European runway fashions.[9]

The styling of *Clueless* undoubtedly kicked off a long-standing trend of on-screen high schools as fantasy spaces unto themselves: miniature kingdoms in which the girls rule, and nothing that bad really happens. As critic Samantha Colling suggests, the production and costume design of such films are exactly how 'a post-feminist, neo-liberal version of girlhood becomes pleasurable... the Hollywood version of girlhood is designed to feel good'.[10]

Alongside figures such as Julie Dash (*Daughters of the Dust*, 1991), Katt Shea (*Poison Ivy*, 1992) and Leslie Harris (*Just Another Girl on the I.R.T.*, 1992), Amy Heckerling was a member of an emerging set of women directors who, thanks to the independent film boom heralded by the Sundance Film Festival, briefly returned to the frontlines of Hollywood in the 1990s. The most lastingly successful and most fashion-literate among these was one Sofia Coppola. Across eight feature films, Coppola has done so much to bring a sense of girl-literacy to screens that an entire aesthetic has come to feel recognisably hers. The 1970s ditsy florals and long 'potato sack' prom dresses of *The Virgin Suicides* (1999); the Ladurée Macaron-toned costumes in *Marie Antoinette* (2006) — all are aspects shaped by the history of art, photography and fashion, and the director has never been shy about wearing those references on her sleeve. While we love to sift through Coppola stills as if they *are* photographs, the director's recognition of the importance of fashion in depictions of girlhood has always gone beyond surface pleasures. Watching *The Virgin Suicides* (1999), we smell the mustiness of girls' pyjamas when they've been lying on top of each other in one room for too long; spending time with *Priscilla* (2023), the chemical itch of hairspray catches in our throats.

Moreover, Coppola intuits that it is not just what is worn that expresses how girlhood feels, but *how* it is worn. When the viewer is transported to 7 May 1769, somewhere between Austria and France, to bear witness to Marie Antoinette's handover ceremony to become the Dauphine of France, Coppola films the ceremony from several distanced angles — including of the character's young naked body from behind. Her removal of her childhood clothes, then gaining those becoming to a wife-to-be, is an historically accurate coming-of-age moment that equally captures the contemporary harshness of being 14 years of age and its attendant sense of being surveilled. After all, you needn't be an eighteenth-century royal princess to feel you have been treated like a doll since childhood by the adults around you.

Out of such beguiling visions, and since the early 2000s, there has been an emergent taste for films that play out in rhythm with real girls' lives, often from screenplays that draw from their real, told experiences. *Thirteen* (2003) came out of director Catherine Hardwicke writing the screenplay together with 14-year-old Nikki Reed, whose experiences it retells (the film is heavily reminiscent of *Christiane F.* in its depiction of a young girl's downward spiral. *Eighth Grade* (2018) saw Bo Burnham collaborating closely with actual eighth graders (and yes: his protagonist's green swimsuit was a tribute to Breillat's *A Ma Soeur!*). But the French filmmaker Céline Sciamma —

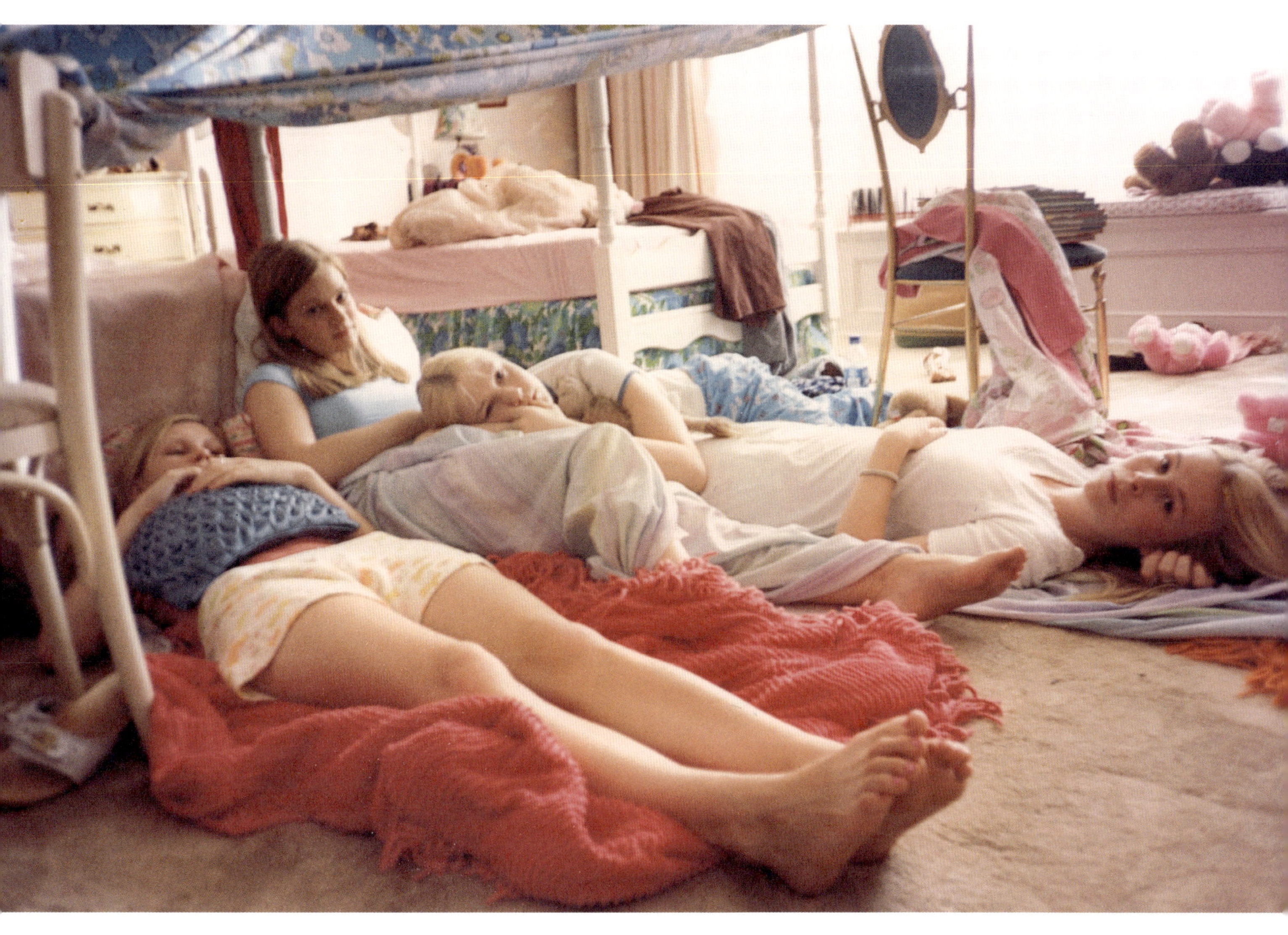

The Virgin Suicides, directed by Sofia Coppola, based on the novel by Jeffrey Eugenides, 1999

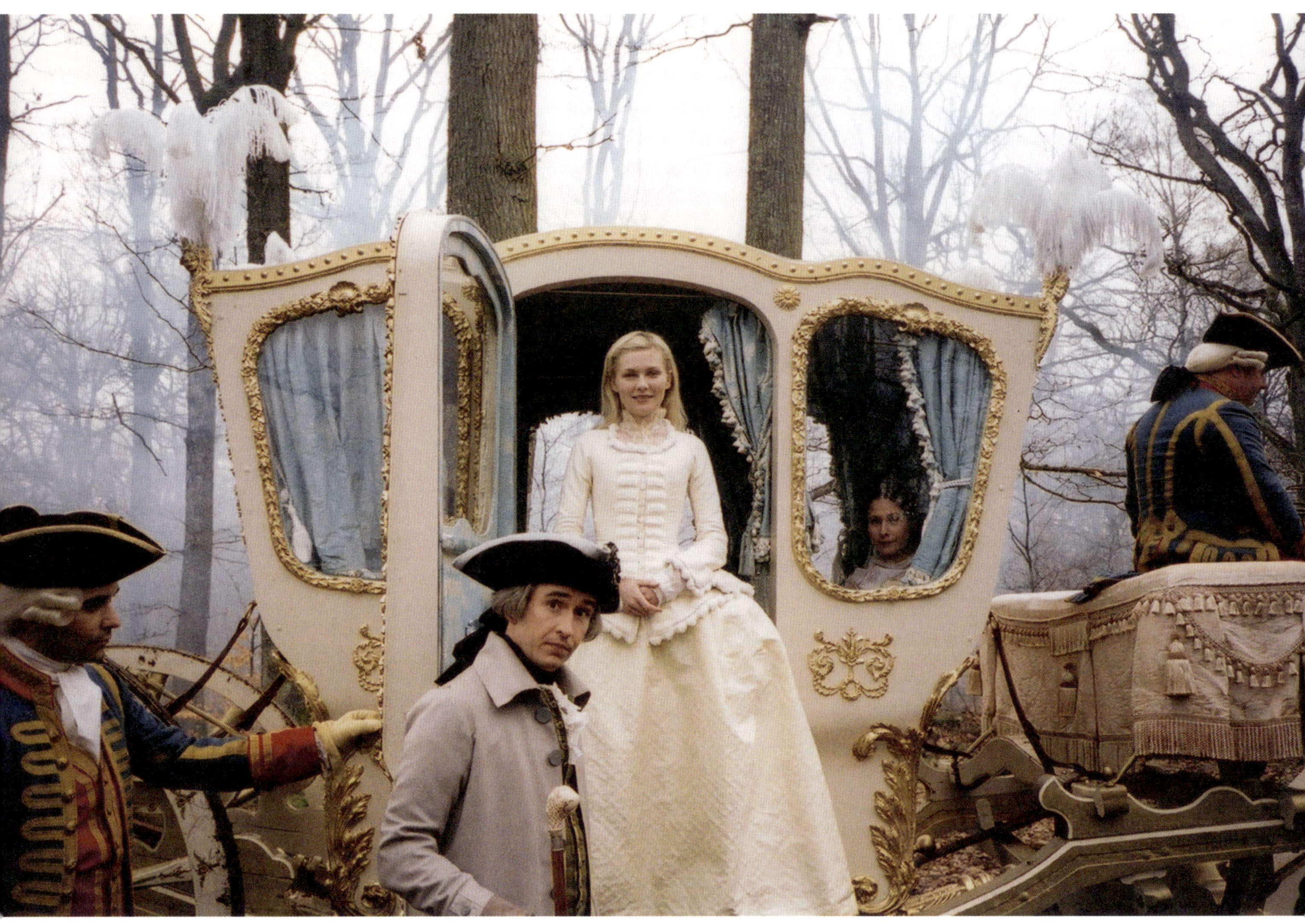

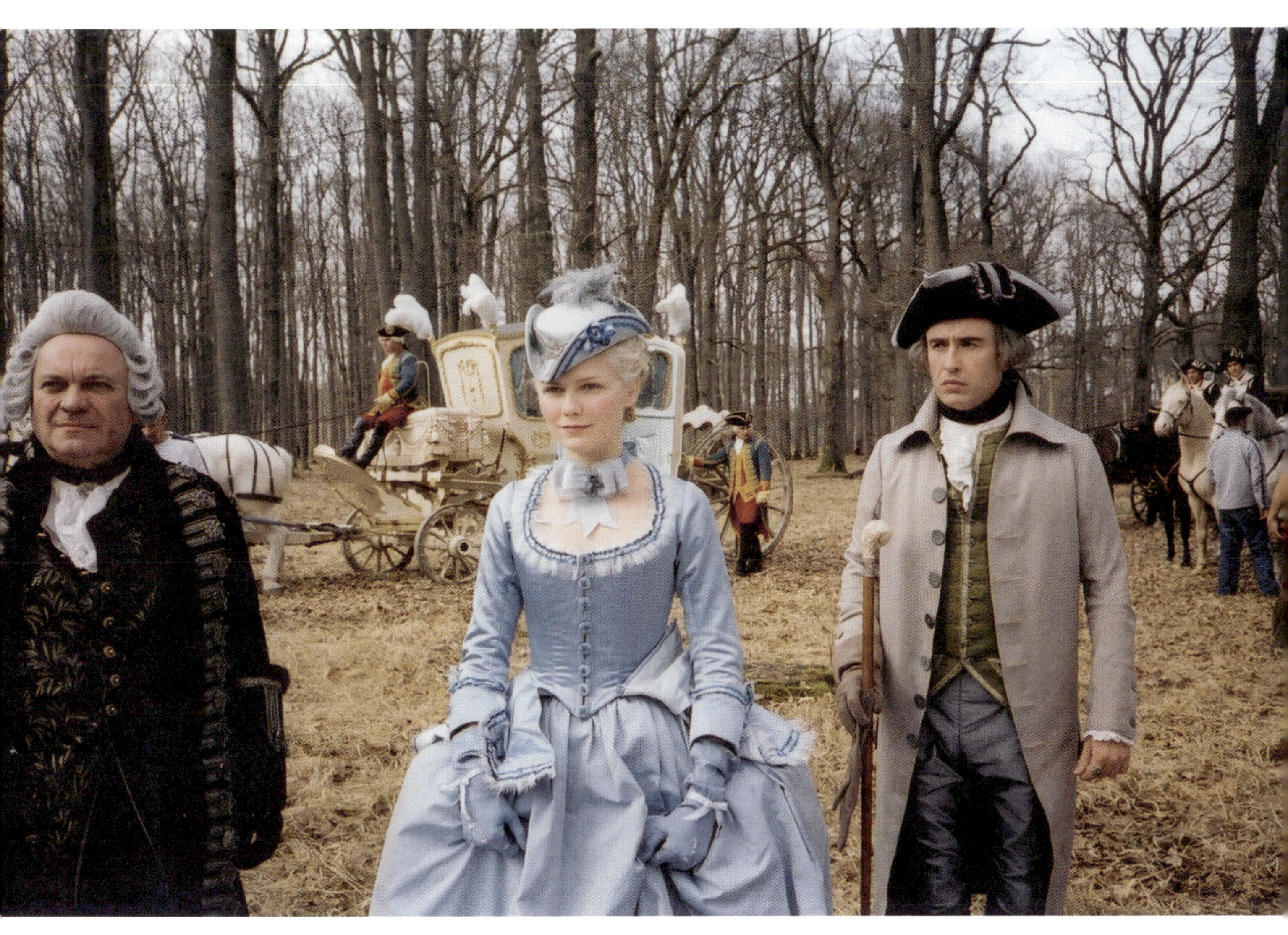

Kirsten Dunst in *Marie Antoinette*,
directed by Sofia Coppola, 2006

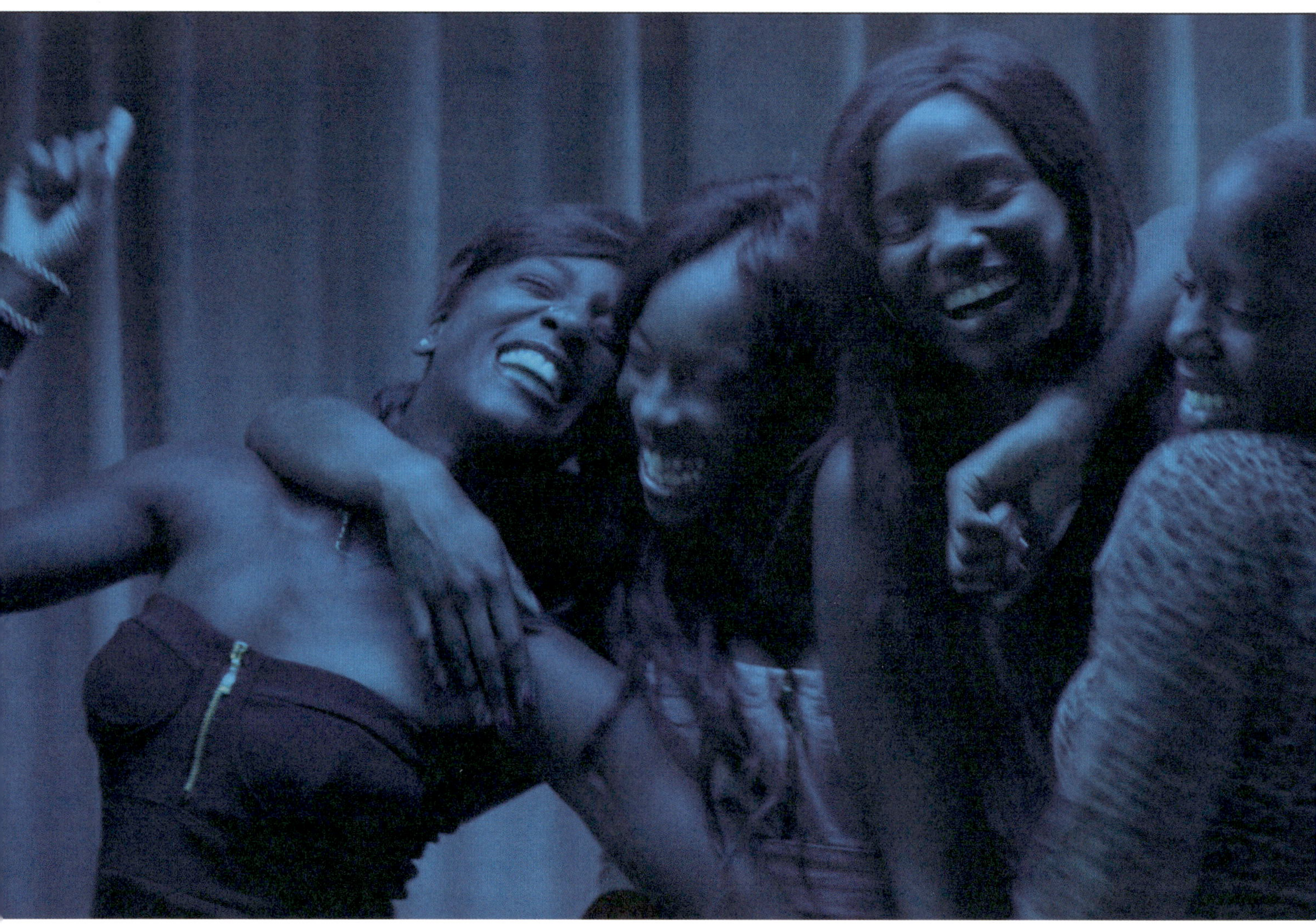

Girlhood, directed by Céline Sciamma, 2014

who the BFI recently identified as one of the 'Big 3' of contemporary storytellers of girlhood in film (along with Greta Gerwig and Coppola) — is a director with an especial interest in achieving such realism, specifically through garments.

'I wanted to go against the folklore of teenage girls in cotton underwear and their mysteries. I wanted the film to be an answer to that undying tradition of fascination,' Sciamma has said of her debut feature, *Water Lilies* (2007), which tells the story of various first loves in the context of a local pool and the synchronised swimming team that practices there one summer.[11] Instead, what Sciamma uncovers in the film's girls' bedrooms and locker rooms are: training bras awkwardly removed under T-shirts; roll-on glitter applied to scraped-back hair; the scratch and scrape of a sequinned costume being pulled over denim jeans. Such details are movingly rendered, and gently lensed.

Later, in *Girlhood* (2014), about a young woman's initiation into a girl gang on the outskirts of Paris, Sciamma develops the operation of her girls' gaze further. In a memorable scene we watch the group of girlfriends dancing in a hotel room they've rented for the night — in bodycon dresses they've shoplifted — to Rihanna's *Diamonds*; soon, the camera flips to reveal that the reason they look so powerful and glittering, in the blue light, is because we are seeing the friends through the admiring gaze of Marieme. Unfortunately, Sciamma would come under criticism for how she depicts a world she had no first-hand experience of, especially for those plot points where the girls' paths feel like they play up to the stereotypes of life in the *banlieues*. While the nature of that critique of *Girlhood* is valid, it also shows how little representation of Black girlhoods — and support for Black filmmakers — there really has been in European and American cinema to date.

25 years into a new millennium, it is hard to figure out where teenage girls end and the moving images of them begin. In fact, it may be precisely because there are so many girls on our phone screens — dressing, undressing, asking us to *get ready with them* — that films which reflect the correlation between coming-of-age and the tools of dress feel freshly important. Much like when filmmakers such as Catherine Breillat or Sofia Coppola were identifying gaps in expressions of girlhood of their own era — and filling them — it feels like there is a filmic response needed to a world where images of girls are not only hyper-visible, but somewhat incessant. I wonder if the cinema of the present moment can come to rest on the aesthetics of coming-of-age, and its realities, with equal attention.

The last film I want to mention feels as though it provides that stillness. It also brings us back to that urtext for modern-day girlhood, *Bonjour Tristesse*. Durga Chew-Bose, a first-time, fashion-literate filmmaker, brings her writerly gaze to Sagan's novel for her cinematic debut (2025). Hers is an editor's point-of-view: she is someone who has grown up inside a reference-heavy and imaged age, who exhibits era-spanning taste; here, she adapts someone else's book as if she's been collecting seeds for its on-screen harvesting forever.

It is to Sagan's text that Chew-Bose's contemporary retelling, which was executive-produced by the author's son Denis, has its allegiance. But clothes are just as important here as they are in the Jean Seberg vehicle. After all, Chew-Bose, who was originally brought in to write the screenplay alone, apparently told producers she would only make *Bonjour Tristesse* if stylist Miyako Bellizzi did the costumes. The result of that partnership is the film's sense of a teenage girl's dailiness that is still quite rarely seen. In the age of Netflix and the algorithmically crafted coming-of-age drama, I can usually see the rack of pulled brands, the accessories table, before I see *the girl*.

With their modern-day Cécile, Chew-Bose and Bellizzi recognise that clothes are not merely covering, but a *way in* to the girl. The director's camera rests with ease on the details of garments both on and off: swimsuits over the patio furniture, a seersucker gingham shirt to protect shoulders from the sun, white headphones that take too long to untangle. She also spends time with Cécile dressing and undressing; creating herself and trying on identities, as in another scene where the character applies blue eyeshadow and takes several pictures of herself on her phone in her bedroom. Unlike the anxiety-inducing *Eighth Grade*, a teenage girl's attachment to her phone — and Cécile's exploration of her own looks through it — is treated with tenderness here.

The most-seen item in *Bonjour Tristesse* is Cécile's yellow swimsuit — its colour brings to mind Seberg's in the Preminger version — with its white harlequin squares that looks thrifted. I love the swimsuit's inherent 'worn-ness', not only by this character but presumably by a girl in the time of Sagan's girlhood, if it is indeed vintage. Otherwise, we see Cécile in Seberg-esque shirts, but also Chloë's ringer tee in *Kids*; in bright red, or royal blue. (Such looks, with the hotpants, make her feel like a Mary Quant ingénue, and we are back to the 1960s once again).

I should mention: Chloë is in this movie too, playing the impossibly chic, potential mother figure of Anne. Chew-Bose enjoys resting her camera on the back of one or the other's neck, placing them side-by-side, locking the pair in a dance of wills. The casting is another perfect looping of time and cinemas of girlhood; speaking to how we overlay our older selves onto our younger selves, and what we might gain in the exercise of closing the gap.

Chew-Bose's subject is a girl who is becoming. But while her character experiences first lust and the pain of self-recognition in the story, it is not depicted as a break from one form to another via a short, sharp shock; even though a short, sharp, tragic shock is what moves the plot to a new place. While we see a different Cécile at the story's closing to its opening, Chew-Bose's subtle approach to Sagan's text lets the viewer exist inside the state of adolescent in-betweenness for the film's runtime, together with the girl.

I began this essay with a statement of how coming-of-age films allow us to bear witness to the self-actualisation of girls: that girls getting dressed on screen should be considered as a drive towards looked-*at*-ness. But if a certain visibility for the girl is present in the very architecture of cinema, then the way the girls get dressed, desire, dance and display in film can also be understood as a kind of cycling away from that inbuilt gaze. It is a distinction made in a moment of dialogue in the recent *Bonjour Tristesse*, when an older woman observes that she thinks Cécile is beginning to imagine how she wants to be seen. 'I'd rather not think about my daughter being looked at,' says the father. She corrects him: 'I said *seen*, not looked at.'

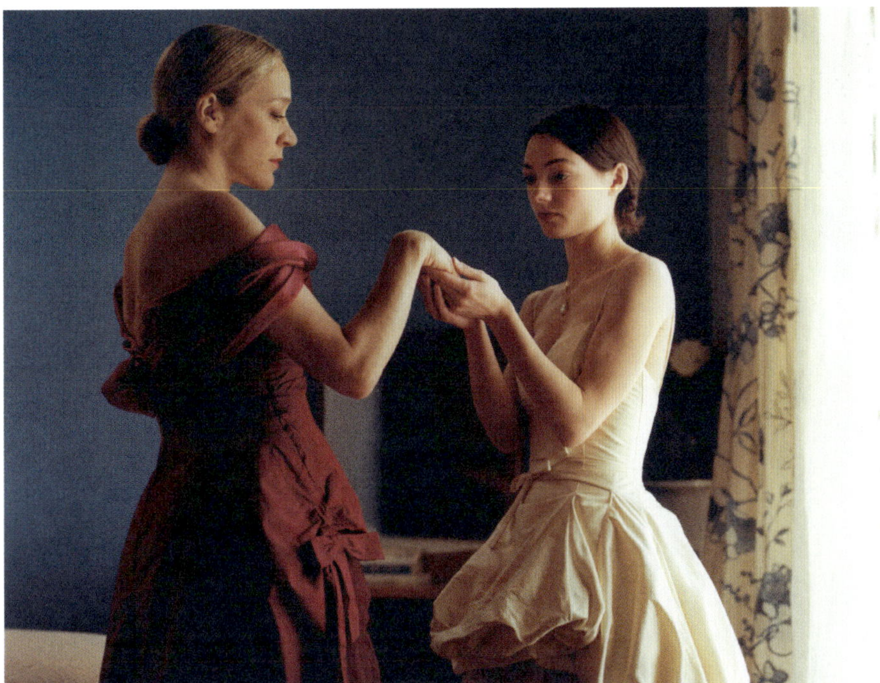

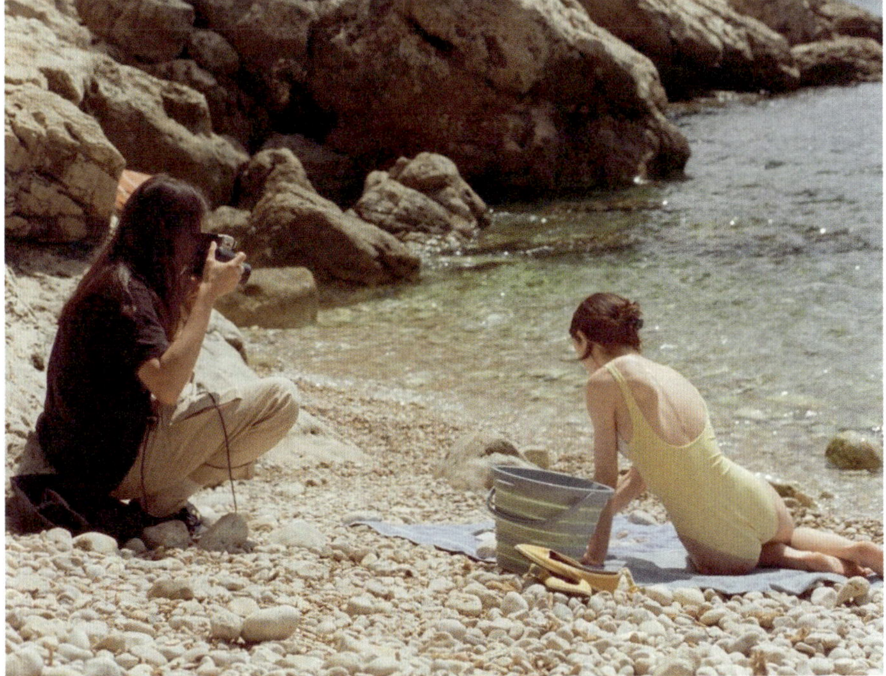

Lily McInerny and Chloë Sevigny in *Bonjour Tristesse*,
directed by Durga Chew-Bose, based on the novel by Françoise Sagan, 2024

notes

1 Cade, M., 'Tumblr Changed How We Watch Movies'. [online] (*Slate*, 2022). Available at: https://slate.com/podcasts/icymi/2022/08/black-film-archive-tumblr-film-online-archiving (accessed 10 March 2025).

2 Rogers, A.B, *Sofia Coppola: The Politics of Visual Pleasure* (New York: Berghahn Books, 2018), 14; De Lauretis, T., *Alice Doesn't: Feminism, Semiotics, Cinema* (London: Macmillan, 1984), 36.

3 The corresponding films to this catalogue of garments are: *Out of the Blue* (1980); *The Last Picture Show* (1971); *The Little Girl Who Sold the Sun* (1999); *Christiane F.* (1981); *The Virgin Suicides* (1999); *Mädchen in Uniform* (1931); *Girlhood* (2014); *The Wizard of Oz* (1939).

4 English, B., *A Cultural History of Fashion in the 20th and 21st Centuries* (London, Bloomsbury, 2013), 94.

5 In this sense, I find the film to be an earlier, girl-centred version of that much-heralded clarion call for disaffected youth: Charles Webb/Mike Nichols' *The Graduate*.

6 In real life, the actress was locked into a kind of twisted daughterhood with her abusive director. At 19, when teased by Hollywood gossip columnist Louella Parsons about whether she was marrying Preminger, Seberg retorted: 'I'm old enough to be his mother!', a moment which brings to mind a line from *Bonjour Tristesse* which blends fiction with the ingénue actress's reality. 'You know where I live? Limbo, with my father.'

7 Brownlow, K., *The Parade's Gone By* (Berkeley: University of California Press, 1996), 11.

8 Haskell, M., *From Reverence to Rape: The Treatment of Women in the Movies* (London: Penguin, 1974), 3.

9 Chaney, J., *As If!* (New York: Simon and Schuster, 2015), 40.

10 Colling, S., *The Aesthetic Pleasures of Girl Teen Film* (London: Bloomsbury Academic, 2017), 16.

11 Soares, A., *Water Lilies: Céline Sciamma Discusses Lesbian Teen Drama*. [online] (Alt Film Guide, 2008). Available at: https://www.altfg.com/water-lilies-celine-sciamma/ (accessed 24 Nov. 2024).

pp. 74–75

Jenny Watson
***Hair / Shopping*, 2023**
A4 coloured paper

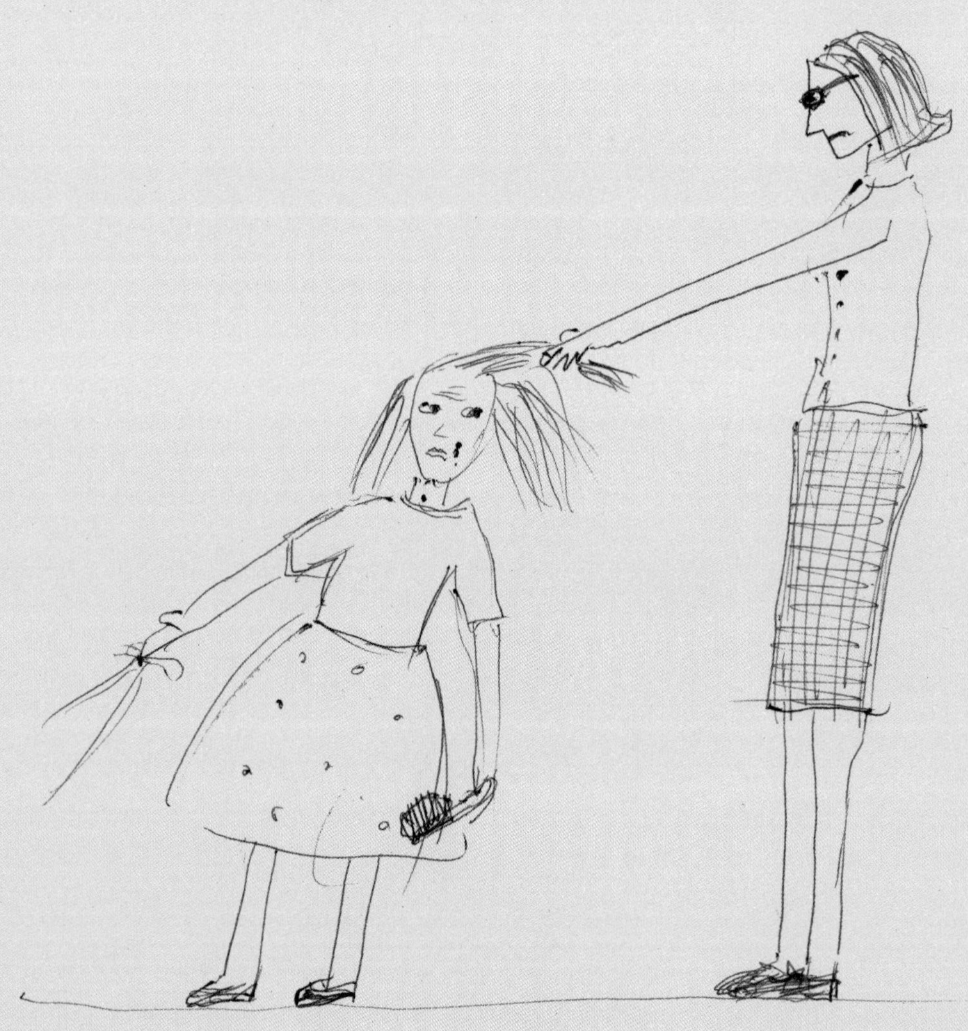

Hair

Jun 2003

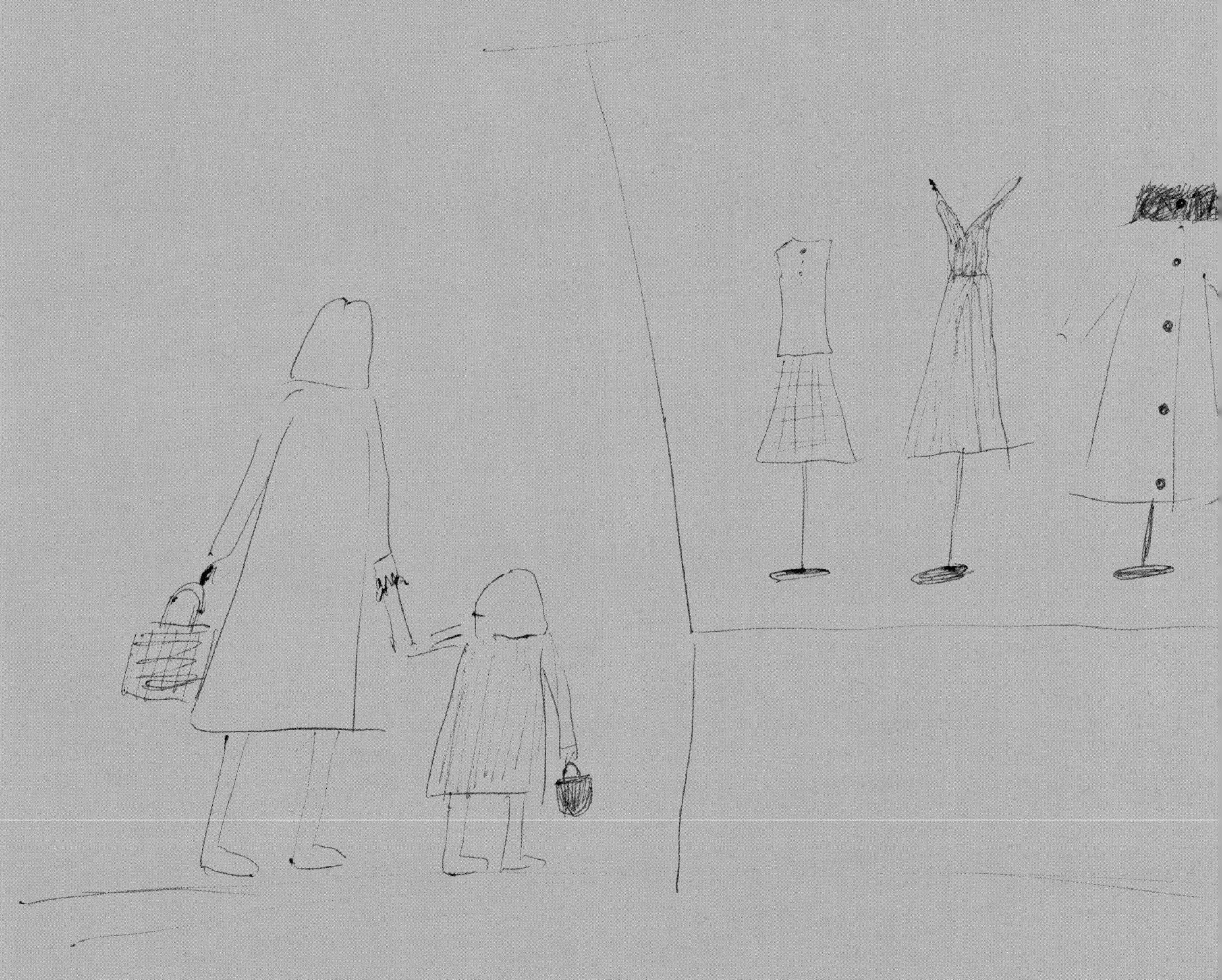

Shopping

Jw 2003

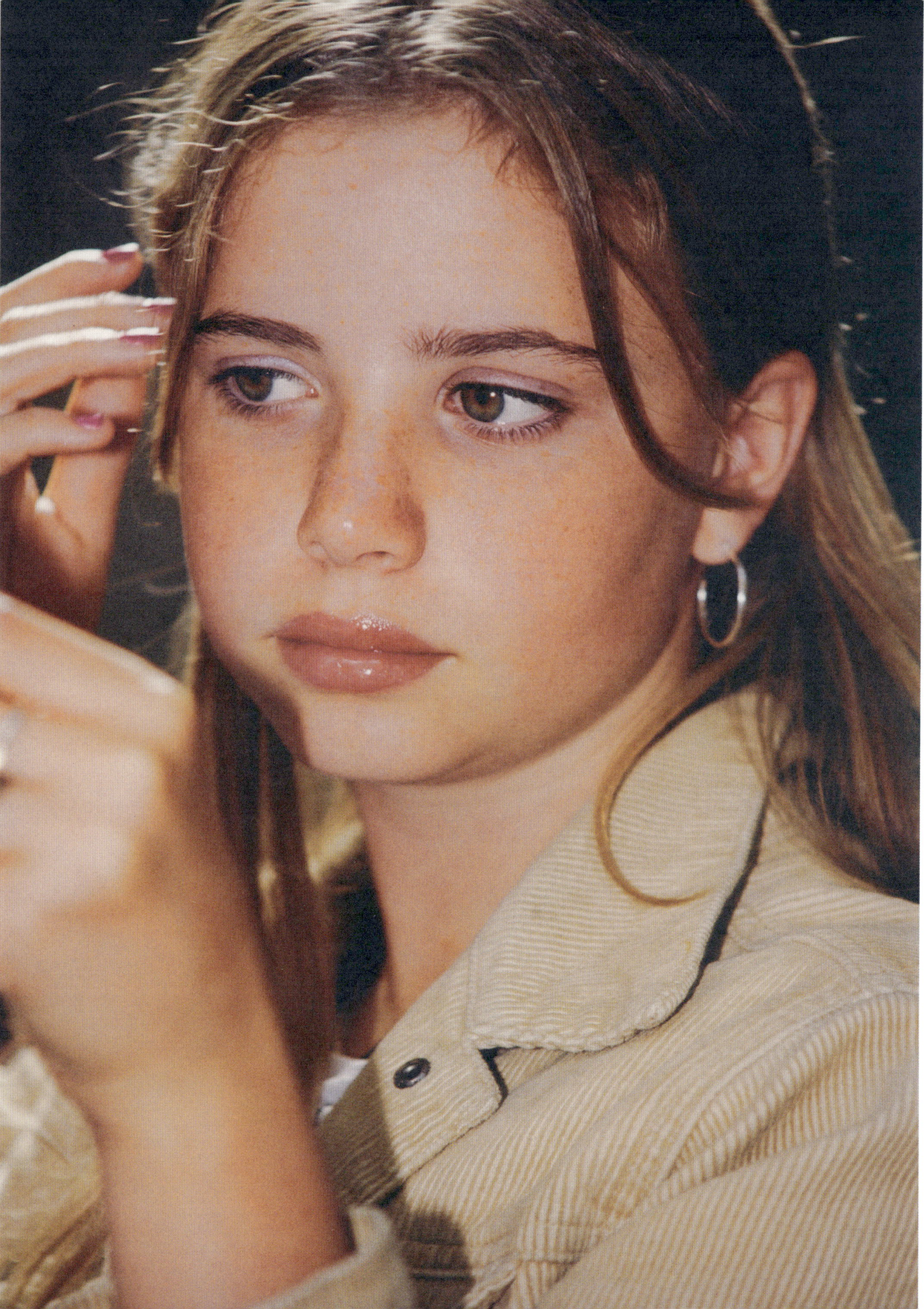

picturing girls

Tina Barney
Eimear Lynch
Nancy Honey
Sofia Coppola
Nancy Steiner
Lauren Greenfield
Leticia Valverdes
& Sofia Lai

in conversation with curator
Elisa De Wyngaert

'We felt the imprisonment of being a girl, the way it made your mind active and dreamy, and how you ended up knowing which colours went together. We knew, finally, that the girls were really women in disguise, that they understood love and even death, and that our job was merely to create the noise that seemed to fascinate them. We knew that they knew everything about us and that we couldn't fathom them at all.'

The boys reflecting on the Lisbon sisters in *The Virgin Suicides* (1999), Sofia Coppola's film adaptation of Jeffrey Eugenides' 1993 novel

Nancy Honey
Girls shopping (Nancy), London, 2001

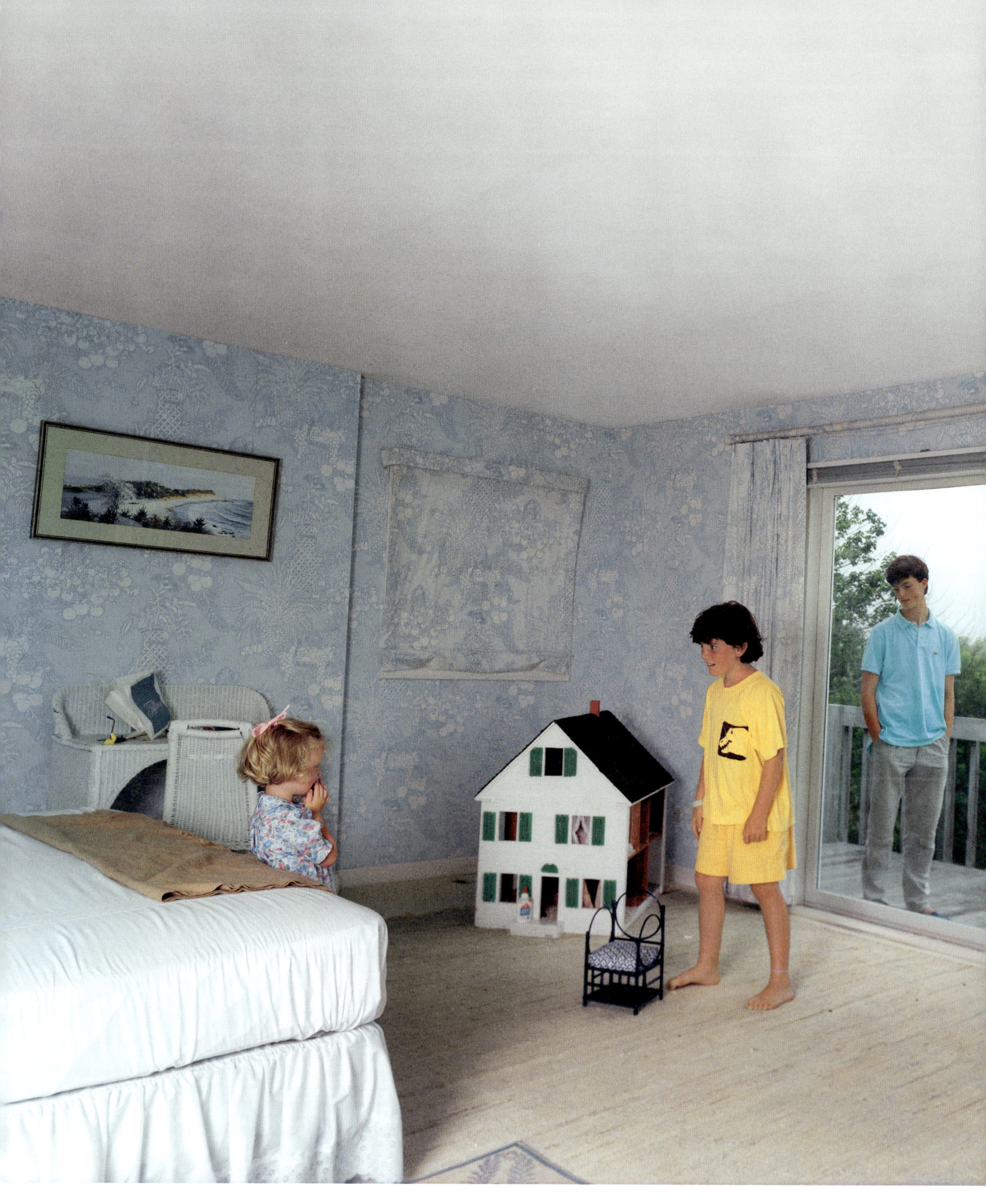

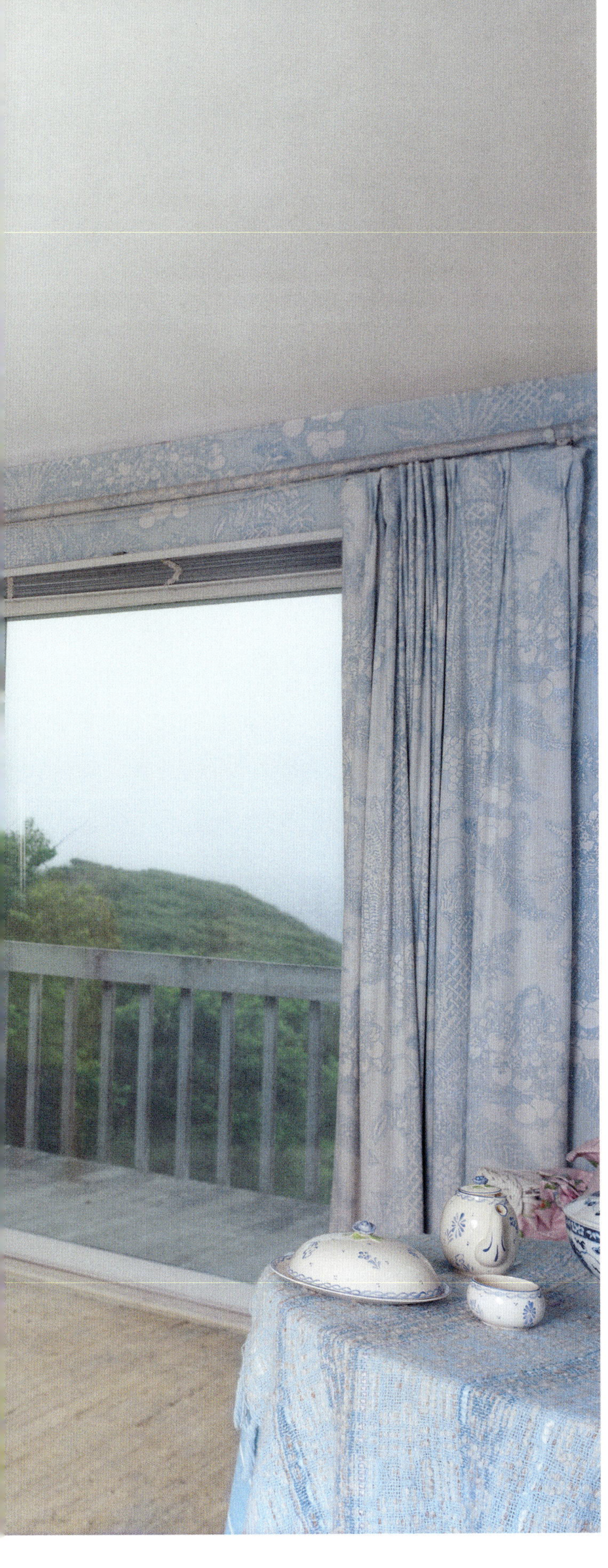

tina barney
the dollhouse, 1986

'The boy standing outside on the balcony and the little girl in the dress are half-siblings. The girl in yellow was a friend whose house they were visiting that day. The dollhouse was already in the room, but I think I placed the tiny wicker chair there to emphasise the difference in scale. I asked the boy to stand outside the room to guide the viewer's eye through the space, and the girl in yellow to look at her little friend. The "gift", as I call it, was the moment when the smaller girl brings her hands to her mouth — a gesture that could mean so many things, evoking the sense of narrative I'm always looking for.'

Tina Barney, *The Dollhouse*, 1986

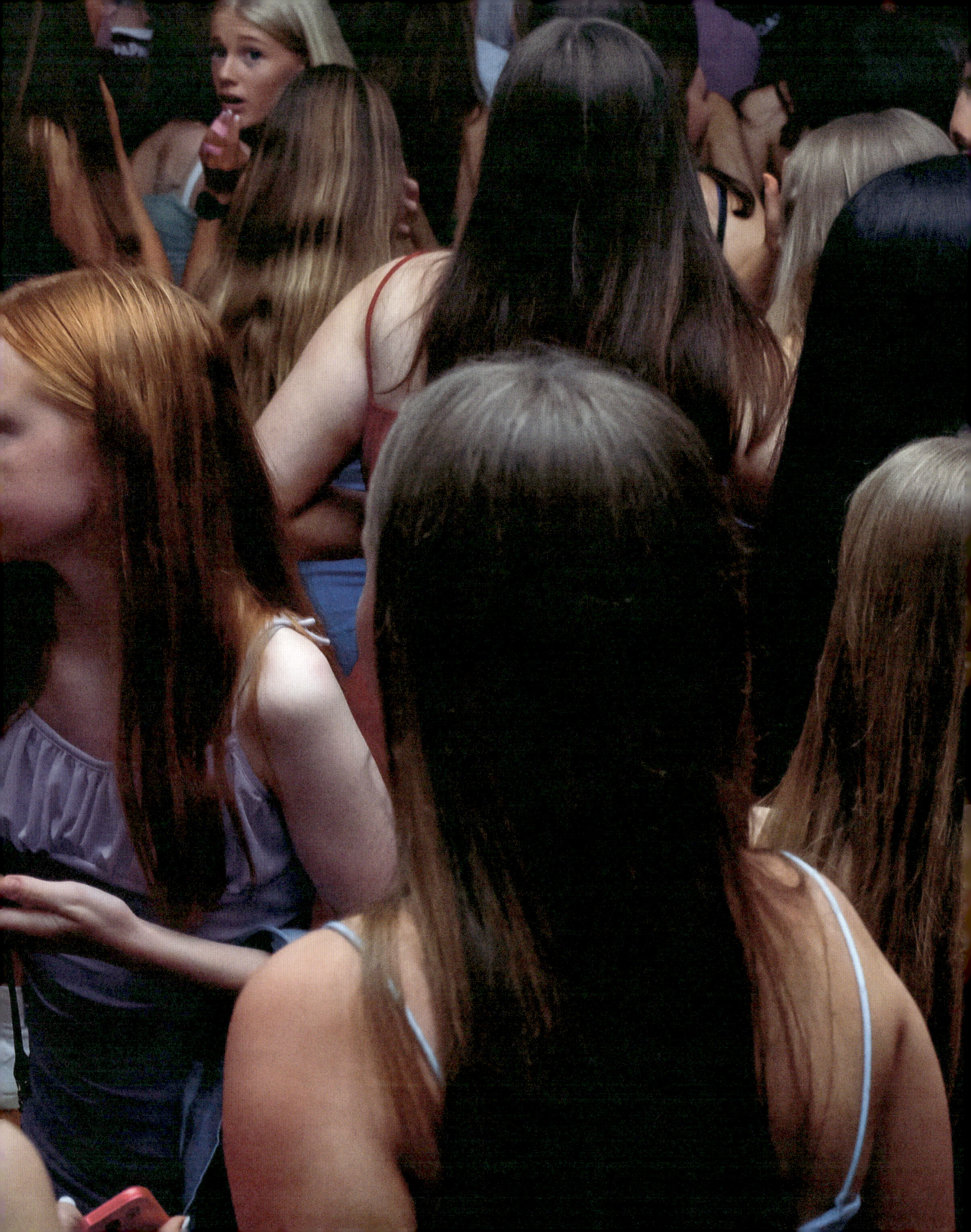

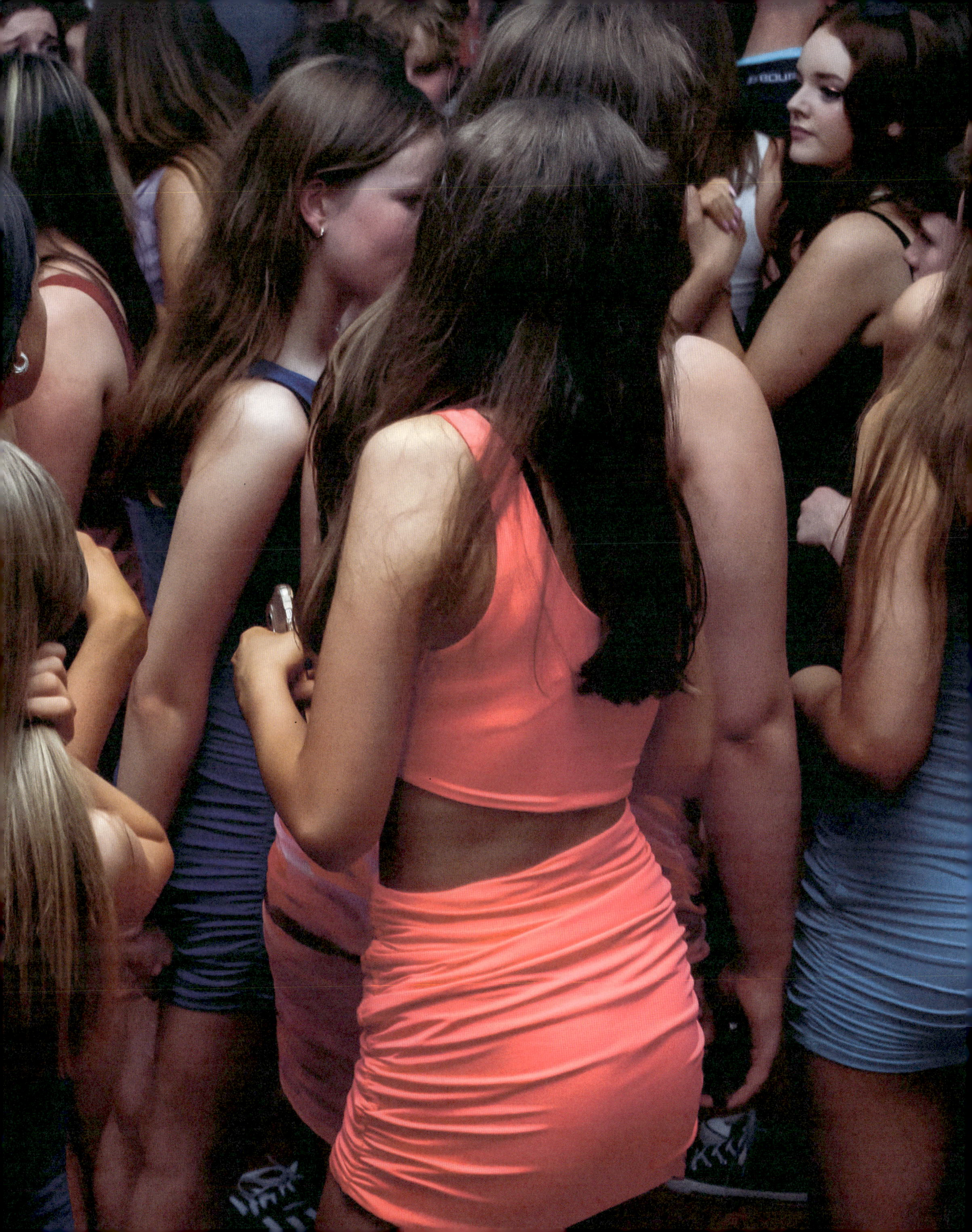

eimear lynch
girls' night, 2023

'For *Girls' Night*, I travelled around Ireland to photograph teen discos. I wanted to try and capture the anticipation of girls as they prepared to go out. In a way, I think I wanted to relive my teenage years. I loved going to discos. I mostly loved the hours of getting ready with friends. We didn't really get ready for the boys. We knew they didn't care what colour eyeshadow we wore or whether we curled or straightened our hair. The discos were more of a place to show off our new make-up skills that we probably learnt from *Kiss* magazine, and to pretend to be women for the first time. We were no longer kids. We were no longer the 12-year-olds who our parents were dressing: we were 13 and allowed to wear the bodycon cut-out dress we ordered from ASOS and pretend we could walk in cheap stilettos.'

'Before a night out, the girls I photographed for my book were spending an hour or two doing their makeup; meanwhile they were chatting and listening to music, and talking about good music. They weren't really talking about boys, which was a lot of what we spoke about when I was a teenager. Getting ready together actually gives girls a lot of time to be together and connect: whereas the boys would all arrive at the same time after being in their own houses and then go home by themselves, the girls would have organised sleepovers. That's how strong friendships are formed.'

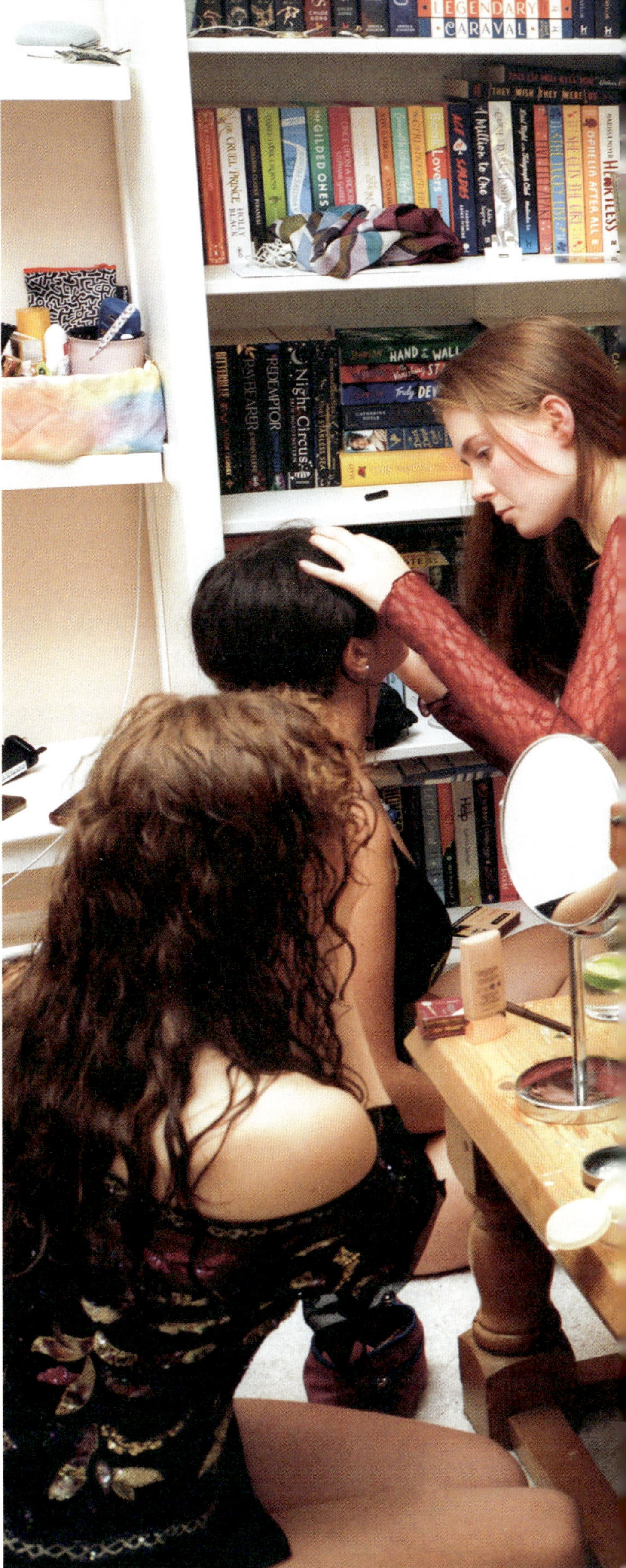

pp. 80–87

Eimear Lynch
Girls' Night, 2023

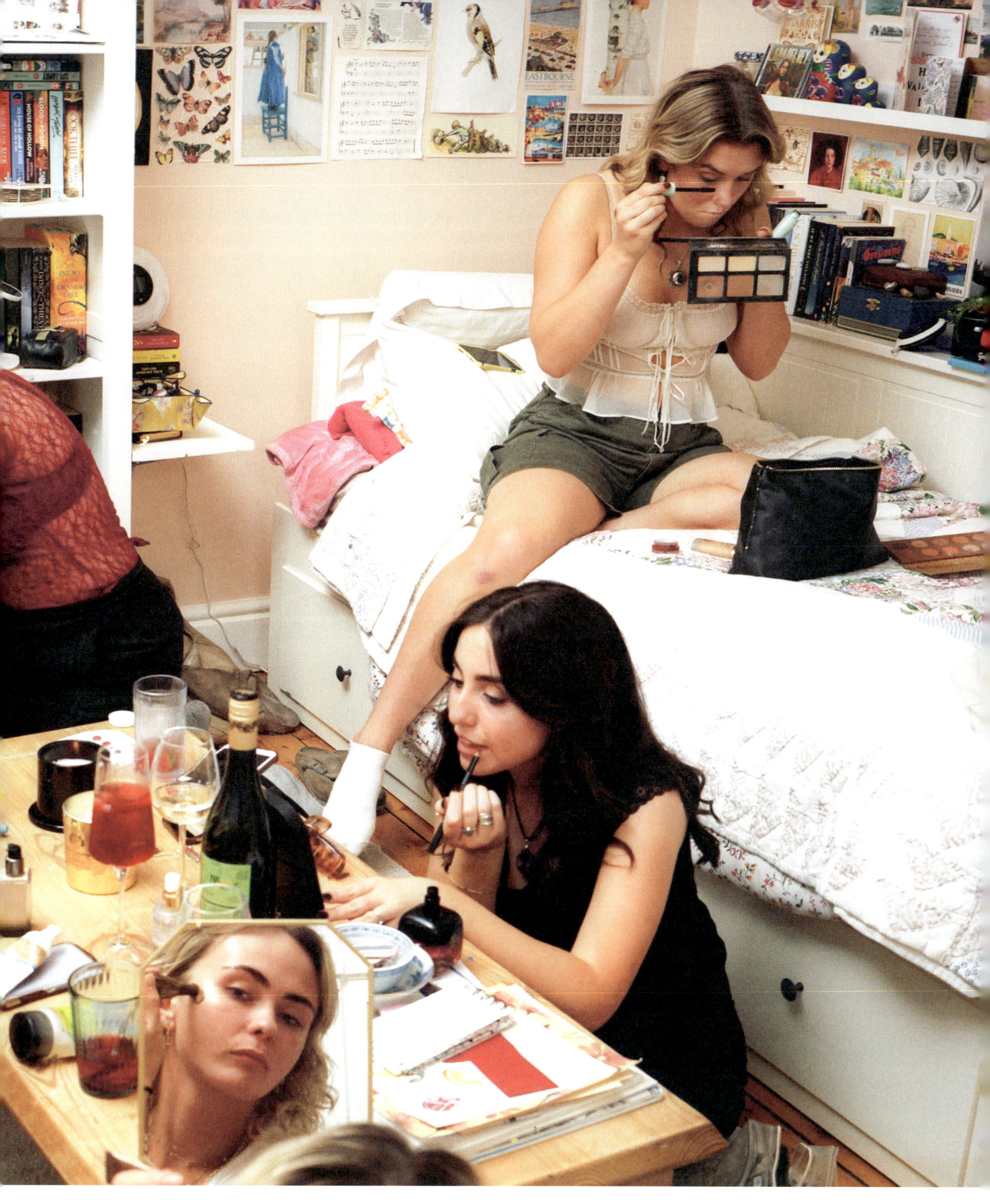
EASTBOURNE
HOUSE OF HOLLOW
SAMANTHA SHANNON
OUTSIDERS

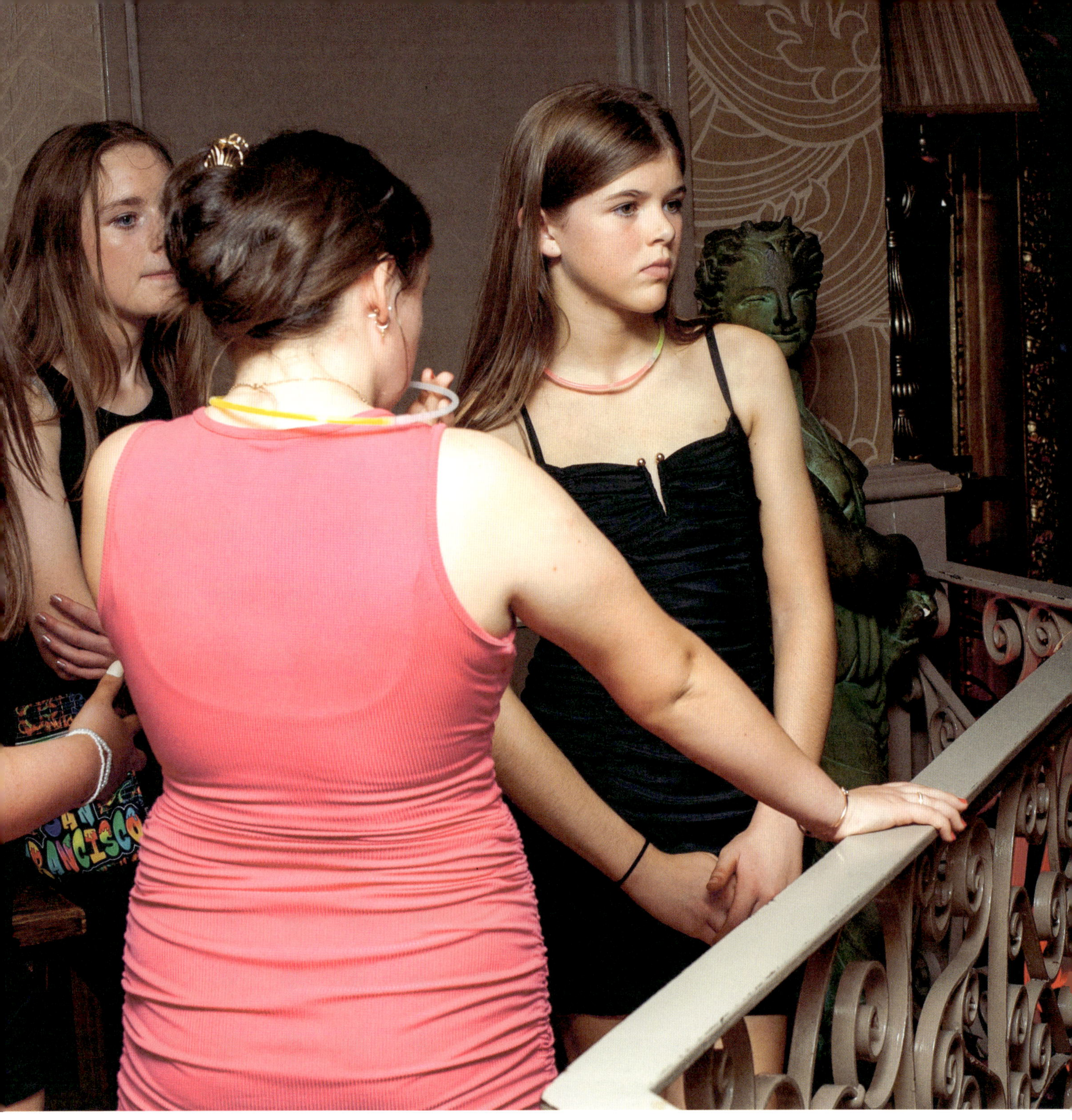

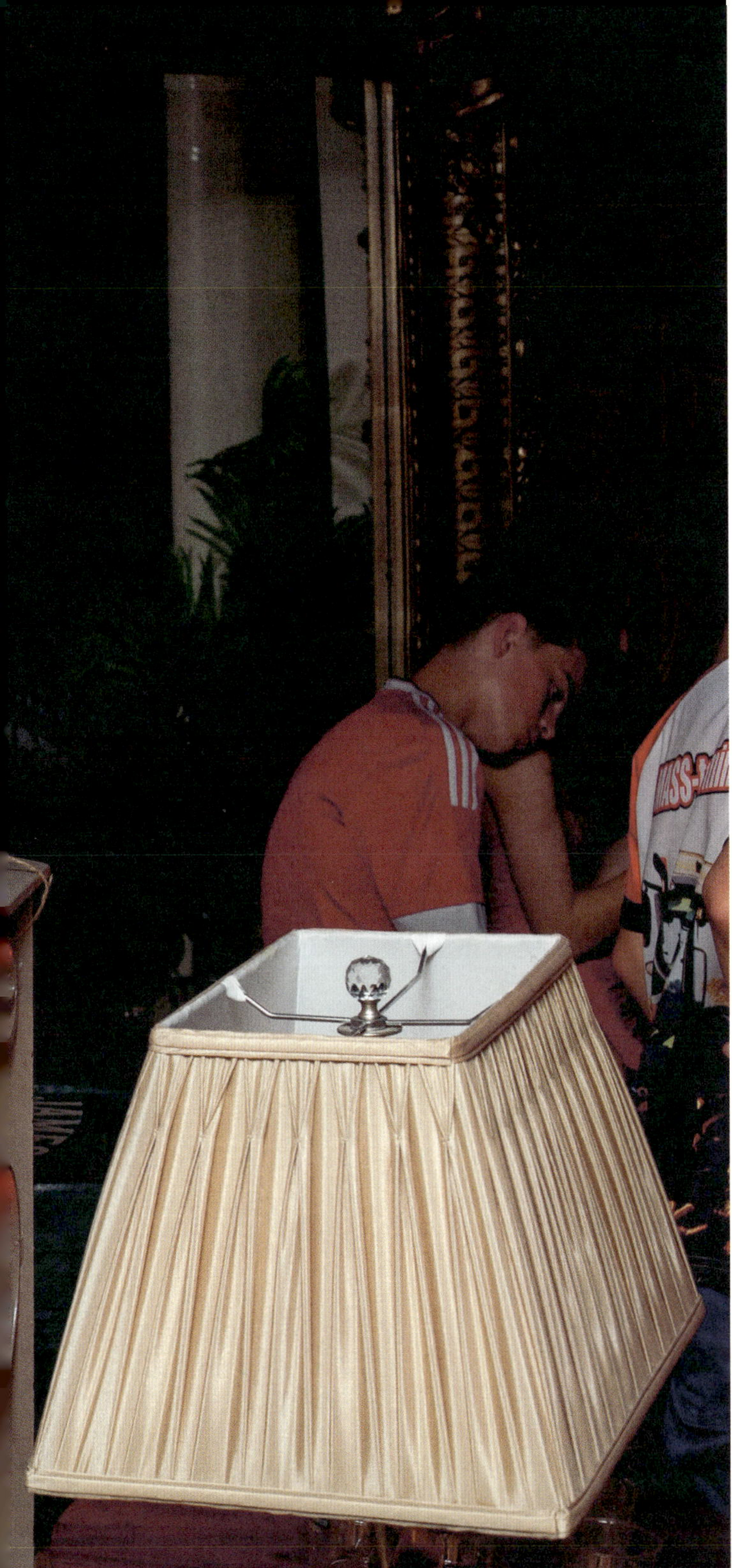

'The transition from child to teenager comes about so fast and suddenly you're completely consumed by your appearance and the first signs of womanhood. Amidst the insecurities and pressures that accompany this transition, there's also an undeniable thrill in the anticipation of growing up. I remember the excitement I had as a teenager to finally be able to partake in the rituals of beauty culture. It was a sweet spot where the positives of womanhood were untainted by the weight of any impending challenges.'

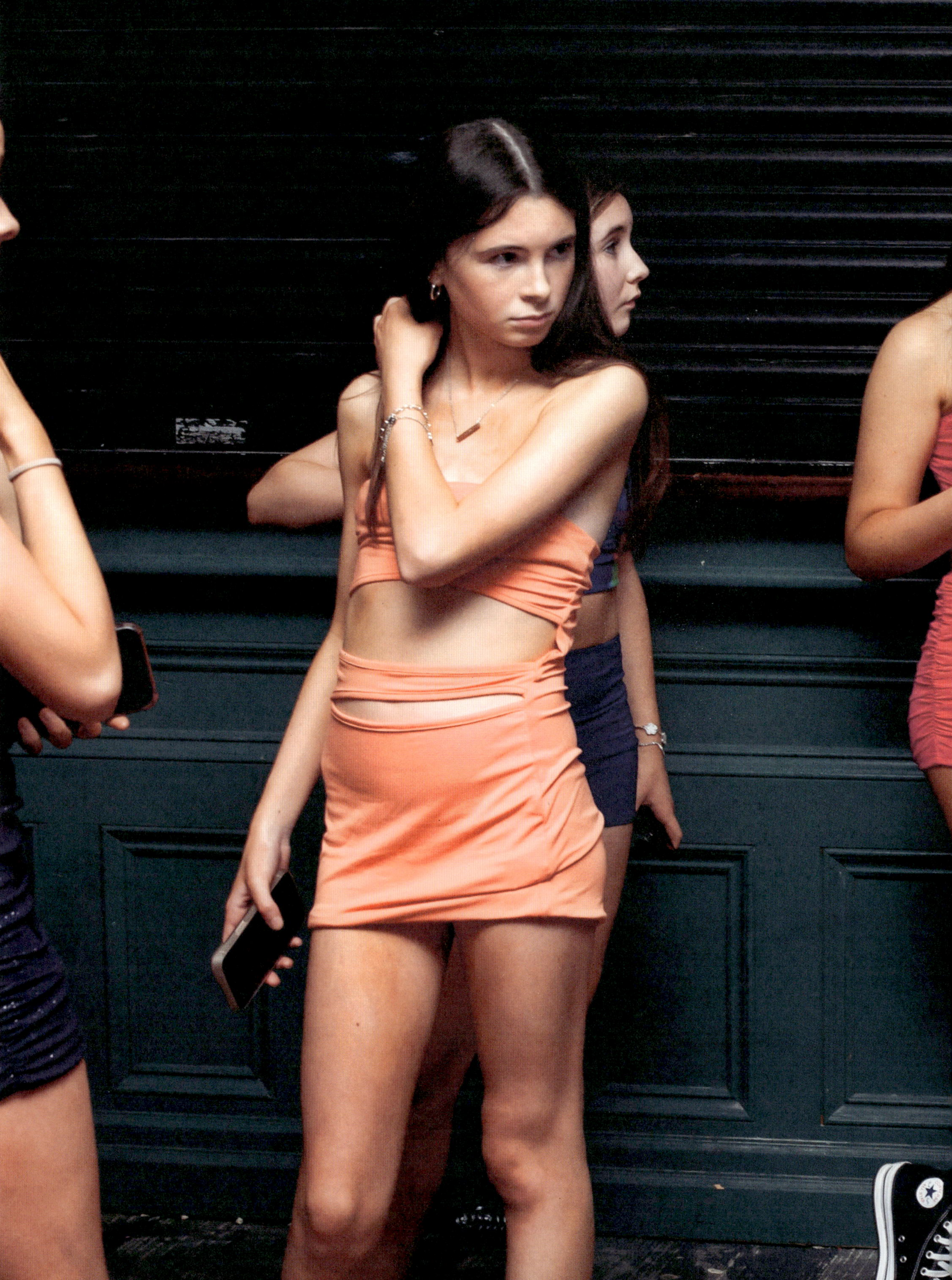

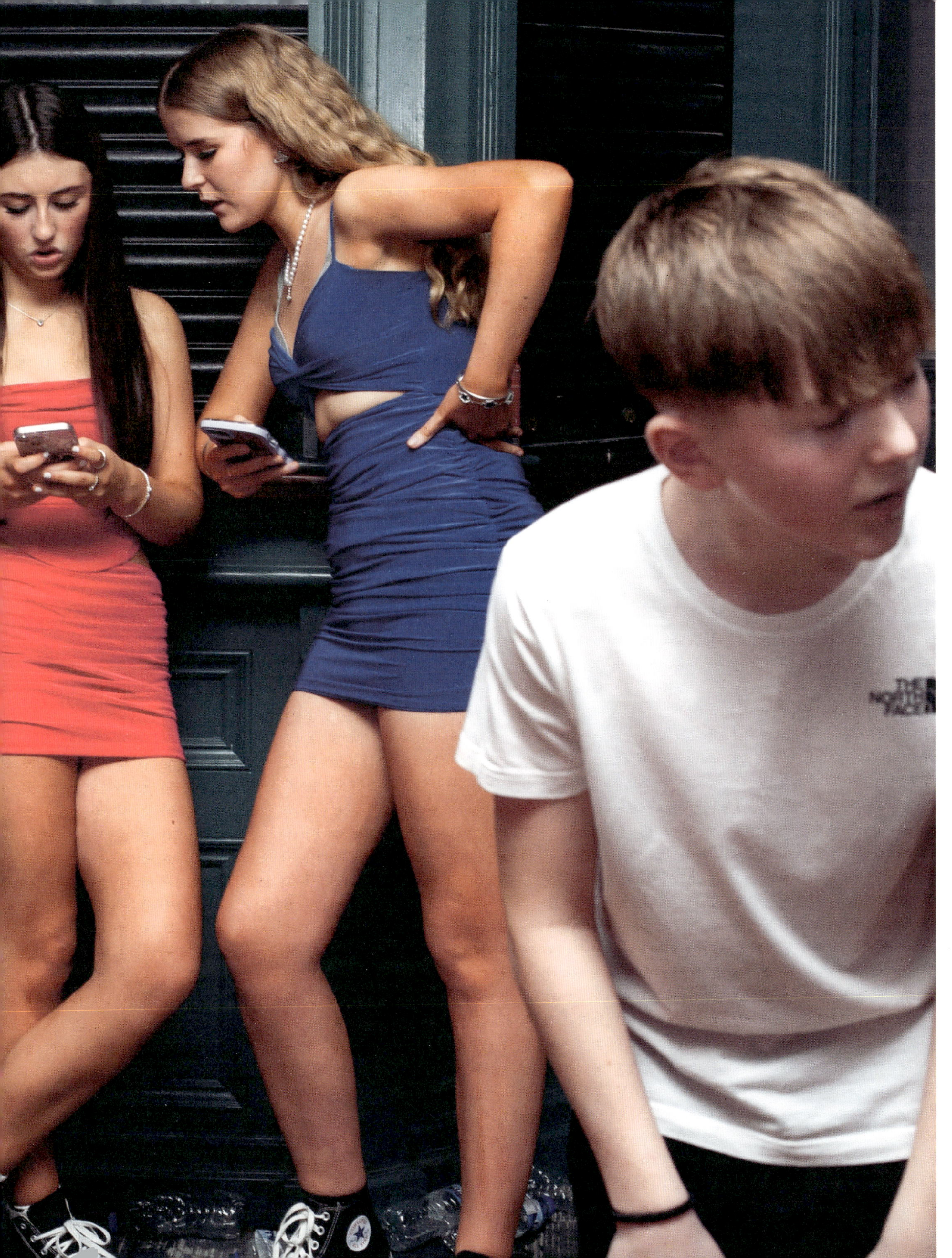
THE
NORTH
FACE

nancy honey
entering the masquerade, 1992

'In 1991, I began photographing adolescent girls in my immediate circle — my daughter Daisy, her friends, my niece — capturing everyday moments in their lives. *Entering the Masquerade* became a documentary project for my Fellowship at The National Museum of Photography, Film and Television (Bradford, West Yorkshire) in 1991–1992, as I started photographing girls at four different British state schools in Bath and Yorkshire. I wanted to capture the emotions of this pivotal stage between the ages of 11 and 14.'

Lynn at school, Bath

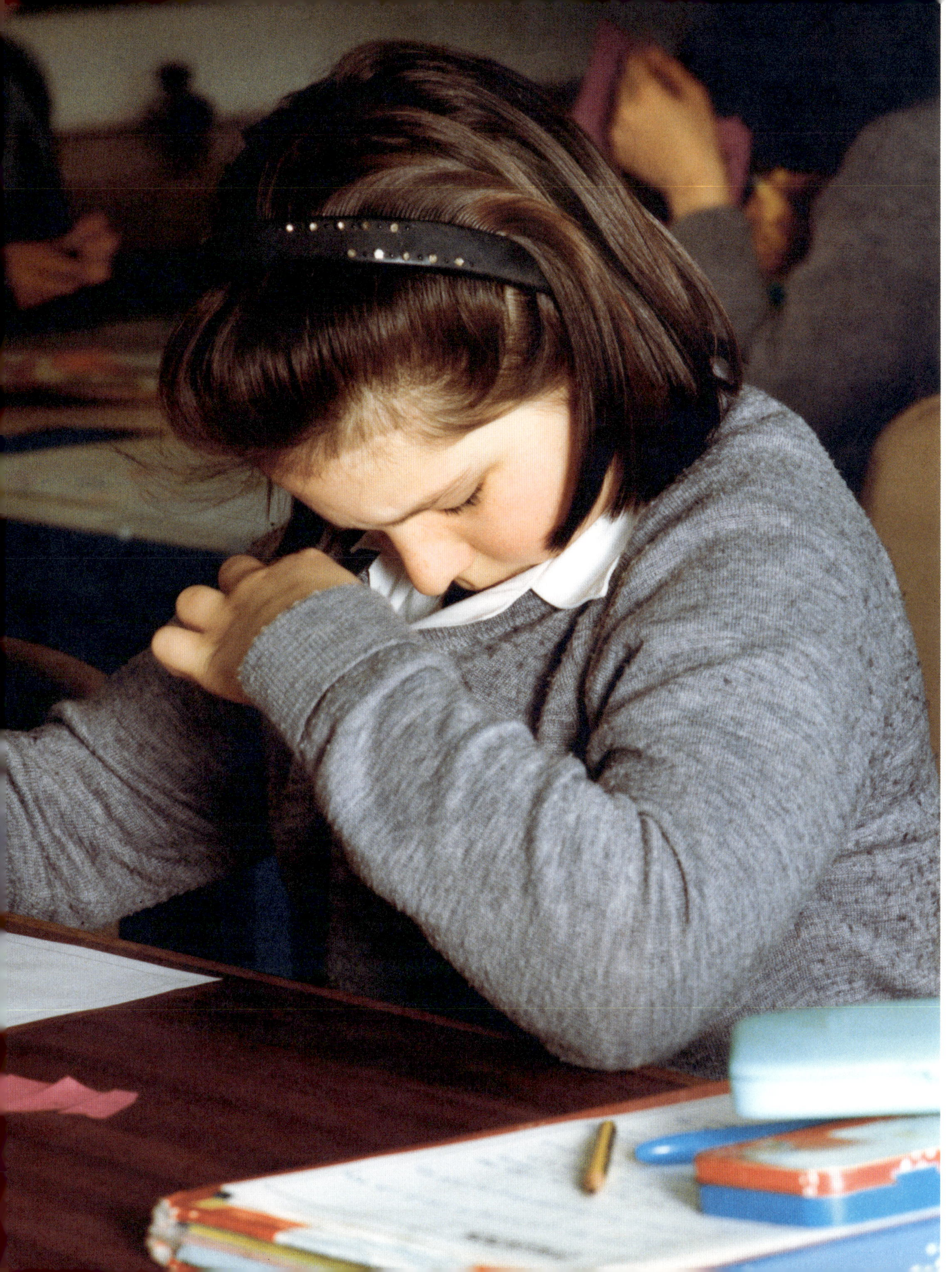

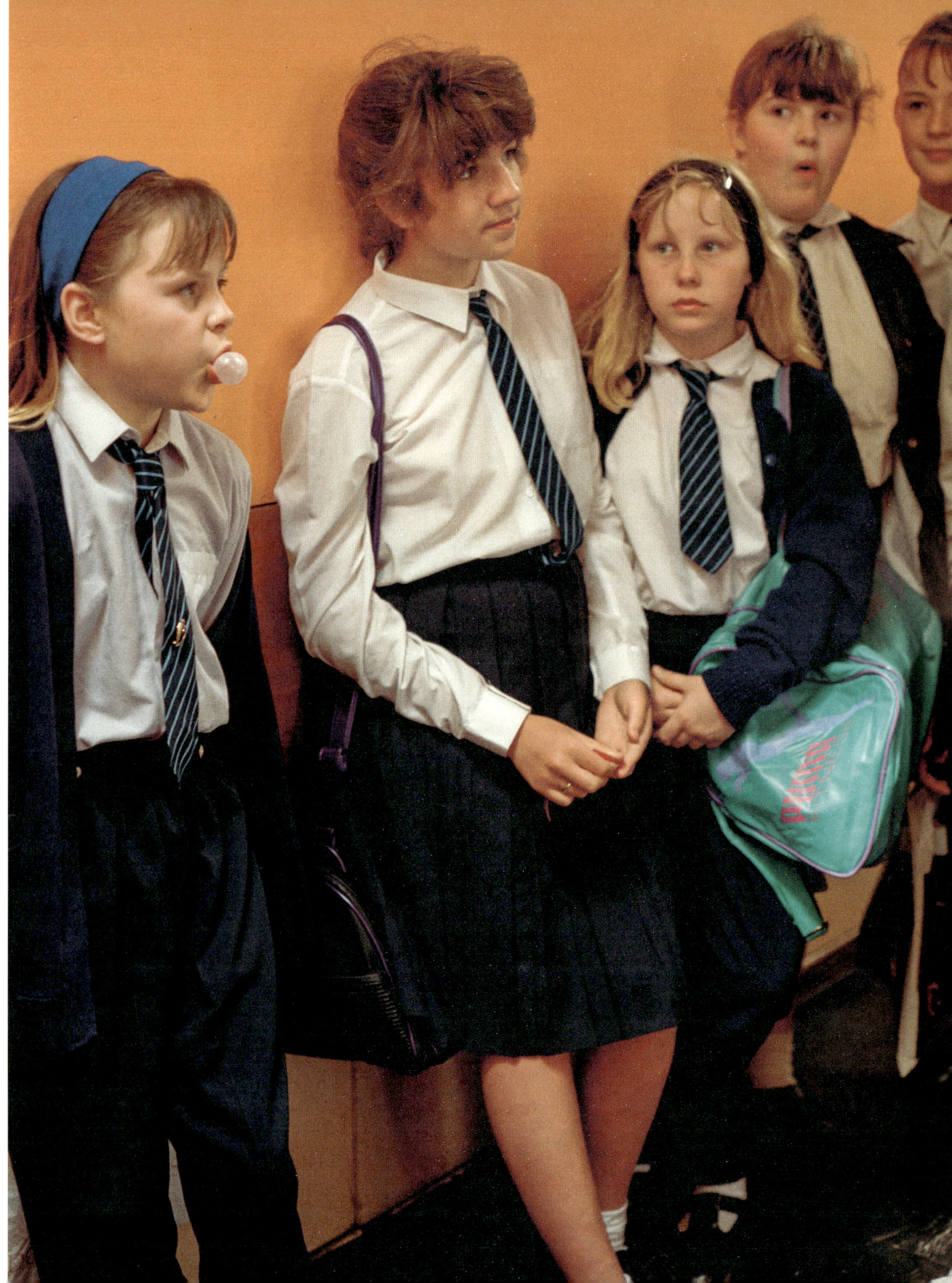
PUMA

‘I observed that, up until the age of 11, girls — to varying degrees — conformed to the expectations of parents and teachers. But from the age of 12, they began to experience new and different pressures from their peers. At 11, most girls were still children; by 14, they were on the cusp of becoming young adults. This brief three-year span plays a crucial role in shaping a girl’s self-image for the future.’

Group of girls, 11 and 12, at school, Knottingley

‘What I love about these photos is that they show how much these girls enjoyed having their picture taken — or, alternatively, how invisible I was to them.’

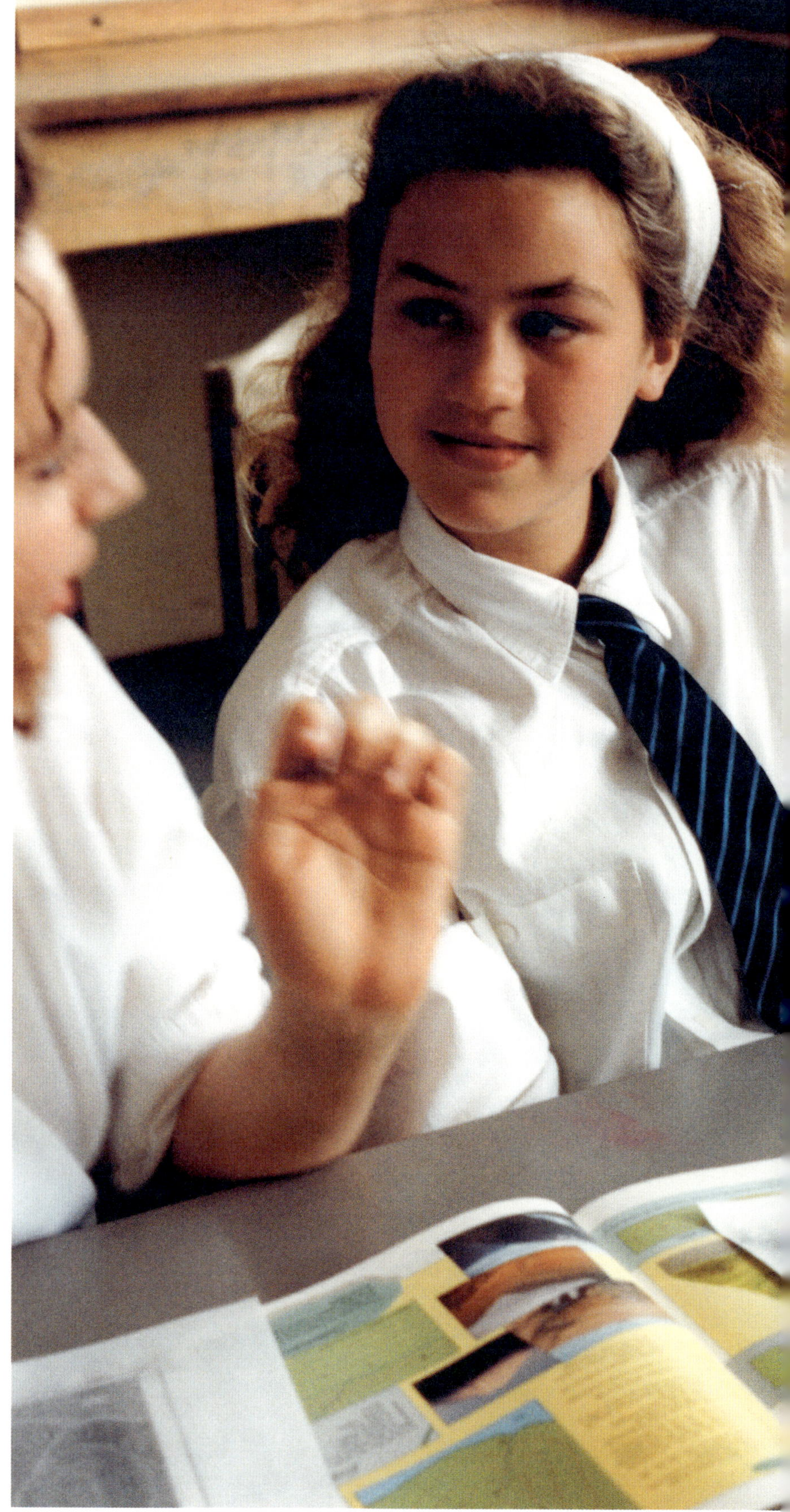

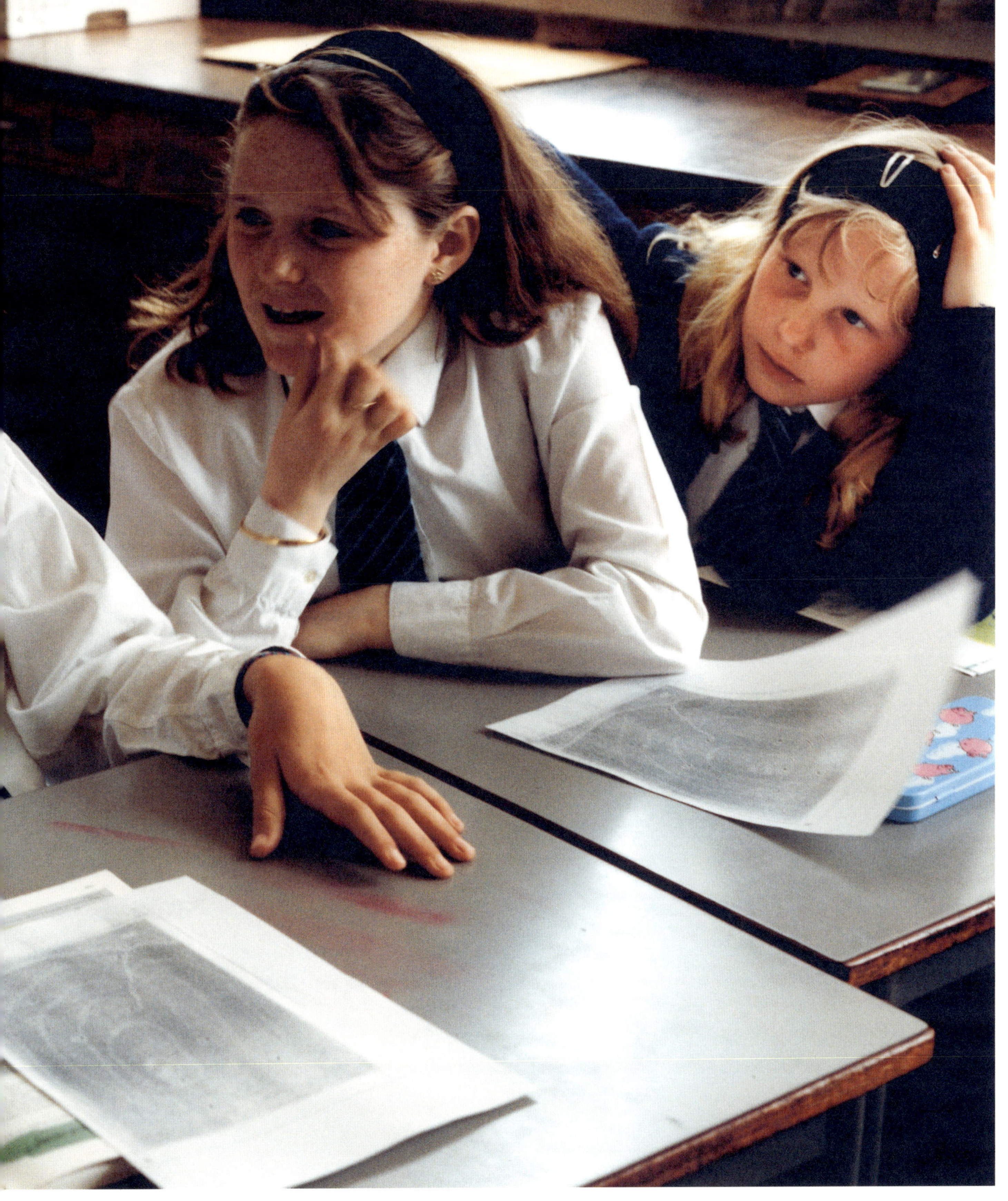

Girls, 11 and 12, at school, Ferrybridge

‘During my photography sessions, I often noticed when someone seemed withdrawn. Whenever I asked, “What’s wrong with her?” the response was always the same: “She’s in a mood.”’

Hannah and Kathy, 11, at school, Bath

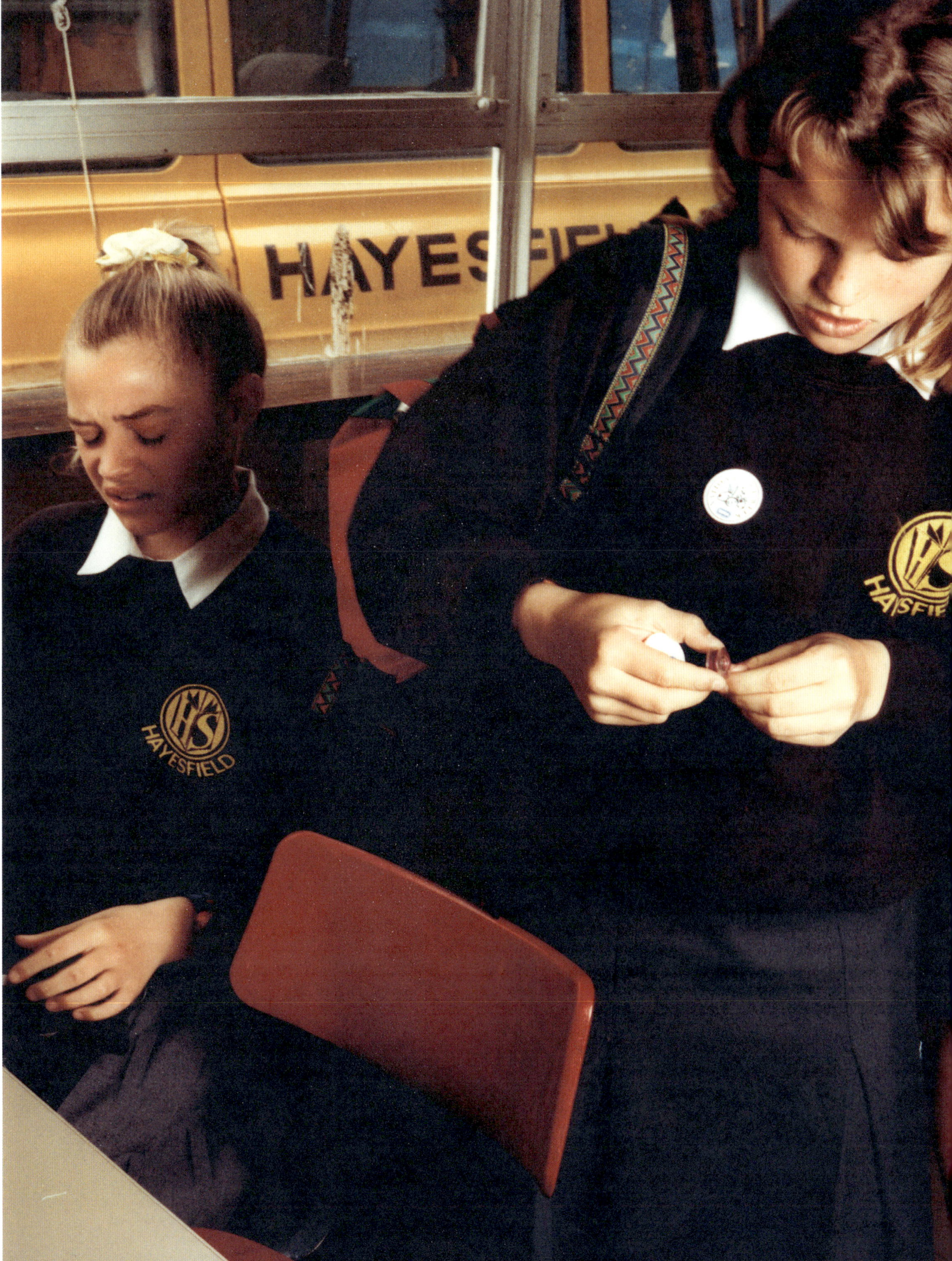
HS
HAYESFIELD

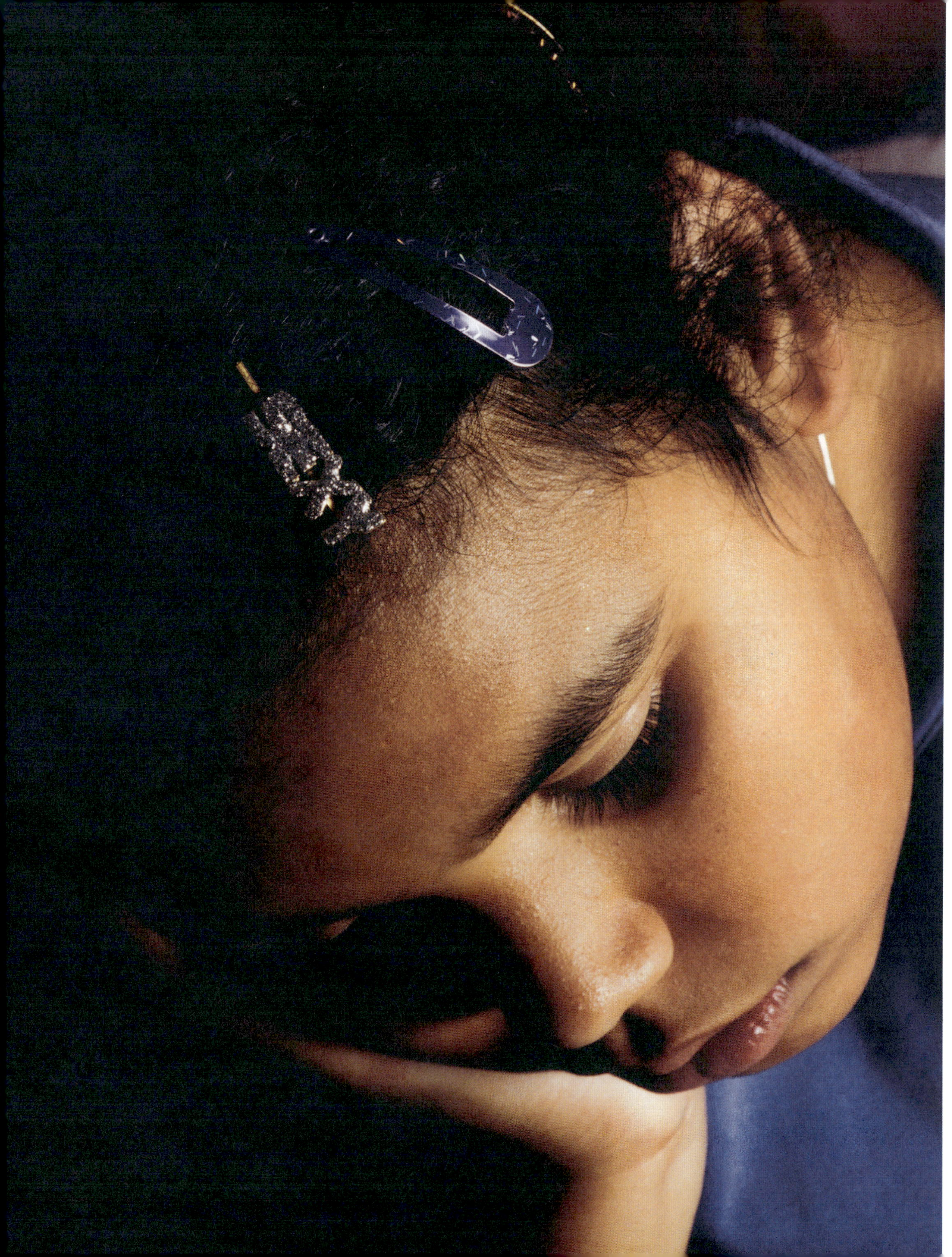

nancy honey
girls shopping, london, 2001

'I knew one of the girls' mothers, and we arranged for me to photograph them on their shopping day in London. They were so animated which made it delightfully difficult to capture them. Since they were young teens they didn't buy much that day — they tried on endless pairs of shoes and clothes and ate sweets. That was the joy of it.'

Ella

‘This shopping series is dear to me as it takes me back to when I was their age. The first time I was allowed to go out on my own was to go shopping with friends at about 12 years old. I grew up in San Francisco, and just the adventure of taking the bus to meet my friend downtown felt exhilarating. I still remember the thrill of that new sense of excitement, freedom and possibility. And, of course, trying on things we never intended to buy — it was all part of the experience. We were posing in front of the mirror in high heels, holding up dresses. It was these girls’ way to bond, to share in the excitement of exploring the adult world together.’

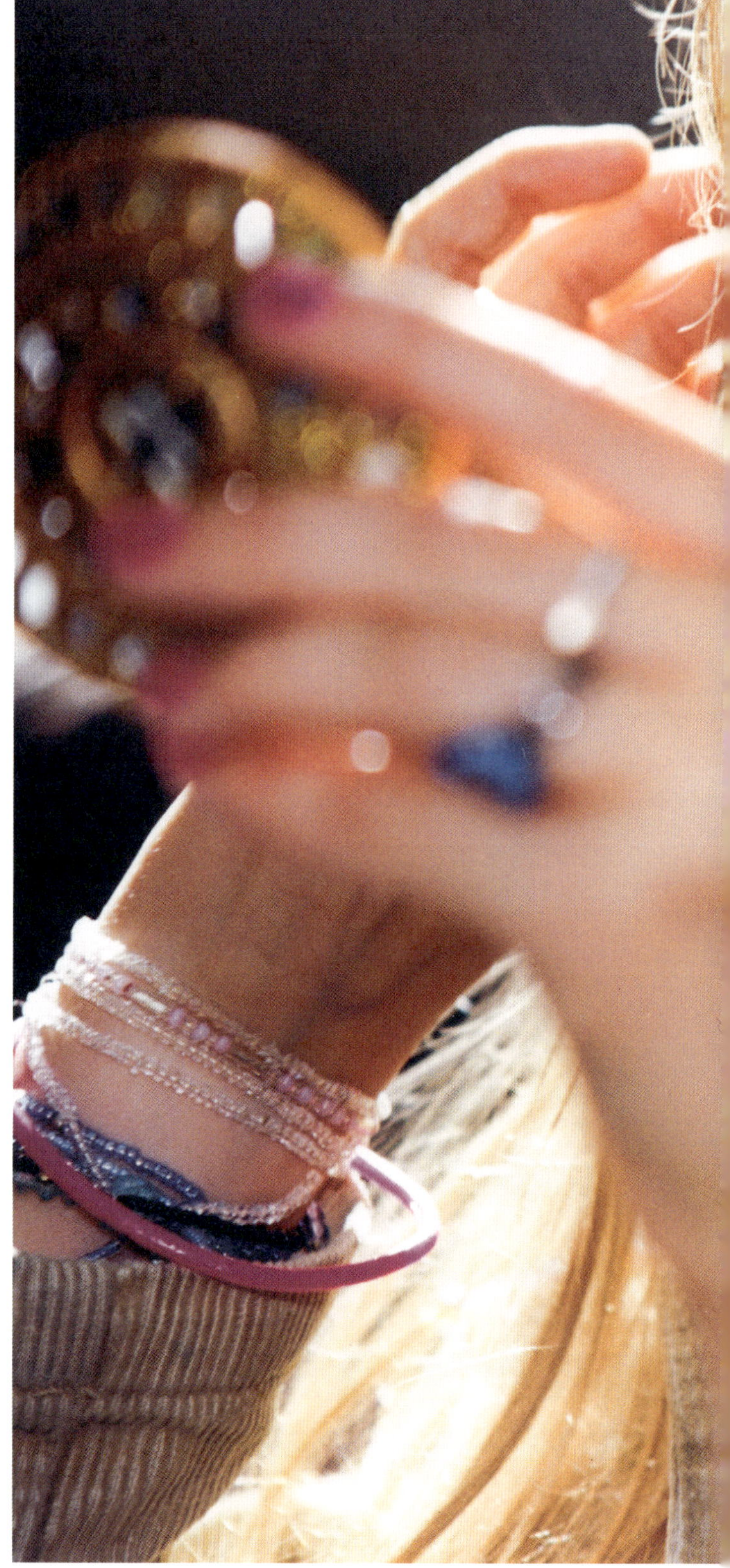

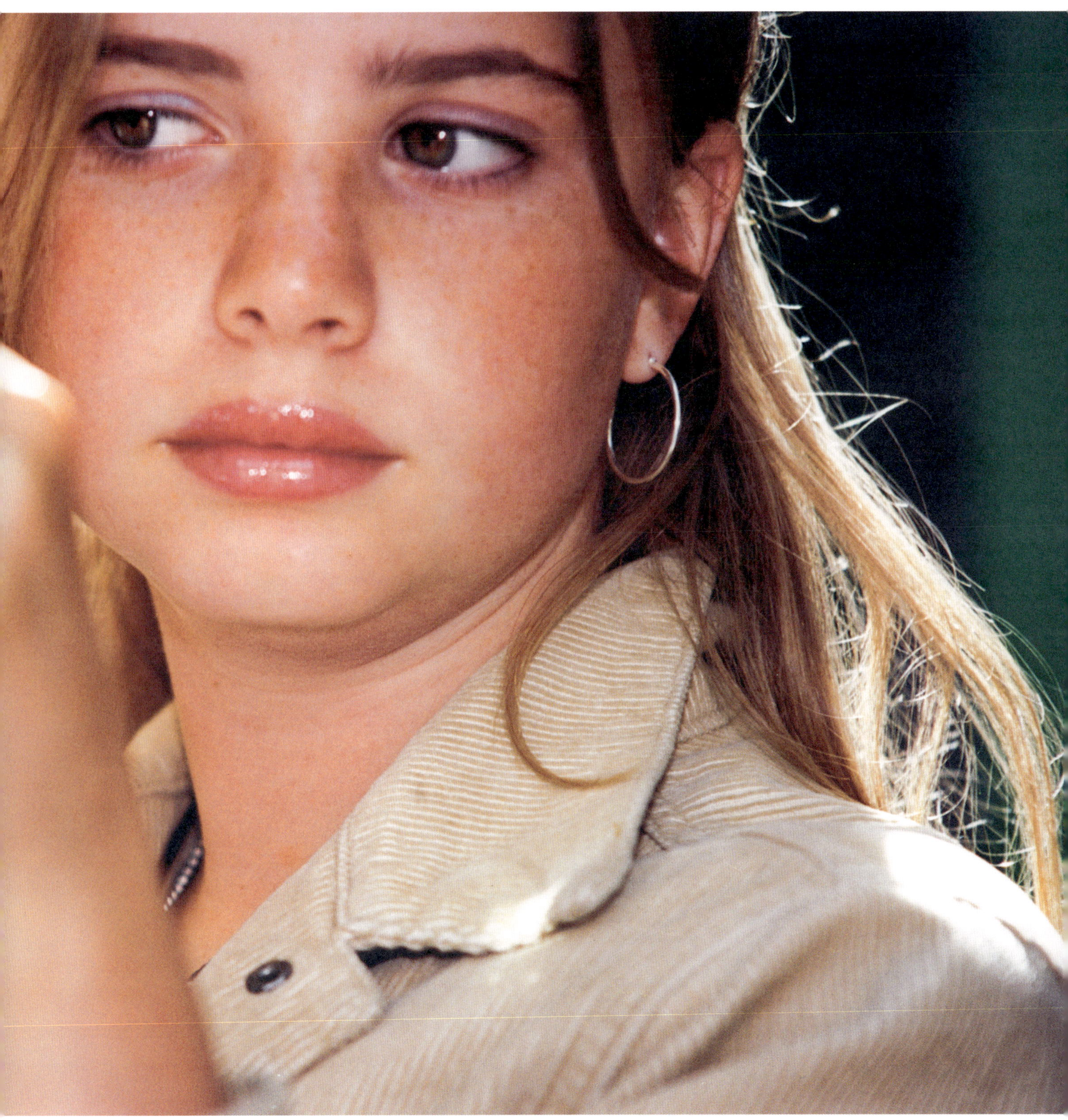

Nancy

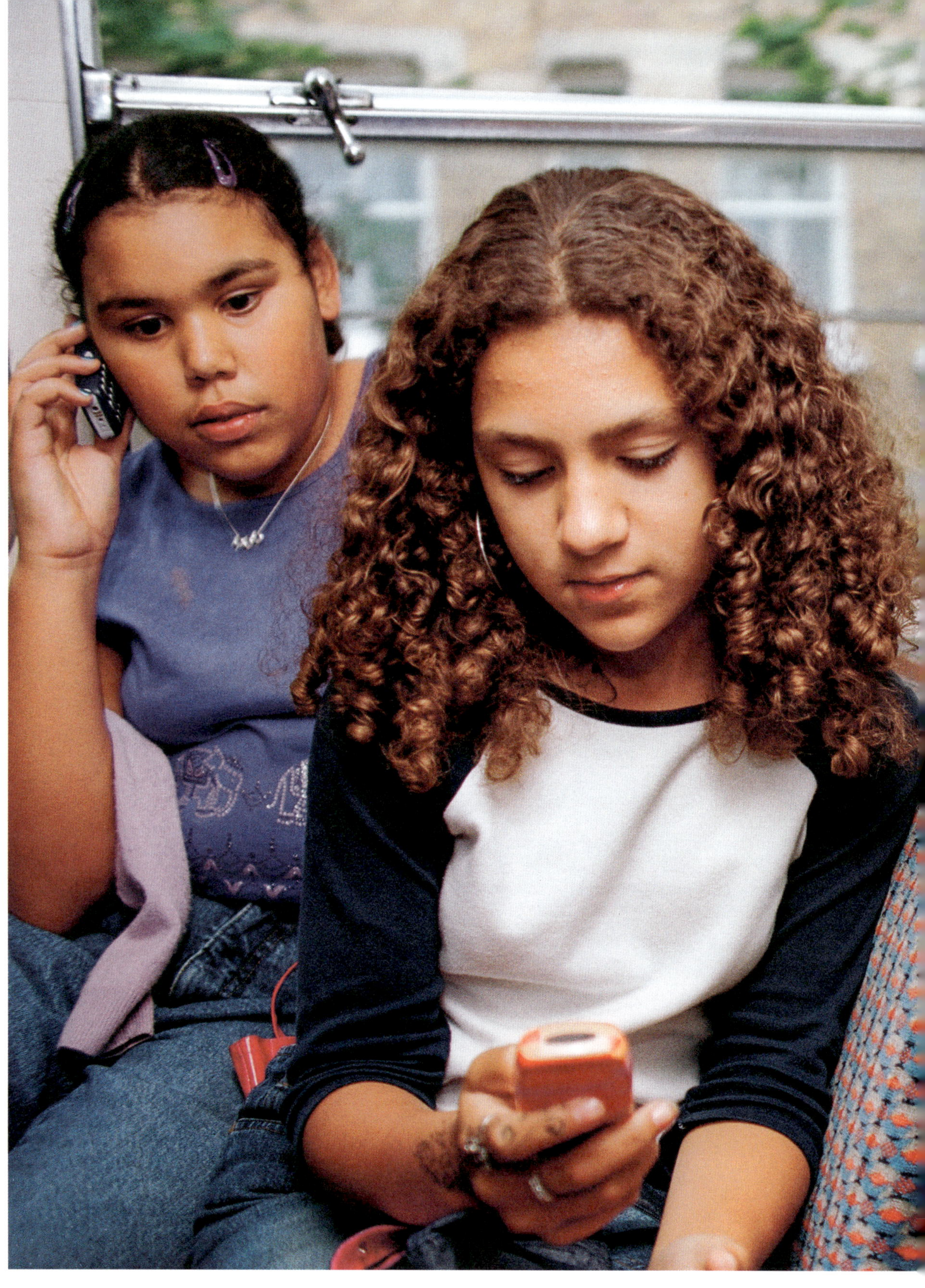

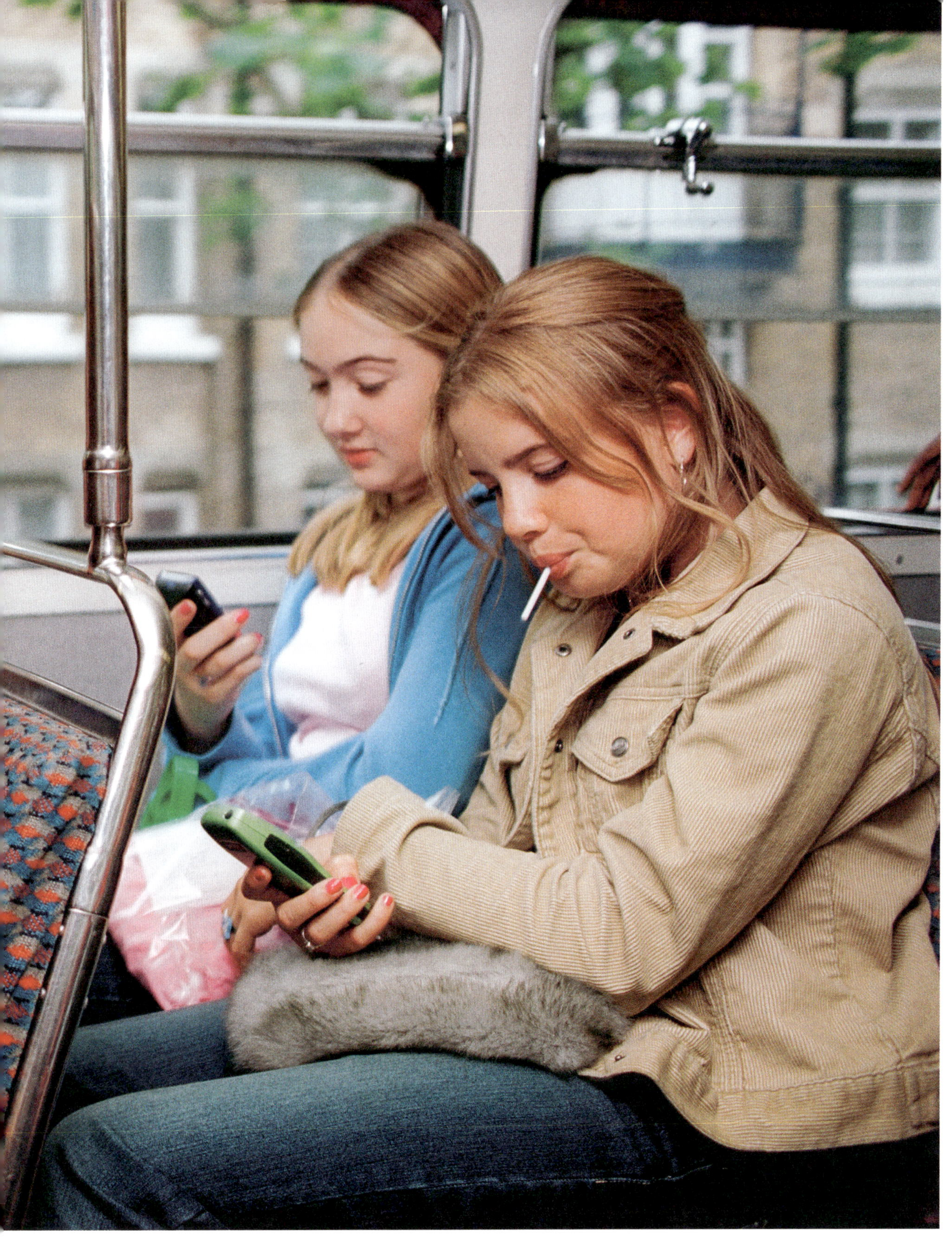

Ella, Lily, Georgia and Nancy

sofia coppola
the virgin suicides, 1999

'It felt like Jeffrey Eugenides — author of *The Virgin Suicides* — really understood the experience of being a teenager. I loved how the boys were so confused by the girls, and I really connected with all that lazing around in your bedroom. I tried to make it feel real to me. I felt that in a lot of movies, the teens didn't feel relatable. Because I was still in my 20s when I directed the film, the idea of school wasn't far away. I wanted their world to look accurate.'

'The story is told as a memory. Costume designer Nancy Steiner and I talked about the prom dresses reflecting the way Eugenides wrote about them as a "four-headed-creature". We wanted them to look accurate for the 1970s, and for them to feel like real kids, while the Lisbon girls were dreamy and mythic in the memory of the boys' minds.'

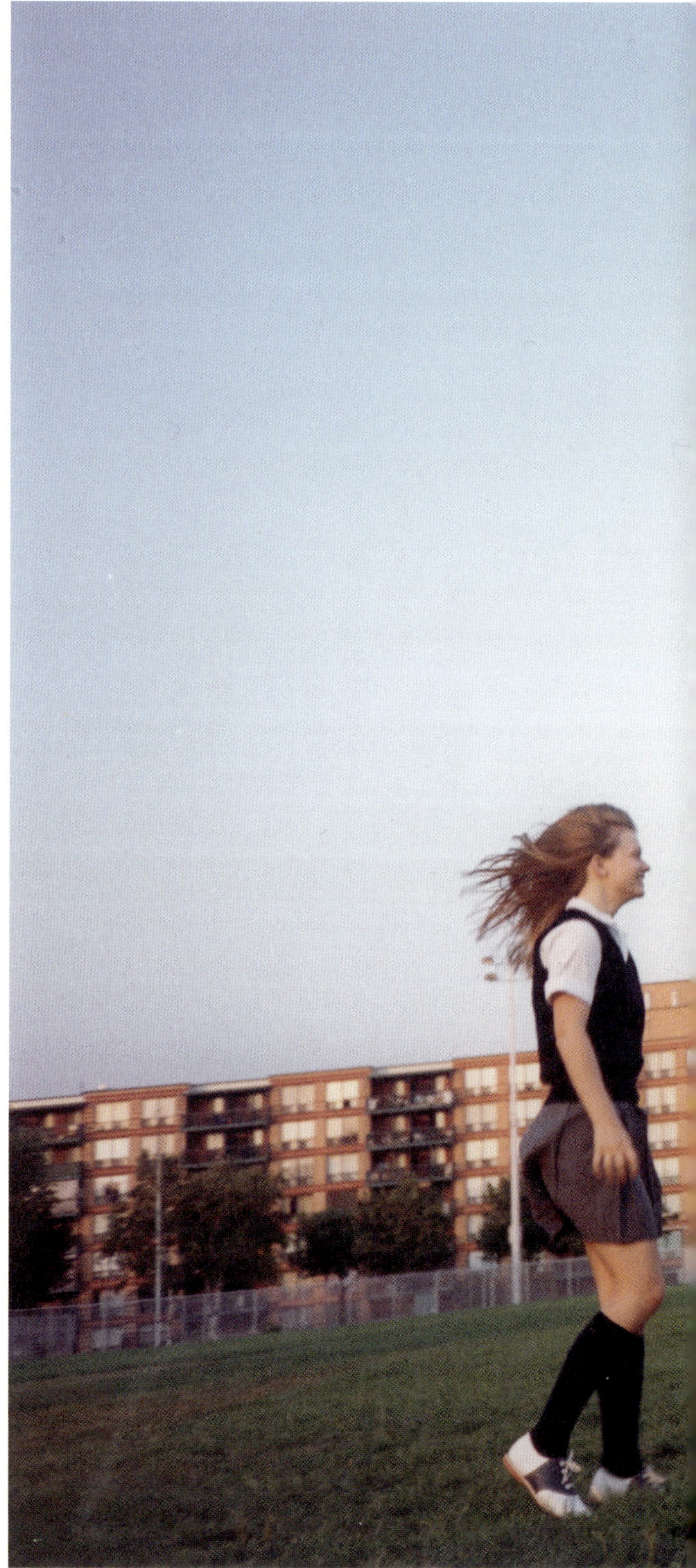

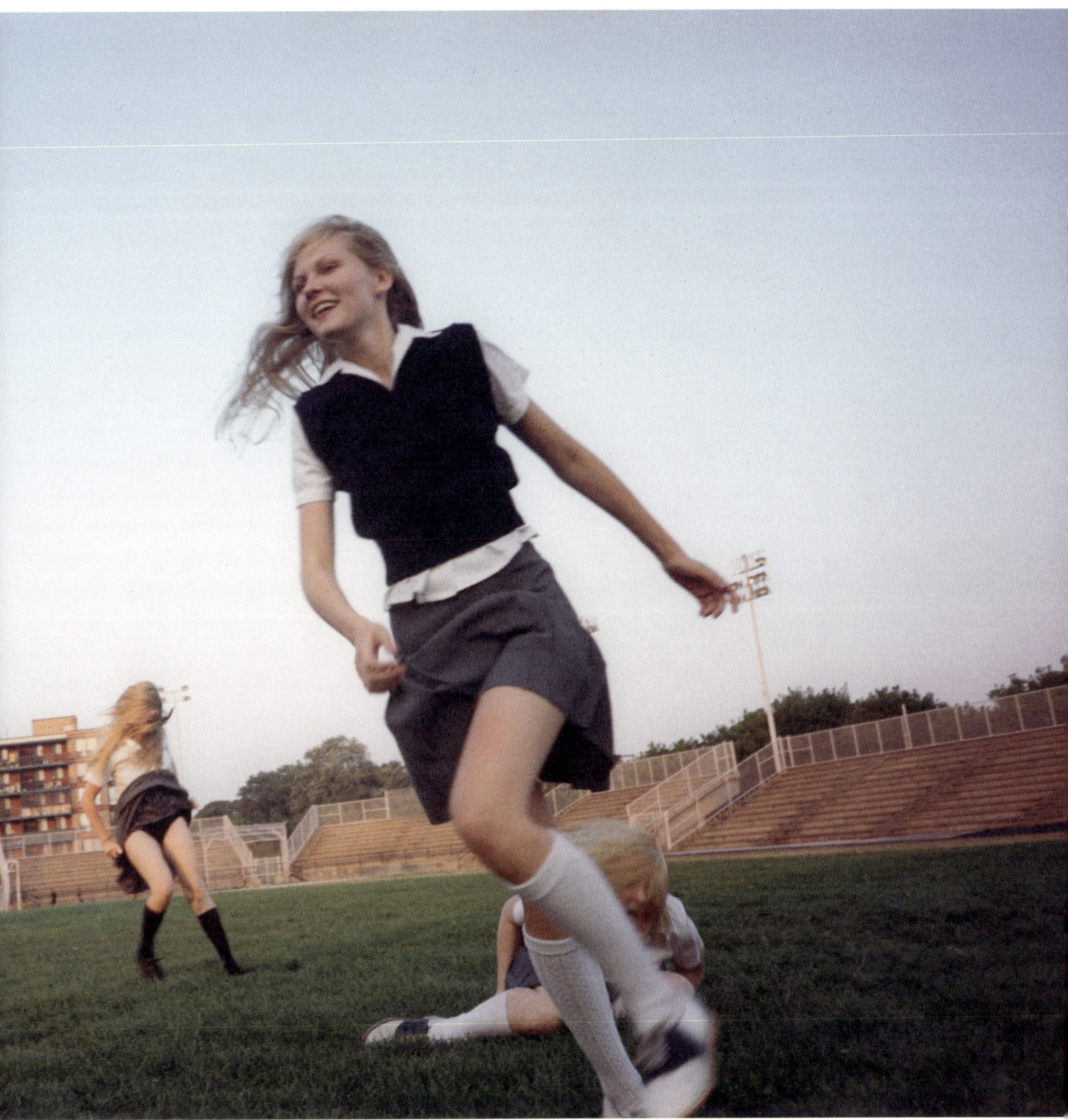

The Lisbon sisters at school, photographed by Sofia Coppola

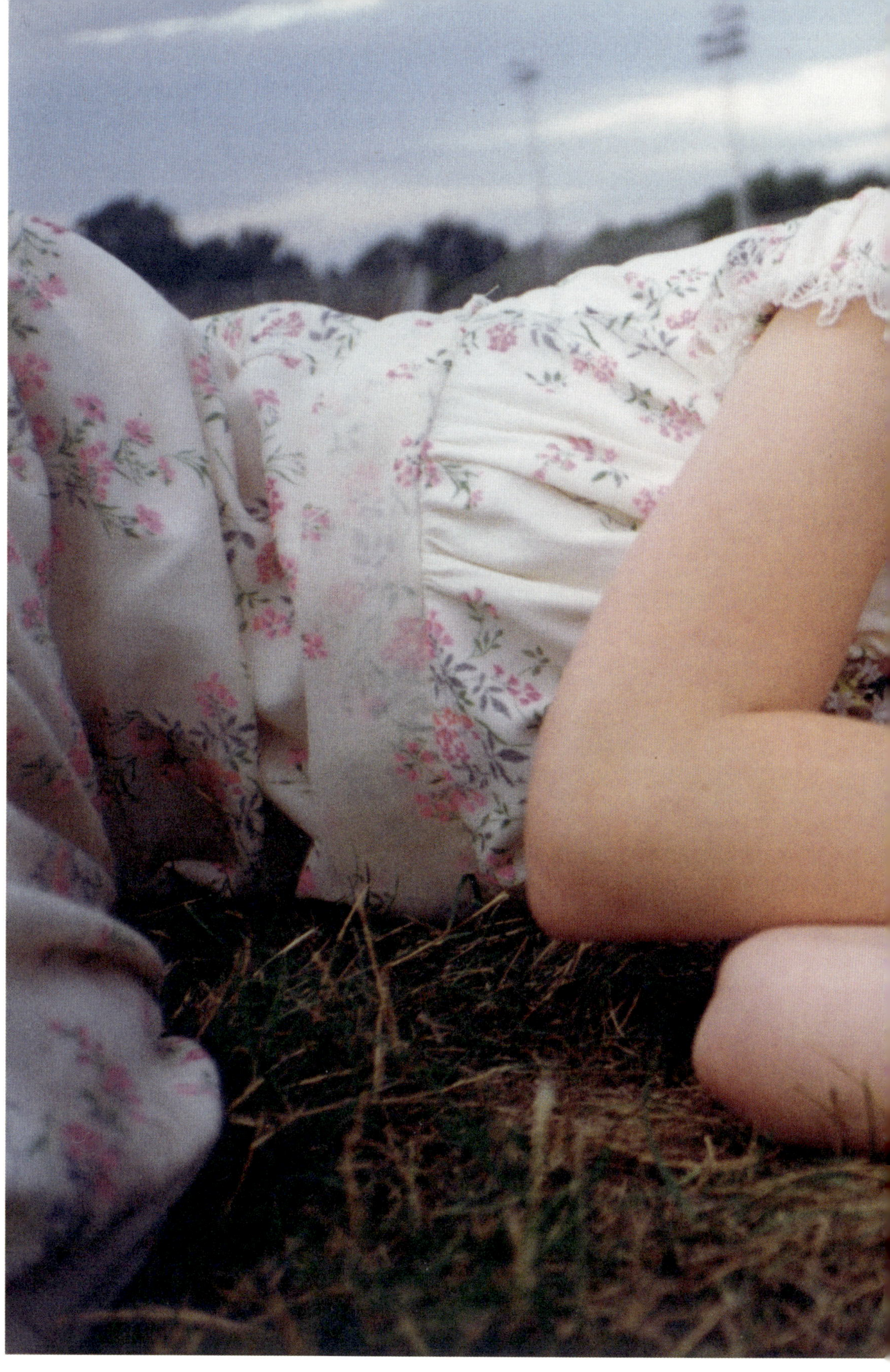

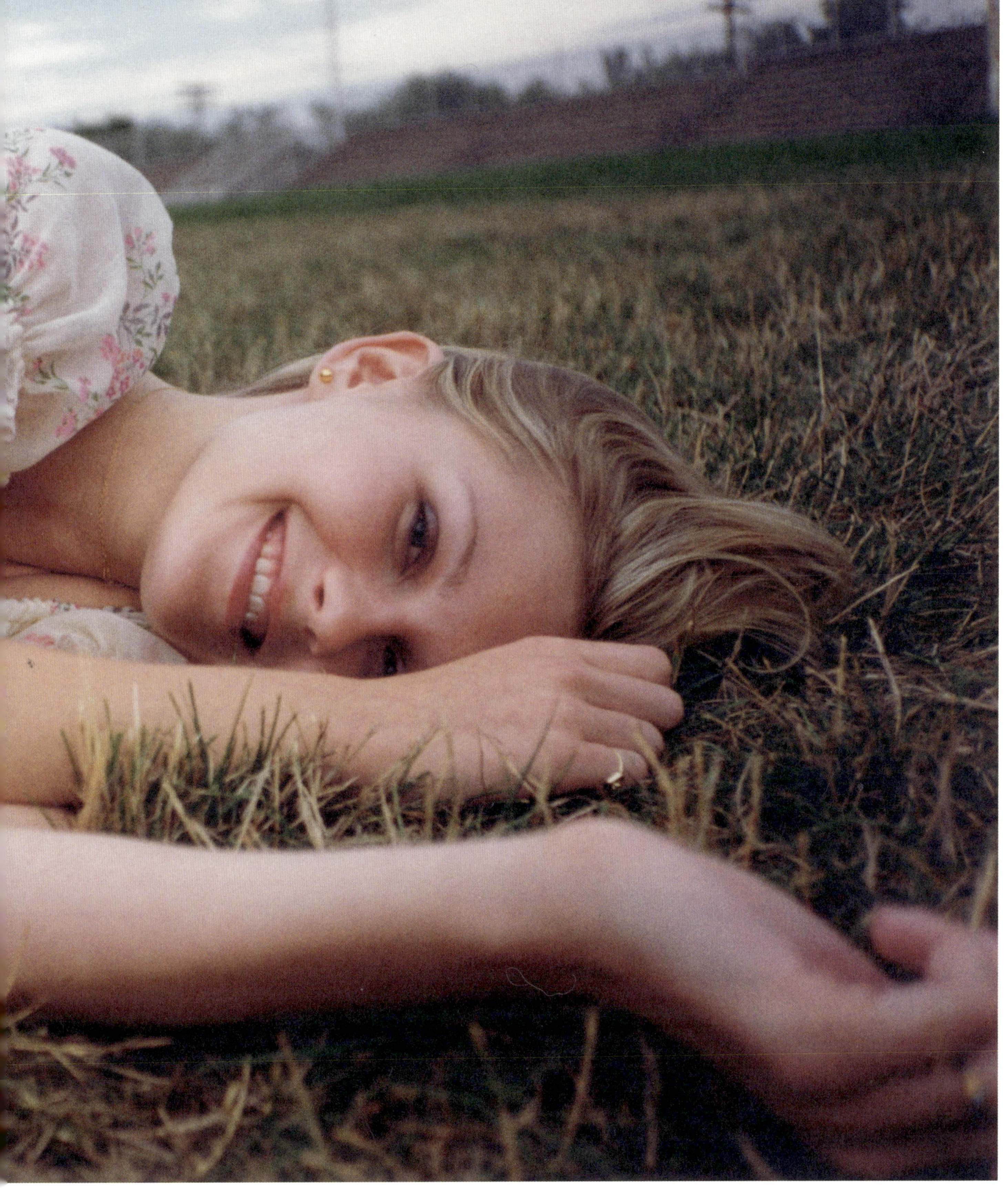

Lux in her prom dress, photographed by Sofia Coppola

nancy steiner
the virgin suicides, 1999

'Sofia approached the aesthetic elements of the film subtly, which I felt very connected with. There is a uniformity to the way the Lisbon girls dress, but we discussed how to adapt the costumes according to each sister's personality. Because Mary is the oldest, her look was slightly more mature and studious. Lux dressed a bit sexy with more low-cuts and form-fitting garments. The youngest sister, Cecilia, was in her own world, with her own style. You see her mostly in the white lace dress. The backstory for that costume was that this dress was their grandmother's wedding dress that had been kept in a box and was rediscovered. I did the math when their grandmother would have gotten married, and it was in the mid-1920s. I wanted the dress to look like it had been in a box for decades.'

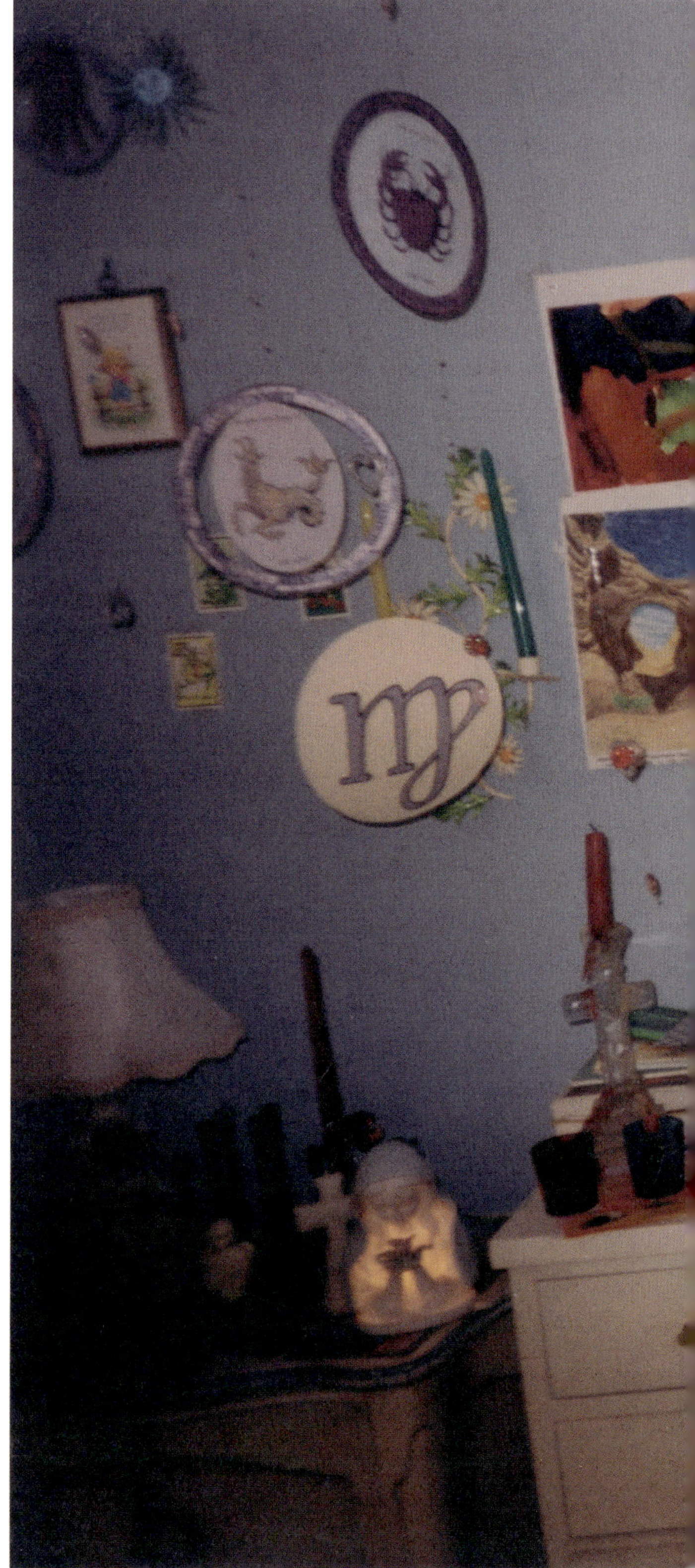

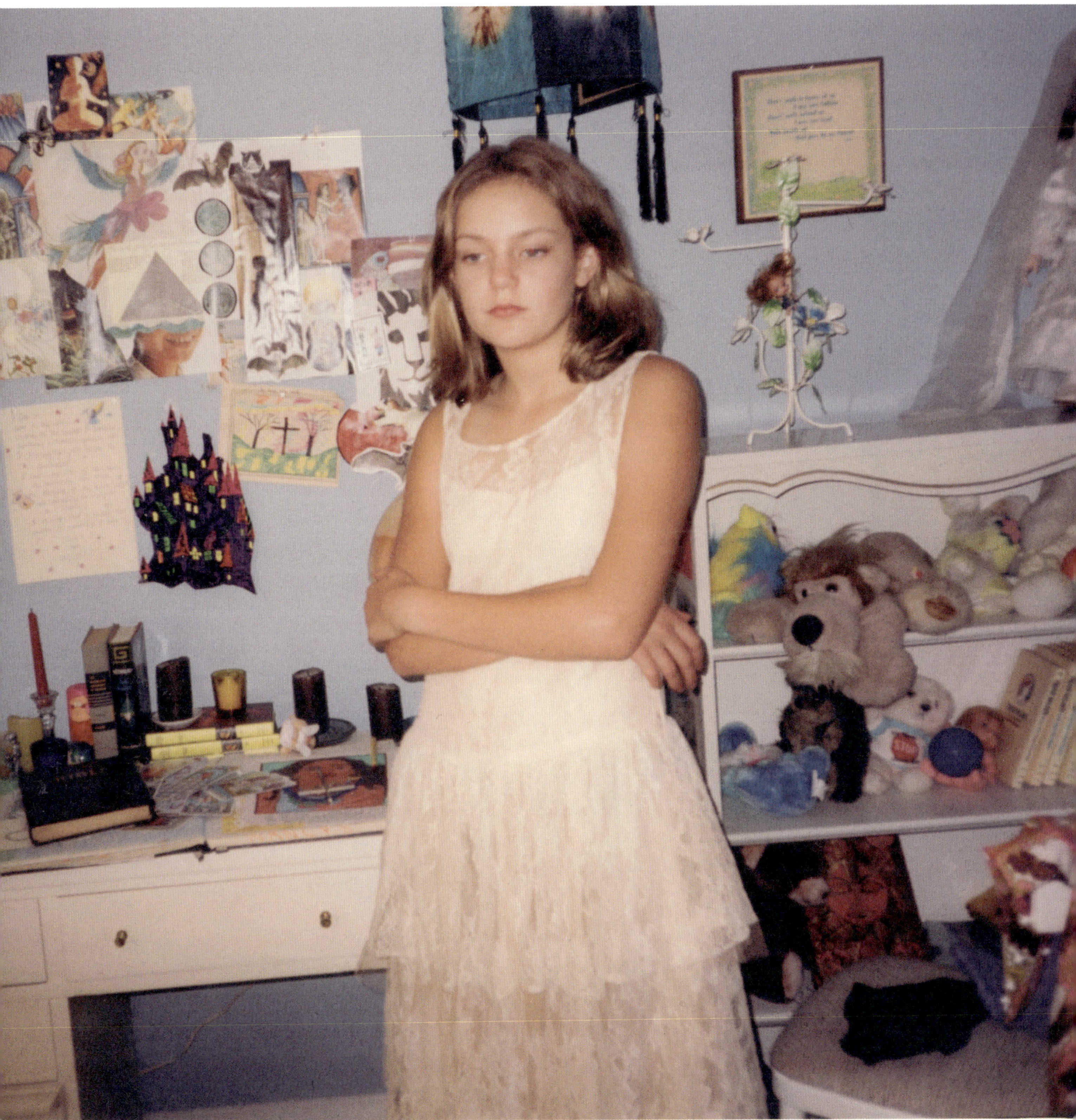

Cecilia in her bedroom wearing her grandmother's wedding dress, photographed by Sofia Coppola

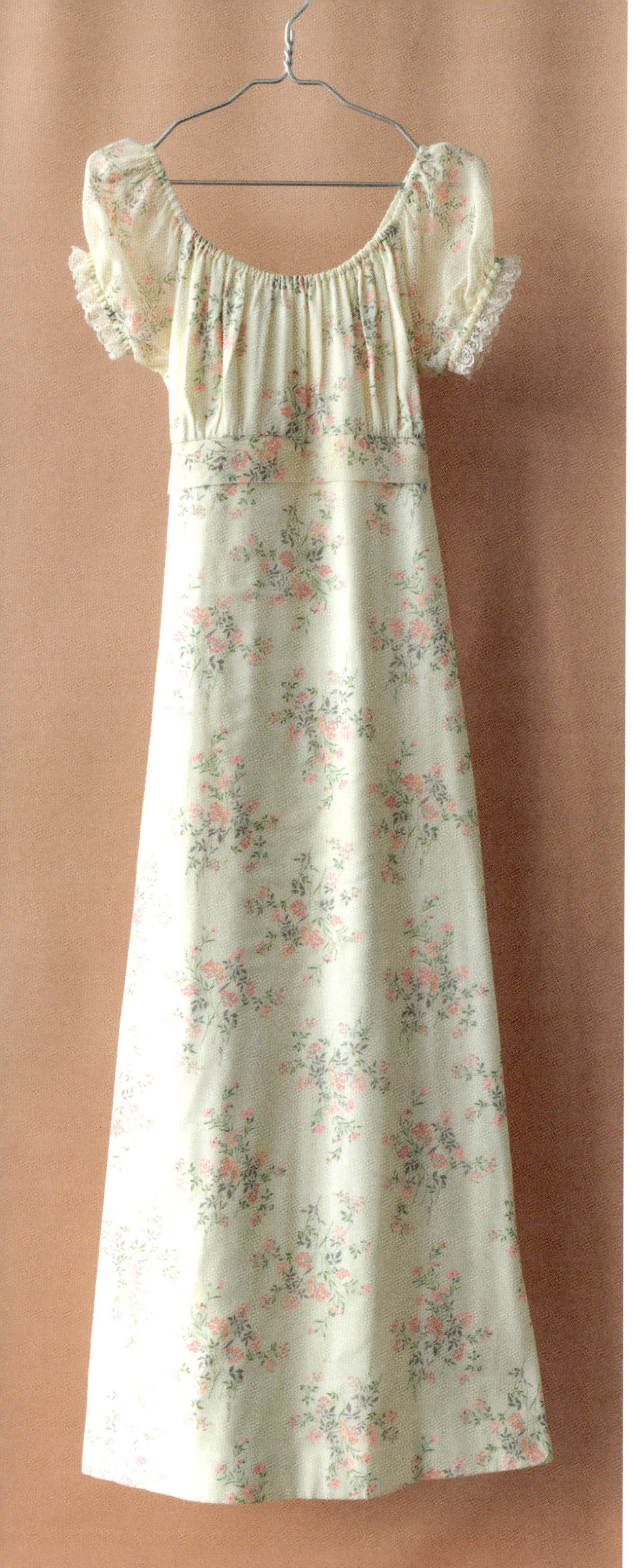

'I had this idea that their mother would make her daughters' modest prom dresses from a pattern. Back in the 1970s, mothers would make clothes for their kids — and their mom would have been way too frugal to go out and buy four dresses. So, in my mind, she just got one pattern at the fabric store and used all the different versions. I was so happy to have found this fabric in three different colours: one has pink flowers, one has blue and one has yellow. I made them all very similar: one dress with long puffy sleeves, one with an open neck, etc. The dresses are definitely not sexy, except maybe the one worn by Kirsten Dunst's character, Lux, which is more form-fitting, but she is still covered. They look how their mother would have wanted. Costume design is like storytelling.'

Lux's prom dress, worn by actress Kirsten Dunst

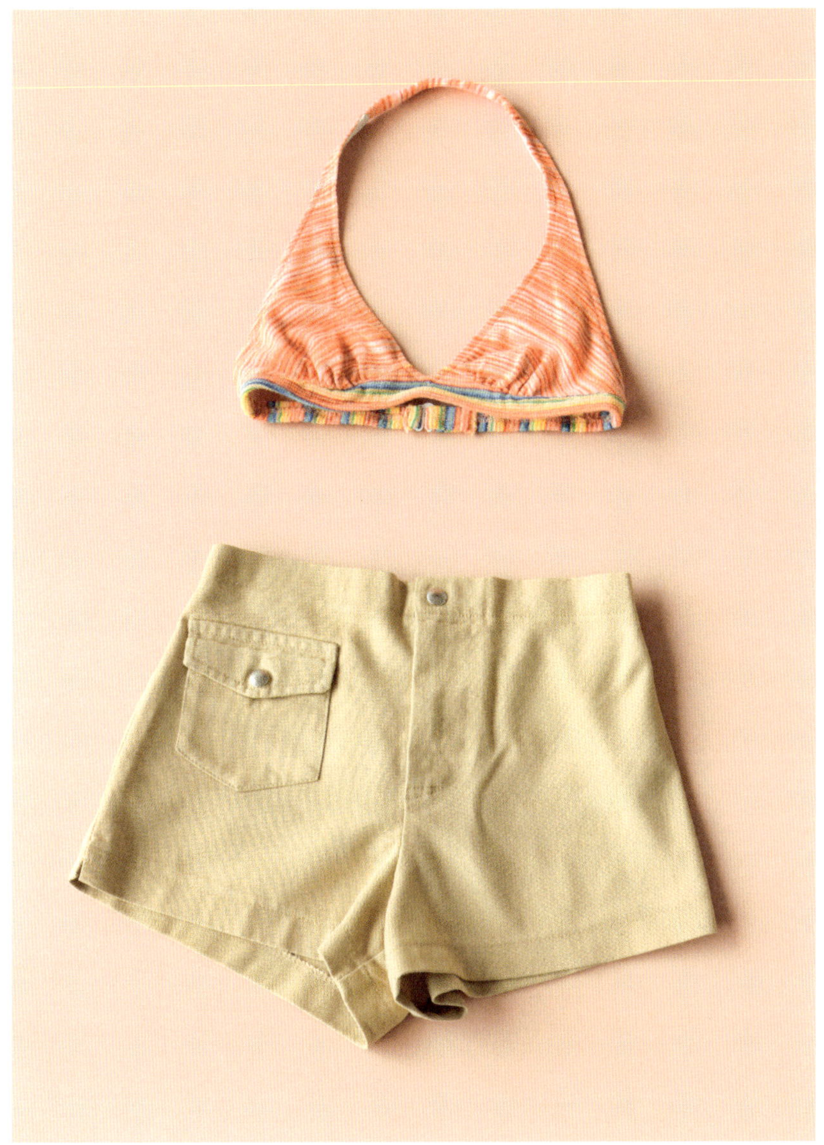

'Kirsten Dunst was 17 when we filmed *The Virgin Suicides*, and I think it was her first time playing a character who is consciously trying to be sexy. As a costume designer, I'm always very protective of the actors. They were all teenagers back then, so you feel like you're their mother or big sister. I have a very maternal quality — and I think a lot of costume designers do. Your actors need to be comfortable in what they are wearing, or uncomfortable because it is supposed to make them feel strange. The girls were thrilled with their costumes. During the filming, the boys were actually more tricky... I kept telling them they had to wear their trousers at their waists because that was fashion in the 1970s. But it was the 1990s, and all the boys were wearing their pants low, so it felt super strange to them. I remember saying "pull up your pants", "pants at the waist", on repeat.'

Lux's knitted bikini top and shorts set, worn by actress Kirsten Dunst

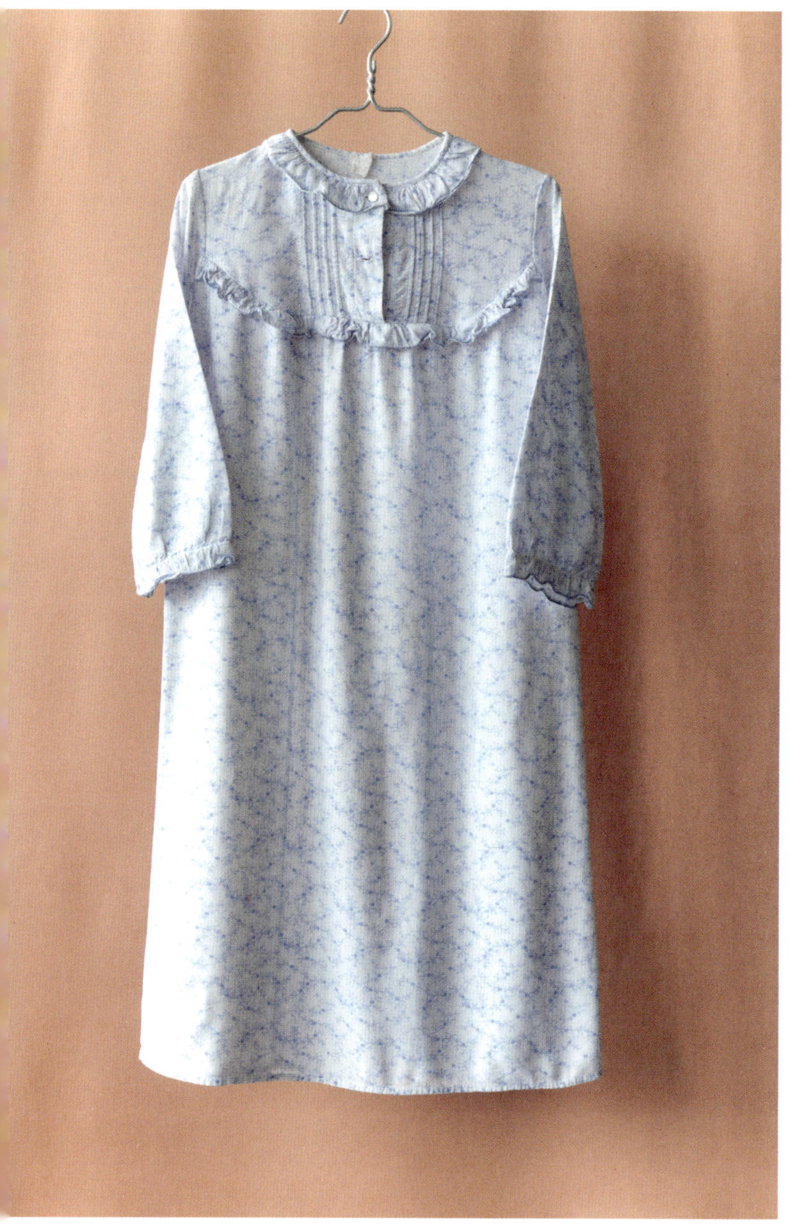

'The vintage flannel nightgowns are by Lanz of Salzburg. When I was a little girl, every Christmas my sister and I would get a nightgown from this brand too. I got the Lisbon sisters those nightgowns because they were appropriate for the period, and very cosy.'

Lux's nightgown, worn by actress Kirsten Dunst

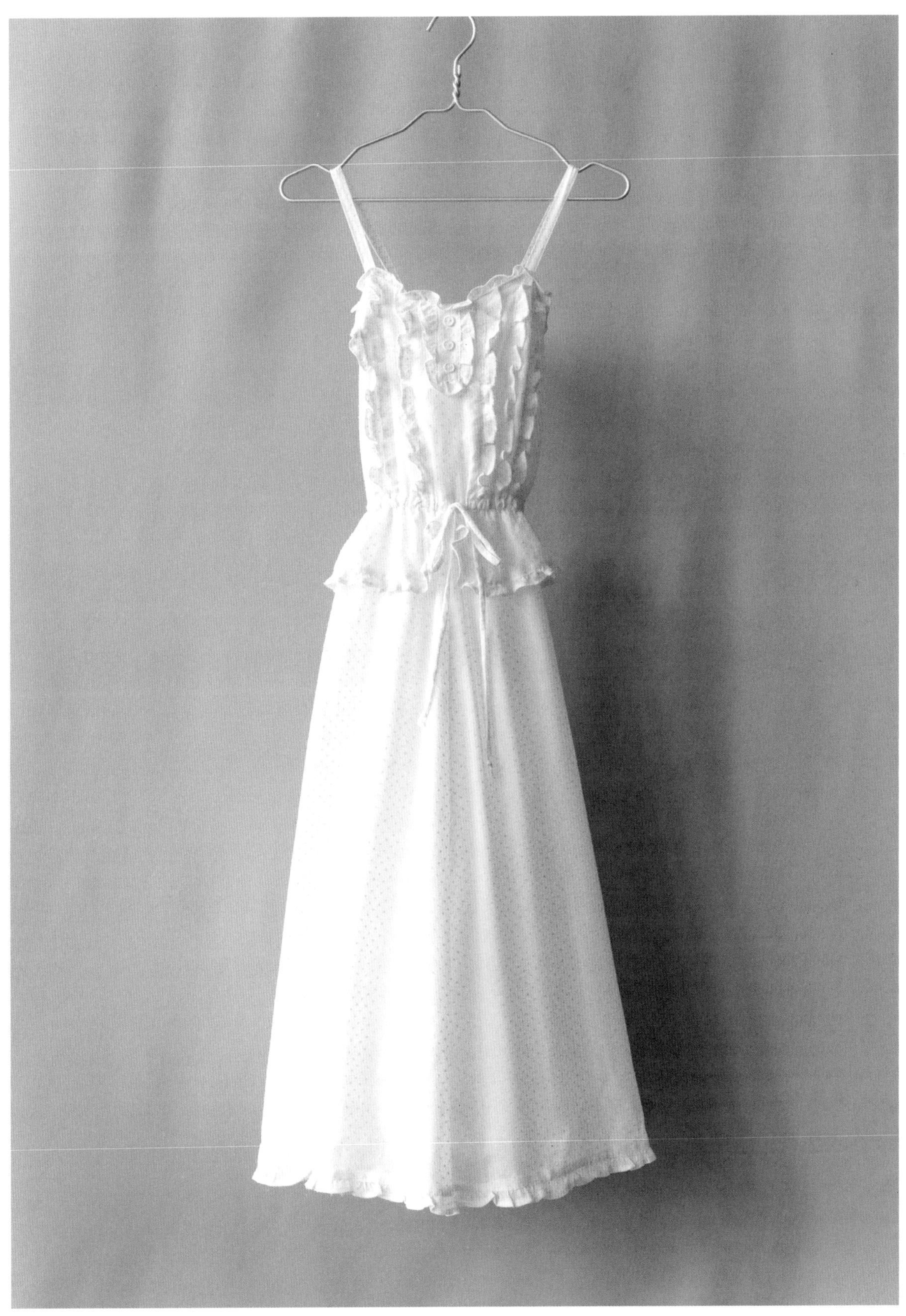

Lux's summer dress, worn by actress Kirsten Dunst

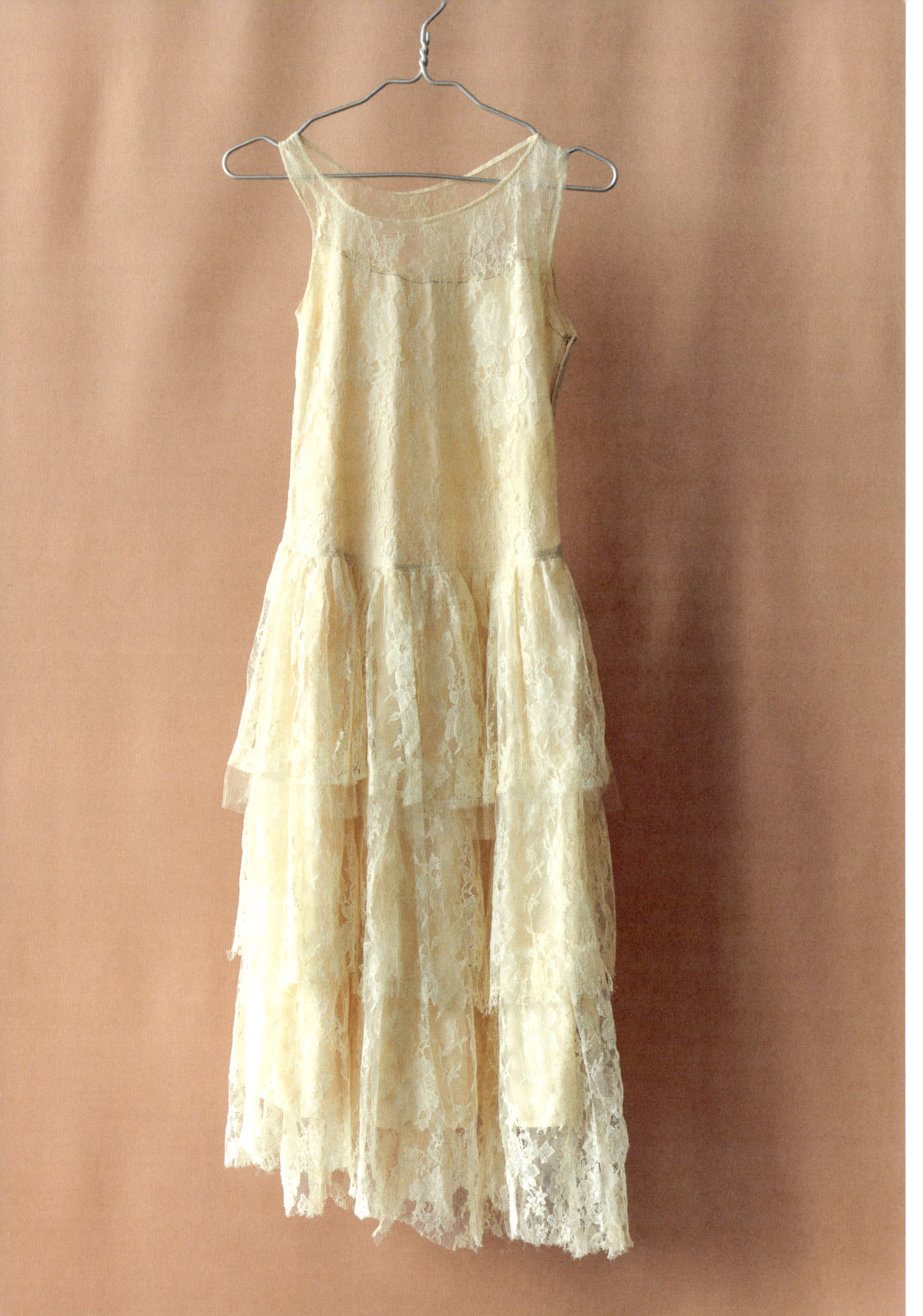

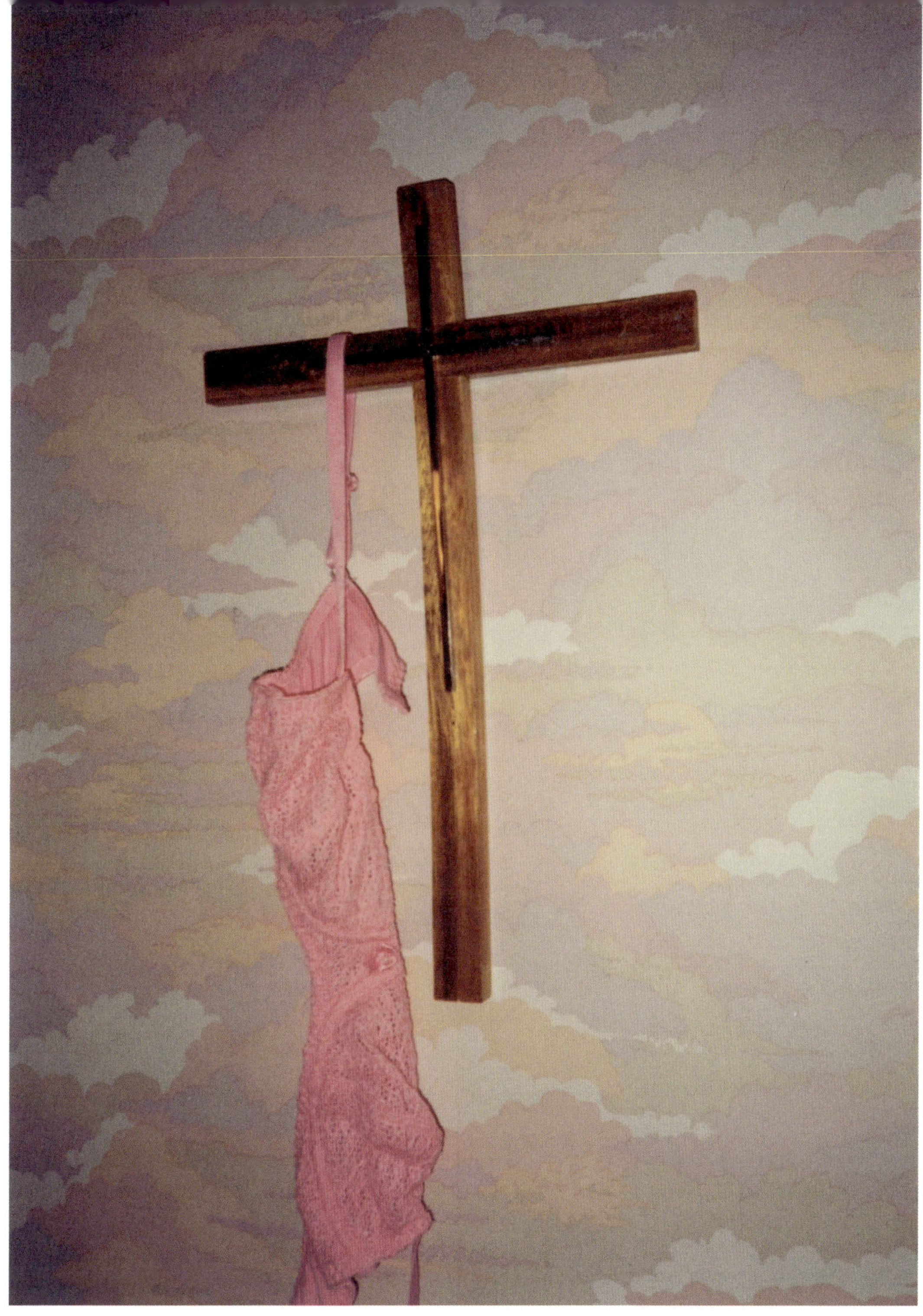

'Kathleen Turner, who played the mother, hated her costumes. She said "I've never looked so ugly in my life." I dressed her in very formulaic 1970s beige polyester dresses — bland and conservative. She thought they were awful, but they were right for her character. She needed strict clothing you don't feel great in. The clothing emphasised how closed off she was from her daughters; she didn't understand them at all.'

Cecilia's 'wedding' dress, worn by actress Hanna Hall

Cross and bra in the girls' bedroom, photographed by Sofia Coppola

lauren greenfield
girl culture, 2002

'My book *Girl Culture* was very much inspired by my own teenage anxieties and body image struggles. I was a chronic dieter and always compared my body and clothes to those of my friends and what I saw in the media. I was very insecure and painfully shy, trying to be part of the popular clique, trying to wear the trendy fashions, and always feeling like an outsider who was not quite measuring up. I think these feelings fuelled my interest in visual anthropology and sociology and my motivation as a photographer looking at society with the privileged and passionate perspective of both an insider and an outsider. In making *Girl Culture*, I was also very influenced by Joan Jacobs Brumberg's book *The Body Project* which examines how girls in contemporary culture turn their bodies into all-encompassing projects and how that contrasted with the 19th century when being a "good girl" was about doing "good work".'

'I was very struck by how girls learnt at an early age that their value was in their body, and then embarked on body projects to maximise that value. I also was very moved by something that Erin, one of the eating disorder patients I photographed at the Renfrew Clinic, told me. She said she didn't know how to use her voice so she used her body instead.'

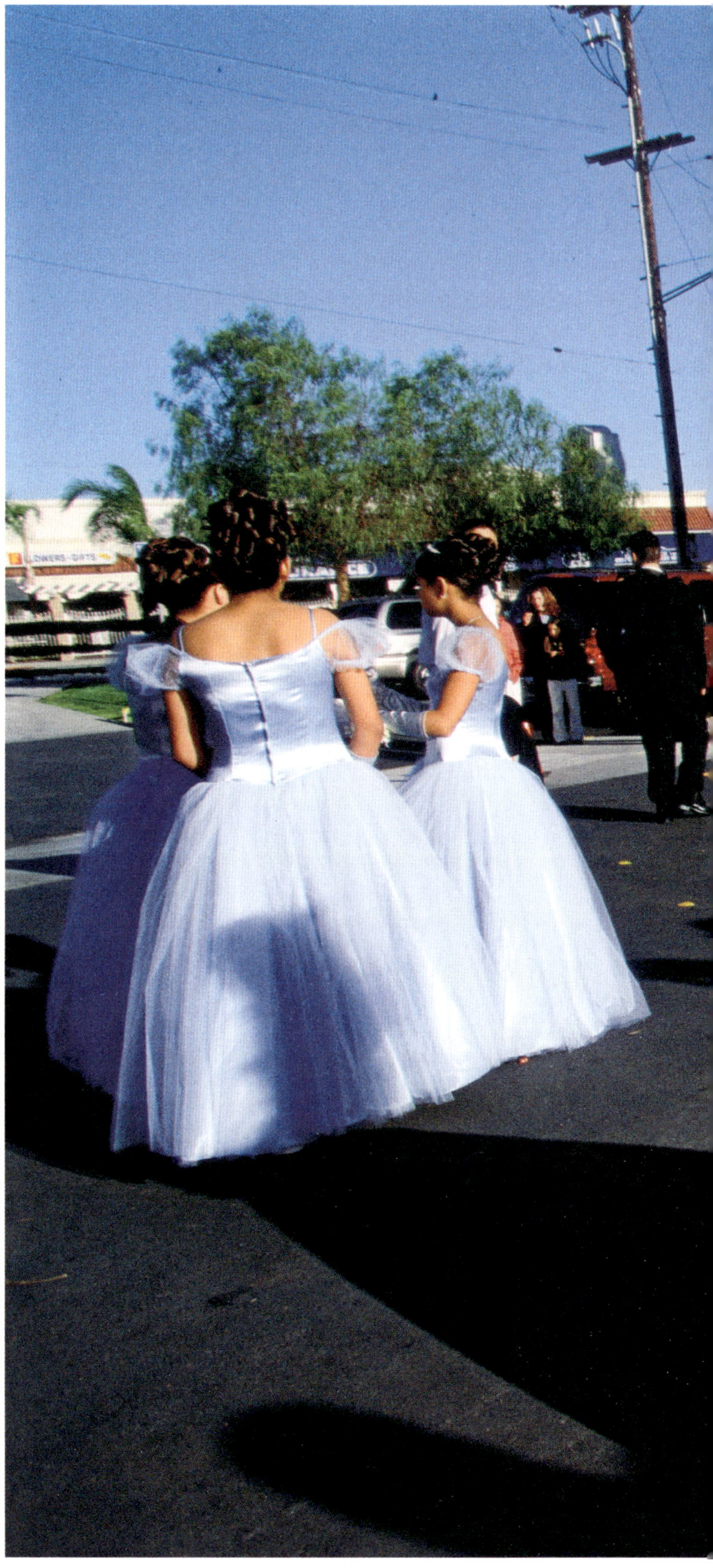

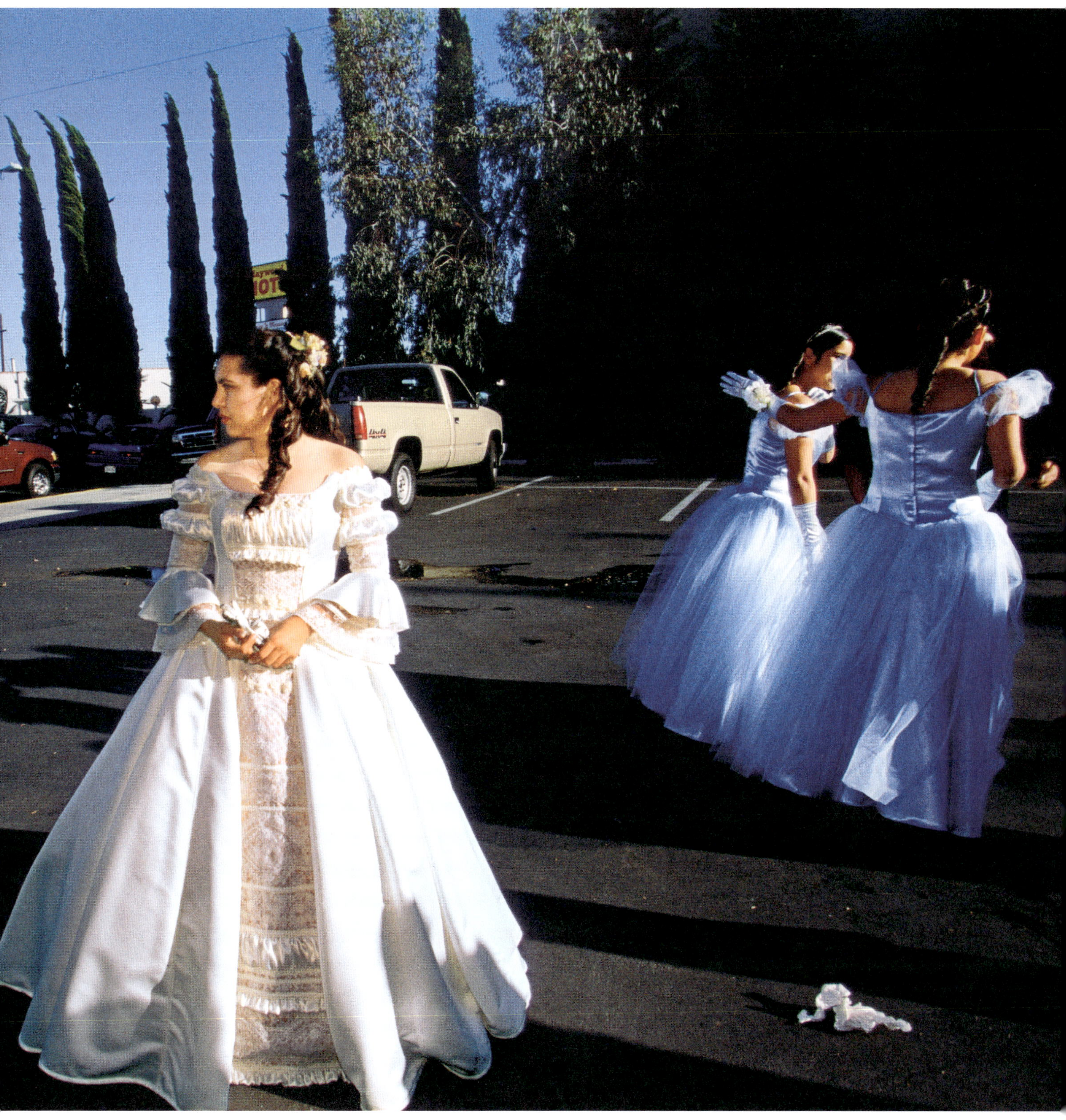

Ruby, 15, on the day of the *quinceañera*, a 'sweet fifteen' ritual in the Hispanic community, Huntington Park, California

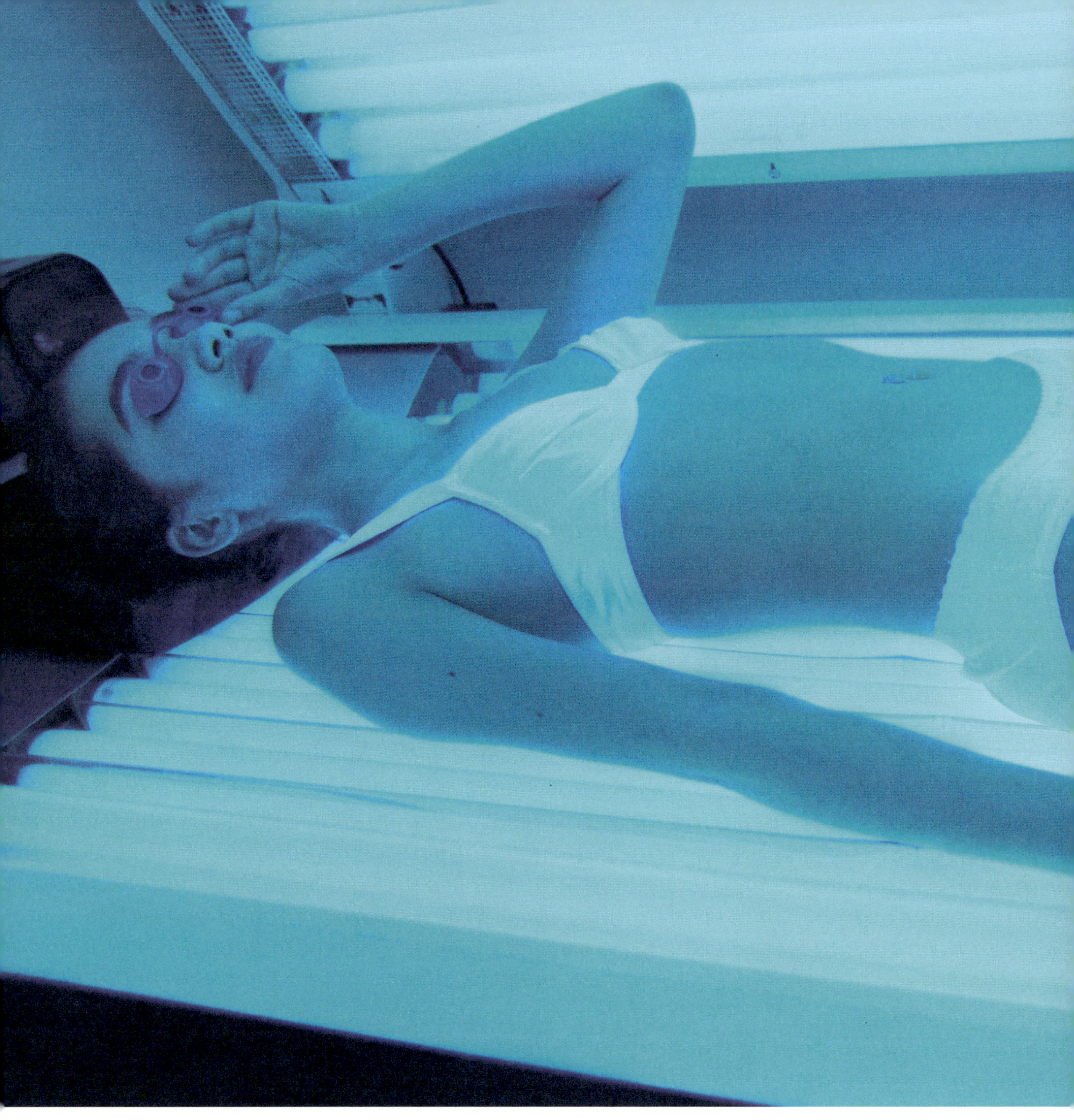

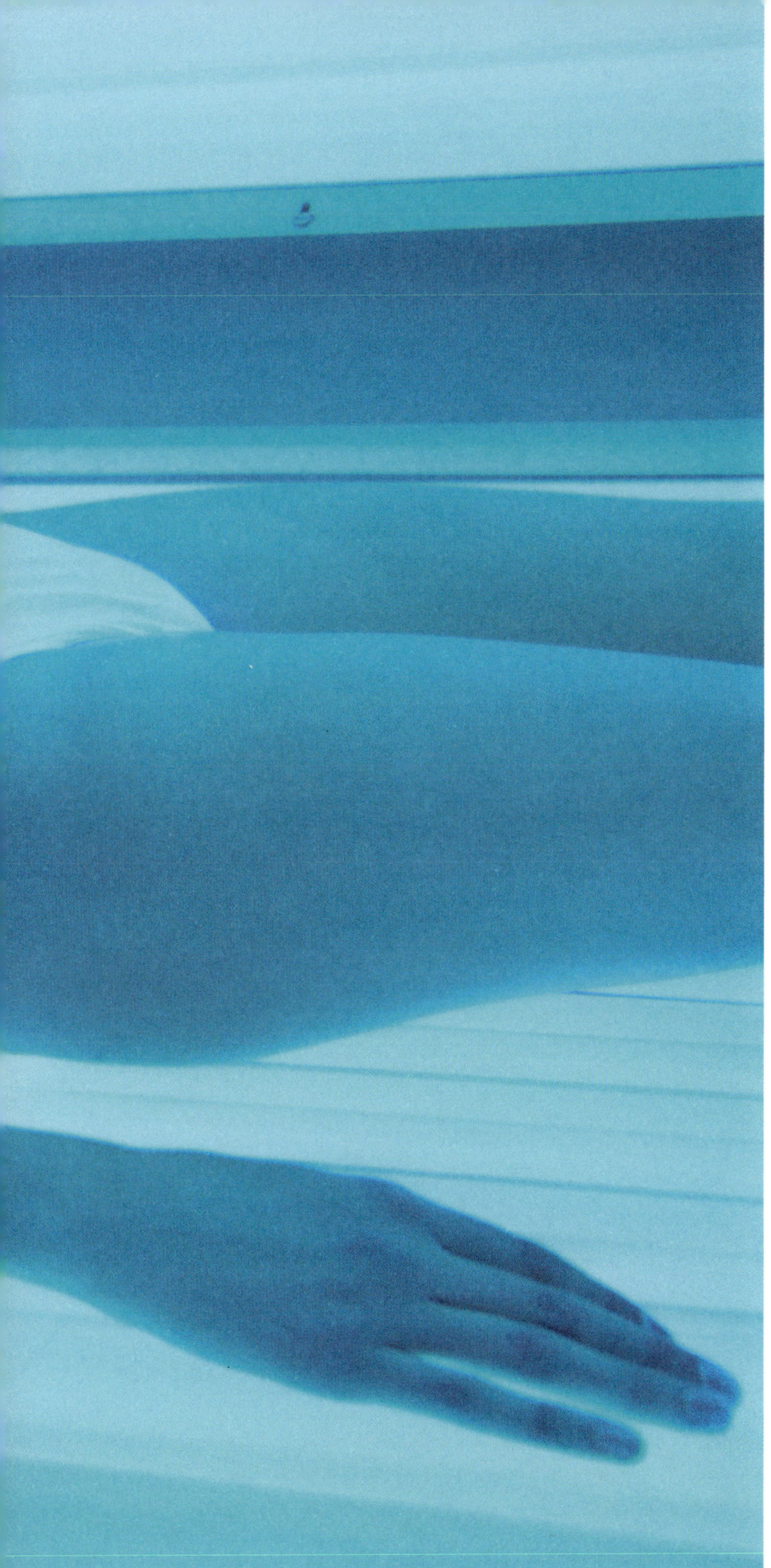

'My dad used to tell me that boredom is the highest state. I didn't get it as a kid but now appreciate his brilliance. Ella, one of the teenagers in my recent project *Social Studies* (which I started filming in 2021), talks about how, when you are on social media, you are never bored. When she went on social media, she stopped doing the creative activities she loved — design, drawing, painting, reading. When she went off social media, she got bored and said that that is when she got creative. Boredom is a source of both creativity and reflection — two things we badly need more of.'

Fina, 13, in a tanning salon, Edina, Minnesota

leticia valverdes
brazilian street girls, 2000

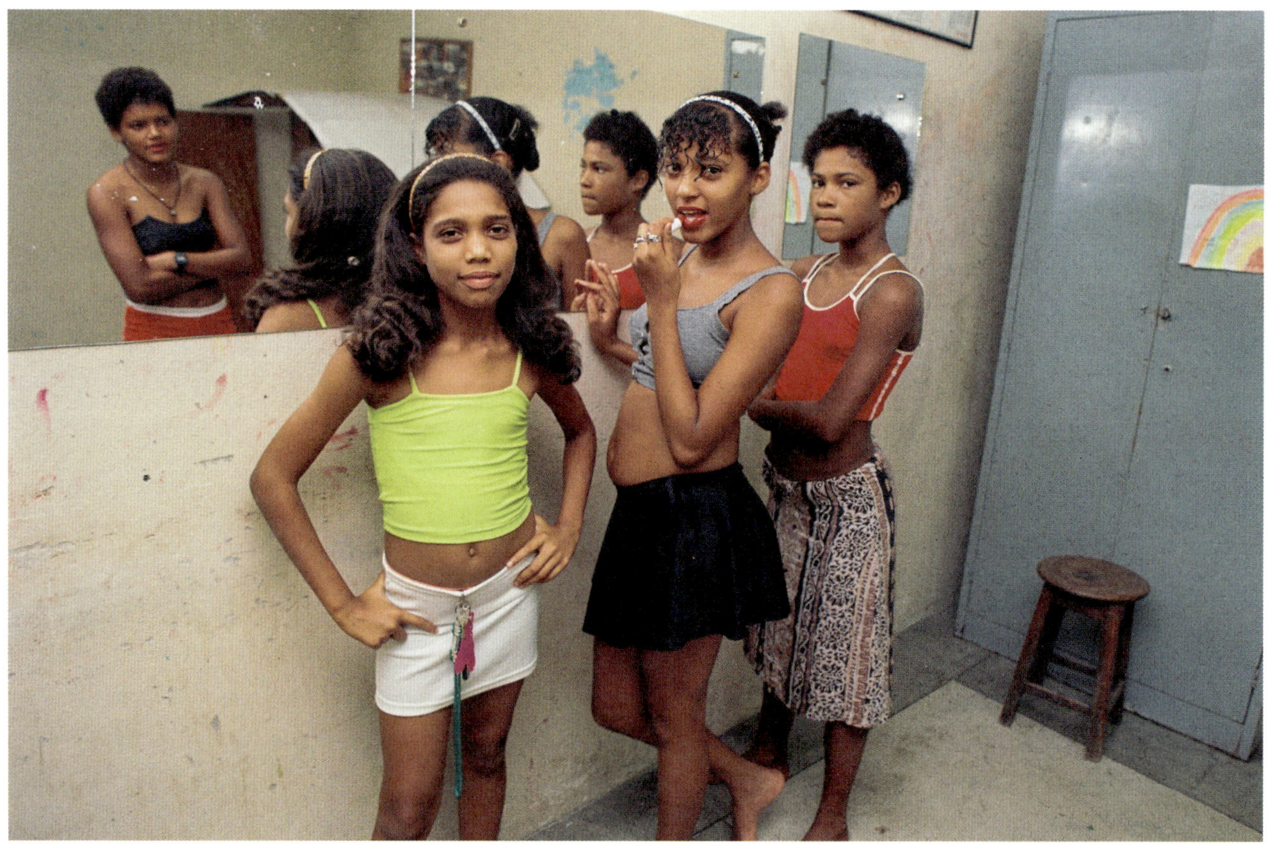

'My book *Brazilian Street Girls* reflects my lifelong commitment to celebrating those who live on the margins of society. In this case, young women and girls whose coming-of-age is neither celebrated nor documented. Growing up, I witnessed the misery of impoverished families and their children as our government failed, year after year, to provide them with even the most basic support. Young people end up trapped in homelessness.'

'I found it striking that in my home country, Brazil, a country obsessed with the body and beauty, street girls had to dress as boys to hide their femininity to feel safe. As I got to know them, they showed me how impossible it can be to explore one's femininity in a space that feels unsafe. I felt their vulnerability and their unspoken longing to be seen, to embrace their femininity, despite their fear of being exposed.'

Casa de Passagem, Recife

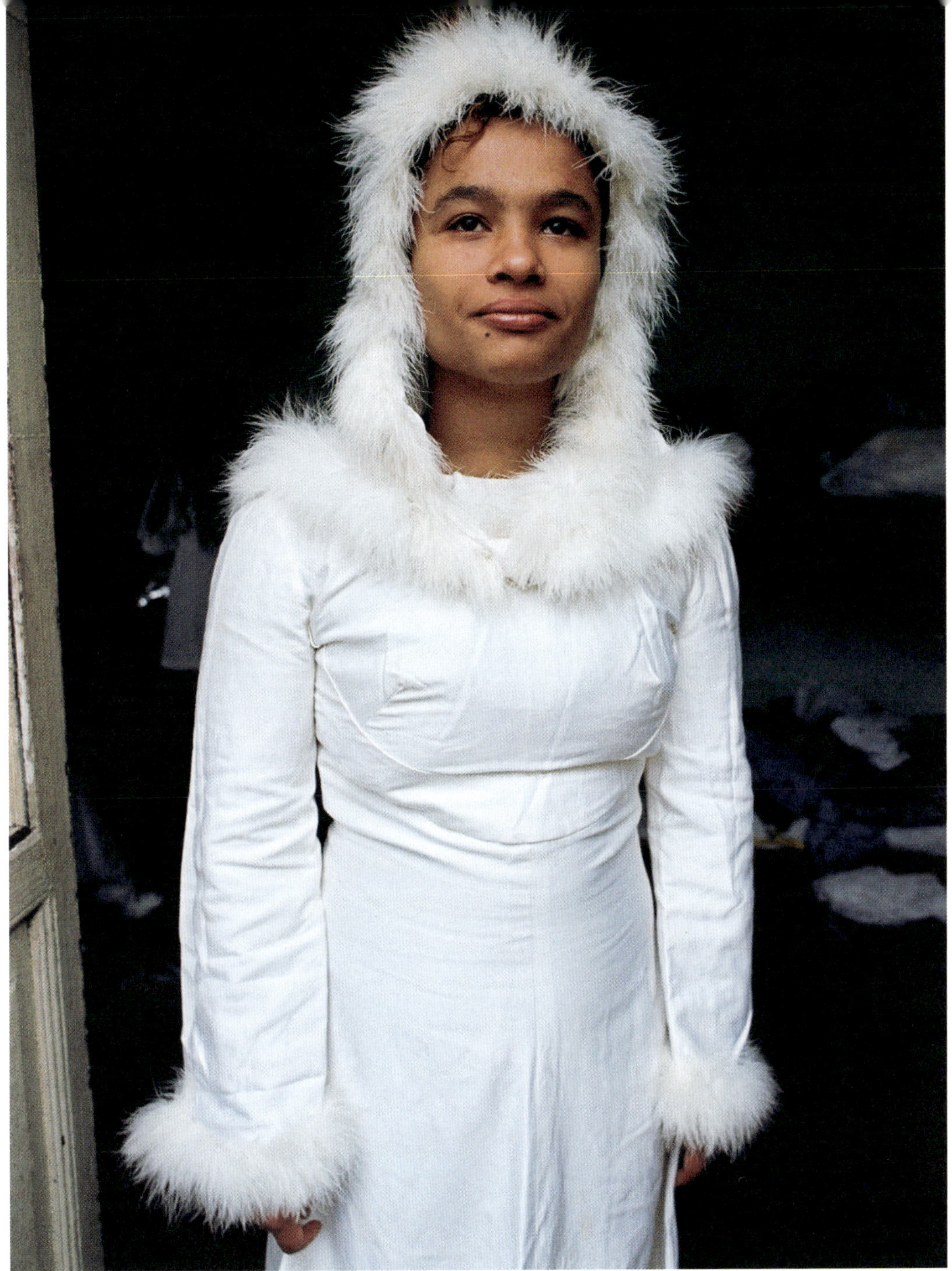

‘When I decided to photograph the reality of street kids, my goal was to avoid extremes, to move beyond stereotypes and to reveal different facets of their lives, of their stories. In their world then, shop windows served as mirrors. Photographs of them were rare, and proofs of identity almost non-existent.’

‘I brought the girls mirrors and the clothes I had played with as a teenager, including my mother’s wedding dress. Together, we dressed up as they might have done with their mothers’ clothes. In the days we spent playing and performing, simply being girls together, we shared moments of intimacy and trust, fleeting yet precious moments of respite and beauty in their otherwise very hard lives.’

Karina (wearing a wedding dress), abandoned house São Paulo

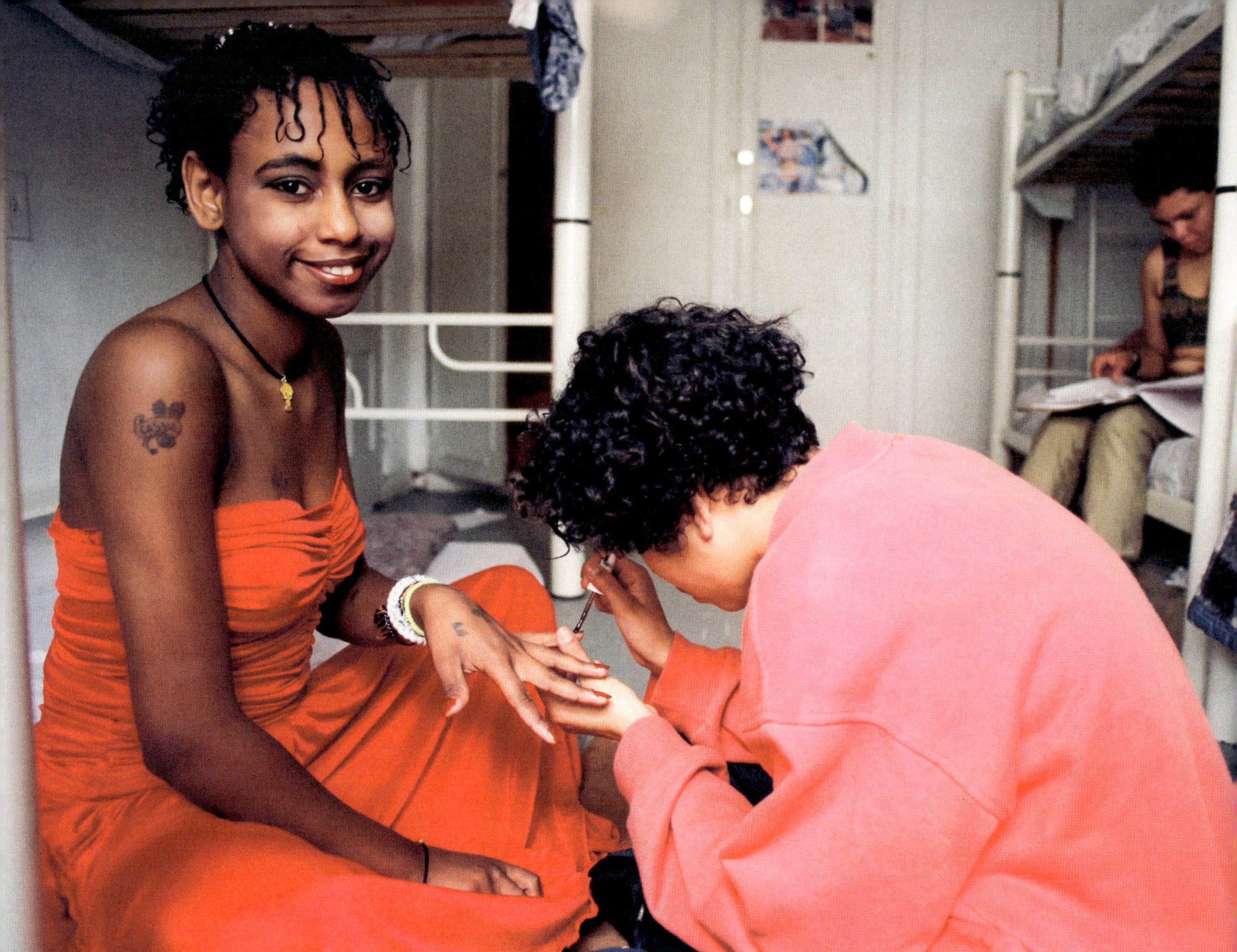

‘Cassia asked me if she could be the first to dress up, as she would soon have to leave the shelter house. A judge had sentenced her to a prison for juvenile “criminals” after she had been caught stealing. She chose the red dress and had Adriana do her makeup. We played and danced. The next day, when I arrived at the shelter, Cassia was gone, taken to prison. She saw the photos from that day only a year later.’

Cassia and Adriana, Casa Taiguara, São Paulo

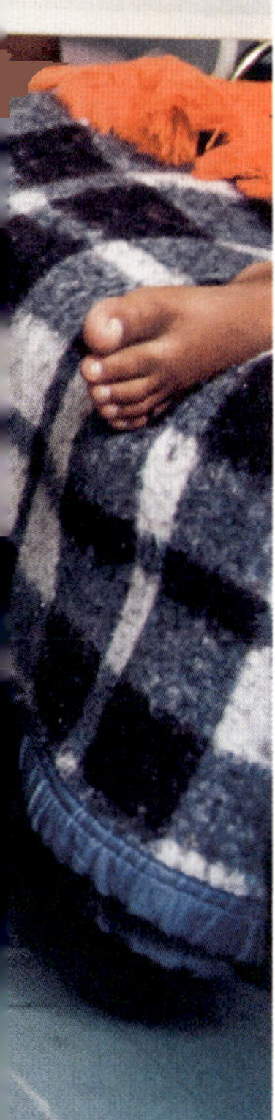

'Adriana was the stylist and makeup artist of our games, helping the girls dress up. One day, I caught her gazing into a small mirror, covering half her face with her hand. Only then did I realise how hard it was for her to face herself, and how difficult it would have been to dress up and feel beautiful.'

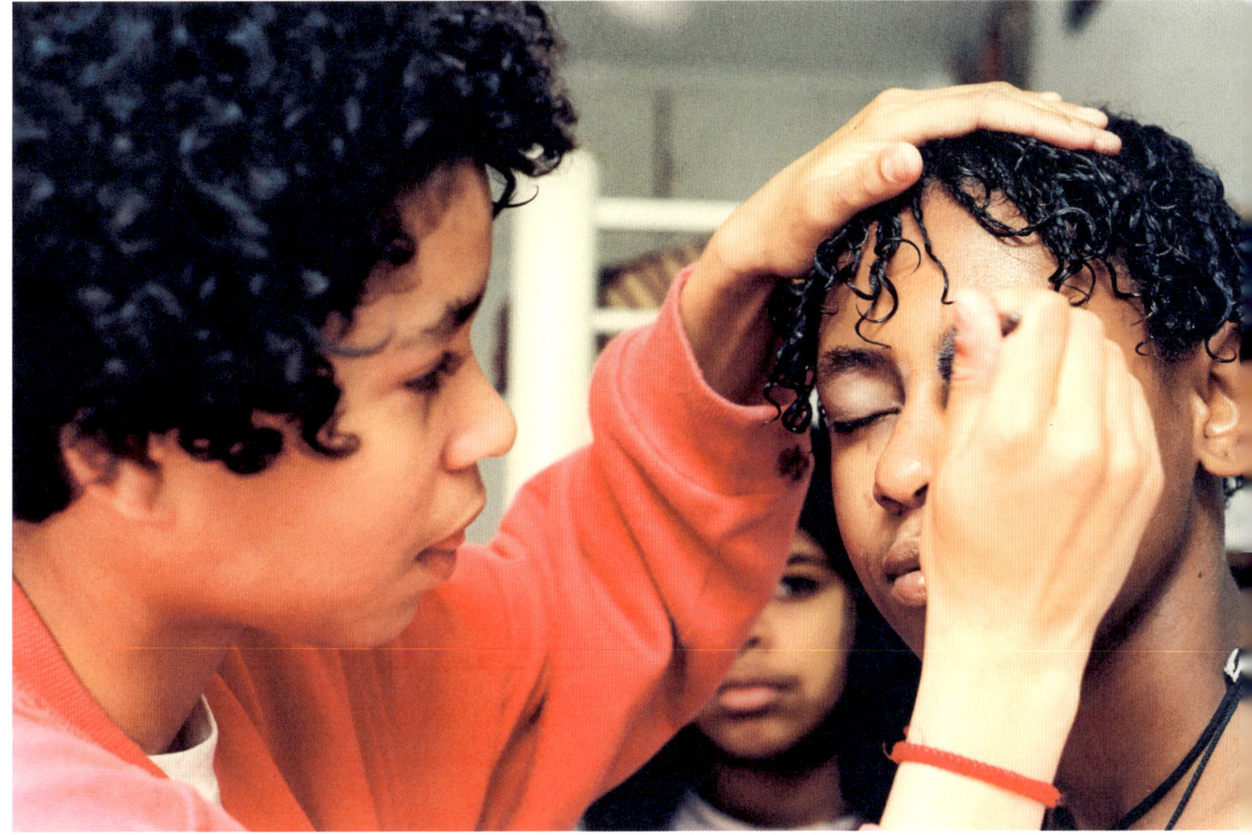

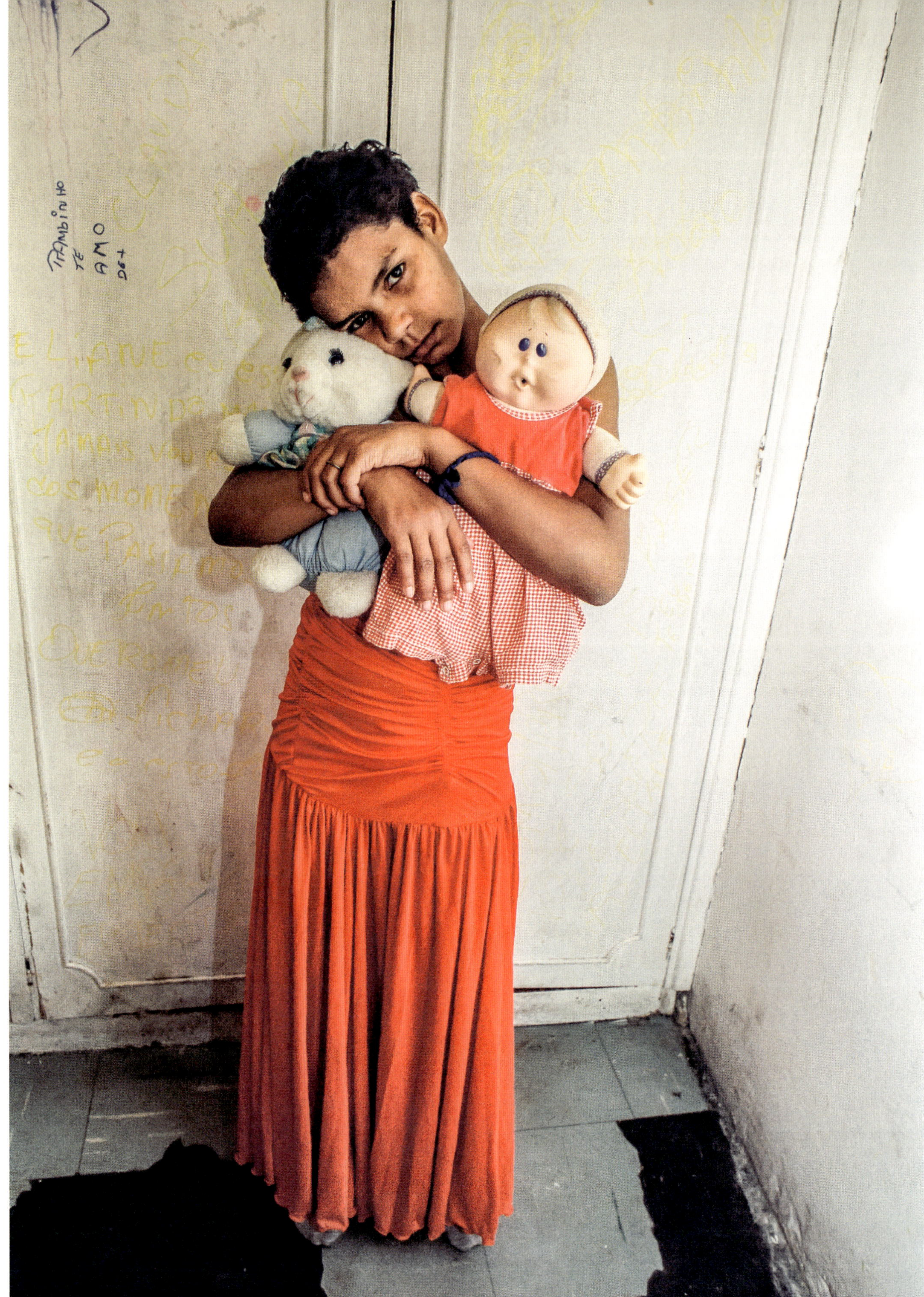
TAMBINHO
TE
AMO
ELIANE eu
JAMAIS VOU

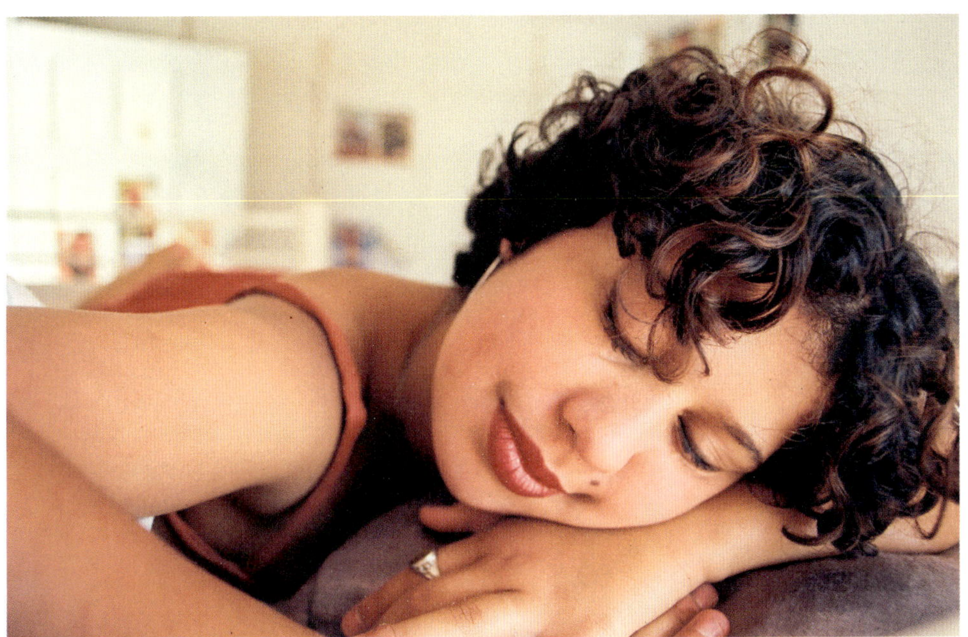

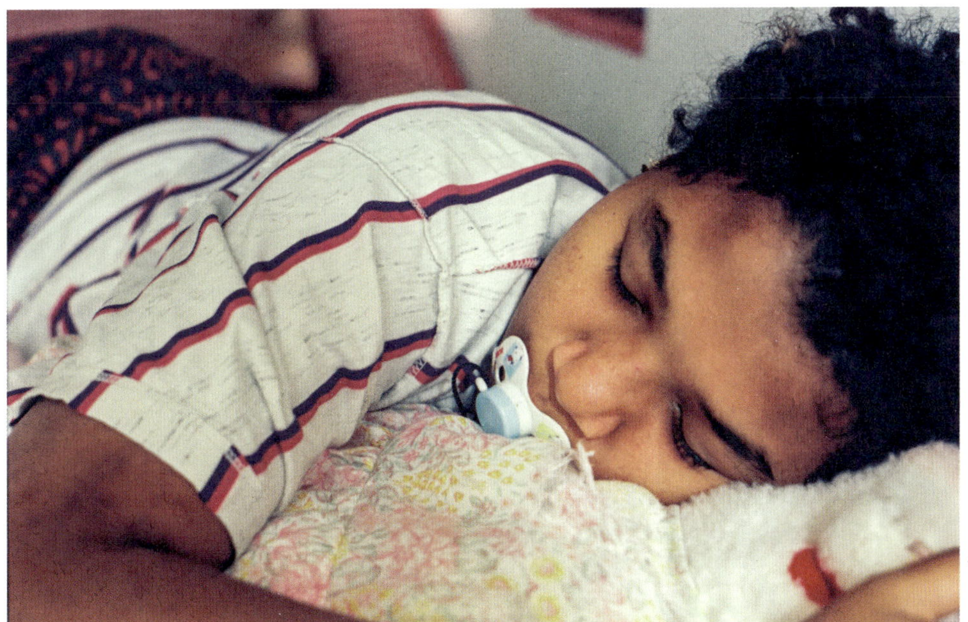

‘I could have not imagined the joyful role-playing that would emerge from our sessions. Looking at these photos now, I wonder how quickly that joy might have vanished again, whether hidden or erased. But I believe the memory of it endured for a while. Whether it helped these girls navigate the daily hardships they faced, I cannot know. I can only hope it did, even if fleetingly.’

Bruna, Casa Taiguara, São Paulo

Marcela & Milena, Casa Taiguara, São Paulo

sofia lai

'When I was a child, I felt a sense of isolation and the pressure to be good enough. My imagination was the tool that helped me. I started using clothes to express different parts of myself. I imagined myself as different characters, and my outfits became the costumes to bring those characters to life. This duality between the weird and the wonderful has always been a part of me.'

The First Bloom, 2025

'*The First Bloom* symbolises a mother being pregnant. The pregnant belly becomes a metaphor for people's potential for transformation, creativity and growth, even in our darkest moments. The sculpture invites viewers to reflect on their own experiences of loss, stillness and renewal. It is about the first bloom of spring after a long winter. A girl is born.'

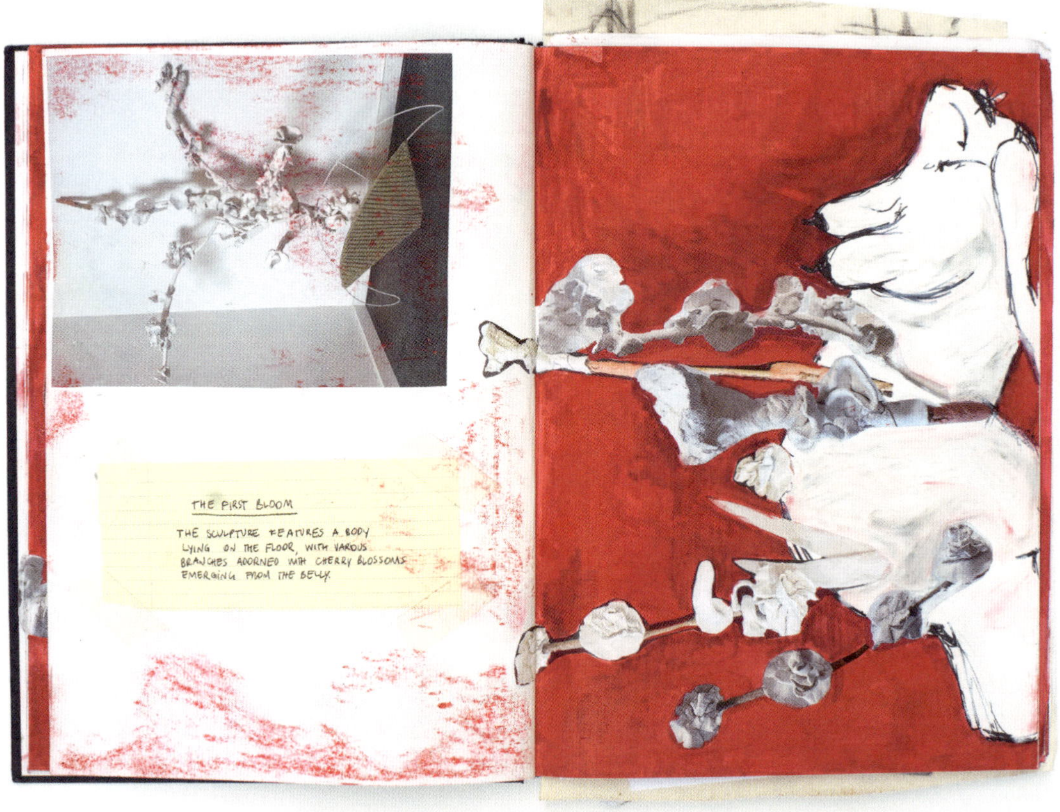

Sofia Lai, drawing of *The First Bloom*, 2025

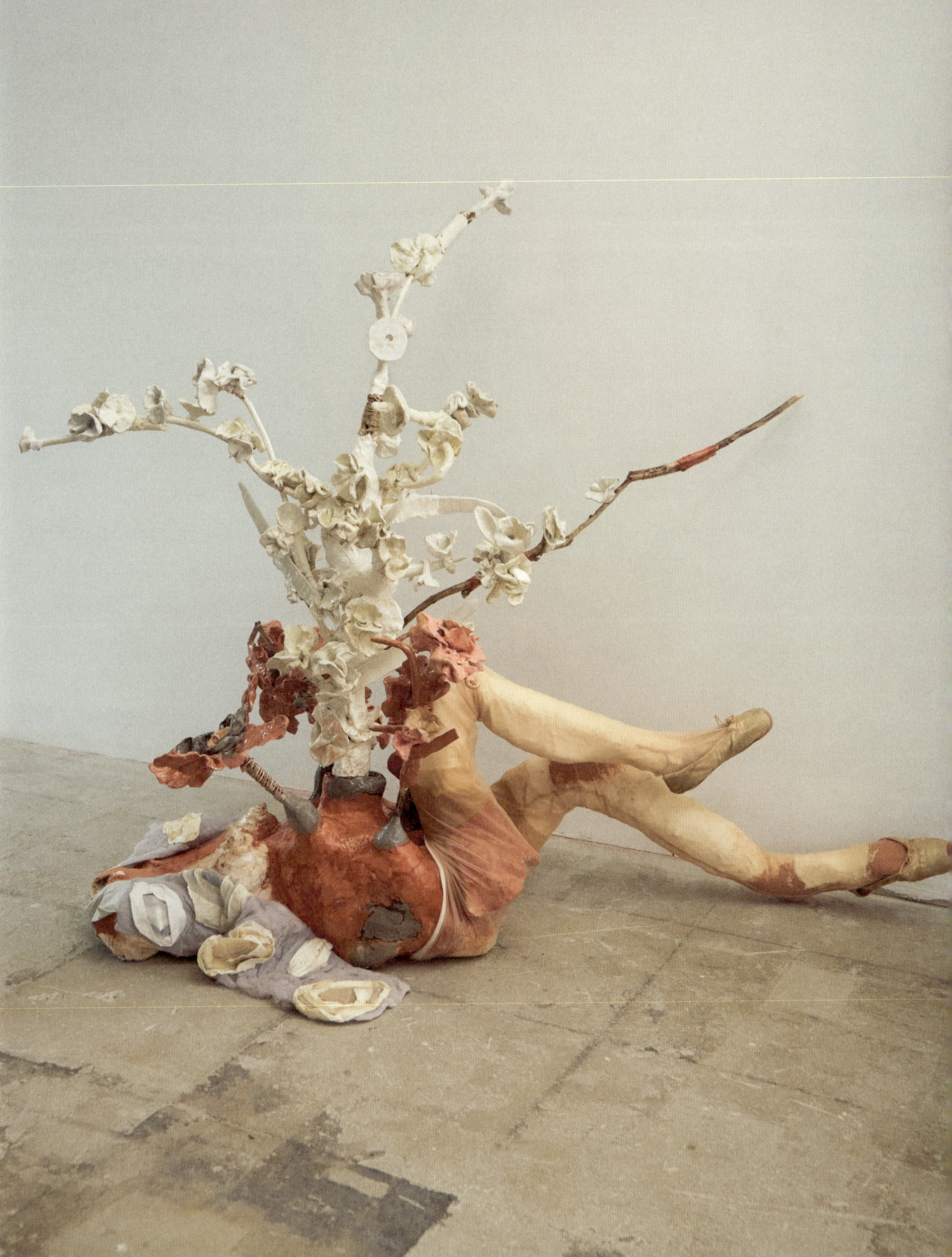

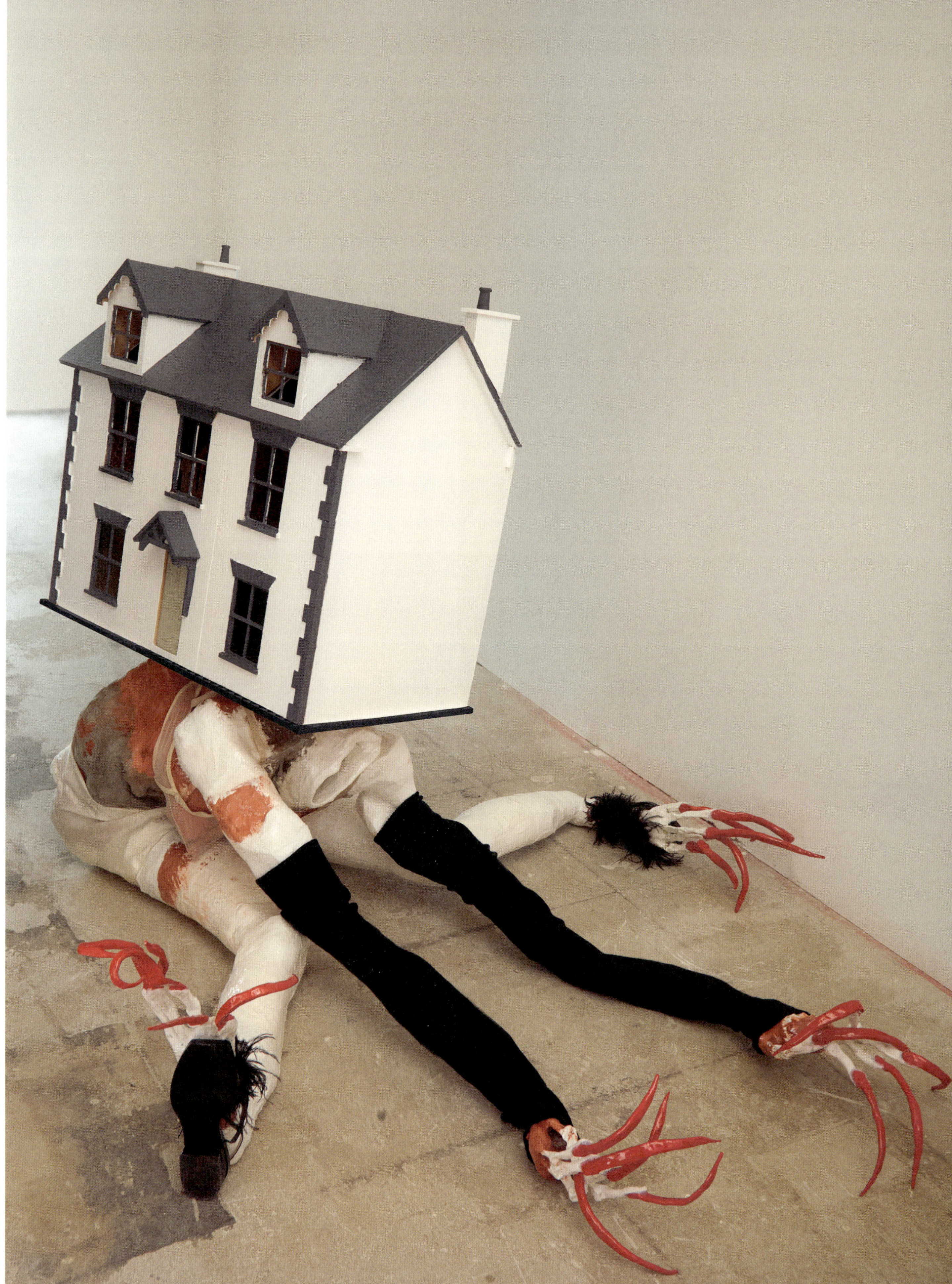

Burden: The Dollhouse, 2025

‘*Burden: The Dollhouse* is a reflection of the emotional and psychological weight of societal expectations. To me, the dollhouse on the figure’s back symbolises the idealised and sometimes rigid structures of family, while the crawling figure represents how one can be weighed down under that burden. The exposed interior of the dollhouse invites you to peer inside to see the disconnect between surface and reality. The figure is still moving, however slowly, showing the resilience of girls in reclaiming their identities.’

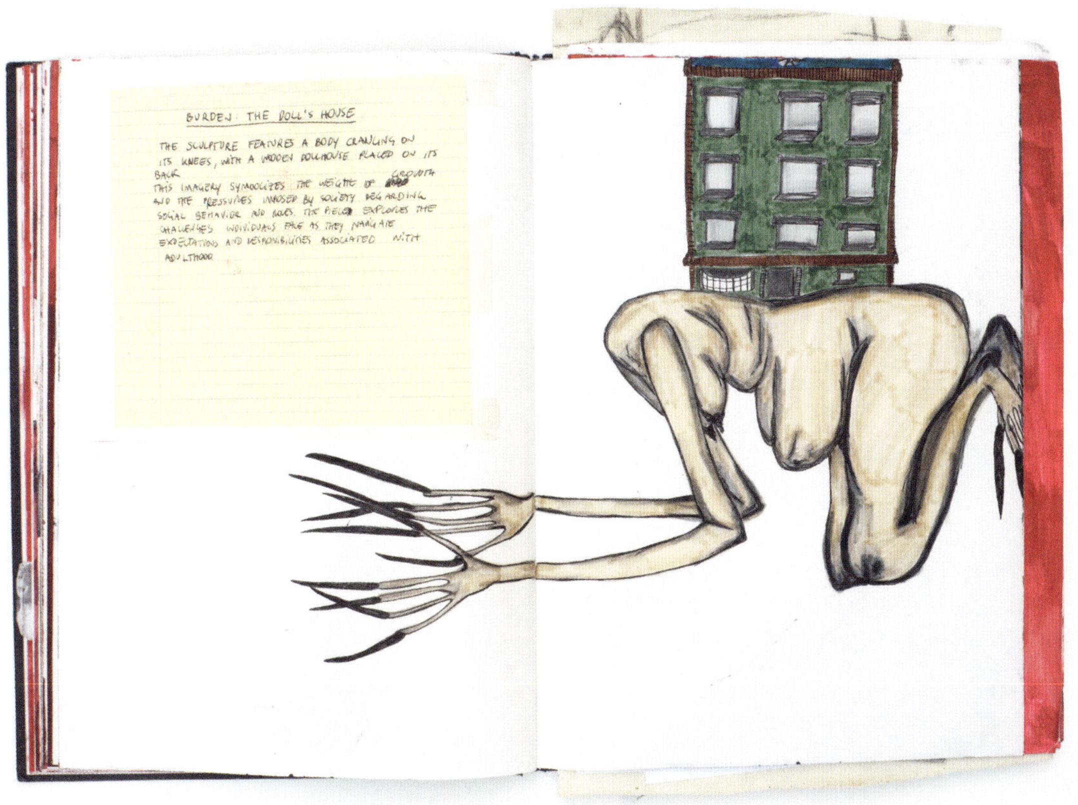

Sofia Lai, drawing of *Burden: The Dollhouse*, 2025

Foreigner in Your Own Body, 2025

'*Foreigner in Your Own Body* is about your changing body during adolescence. The two identical figures symbolise the duality between the inner, authentic self and the external, performative self. Their tender, mirrored forms reflect the struggle to reconcile who we are with who we are expected to be.'

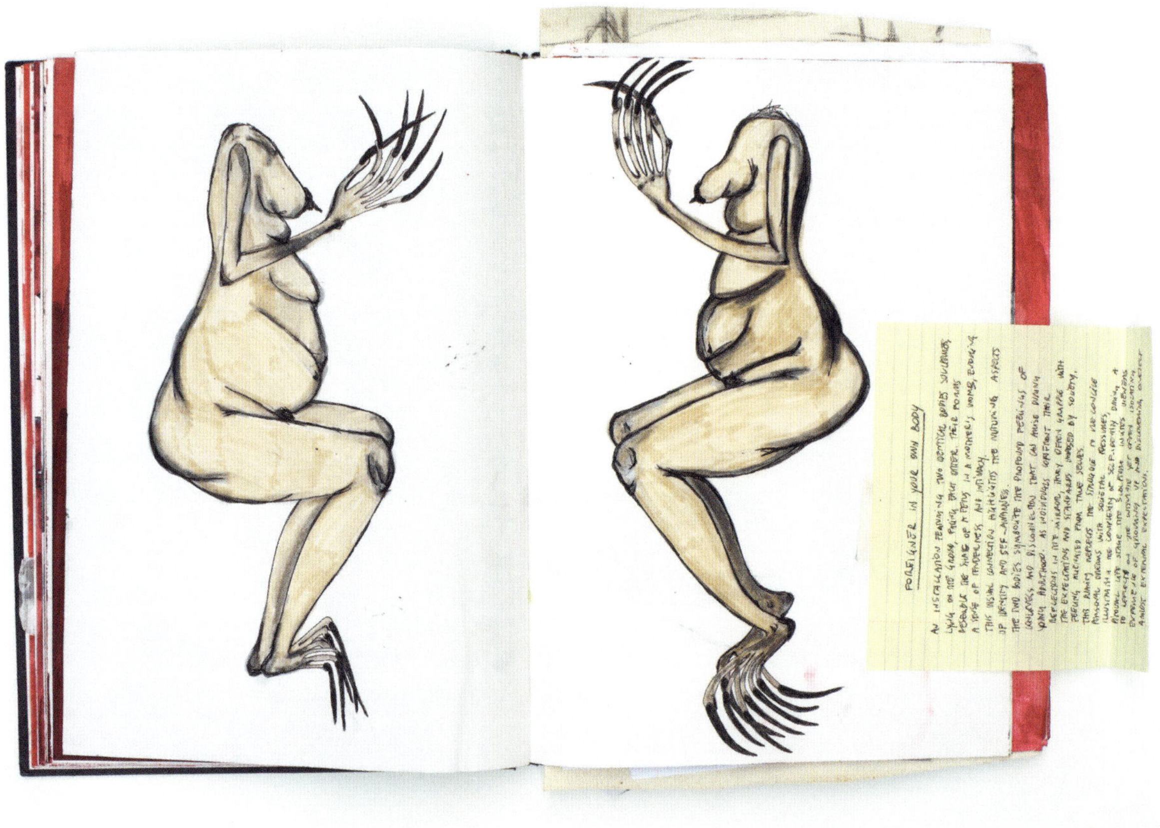

Sofia Lai, drawing of *Foreigner in Your Own Body*, 2025

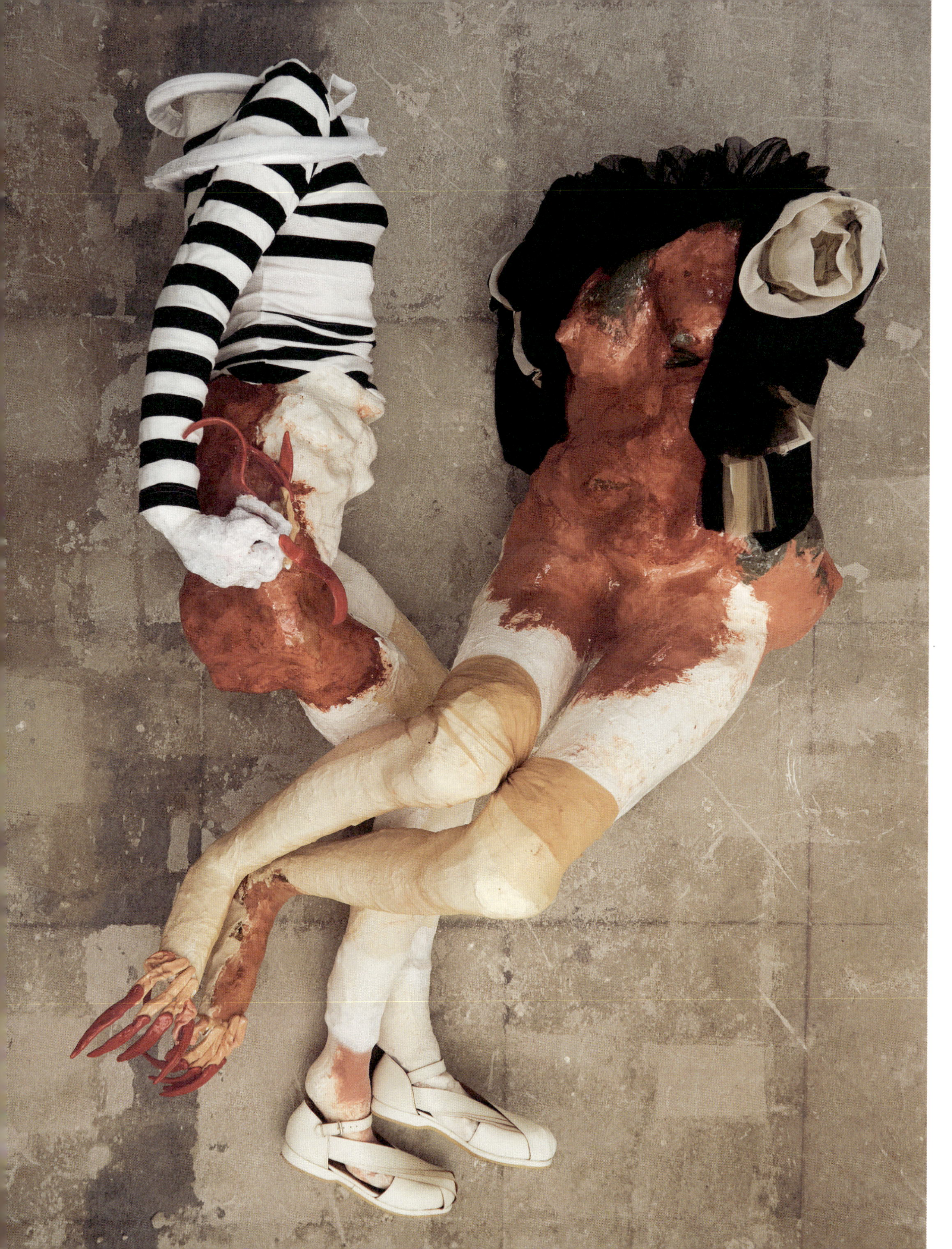

Sofia Lai, drawing of *Foreigner in Your Own Body*, 2025

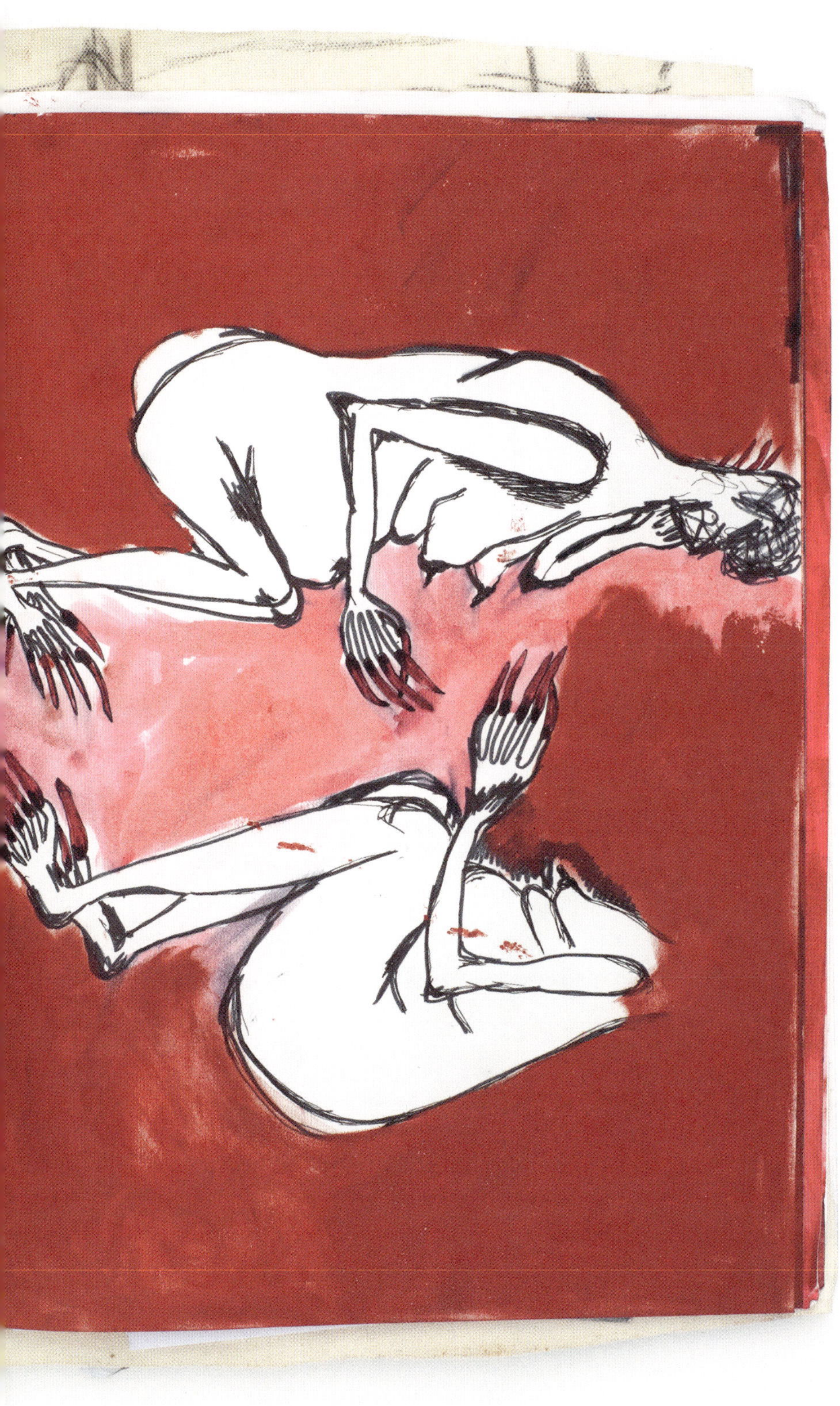

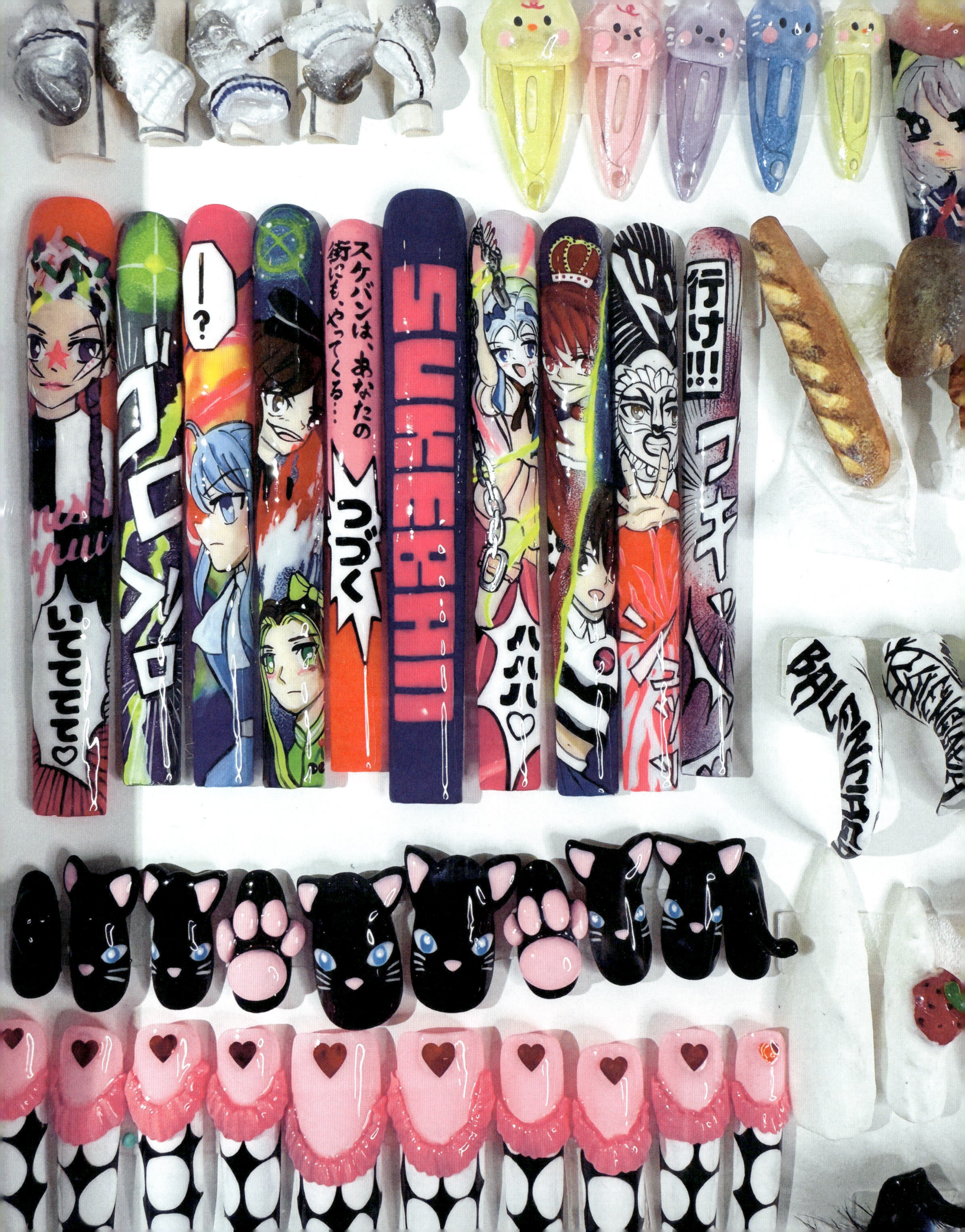

スケバンは、あなたの
街にも、やってくる…
つづく
SUKEBAN
行け!!!
BALENCIAGA

Alex Quicho

good 4 u

'Breakfast at Tiffany's and
bottles of bubbles,
girls with tattoos who like
getting in trouble,
lashes and diamonds,
ATM machines.'[1]

The recipes for crafting a 'girl' are myriad; the ingredients countless yet so specific. She materialises out of thin air and a shopping list, taking shape inside a carapace of pearls and silk, or rhinestones and bodycon spandex, or sterling silver and male tears. She looks like she tastes of lip gloss and sugar, or diesel and sunshine, or dried flower petals, hair and candlewax — but to touch or taste her would disturb the image. It would get complicated. Her human body is incidental — or, her human body is the most dangerous part.

In my previous work, I diagrammed one recipe for making a girl: the (1) symbolic, (2) consumer, and (3) inhuman elements that converge into the compelling subject that we all instantly recognise.[2] I make it clear that 'girl' is not attached to a human of a certain biological sex or age — the ornaments and performance of femininity, the eternity of forever-youth, and the seduction of the void are imperatives for all, regardless of identity or biography. Refreshing the familiar Butler refrain — where 'gender is a kind of imitation for which there is no original'[3] — is possible, not only through close attention to how 'imitation' has changed and progressed, but through cataloguing the instances where eternal questions about perception and persona are shaken up by a world shared with sensing machines. Since their invention, girls have been creators and products of media; or, girls themselves are media — especially today, as mood boards blur with memories, private journals become public writing, and individual taste forms through swarm consensus. That leaves us at an elusive crossroads: does 'girlhood' — as a set of feelings and experiences, and as a phase that one can live through and leave behind — exist?

An argument in favour of 'girlhood' would focus on living individuals with specific memories, yet the problem of 'imitation' would follow us down the rabbit hole. Do you still have a girlhood if you do it wrong? What about a girlhood that is empty of its accoutrements? Is there a girlhood without innocence, without the adoration, envy and brutality of others, and must it take place early in life — or could it go on forever? Yes; no; maybe. While the iconography of girlhood is preciously specific to each person who has lived as 'a girl', there is a simultaneous drive to think of one's own canon as universal — that everyone should get your references, or share in your memories. That is often not the case. Still, the volatility of the girl-canon doesn't diminish its value. An emotional pull that is so powerful — with formal qualities so pronounced — accomplishes the feat of *feeling* universal. What are those emotional, formal qualities? Perhaps they are best defined according to their — *tuck the tailbone, and scoop the abdominals* — core tensions.

Nail art by Mei Kawajiri (Nails by Mei), 2025

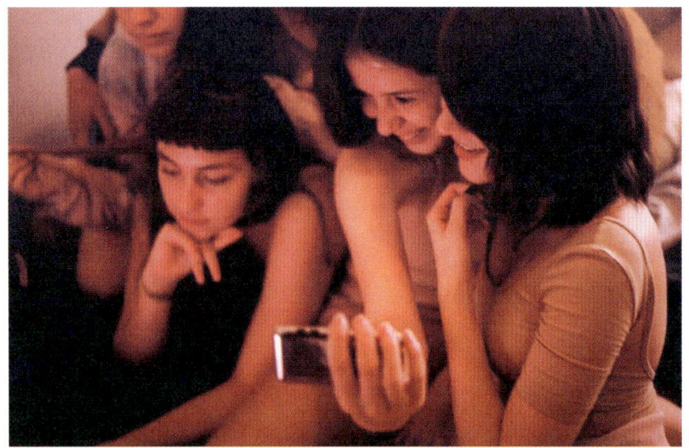

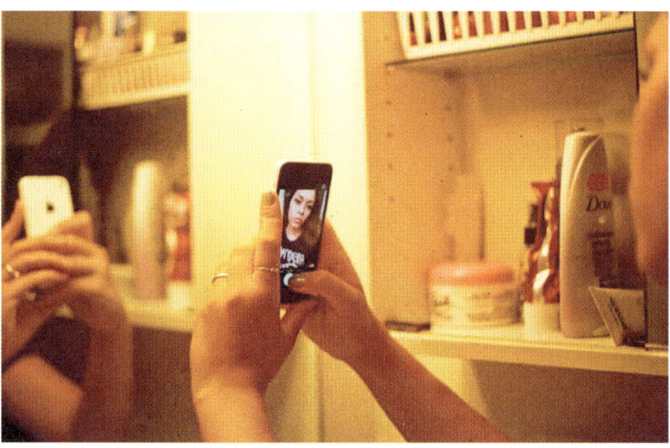

sweet vs toxic

Sweetness makes poison appetising. It's also a way to intoxicate the poisoner in return, inducing a delirium easily confused with love. Anonymous French collective Tiqqun's *Preliminary Materials for a Theory of the Young-Girl* has been chopped and screwed, incanted and broadcast, cited and rewritten in thousands of instances since its publication.[4] The text's inherent hatred of the girl has not stopped its circulation among living girls, who have finally assembled a complete 'girl theory' derived, but autonomous from, those 'preliminary materials'. Girls, after all, are accustomed to living with hate: finding flowers to adore in hostile territory, squeezing diamonds out of toxic waste. 'A female is one who has eaten the loathing of another, like an amoeba that got its nucleus by swallowing its neighbour', writes Andrea Long Chu in *Females*.[5] Metabolising hatred is a survival strategy, but it still turns the stomach when one reaches their limit.

vulnerable vs vicious

Is it any wonder that Harmony Korine's *Spring Breakers* accessorised with semi-automatics? The tragedy of a girl's existence — the violent and violating consequences of being a seemingly easy mark — is often met, with matching intensity, with disgust at tragedy itself. Tears are cut with tight smiles and/or screaming rage. Contrary to appearances, vulnerability spring-loads girls with viciousness. Consider the explosive triple-axels of figure skaters, who drill into reality blade-first — or the propulsion behind cheerleader backflips, where miniskirts are ancillary to frightening precision.[6] In an act of emotional realism, Petra Collins puts Olivia Rodrigo in a cute uniform and elbow-length black rubber gloves for the *good 4 u* music video:[7] all the better to handle a canister of kerosene so she can torch the house of whoever wronged her.

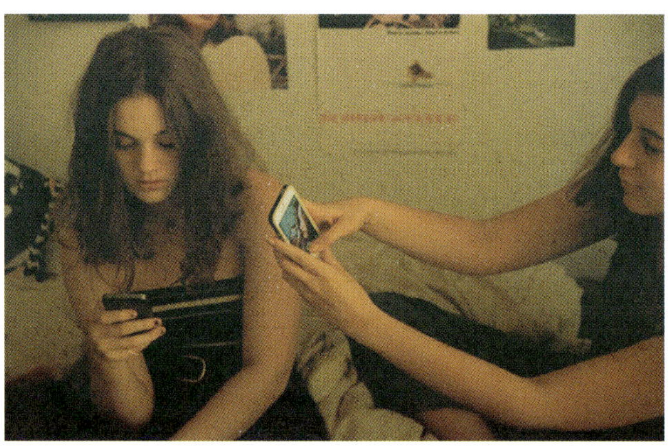

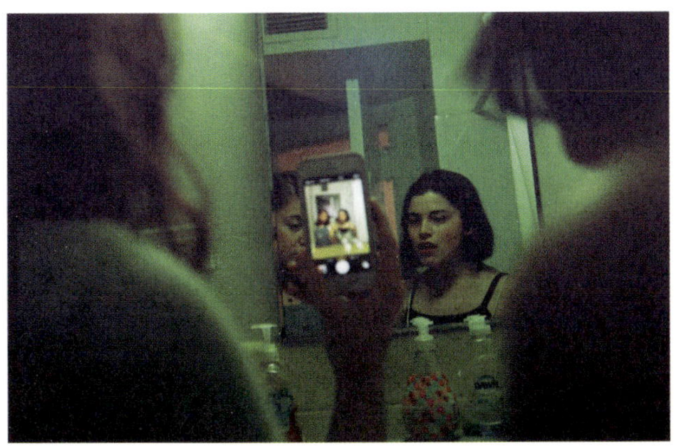

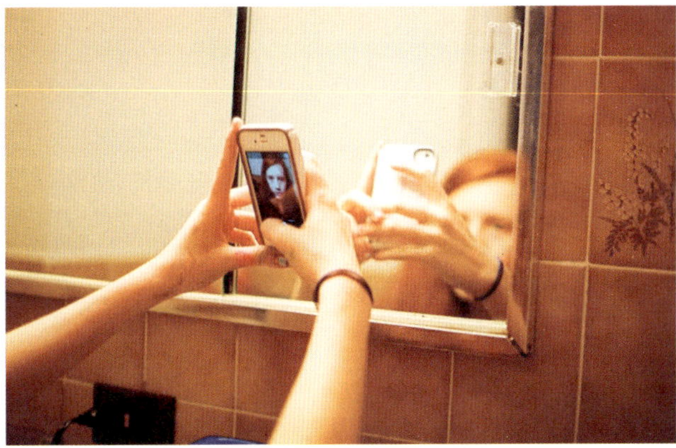

consumed vs consumer

Girls are good consumers, supposedly because they are the embodiment of consumption itself. Tiqqun argues that girls primarily exist as an ad category: a distillation of the global expectation for market-ready prettiness, youthfulness and limited availability. Without a doubt, girls *do* consume with a systematic frenzy and at an apocalyptic scale. Polyester ribbons, plastic glitter and undissolvable cosmetic filler mean that girly accoutrements will outlive human bodies. Fast fashion packages pile up, couriered overnight in a cloud of CO_2. The relationship is mutual. The details of girls' consumption are finely assessed and documented, amounting to 'deliberate self-design'[8] at a truly planetary scale — from patented molecules to seasonal trends to cities reshaped by logistical shopping flows. Many industrial, medical, artistic and pornographic innovations are the by-products of girls eating girls.

basic vs unfathomable

Girls wearing pageant ribbons, mass-produced swimsuits, first-place medals, debutante tulle and virtual verification badges deftly contend with the contradictory demand to be exceptional and replicable. Copies of copies stride through clouds of self-doubt and external criticism to actualise their ambitions — besting past performance fuelled by iced oat matcha, reformer Pilates, and the journals that outline unflinching progress toward set goals. Tiqqun was suspicious of girls' 'mechanical self-sufficiency or an indifference to the observer, like the insect, the infant, the automaton'.[9] Unknowable depths are concealed by a deflective carapace. 'Basic girls', 'non-playable characters', and any number of perennial girl-forms game commercial systems designed to observe them — selecting the archetype that allows them the smoothest passage through the tribulations of life on Earth, without exposing too much of their inner world. 'Isn't that the whole point of gender', writes Long Chu. 'Letting someone else do your living for you?'[10]

Petra Collins
***Selfie*, 2013**

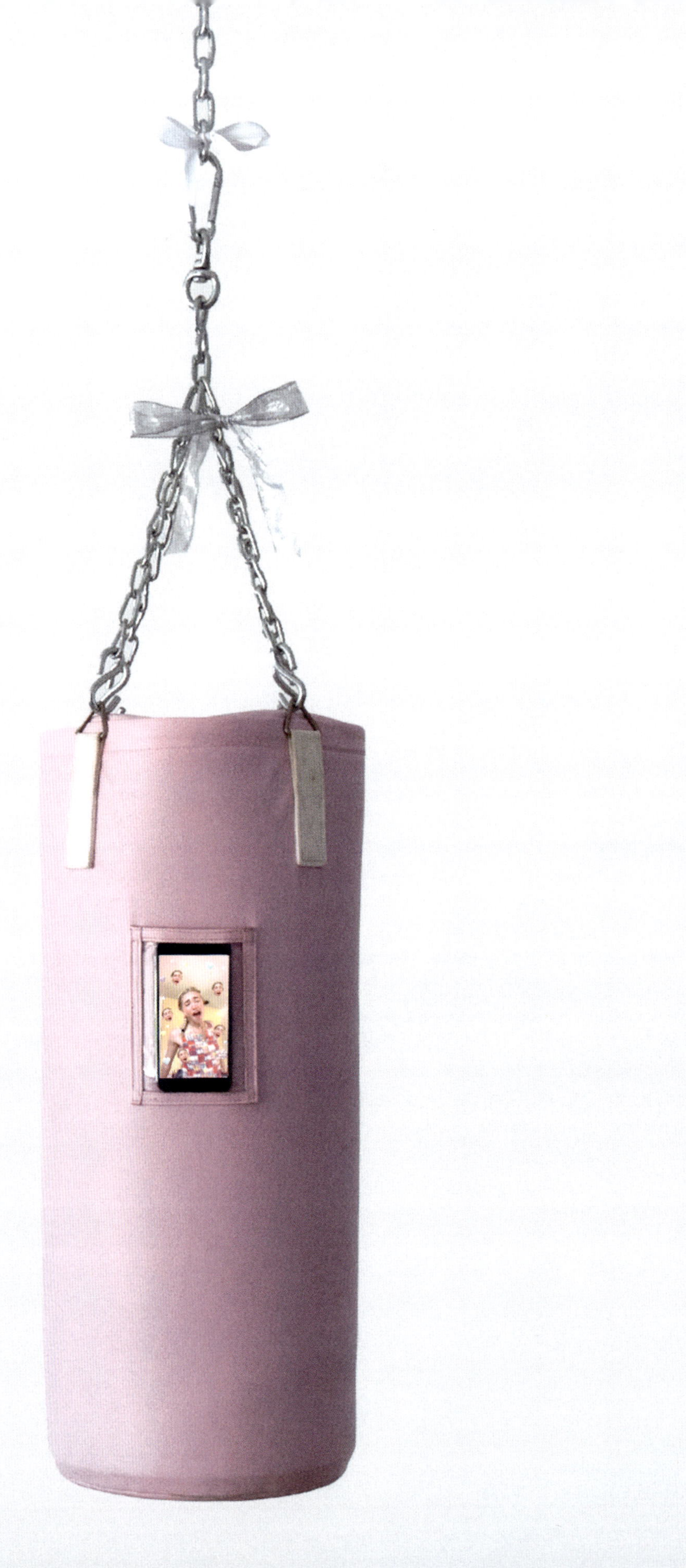

fake vs real

Tans, lashes, lips, breasts and personalities number among easily attainable 'fakes', prosthetics for sexy social dominance. Anyone who has lived as a girl has felt another plumb them for a glimpse of 'authenticity'. 'You're just acting', one might hear, after delivering a heartfelt confession on a date. Fail the test and risk getting booted out of the inner circle: 'Don't trust her; she's fake.' But fakes *are* real, as thriving dupe industries can attest, and life itself is synthesis. The borders between act and instinct, authenticity and artificiality, are as man-made as a silicone implant. Activities that deliberately fool around with these distinctions — from writing in a diary, to crying in the mirror, to staging a scene for a phone camera — are classed as 'girly', meaning that girls are the arbiters of the real fake: that is, our material world, crowded with media, decoration and simulations.

'New York, Sydney, Paris, London...
ice cream, chocolate, coffee, sugar...
candy, lollies, kitties, bunnies,
knee highs, stockings...
vintage, dresses, vodka, whiskey,
kitty, bunny, Paris, London,
sweet girls, cute boys, vodka,
whiskey, cameras, pictures...'[11]

notes

1 Ariana Grande, '7 Rings' (2019).
2 Quicho, A., 'Everyone Is a Girl Online', *WIRED* (2023).
3 Butler, J., *Gender Trouble* (London: Routledge, 1990).
4 Warren-Crow, H., & Jonsson, A., *Young-Girls in Echoland* (Minneapolis: University of Minnesota Press, 2021).
5 Long Chu, A., *Females* (London: Verso, 2019).
6 Cook, C., *Be Aggressive*, NYU Shanghai: IMA Speaker Series (26 March 2025), https://ima.shanghai.nyu.edu/events/ima-speaker-series-be-aggressive-connor-cook (accessed 21 April 2025).
7 https://www.youtube.com/watch?v=gNi_6U5Pm_o (accessed 21 April 2025).
8 Bratton, B., 'Planetary Sapience', *Noema Magazine* (17 June 2021).
9 Tiqqun, *Preliminary Materials for a Theory of the Young-Girl* (trans. A. Reines), (Los Angeles: Semiotext(e), 2012).
10 Long Chu, A., *Females*.
11 The Golden Filter, 'Favourite Things' (2024).

Maya Man
***love/hate*, 2022**
Punching bag, chains, ribbon, smartphone, video

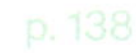
p. 138

Jenny Watson
***Skip*, 2023**
A4 coloured paper

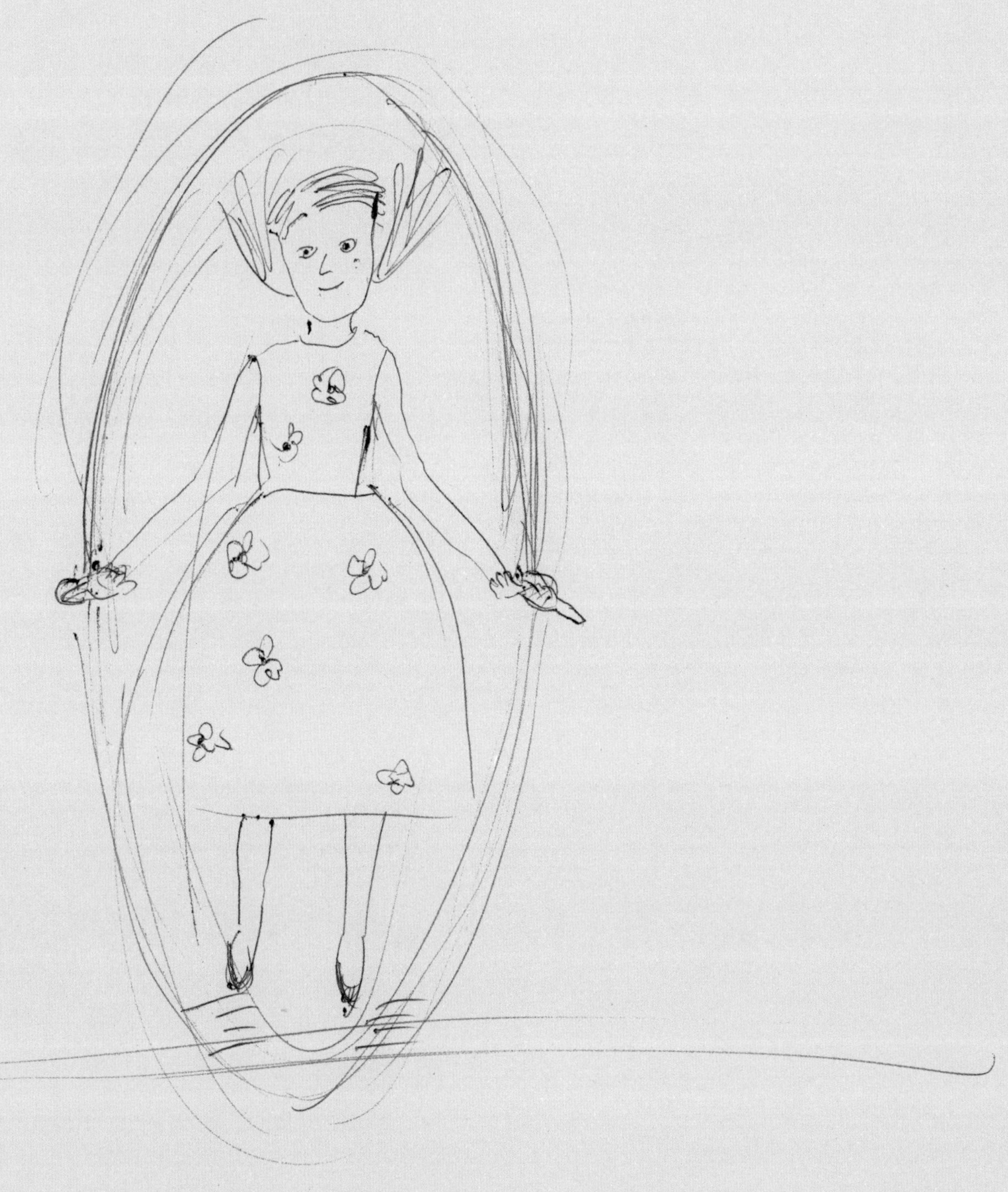

Skip

2003

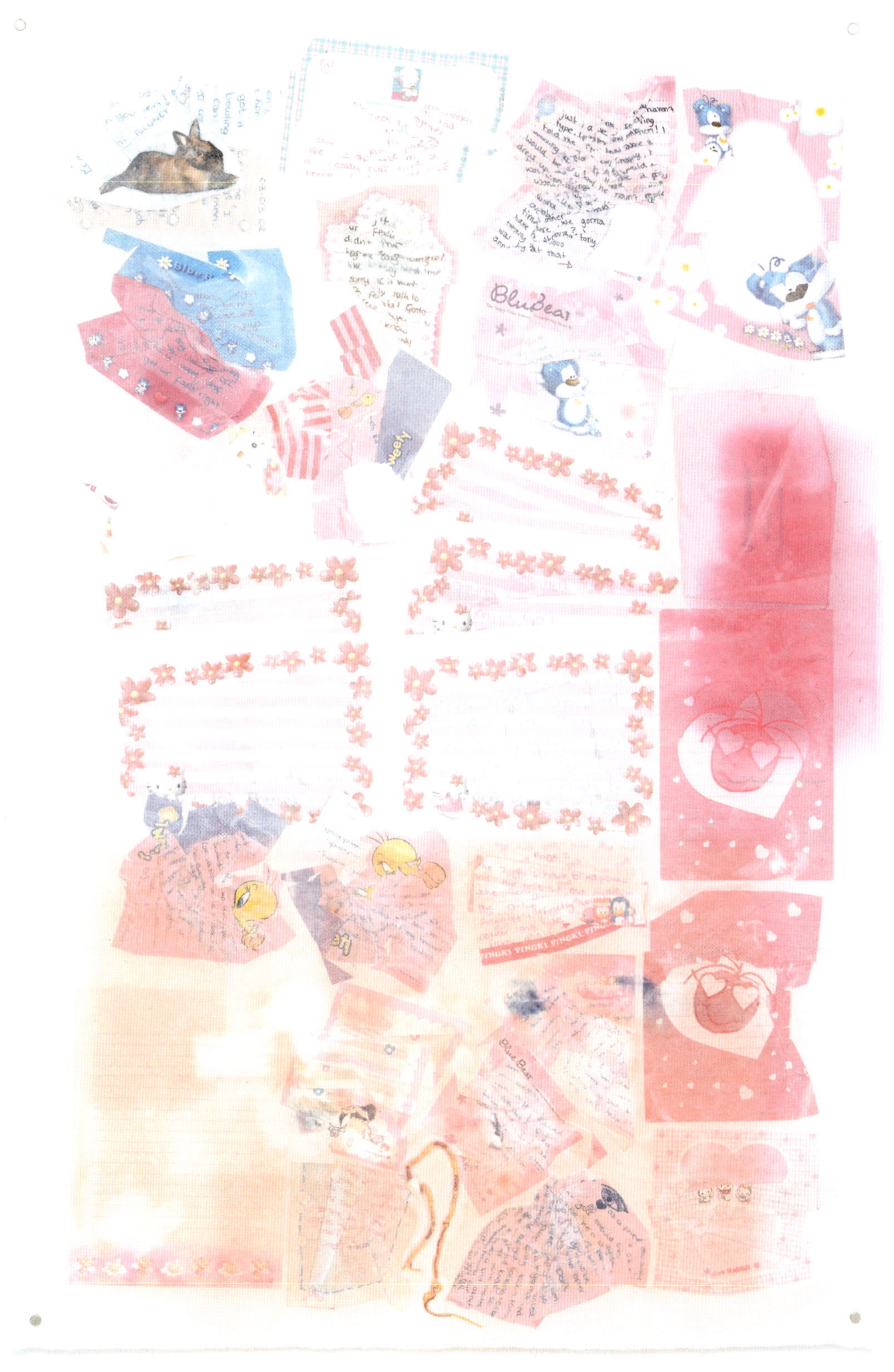

Harley Weir
i love you as a friend, 2025
Archive embedded in handmade paper

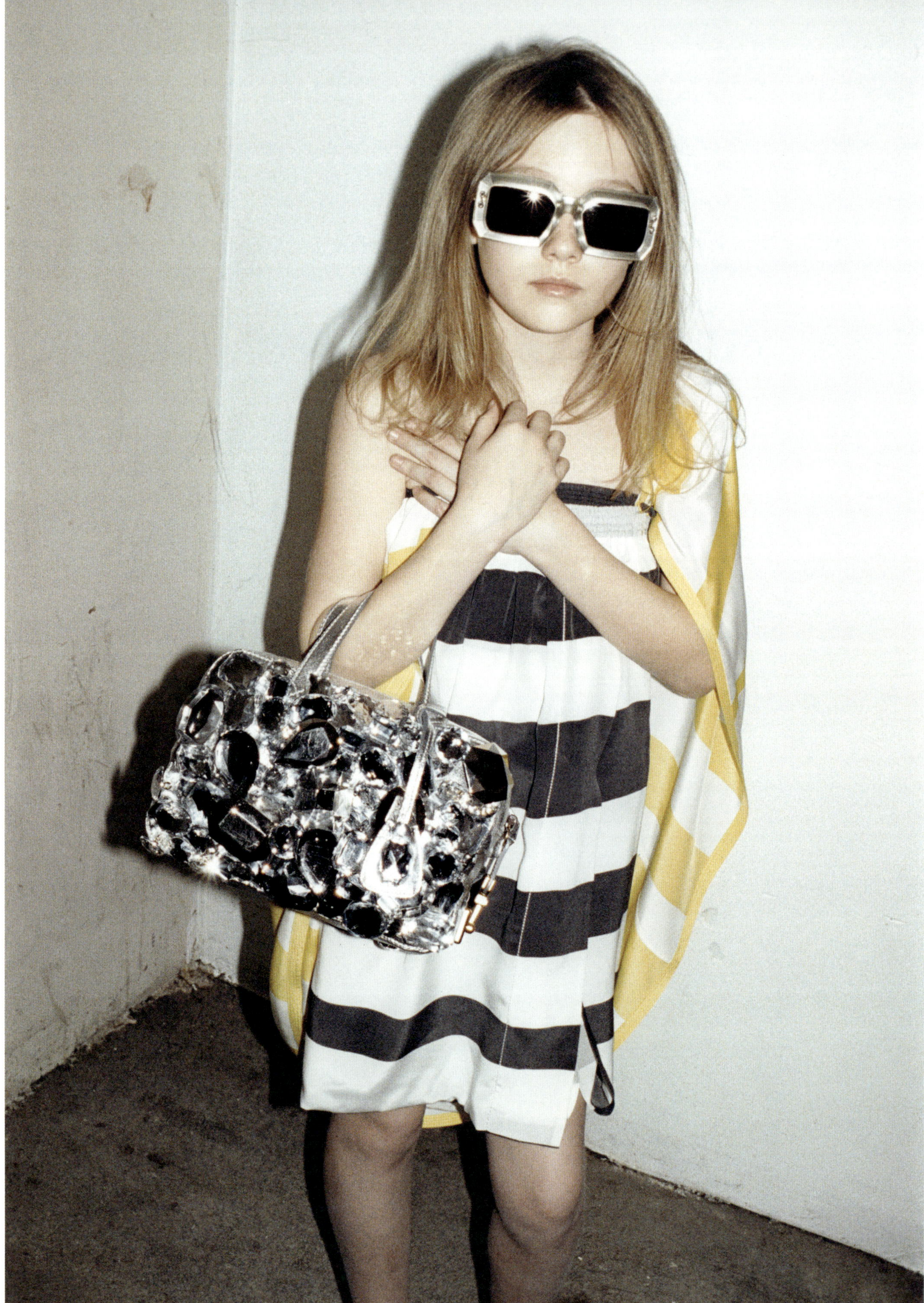

Morna Laing

girl code: conceptualising the girl of fashion

Who counts as a girl? And what does the girl of fashion stand for? These questions are incredibly loaded since the concept of 'the girl' has elastic boundaries, used as it is to refer to anyone from girl-children to women in their later years.[1] The term is not easily pinned down by chronological age, since one can remain a girl long after leaving girlhood; or at least that is what language would have us believe. Given the historical backdrop of women being infantilised — and thus excluded from public life — feminists of the Second Wave tended to insist on the use of the term 'woman' or 'young woman' to underline women's equal adult standing alongside men. Yet, the 1990s marked a point of departure, with certain feminists seeking to reclaim and re-signify the term 'girl', celebrating the culture of young femininity rather than denigrating it.[2] It is tempting, by contrast, to suggest that girlhood is more straightforwardly defined, referring to a fixed period of development when a female person is a legal minor. But a more nuanced view would see both girlhood and the figure of the girl as culturally mediated categories, subject to ongoing redefinition.[3]

The ambiguity built into the word 'girl' is paralleled in her visual manifestations. Fashion plays a central role in coding that figure: sometimes locating her squarely in the realm of childhood whilst at other times troubling her status, meaning that she fails to fall neatly into one category or another. This has led Paul Jobling to describe the girl of fashion as 'a woman who is also a child… a girl who could also be a boy'.[4] In the context of the West, the girl often signifies something beyond herself: from modernity in the 1920s; youth culture and sexual revolution in the 1960s; despondency in the 1990s; and a playful hyper-femininity in the 2010s.[5] This interpretative flexibility positions the girl as something of a 'cipher':[6] a vessel that can be filled up with new meanings which never entirely succeed in eclipsing older ones. This rich textual history represents a repository from which different mythologies of the girl can be mined by image-makers and spectators.[7]

In this essay I build upon the idea of the girl as cipher — or multi-layered code — who holds spectacular currency in the fashion media.

Dakota Fanning by Juergen Teller,
Marc Jacobs Campaign Spring-Summer 2007,
Los Angeles, 2006

One might even argue that the girl is fashion's protagonist *par excellence*. Girl code is a heavily sedimented terrain, influenced by longstanding narratives that align women with children. To understand this better, we first need to theorise the concept of childhood, looking at how it was feminised and romanticised in the eighteenth century. As will become clear, the feminisation of childhood and the infantilisation of women are phenomena that go hand in hand. While the normative code would posit adult/man in opposition to child/woman there are nevertheless fissures — or noise — in the binary system.[8] Certain sartorial forms operate as free-floating signs of childhood or adulthood – signifying innocence or knowledge, respectively. Those elements then serve either to reinforce or trouble the wobbly dividing line between girl-children and adult women in western fashion media, and beyond.

defining childhood: woman/child vs man/adult

While in progressive circles gender is now widely understood as a social construct, what is less readily accepted is the idea that childhood, too, is defined through words and images.[9] The idea of childhood as a social construct is widely attributed to French historian Philippe Ariès and his work *Centuries of Childhood* (1960).[10] Ariès argues that the idea of childhood was invisible in medieval society and gradually started to appear in iconography and religious texts from the fourteenth century.[11] This invisibility in the Middle Ages meant there was infancy, which lasted until the age of five to seven, then there was adulthood.[12] This is the idea of a 'short childhood'. A distinction should be made between biological children and the concept of childhood. Children have always existed. By contrast, it is the concept of childhood — as a set of sensibilities and behaviours, discrete from those of adults — which Ariès identified as appearing from the Renaissance onwards.[13]

The aforementioned shift was gradual, meaning that we can find traces of 'short childhood' in visual culture even after the medieval period. The portrait on page 143 depicts a wealthy Protestant family from 1559. Thomas Gerritszn Doesburch of Amsterdam is presented alongside his wife, Claesje Hendricksdr Roeclaes and their two daughters who, for all intents and purposes, look like miniature adults.[14] In the background we see the couple's respective coats of arms, speaking to the painting's function as a demonstration of lineage and succession.

Anonymous
***Thomas Gerritszn Doesburch and Claesje Hendricksdr Roeclaes with their Daughters*, 1559**
Oil on panel

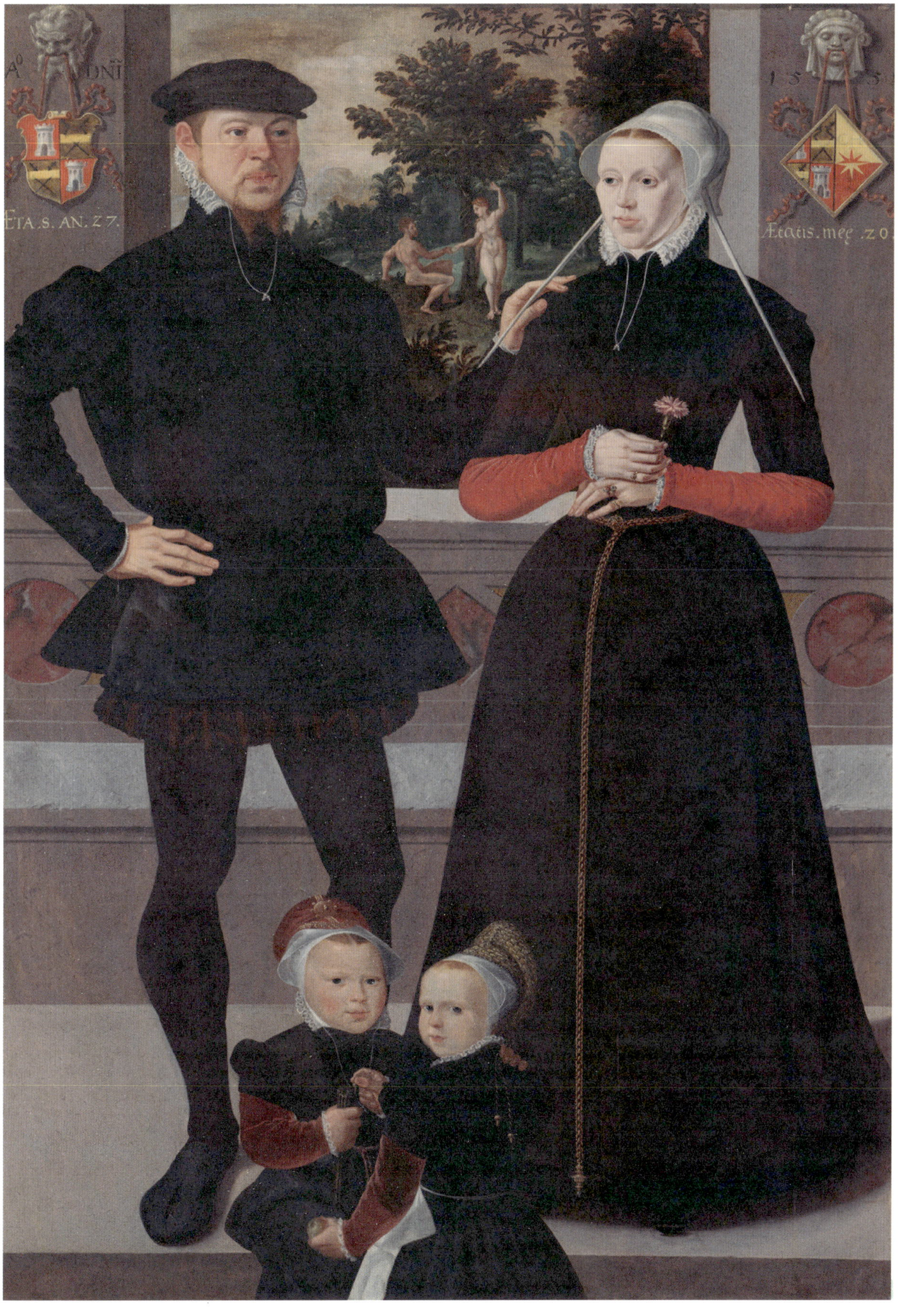
ETA.S. AN. 27.
Ætatis. meę. 20.

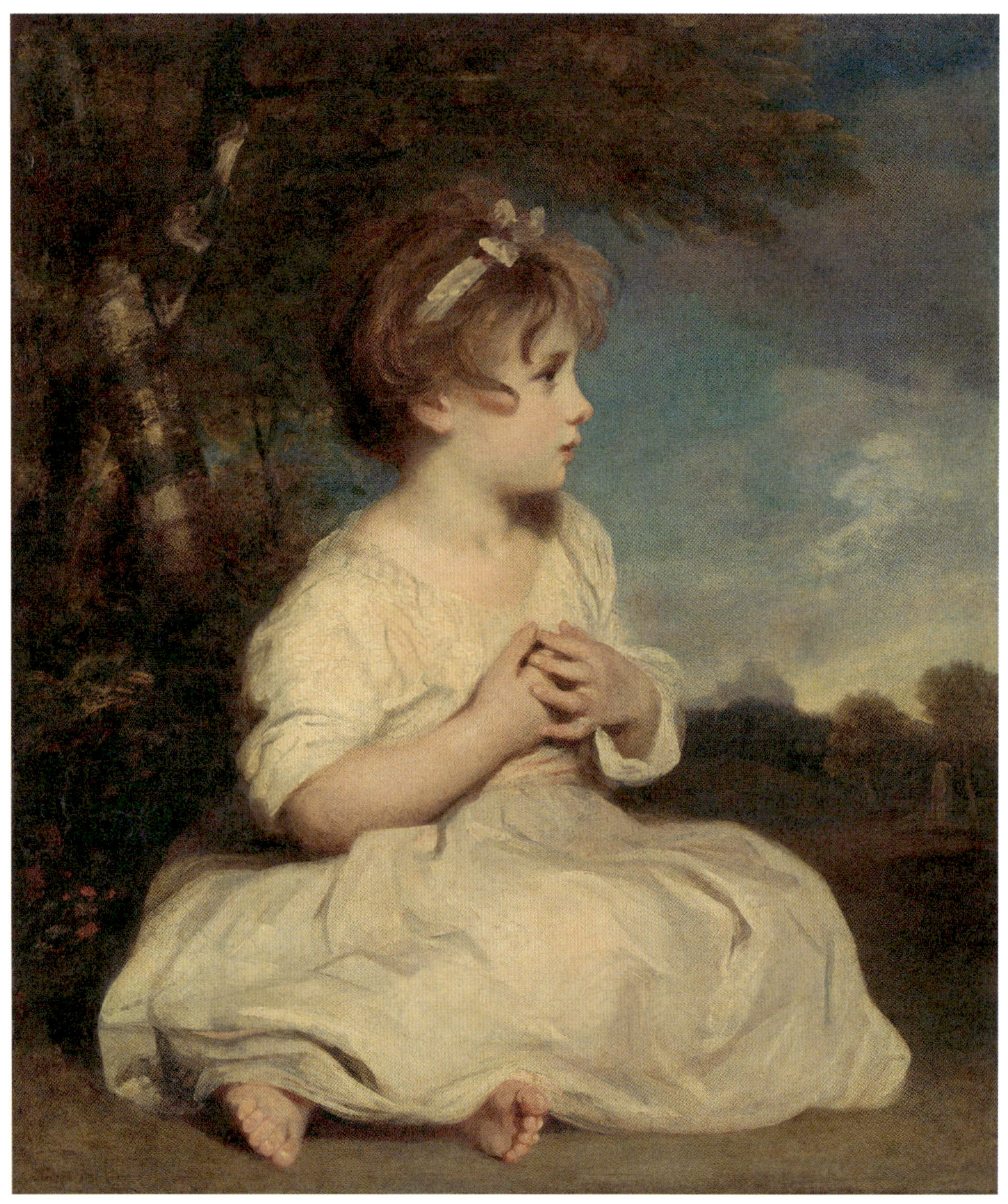

Sir Joshua Reynolds
The Age of Innocence, c. 1788
Oil on canvas

The girls are thus positioned as recipients of the family name and fortune. The daughters gaze directly out at the viewer, conferring on them a sense of control, composure and even authority. In keeping with the Spanish-influenced fashions of the day, the girl-children are soberly dressed in black, with their white chemise frills echoing the dress of their mother and father.[15] Their forearms are sheathed in what looks like burgundy velvet: a muted echo of their mother's crimson. The daughters' attire thus aligns them with the adult sitters rather than differentiating them as girl-children, as we are accustomed to seeing today.

The sobriety and stiffness of the daughters' dress sits in stark contrast to the flowing wafts of ivory fabric in Joshua Reynolds's *The Age of Innocence* (1788). The painting depicts the ideal of Romantic innocence which crystallised in art and literature from the eighteenth century.[16] It is closely connected to the idea of 'long childhood', where greater distance is placed between the norms of adulthood and childhood in the West. That distance was augmented by the rolling out of education, which extended the 'apprenticeship' required for children to become adults: at first for the upper classes in the seventeenth century, then later for the middle and working classes with access to education.[17]

Educational ideals were elaborated by the Enlightenment thinkers Jean-Jacques Rousseau and John Locke, each in his own distinct way. Rousseau presented his Romantic conception of childhood in his lengthy treatise, *Émile* (1762). Here, he argues that 'childhood has its own ways of seeing, thinking and feeling; nothing is more foolish than to try and substitute our [adult] ways'.[18] This set up a binary opposition between adulthood and childhood, which in turn mapped onto binaries between men and women, as we will see.

Childhood, for Rousseau, was characterised by innocence and purity, with children having a special capacity for curiosity and *joie-de-vivre*. Reynolds's *The Age of Innocence* can be read as an 'illustration' of Rousseau's proposals, with innocence being coded through the child's ivory dress and her gently clasped hands.[19] The pastoral backdrop makes nature childhood's home, echoing Rousseau's sentiment that children were closer to the 'state of nature', unlike adults who had been spoilt by society and culture.[20] The painting thus grants 'poetic significance'[21] to the girl-child, quite apart from the demonstration of lineage and succession, which we now consider adult concerns.

While Romantic childhood might masquerade as neutral or blank, it is in fact highly ideological. The girl's immaculate dress and her pale skin speak to a certain privilege on the part of the sitter.[22] This is an image of childhood which excludes labouring children and children of colour from its ambit.

As such, the long conception of childhood is by no means universal.[23] Even today, Susan Neiman reminds us that 'in poor countries around the world, children as young as five are expected to labour at tasks that make real contributions to their families' lives'.[24] Romantic childhood was not only exclusionary, it was also feminised. Following the Industrial Revolution, middle-class women were increasingly located in the private sphere along with their children, while their husbands inhabited the public sphere.[25] A child's place in the family economy was also changing.[26] In the past, the strategic marriage of children could augment a family's wealth and status. But the shift away from a land-based economy meant that education became an increasingly important determinant of future prosperity. In turn, children gradually shifted from being 'an economic to an emotional asset for parents', transforming them into a female concern in the process.[27] This feminisation, combined with the adult/child binary baked into the image of Romantic childhood, culminated in a cultural code (for affluent society) which posited adult/man/culture/knowledge in opposition to child/woman/nature/innocence.

noise in the system: innocence and knowledge

Feminised representations of childhood were, however, soon interrupted by the subtle assignment of gender roles, meaning 'boys, apparently, quickly become men, while girls remain girls', as Higonnet puts it.[28] Indeed, Rousseau was quite explicit in his view that when children approach puberty, boys become men, whereas women 'seem in many respects never to be more than children'.[29] This belief influenced his educational proposals which did not extend to girl-children: a fact lamented by his contemporary Mary Wollstonecraft.[30] She critiqued the way women were encouraged to remain 'innocent' (which she read as code for ignorance) with beauty being their cardinal virtue, alongside gentleness, docility and coquetry.[31] Ultimately, she argued that girlish ideals positioned woman as 'the toy of man, his rattle, and it must jingle in his ears whenever, dismissing reason, he chooses to be amused'.[32] As a consequence, Wollstonecraft, like feminists after her, would campaign for equal — adult — standing for women alongside men.[33]

The ideal of Romantic childhood, and the alignment of women with children, continues to influence the way images of girls are read today. Yet, that narrative now co-exists with other competing discourses: from Freud's early writings on children's pleasure-seeking to more recent discourses on 'knowing childhood' that emerged in the 1960s.[34] These narratives attribute a more complex palette of emotions and behaviours to children, including some that had been relegated to the 'adult' side of the binary set up in the eighteenth century. These qualities include sensuality, rage and knowledge (in its many forms), that trouble the 'blankness' and absolute innocence of the Romantic child in representation.

We see this at play in the work of North American artist Jas Knight. The young girl wears a high-necked cream dress, with cap sleeves and a tiered hem. The shape and colour are reminiscent of *The Age of Innocence*, only this time the girl-child is Black — challenging the narrowness of the Romantic ideal. She clasps a smartphone in both hands: a portal to all manner of knowledge, yet a symbol of adult anxieties about safeguarding children in the digital age. A similar dress is worn by a 12-year-old Dakota Fanning, photographed by Juergen Teller for Marc Jacobs. The garment's ethereality is undercut by Fanning's direct gaze and status as a child celebrity. Further complicating the image is the fact that Fanning is a girl-child approaching adolescence, and one who is playing tentatively with the codes of adulthood through fashion and pose.

Jas Knight
***Croquis for Fugue 14*, 2023**
Oil and linen on chalkboard

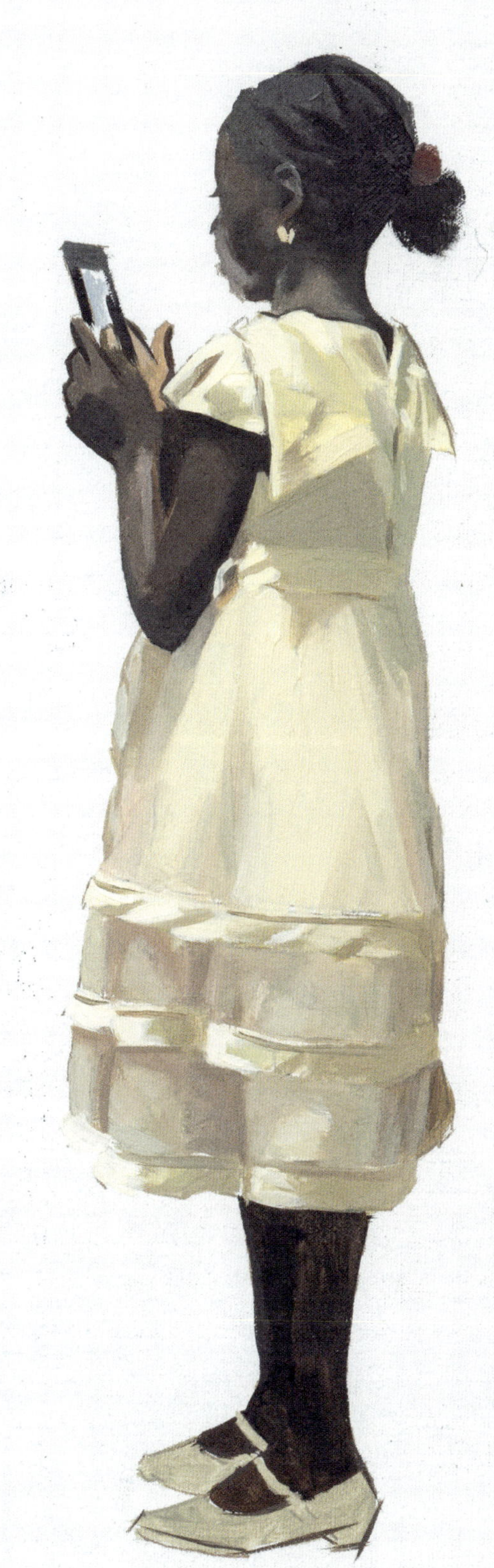

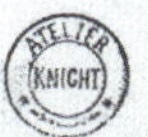
ATELIER
KNIGHT

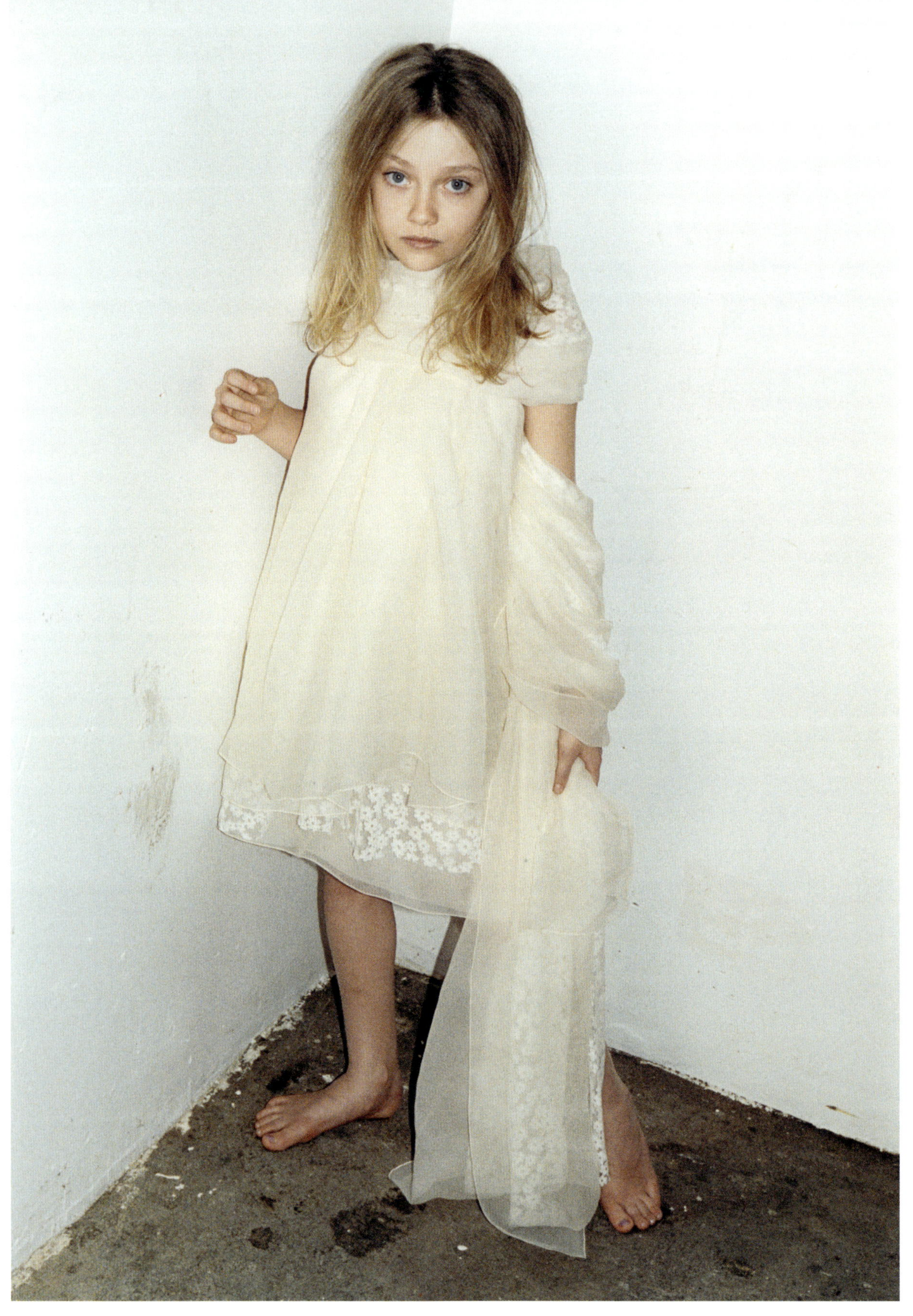

Dakota Fanning by Juergen Teller
Marc Jacobs campaign Spring-Summer 2007,
Los Angeles, 2006

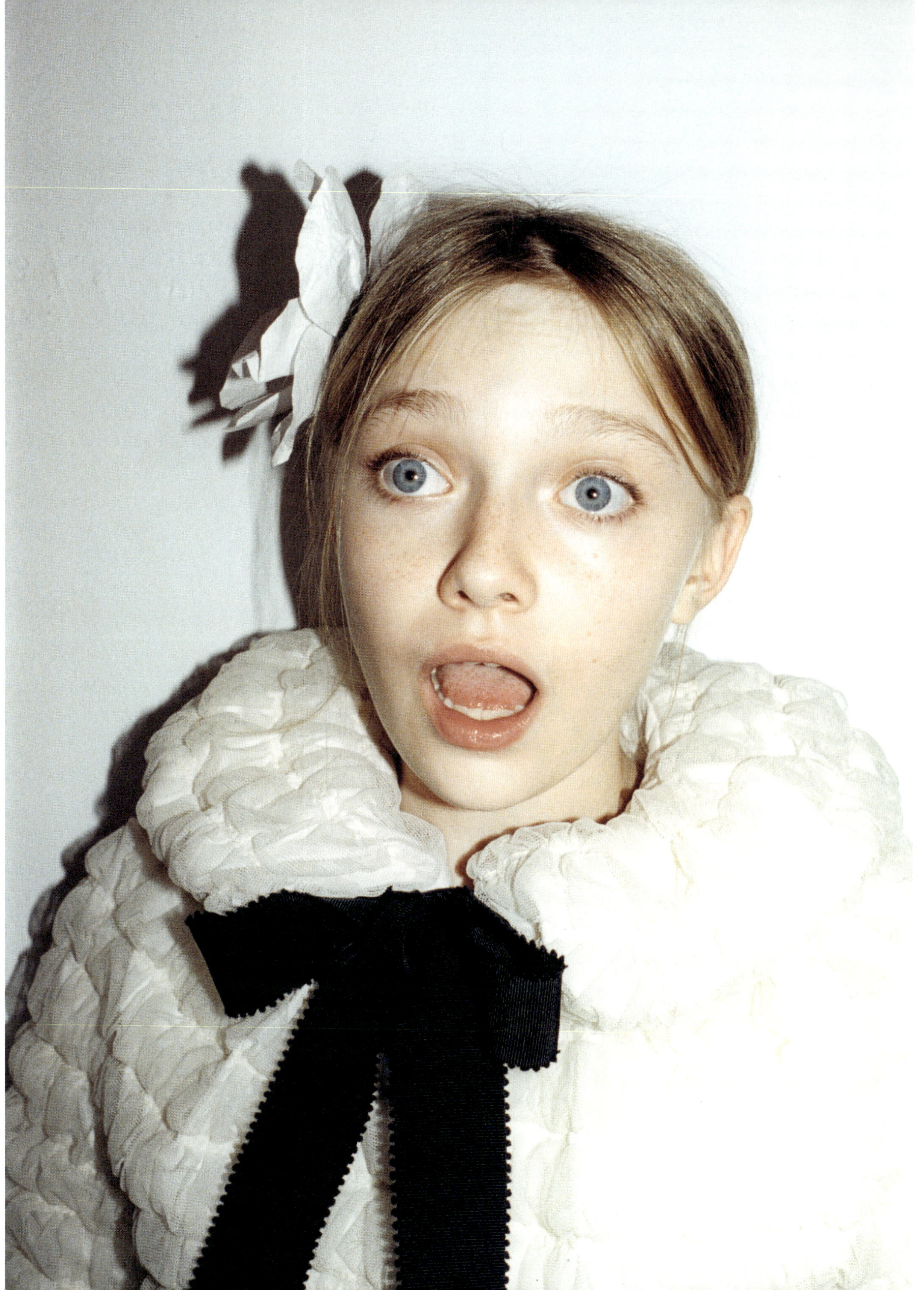

girly fashion for women: from infantilisation to feminist recuperation

The cusp separating girlhood from womanhood can be understood as a sort of symbolic danger zone. Patricia Holland has argued that girls approaching puberty tend to become 'a taboo image, surrounded by signals, fears and warnings'.[35] This is the wobbly dividing line to which I referred in the introduction. In order to draw a distinction between the categories of woman and girl-child there requires a 'threshold above which there is a difference and below which there is a similitude', as Michel Foucault puts it.[36] Fashion and body language have the potential to muddy that boundary. The presence of ambiguity or 'matter out of place' can thus provoke anxiety on the part of the viewer.[37] This is true of imagery featuring girl-children but also, young women. A later Marc Jacobs campaign for *Oh, Lola*! in 2011 also featured Dakota Fanning, only this time she was 17 and sat on the other side of the adult/child divide. The image was seductive, conveyed through smoky eye make-up and a provocative pose, but this was combined with contrasting codes of innocence, through a pale pink polka-dot dress and an oversized perfume bottle of cartoonish dimensions.[38] Fashion's capacity to trouble the dividing line between girl-children and young women thus works in both directions.

In light of the way women have historically been aligned with children, how should we make sense of women who wear the codes of childhood? We have seen how early feminists, such as Wollstonecraft, viewed 'coquettish' fashion and beauty ideals as part and parcel of the infantilisation process.[39] The visual alignment of girl-children with women sat alongside socio-cultural practices that limited women's access to education and public life. Yet, in the 1990s, some feminists began to reclaim girly fashion as a source of empowerment, in parallel with the reclamation of the word 'girl', by movements such as Riot grrrl.[40] Although not universally embraced, the idea was that girls and women should not have to emulate sober masculinity in order to be taken seriously.[41]

Kinderwhore was one such sartorial strategy which emerged in the 1990s, most famously associated with Courtney Love. There, signifiers of childhood such as gingham, bows and knee-high socks were combined with signifiers of womanly sexuality in what amounted to a parody of the contradictory demands of idealised femininity.[42] A muted rendition of this can be seen in Prada's Spring-Summer 1994 show. One of the models is wearing gauzy white fabric, perhaps linen or cotton, with her blonde hair pinned back with a hair slide. Her ankle socks are reminiscent of a schoolgirl's, only this time they are black and paired with sturdy masculine lace-ups. This undercuts the innocence conveyed by her fresh, white garments, as does the emphasis on the model's sexuality, with her nipples pressing visibly against her slightly sheer top.[43]

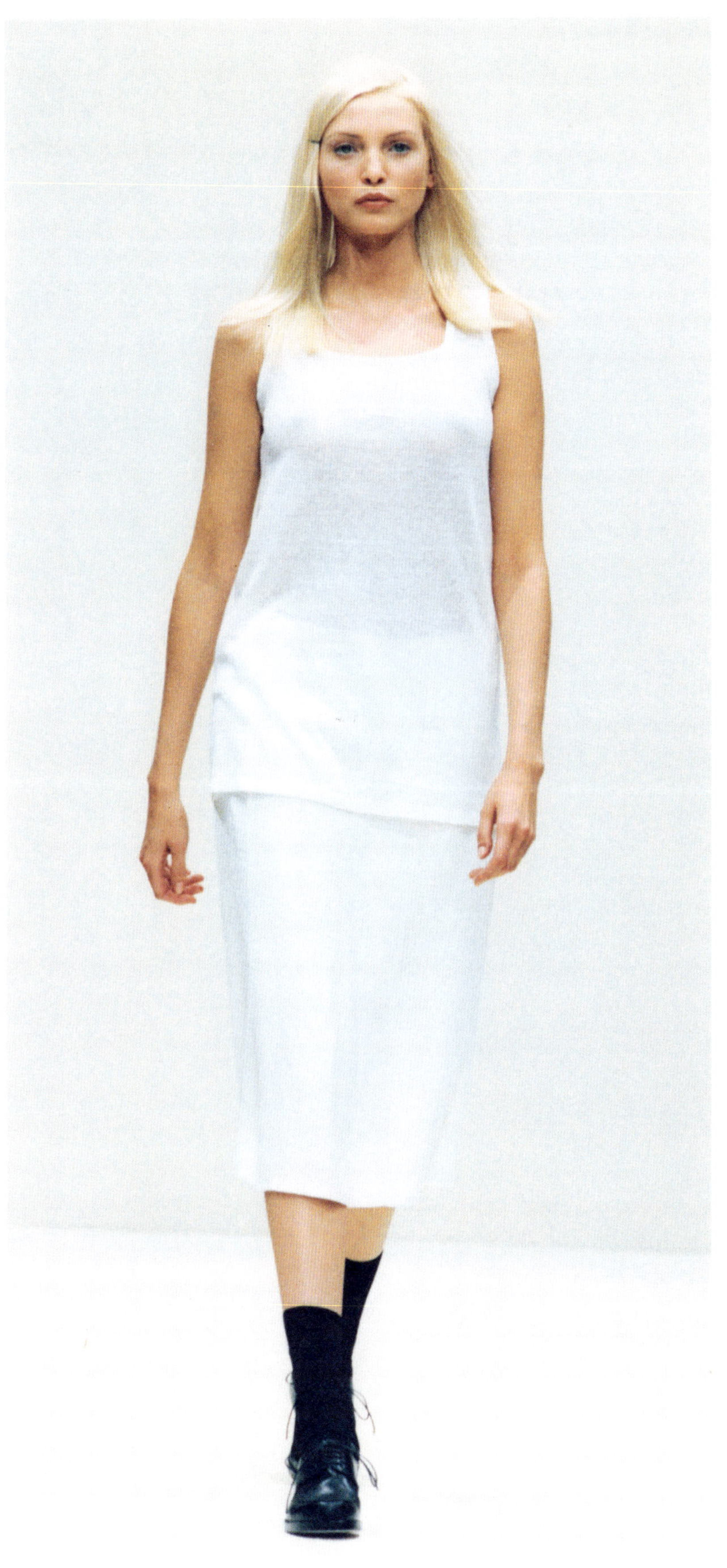

Prada
Spring-Summer 1994

What proved paradoxical is that, during the 1990s, as in earlier historical moments, childlike femininity played out on privileged bodies: young, white, thin, cisgender women. This was true of the 'super waif', embodied by Kate Moss, as well as the wave of Russian and East European models in the new millennium, such as Natalia Vodianova and Sasha Pivovarova.[44] In this sense, the visual codes of infantilisation became, ironically, a marker of bodily privilege within the industry. A shift did occur in the 2010s and early 2020s when the codes of girlhood began to play out on a slightly more diverse range of adult bodies. Miu Miu's reinterpretation of the schoolgirl aesthetic for Autumn-Winter 2022–2023 featured non-binary models (such as Maty Drazek, who uses they/them pronouns) as well as models of colour (such as Anyiel Majok and Diana Achan). There was continuity, however, in the emphasis on androgynous frames — ambiguous both in terms of gender and age. This leads us back, full circle, to Jobling's vision of the girl as 'cipher', always open to recoding, renewal and reinterpretation.[45]

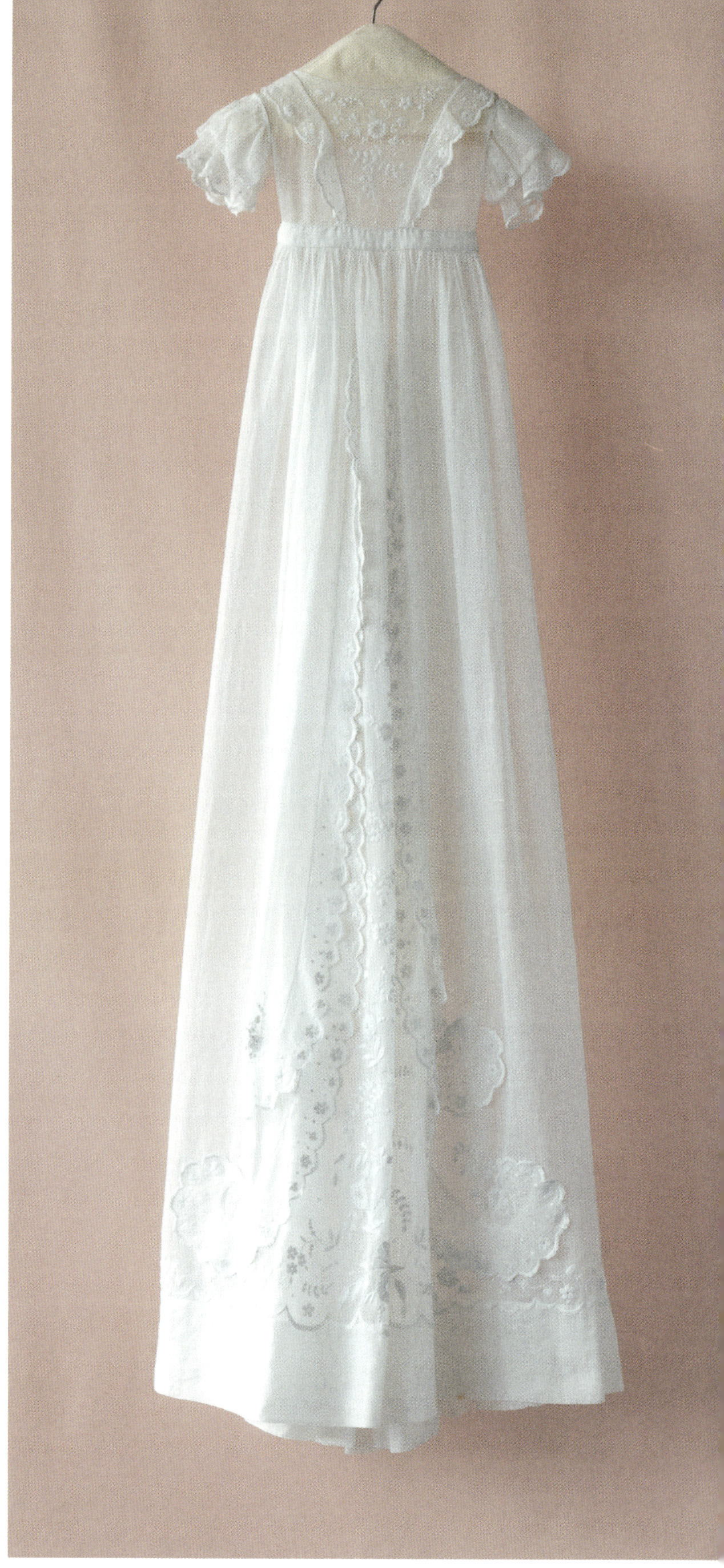

Baby dress, c. 1830–1850

1 Aapola, S., Gonick M. and Harris A., *Young Femininity: Girlhood, Power and Social Change* (Basingstoke: Palgrave Macmillan, 2005).
2 Aapola, Gonick and Harris, *Young Femininity*, 5.
3 Aapola, Gonick and Harris, *Young Femininity*, 1.
4 Jobling, P., *Fashion Spreads: Word and Image in Fashion Photography since 1980* (Oxford: Berg, 1999), 111.
5 For further discussion of each, see: McRobbie, A., *The Aftermath of Feminism: Gender, Culture and Social Change* (London: Sage, 2009); Radner, H., 'On the Move: Fashion Photography and the Single Girl in the 1960s', in: Bruzzi, S. & Church Gibson P. (eds.), *Fashion Cultures: Theories, Explorations and Analysis* (London: Routledge, 2000); Arnold, R., 'Heroin Chic' in *Fashion Theory*, 3, no. 3 (1999), 179–296; Laing, M., *Picturing the Woman-child: Fashion, Feminism and the Female Gaze* (London: Bloomsbury, 2021).
6 Jobling, *Fashion Spreads*, 112.
7 For a discussion of mythologies, see Barthes, R., *Mythologies* (trans. A. Lavers), (London: Vintage, 2000 [1957]).
8 'Noise', here, is a reference to Donna Haraway who uses it to describe the troubling of binaries that have underpinned normative subjectivities in the West. See Haraway, D., 'A Cyborg Manifesto: Science, Technology and Socialist-Feminism in the Late Twentieth Century' in Bell, D. and Kennedy, B.M. (eds.) *The Cybercultures Reader* (London and New York: Routledge, 1991), 312.
9 This is the central premise of the new sociology of childhood, a paradigm which emerged in the 1990s and emphasised the role of discourse in the way we understand children. For a discussion see: Jenks, C., *Childhood*, 2nd ed. (Oxford: Routledge, 2005).
10 Ariès, P., *Centuries of Childhood* (trans. R. Baldick), (London: Pimlico, 1996 [1960]).
11 Ariès, *Centuries of Childhood*, 10–11.
12 Ariès, *Centuries of Childhood*, 316. See also 31, 125.
13 Ariès, *Centuries of Childhood*, 10–11.
14 KMSKA (2025), *Thomas Gerritszn Doesburch and Claesje Hendricksdr Roeclaes with their Daughters*. Available online: https://kmska.be/en/masterpiece/thomas-gerritszn-doesburch-and-claesje-hendricksdr-roeclaes-with-their-daughters (accessed 27 March 2025).
15 Ashelford, J., *A Visual history of Costume: The Sixteenth Century* (London: Batsford, 1983).
16 For Ariès, education thus plays a pivotal role in the establishment of a 'long' childhood (see 316).
17 Ariès, *Centuries of Childhood*, 316. See also Elias, N., *The Civilizing Process* (trans. E. Jephcott), (Oxford: Blackwell, 2000).
18 Rousseau, J., *Émile* (London/Vermont: Everyman, 1993 [1762]), 64.
19 Higonnet, A., *Pictures of Innocence: The History and Crisis of Ideal Childhood* (London: Thames and Hudson, 1998). See also, Steward, J.C, *The New Child: British Art and the Origins of Modern Childhood, 1730–1830* (Berkeley: University Art Museum and Pacific Film Archive, University of California, 1995), 81.
20 Rousseau, *Émile*.
21 Ariès, *Centuries of Childhood*, 125–26.
22 For further discussion, see Higonnet, *Pictures of Innocence*.
23 Steward, *The New Child*, 26, 84–5, 206–07, 173–81.
24 Neiman, S., *Why Grow Up?* (London: Penguin, 2014), 163, building on Mead.
25 The same was not, of course, true of working-class women and children. For a discussion, see Steward, *The New Child*.
26 Jensen, A., 'The Feminization of Childhood' in Qvortrup, J., *et al.* (eds.), *Childhood Matters* (Aldershot: Avebury, 1994), 59.
27 Jensen, 'The Feminization of Childhood', 59.
28 Higonnet, *Pictures of Innocence*, 27.
29 Rousseau, *Émile*, 206.
30 Wollstonecraft, M., *A Vindication of the Rights of Woman* (London: Penguin, 2004 [1792]); Wollstonecraft, M., *Thoughts on the Education of Daughters* (Whitefish MT: Kessinger, 2010 [1787]).
31 Wollstonecraft, *A Vindication of the Rights of Woman*.
32 Wollstonecraft, *A Vindication of the Rights of Woman*, 45.
33 For further discussion, see Laing, *Picturing the Woman-child*.
34 Freud, S., 'Three Essays on Sexual Theory' in Freud, S., *The Psychology of Love* (trans. S. Whiteside), (London: Penguin, 2006 [1905]). For a discussion of 'knowing childhood', see Higonnet, *Pictures of Innocence*.
35 Holland, P., *Picturing Childhood: The Myth of the Child in Popular Imagery* (London: I.B. Tauris, 2004), 191. There are some exceptions to this with regard to the representation of boy-children, as Annamari Vänskä has argued: Vänskä, A., 'Seducing Children?', in: *Lambda Nordica*, 2–3 (2011), 69–101.
36 Foucault, M., *The Order of Things* (trans. unknown), (London: Routledge, 2002 [1966]), xix.
37 Douglas, M., *Purity and Danger: An Analysis of Concepts of Pollution and Taboo* (London: Routledge, 2002 [1966]), 50.
38 For a discussion, see Laing, *Picturing the Woman-child*.
39 Wollstonecraft, *A Vindication of the Rights of Woman*, 16.
40 Aapola, Gonick and Harris, *Young Femininity*, 20.
41 Susan Faludi, for instance, saw girlish fashion as part of a backlash against the gains of Second Wave feminism. See: Faludi, *Backlash: The Undeclared War Against Women* (London: Vintage, 1992), 92.
42 Arnold, 'Heroin Chic'. Kinderwhore would take on a different guise in the 2010s, reaching almost cartoonish dimensions in the work of designers such as Meadham Kirchhoff. SHOWstudio (2014) 'Project Girly', SHOWstudio, http://showstudio.com/project/girly (accessed 4 September 2015).
43 For a discussion, see: Wallerstein, 'Thinness and Other Refusals in Contemporary Fashion Advertisements', in: *Fashion Theory*, 2, no. 2 (1998), 129–50.
44 Laing, *Picturing the Woman-child*.
45 Jobling, *Fashion Spreads*.

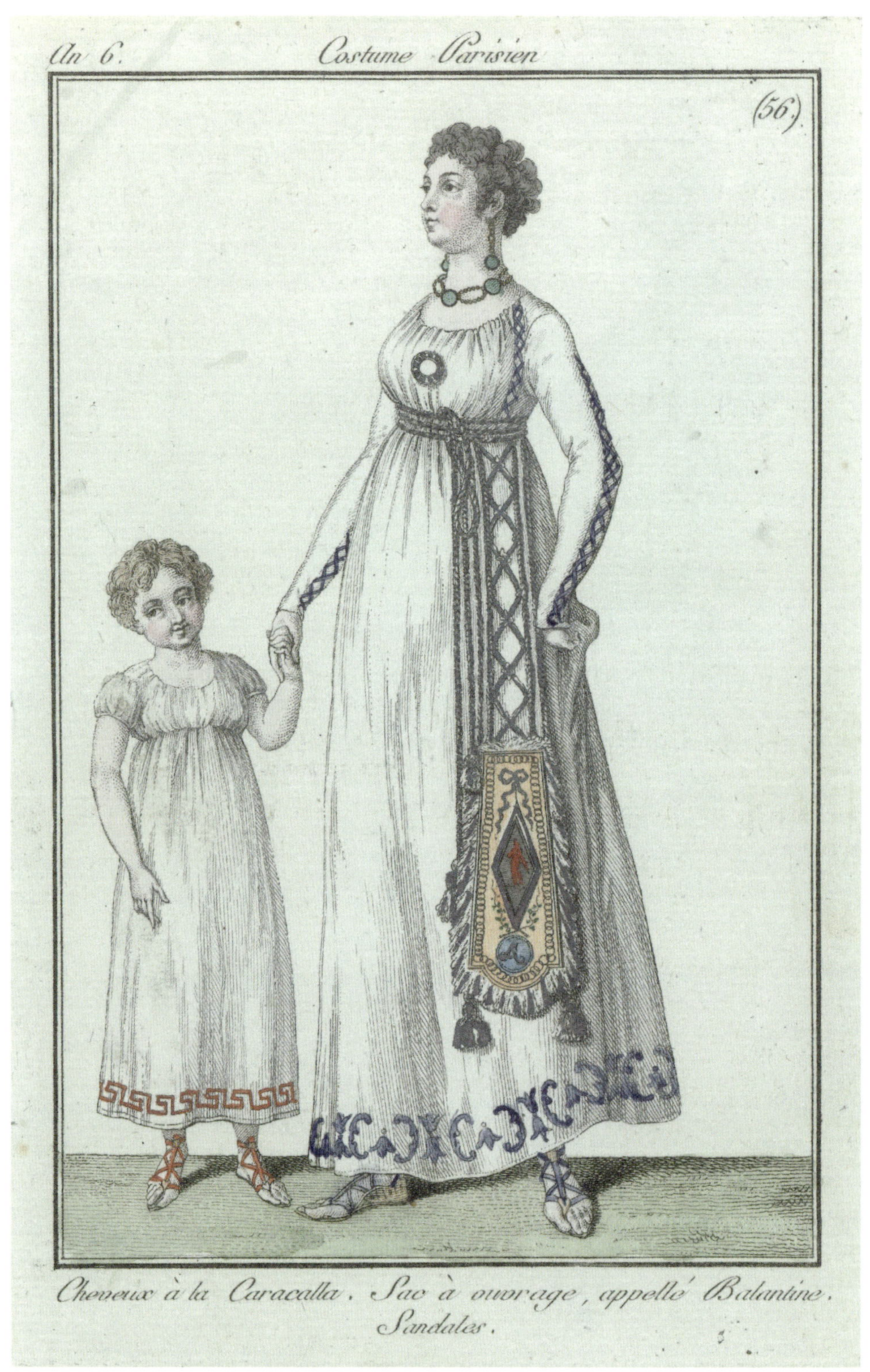

Anonymous
Costume Parisien,
in *Journal des Dames et des Modes*, An 6, 17 August 1798

Wim Mertens

girls in white dresses

Or how an archetype became encoded during the nineteenth century in western society.

In 'My Favorite Things', a song from the iconic 1965 musical *The Sound of Music*, Maria, who is the governess of the Von Trapp children, lists the things she thinks about when she is scared, things that make her feel happy. One is girls in white dresses. The Von Trapp children, who are being raised in a wealthy household, are familiar with the image that their governess evokes. Girls in white dresses remind them of spring and summer, of parties, and probably of pivotal events in their lives that they have already experienced or that they know will happen. In the late 1930s, the period in which this story is set, girls and young women wore white dresses at several milestones in their lives.

White dresses became highly fashionable in the late eighteenth and early nineteenth centuries. They were synonymous with wealth because they were delicate and precious — and difficult to keep clean. Like adults, young girls also began to wear white dresses, often for festive or more formal occasions.[1] During the nineteenth century, they became archetypes and a must-have.

This is illustrated in a short article in *La Mode Illustrée* (1 March 1903), entitled '*Robes blanches*', by the French fashion magazine's editor-in-chief Aline Raymond.[2] In a veritable lyrical reverie, she reflects on three key moments in a mother's life: baptism, first Communion, and the marriage of her daughter(s).[3] The author captures the spirit of an era when faith and the role of women played a central role in life and society, manifested in white dresses as the embodiments of innocence and purity.

If this article is to be believed, in those days white dresses gradually became standard attire in well-to-do Catholic families in western society for the celebration of the sacraments of baptism, receiving one's first Communion as part of the Eucharist, and marriage.[4] This article was thus not a coincidence. Originally a disseminator of the latest fashion trends, in the second half of the nineteenth century these magazines became the forerunners of lifestyle magazines. This meant they also featured contributions and opinion pieces on *savoir-vivre* (the art of living well and with elegance), which targeted the upper and middle classes.

From the 1830s, but even more so after 1850, fashion magazines promoted white Communion and wedding dresses.[5] Every March, *La Mode Illustrée*, which became a weekly magazine in 1860, featured a print of a Communion dress with a brief description and the name of the *couturière* who made it. Traditionally, this was the time of year when dutiful mothers would have already been preparing the celebrations of the first Communion of their child for months. For centuries, this ceremony has taken place during the Easter season, which also happens to coincide with spring, a period of blossoming and resurrection.[6] In the nineteenth century, children took their first Communion in their early teens. This is confirmed by fashion prints of the period, and later by photographs of the occasion, none of which feature little girls or young women. This is also consistent with Aline Raymond's article, in which she writes: 'The dress (Communion dress) is no longer the dress of a little girl... The skirt is long, and the corsage has a pleated waist panel. The child will seem transformed in this dress, with pinned-up hair and a veil and crown... The little girl of yesterday is blossoming into the young lady of the future.'[7]

Throughout ecclesiastical history, the age of the communicant has been a subject of debate.[8] The primary concern was that the faithful should receive their first Communion when their mind was still pure on the one hand, yet sufficiently formed to understand the spirituality of this sacrament on the other. Many clerics expressed concerns about the unchaste and sinful thoughts that might taint the brain of innocent children at a certain age. As such, the Catholic Church considered the first Communion to be a rite of passage from childhood to young adulthood. The crown that young girls wore for their Communion supposedly referred to this, while the veil symbolised virginity and humility.[9]

White, meanwhile, became the preferred colour for emphasising the purity of the child and communicant. Since the Middle Ages, white has epitomised purity and innocence in Catholic liturgy.[10] A Roman catechism from 1725 first mentions a white robe as being most suited for communicants, in reference to the robes of angels — *in habitu angelorum*.[11] It is worth noting in this context that, for many decades, only the wealthy elite wore specific outfits for this occasion. From the second quarter of the nineteenth century, however, broader swathes of the population could also afford them, thanks to the increased availability of textiles following industrialisation and increasing prosperity.

As well as the colour of these Communion outfits, the church authorities also wanted Communion outfits to be understated and simple. Cotton, which was already used for secular white dresses, became the fabric of choice for Communion dresses in the nineteenth century. Muslin was also popular, as were percale and cambric. In the 1870s, however, Communion dresses became more luxurious, with attention paid to the fabric, cut and trimmings. Occasionally, the veil was made of silk tulle, with the dress made of silk chiffon or silk muslin and trimmed with lace or silk.[12] This was consistent with the prevailing fashion trends and the social phenomenon of conspicuous consumption, where people's newly acquired status was externalised in excessive and ostentatious consumption. Department stores and *couturières* readily seized upon this development, using fashion magazines to tout their wares. As well as dresses, these magazines also featured illustrations of the proper undergarments, accessories, jewellery and gifts, listing their prices.[13] Dresses also came in different price brackets. Poorer households, however, sometimes had to save for years for an outfit, and even then

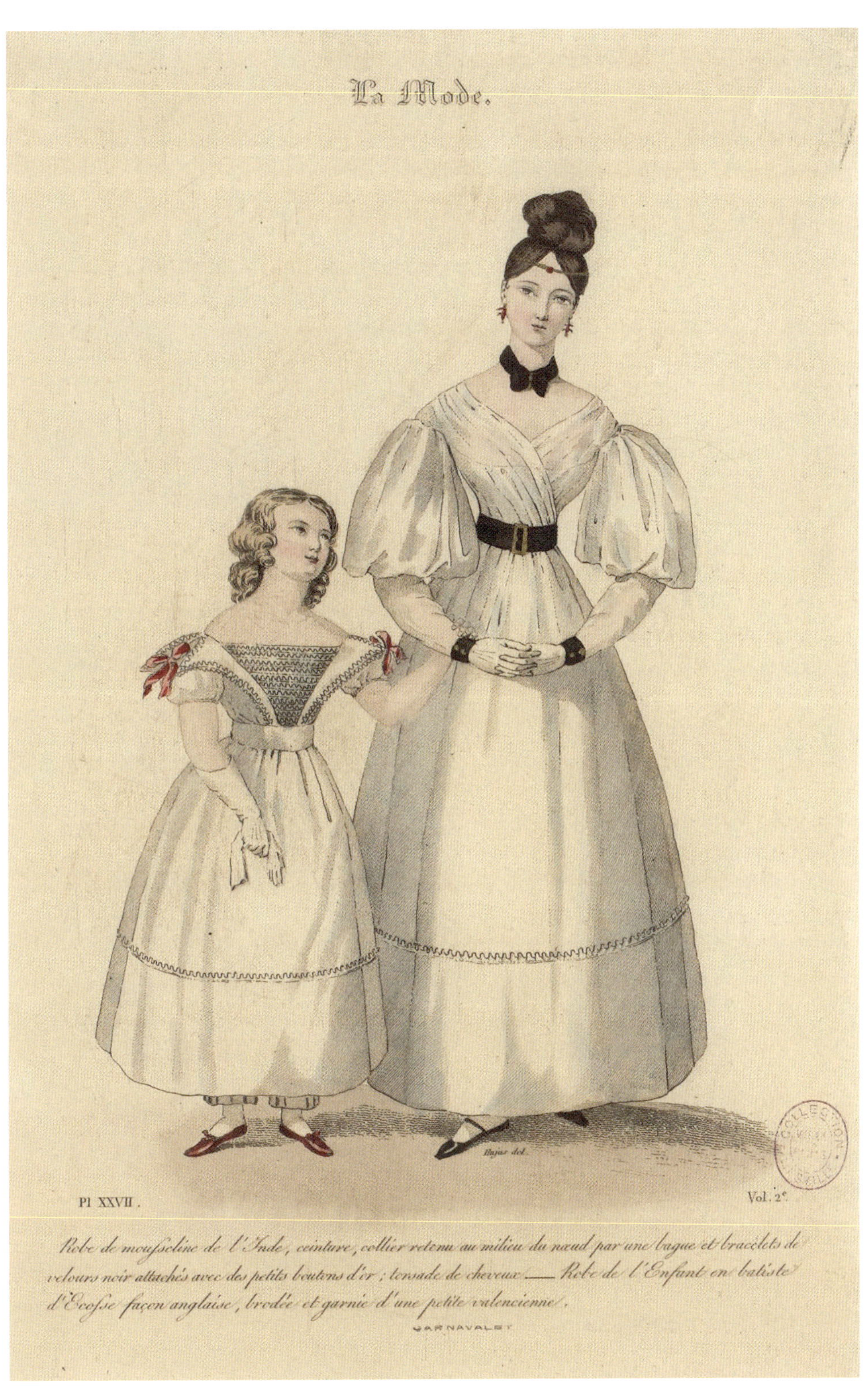

Anonymous
La Mode, 1830

the white Communion dress and accessories still remained out of reach. In these instances, they might rent a dress, appeal humbly to the parish's charity, or rely on the gift of a benefactor or seamstress.[14]

In principle, the first Communion is followed some years later by confirmation. Interestingly, French fashion magazines rarely featured illustrations of confirmation outfits. Moreover, the dresses were not white, but dark in colour and usually very plain and simple. The wearers were young women. This is completely different from the Anglican Church, where the white confirmation dress became all the rage in the second half of the nineteenth century. From the 1870s, British fashion magazines began to publish French prints featuring Communion dresses but calling them confirmation dresses.[15] Like the first Communion in the Roman Catholic Church, confirmation is a rite of passage in the Anglican Church.

For several decades in the nineteenth century, girls also wore a white dress for another, more secular rite of passage: the *entrée dans le monde* or formal entrance into society ('coming out'), when young women went to their first ball, usually when they were between 15 and 18 years of age. The ball gown was often made of tarlatan, a cotton fabric, and trimmed with silk ribbon. The white tarlatan ball gown was especially popular around the mid-nineteenth century. In March 1881, however, Emmeline Raymond wrote the following in the fashion pages of *La Mode Illustrée*: 'young girls no longer have to wear a white ball gown'.[16] White still proved popular, however, albeit increasingly as a transparent top layer over a gown in another colour. Nineteenth-century white girls' dresses were all about unity in diversity. They simultaneously represented simplicity and preciousness, were fashionable yet also timeless, and were both spiritual and worldly. They were worn on occasions that symbolised the transition from childhood to young adulthood, partly due to the connotation of white with innocence and purity. They were also an intrinsic part of social conventions and thus something on which the fashion industry could capitalise.

notes

1 De Jonge, J., 'In de wolken: trouwen en dopen in het wit', in *Kostuum. Jaarboek Nederlandse Kostuumvereniging* (2004), 47.
2 Raymond, A., 'Robes blanches', in: *La Mode Illustrée. Journal de la famille*, 44, 9, 1 March 1903, 98.
3 The author wrote this from a Roman Catholic perspective.
4 In other faith communities, including Protestant churches, white also became the colour of choice for baptisms and, increasingly, marriages. See De Jonge, 'In de wolken', 45–56.
5 Coppens, M., 'Origine et évolution d'une tenue rituelle: la robe de communion solenelle', in *Bulletin van de Koninklijke Musea voor Kunst en Geschiedenis*, 69 (1998), 199; and De Jonge, 'In de wolken', 50.
6 The Fourth Lateran Council, which was convened in 1215 by Pope Innocent III, ordered all the faithful to receive Communion at least once a year, preferably at Easter. Fraikin, J. and Fontaine, P., *La Communion solenelle. Fête religieuse, fête profane* (Brussels: Traditions et Parlers populaires Wallonie-Bruxelles asbl, 1997), 12–13.
7 'Cette robe n'est plus le vêtement que la petite fille a porté jusque-là, la jupe courte, ... La jupe est presque longue, le corsage plissé à la taille. Ainsi vêtue, avec ses cheveux relevés sous son voile et sa couronne, l' enfant apparaîtra transformée, ... Pour la première fois, de la petite fille d'hier, elle croira voir se dégager la jeune fille de demain,...' in: Raymond , 'Robes blanches'.
8 See Fraikin and Fontaine, *La Communion solenelle*, 15–18.
9 Coppens, 'Origine et évolution d'une tenue rituelle', 200. The veil as part of the Communion dress became more commonplace in the late 18th century.
10 Segeren, A-M., 'Trouwen in het wit', in *Ja, ik wil. 250 Jaar Trouwjurken*, exh. cat. (Zwolle: Waanders, 2024), 17.
11 Coppens, 'Origine et évolution d'une tenue rituelle', 196.
12 'Toilettes de première communion', in *La Mode Illustrée. Journal de la famille*, 18, 12, 25 March 1877, 89–93.
13 Ibidem.
14 Coppens, 'Origine et évolution d'une tenue rituelle', 203–04; Fraikin and Fontaine, *La communion solenelle*, 37–38.
15 Jarvis, A., 'The Dress Must Be White, and Perfectly Plain and Simple: Confirmation and First Communion Dress, 1850–1900', in *Costume*, 41 (2007), 86.
16 'Dans les réunions dansantes [...] le blanc n'est plus imposé à toutes les jeunes filles', in: Raymond, E., 'Modes', in *La Mode Illustrée. Journal de la famille*, 22, 11, 13 March 1881, 86.

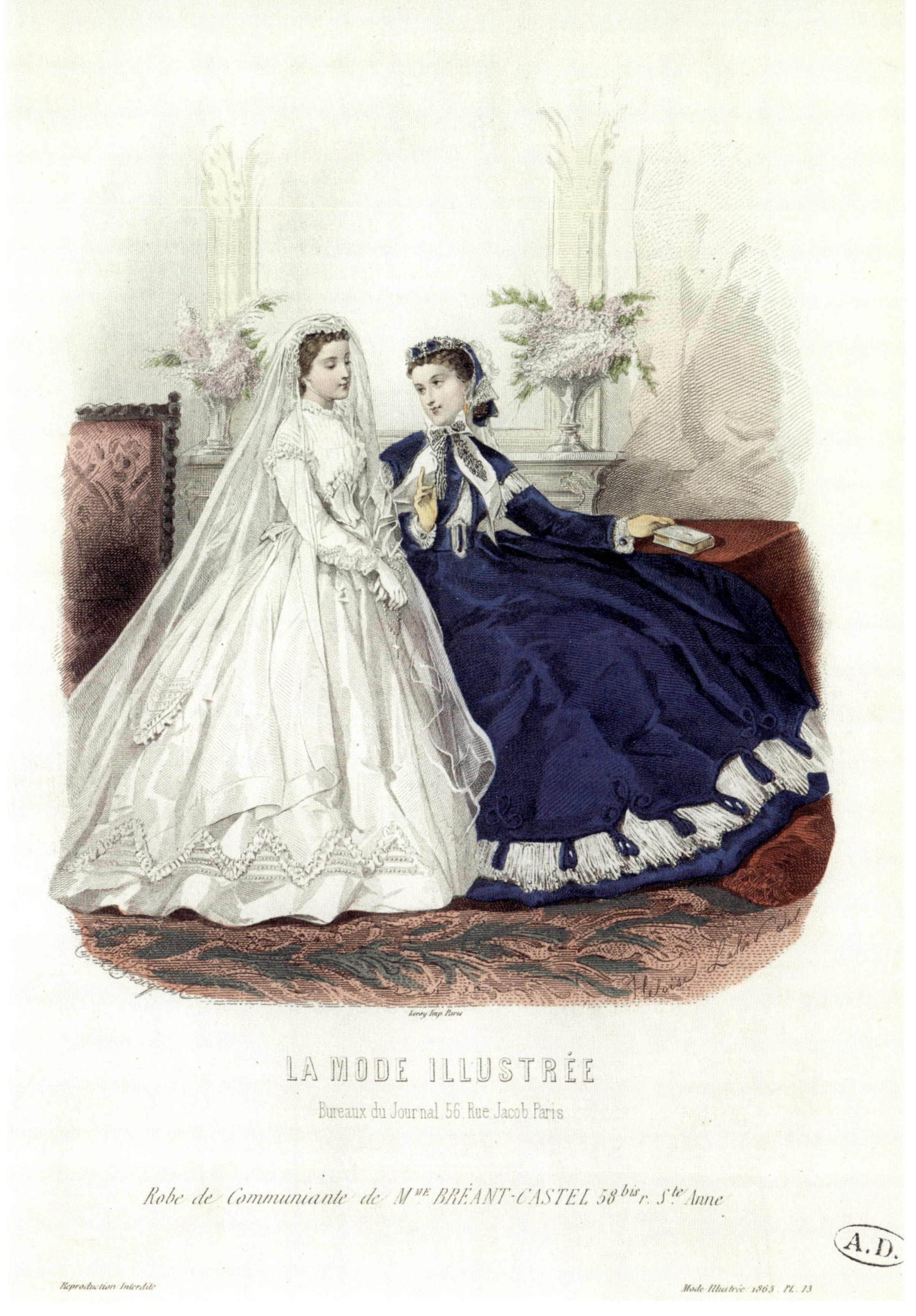

Didot Frères, *Robe de communiante de Mme Bréant-Castel*, in *La Mode Illustrée*, 1865

N° 9 (*avec patrons*). DIX-NEUVIÈME ANNÉE. Dimanche 3 mars 1878.

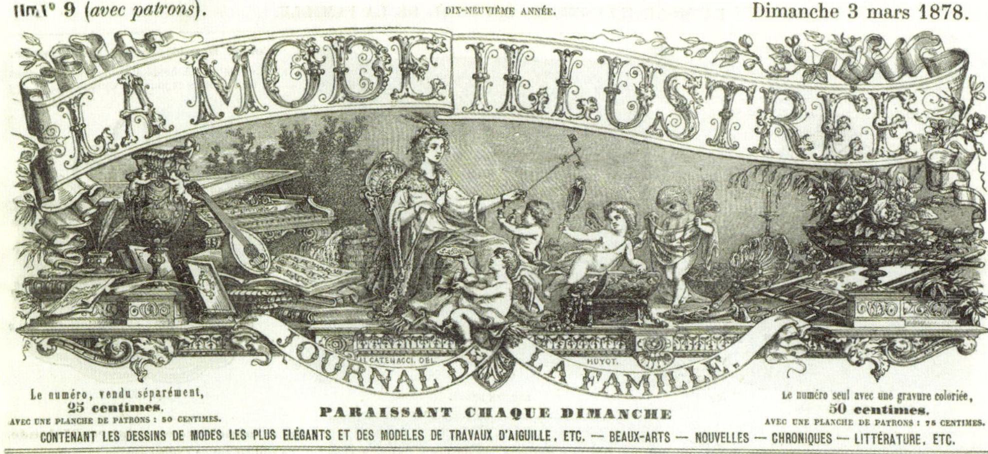

Le numéro, vendu séparément, **25 centimes.** AVEC UNE PLANCHE DE PATRONS : 50 CENTIMES.

PARAISSANT CHAQUE DIMANCHE

Le numéro seul avec une gravure coloriée, **50 centimes.** AVEC UNE PLANCHE DE PATRONS : 75 CENTIMES.

CONTENANT LES DESSINS DE MODES LES PLUS ELÉGANTS ET DES MODELES DE TRAVAUX D'AIGUILLE, ETC. — BEAUX-ARTS — NOUVELLES — CHRONIQUES — LITTÉRATURE, ETC.

PRIX DE LA MODE ILLUSTRÉE :
PARIS.
Un an, 12 fr. — Six mois, 6 fr. — Trois mois, 3 fr.
DÉPARTEMENTS (*frais de poste compris*).
Un an, 14 fr. — Six mois, 7 fr. — Trois mois, 3 fr. 50 c.
POUR L'ANGLETERRE.
Un an, franc de port, 18 s. — Cahier mensuel, 1 s. 6 pence.

RÉDACTION ET ABONNEMENTS, RUE JACOB, 56.
S'adresser pour la rédaction à
Mme EMMELINE RAYMOND,
Et pour les abonnements et réclamations à
M. A. FIRMIN-DIDOT.
Toutes les lettres doivent être affranchies.

PRIX DE LA MODE AVEC GRAVURES COLORIÉES :
PARIS.
Un an, 24 fr. — Six mois, 13 fr. — Trois mois, 6 fr. 75 c.
DÉPARTEMENTS (*frais de poste compris*).
Un an, 25 fr. — Six mois, 13 fr. 50 c. — Trois mois, 7 fr.
POUR L'ANGLETERRE.
Un an, franc de port, 30 s. — Cahier mensuel, 2 s. 6 pence.

Toute demande non accompagnée d'un bon sur la poste ou d'un mandat à vue sur Paris, à l'ordre de MM. Firmin-Didot et Ce, sera considérée comme non avenue.
— On s'abonne également chez tous les Libraires de France et de l'Étranger. (*Pour l'étranger le port en sus.*) — LONDRES : ASHER ET Co, 13, Bedford Street, Covent Garden, C. W. —

Sommaire. — Toilettes de première communion et de renouvellement de communion. — Corbeille à ouvrage. — Coussin brodé. — Vide-poches. — Suite de l'alphabet. — Fichu à plastron. — Corsage en faye. — Robe en cachemire de l'Inde uni avec et sans mantelet. — Mantelet court. — Mantelet-visite. — Mantelet de demi-saison. — Col en toile. — Col et manchette en lacet et dentelle. — Col et manchette en guipure d'Irlande. — Col et manchette en dentelle. — Col et manchette en lacet russe. — Deux toilettes de première communion. — Mantelet avec manches simulées. — Mantelet pour dame âgée. — Toilette de diner. — Robe en cachemire de l'Inde crêpé. — Description de toilettes. — Modes. — TYPES ET CARACTÈRES : la Femme pratique. — NOUVELLE : la Future du baron Jean.

Corbeille

A OUVRAGE.

La figure 62 (*verso*) appartient à cet objet.

En baguettes de jonc noir verni à boules dorées. Doublures en reps de soie rose formant des bouillonnés entre les baguettes. Le bord supérieur est garni d'un lambrequin en drap blanc découpé à l'emporte-pièce, sur lequel on a brodé au passé et point russe le dessin que représente la figure 62. Les myosotis sont exécutés avec de la soie bleue et jaune d'or. Les boutons de rose sont en soie rose et soie olive. Une ruche de ruban olive, ornée de boutons roses, cache la couture du lambrequin. Le fond se compose d'une feuille de carton recouverte de reps rose. Nœuds en ruban rose.

Vide-poches.

La figure 61 (*verso*) appartient à cet objet.

En osier verni noir et or. Le dos est garni d'un ornement en jonc doré ; le lambrequin en satin nuance *bordeaux* doublé de gaze raide, bordé de bandes de drap blanc découpé. Après avoir appliqué ces bandes sur le fond de satin, on reporte sur celui-ci le dessin que représente la figure 61. Les étoiles, en drap blanc, sont fixées par des brins croisés de soie nuance bordeaux, puis ornées de points noués en même soie. Le reste de la broderie est fait avec de la soie blanche au point d'arête, point-chainette et point russe. La broderie des bandes de drap blanc est faite sur le bord inférieur au passé, point d'arête et point-chaînette, avec de la soie de cordonnet ; sur le bord supérieur, avec du cordonnet d'or fixé par des points transversaux de soie noire. Le reste de la broderie, au point russe, point noué et double croix, est fait avec de la soie nuance bordeaux. Une ruche en ruban de satin nuance bordeaux couvre la couture du lambrequin. Sur le couvercle, nœud en même ruban.

Coussin brodé.

La figure 33 (*recto*) appartient à cet objet.

En satin nuance bordeaux. Encadrement capitonné ayant 7 centimètres de largeur. Le

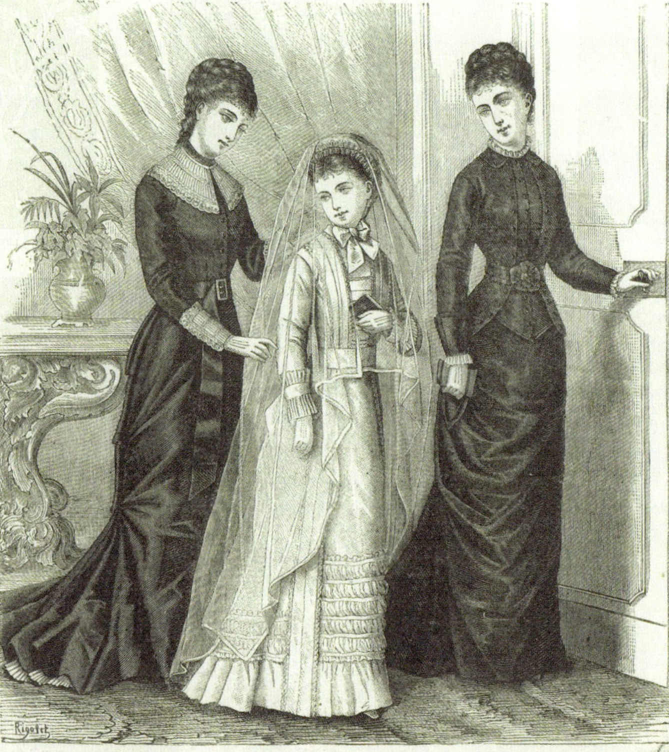

TOILETTE DE RENOUVELLEMENT. TOILETTE DE PREMIÈRE COMMUNION. TOILETTE DE RENOUVELLEMENT.
Modèles de chez Mme Fladry, rue Richer, 43. (Explications sur la planche de patrons.)

Anonymous, *Toilettes de renouvellement, toilette de première communion*, in *La Mode Illustrée*, Vol. 19 No. 9, 3 March 1878

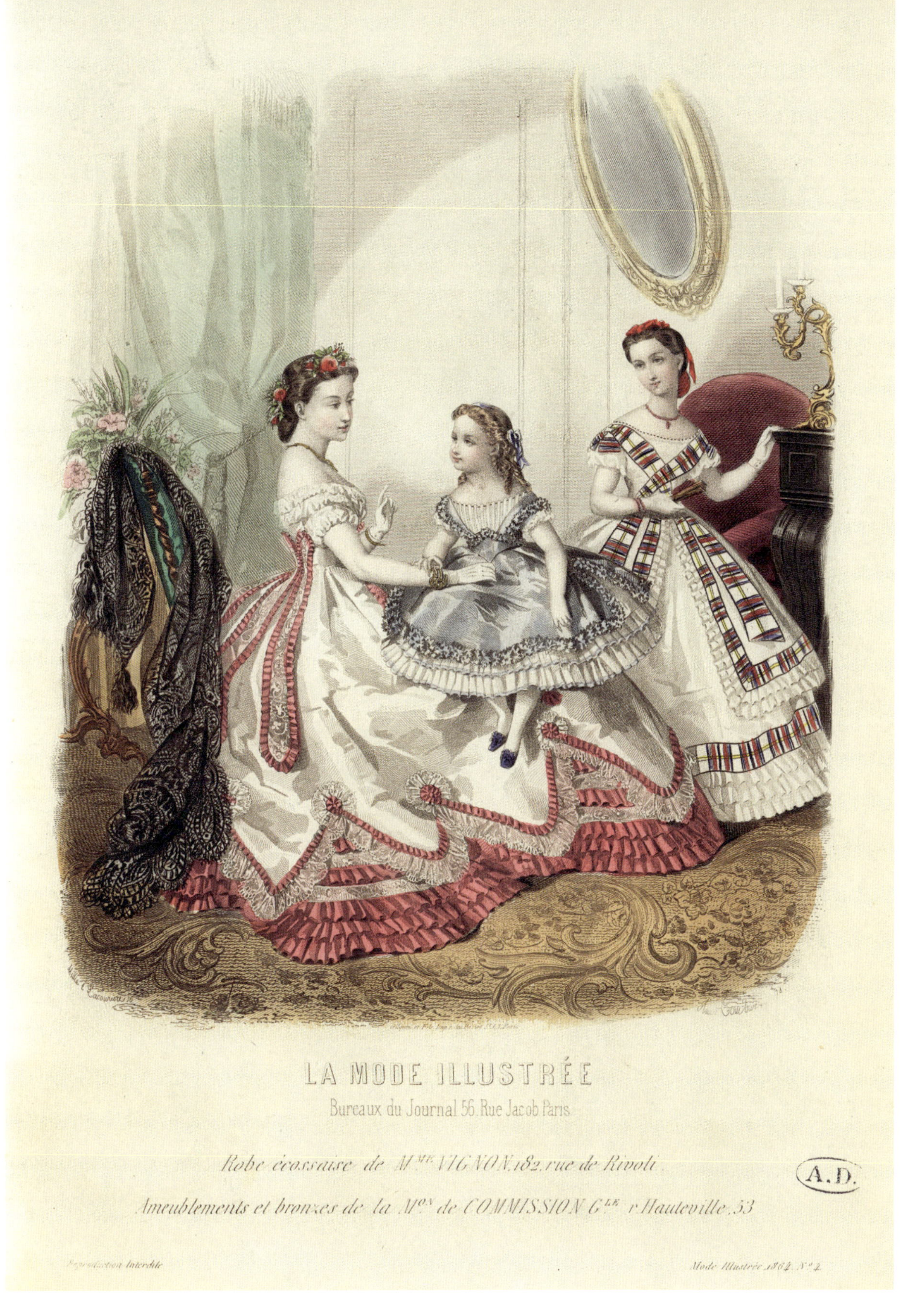

Didot Frères, *Robe écossaise de Mme Vignon, 182 rue de Rivoli*, in *La Mode Illustrée*, No. 4, 24 January 1864

Veil of a Communion dress, 1955–1960

Communion crown, 1940–1950

Communion crown, Lier, 1950–1960

Unfinished Communion crown, Lier, 1950–1960

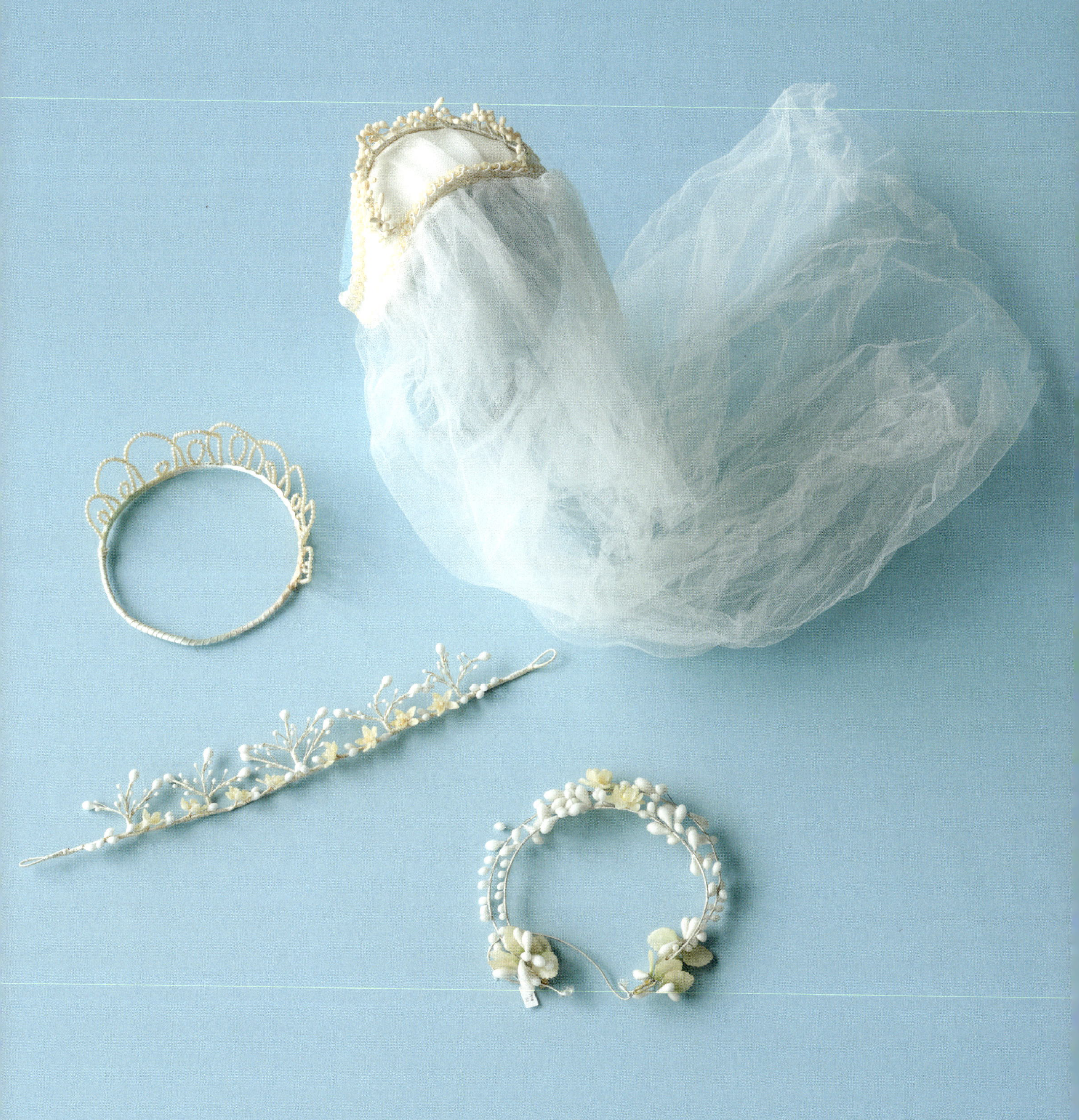

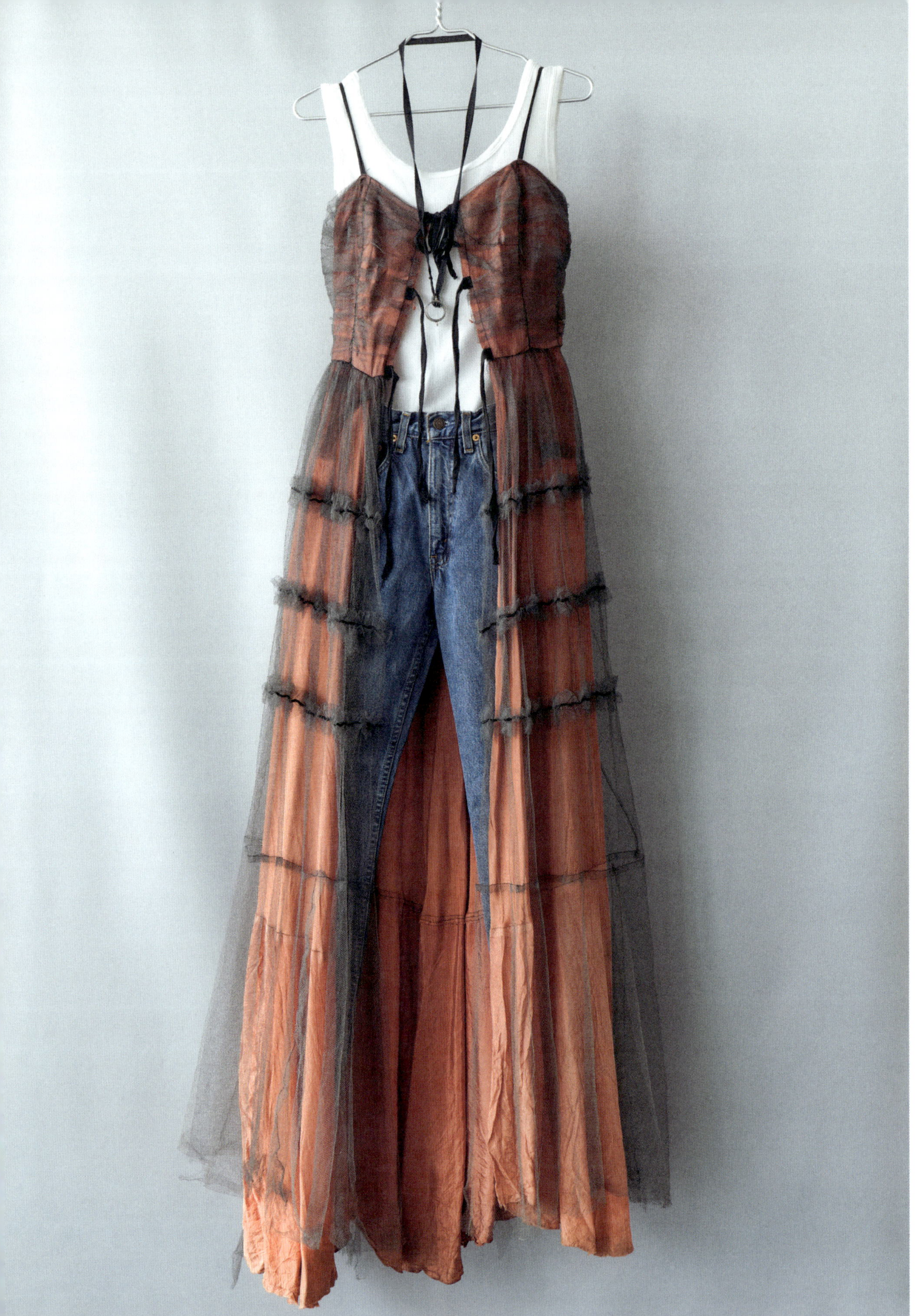

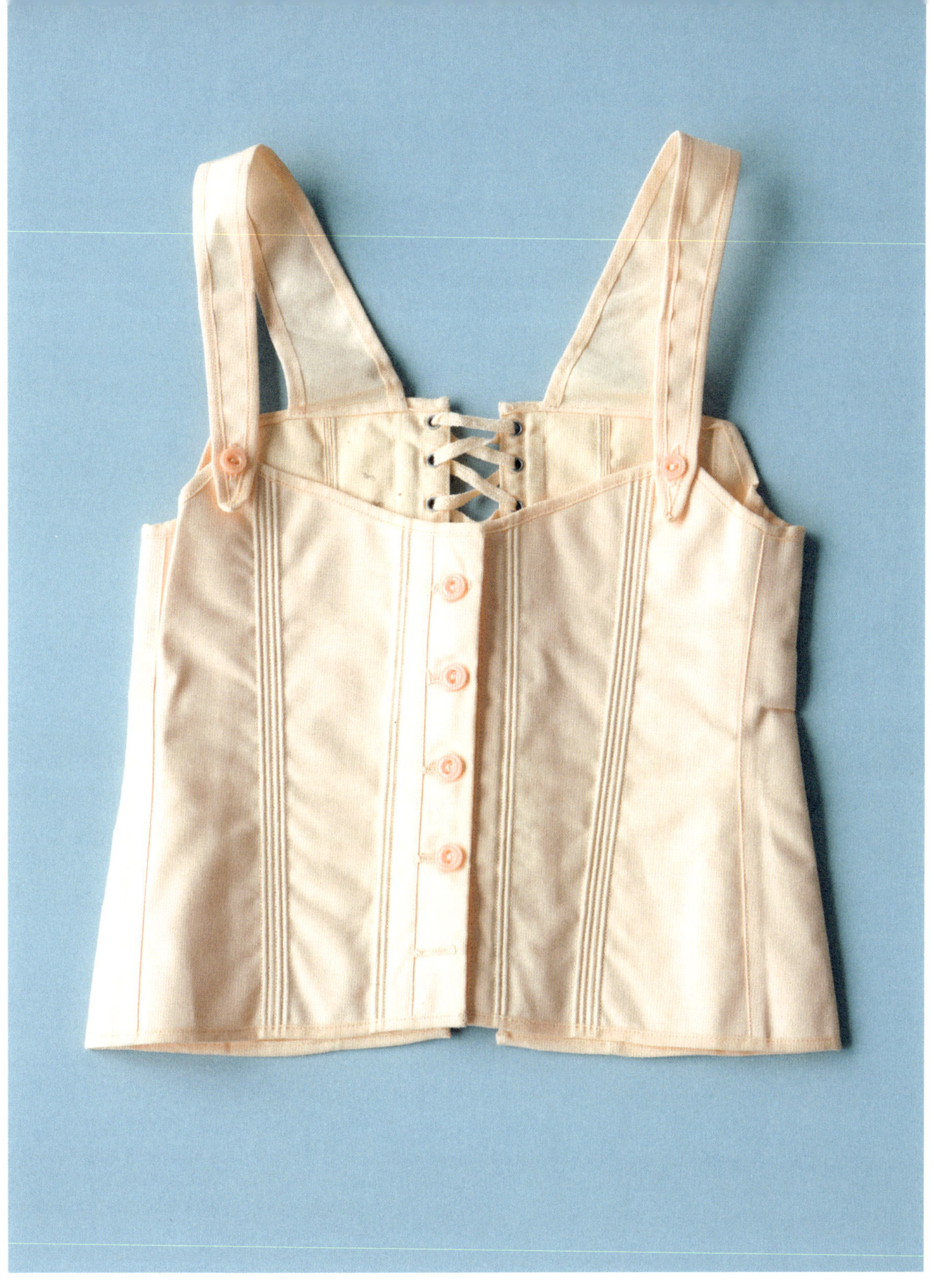

Maison Martin Margiela
Spring-Summer 1991

Child's corset in pink cotton satin,
reinforced with boning, 1920–1930

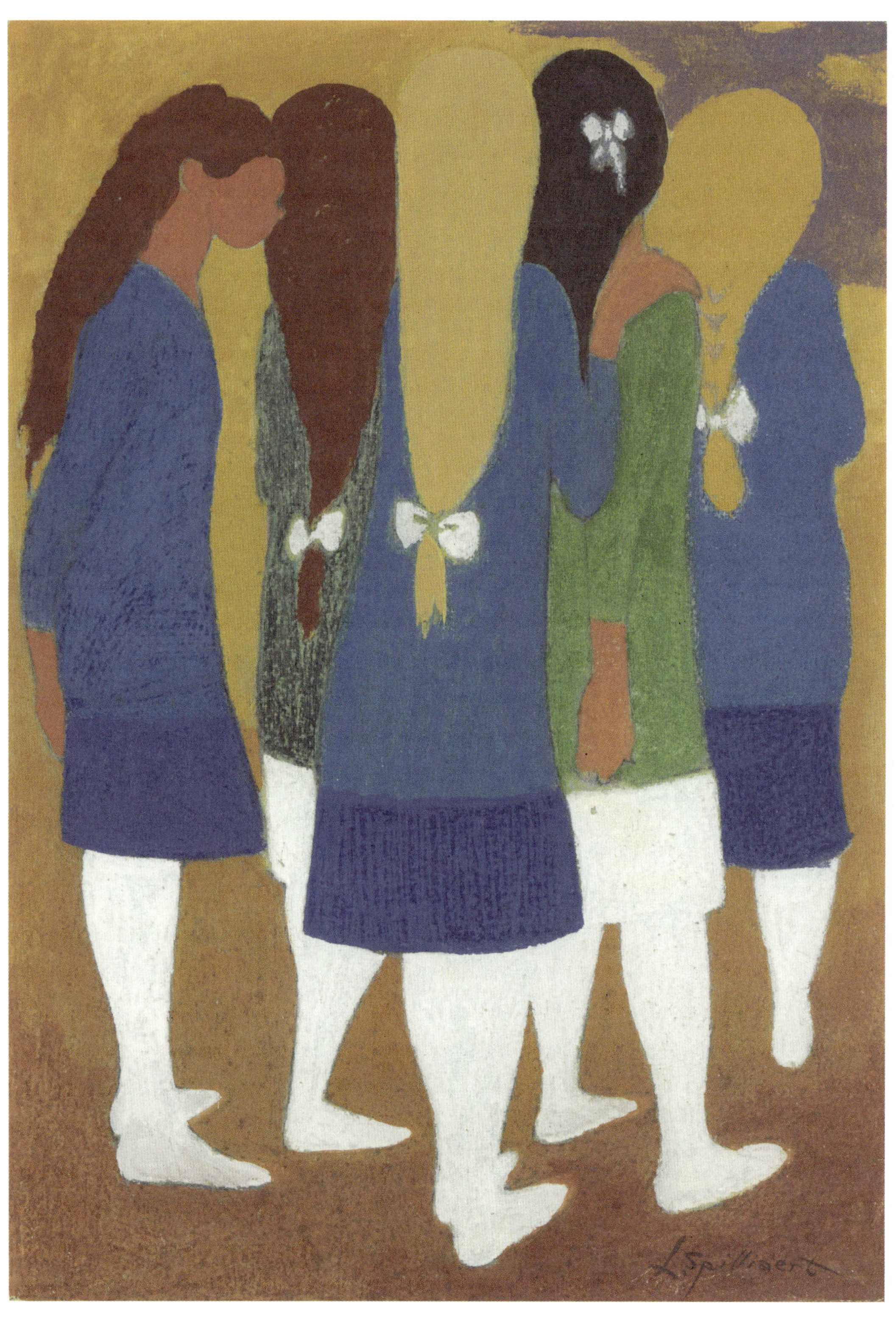

Léon Spilliaert
Girls with white stockings, 1912
Pastel, coloured pencil and oil pastel on paper

Frida Orupabo
On Her Mind, 2022
Collage with paper pins

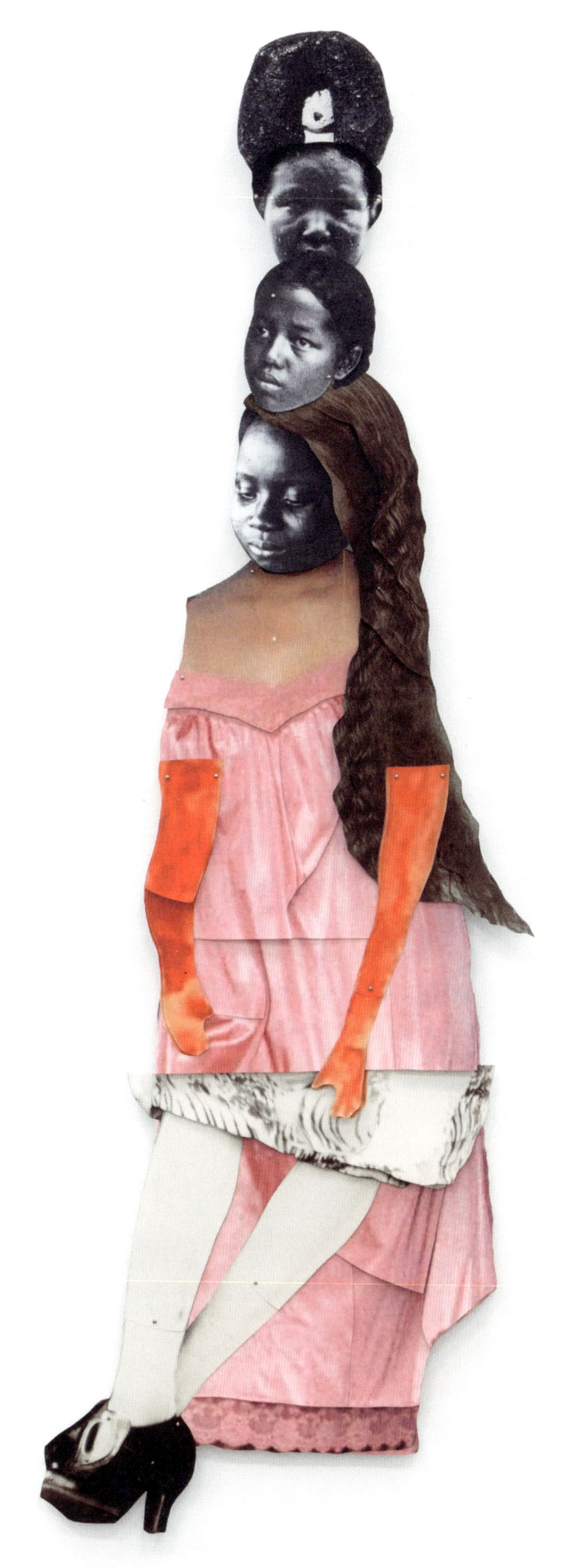

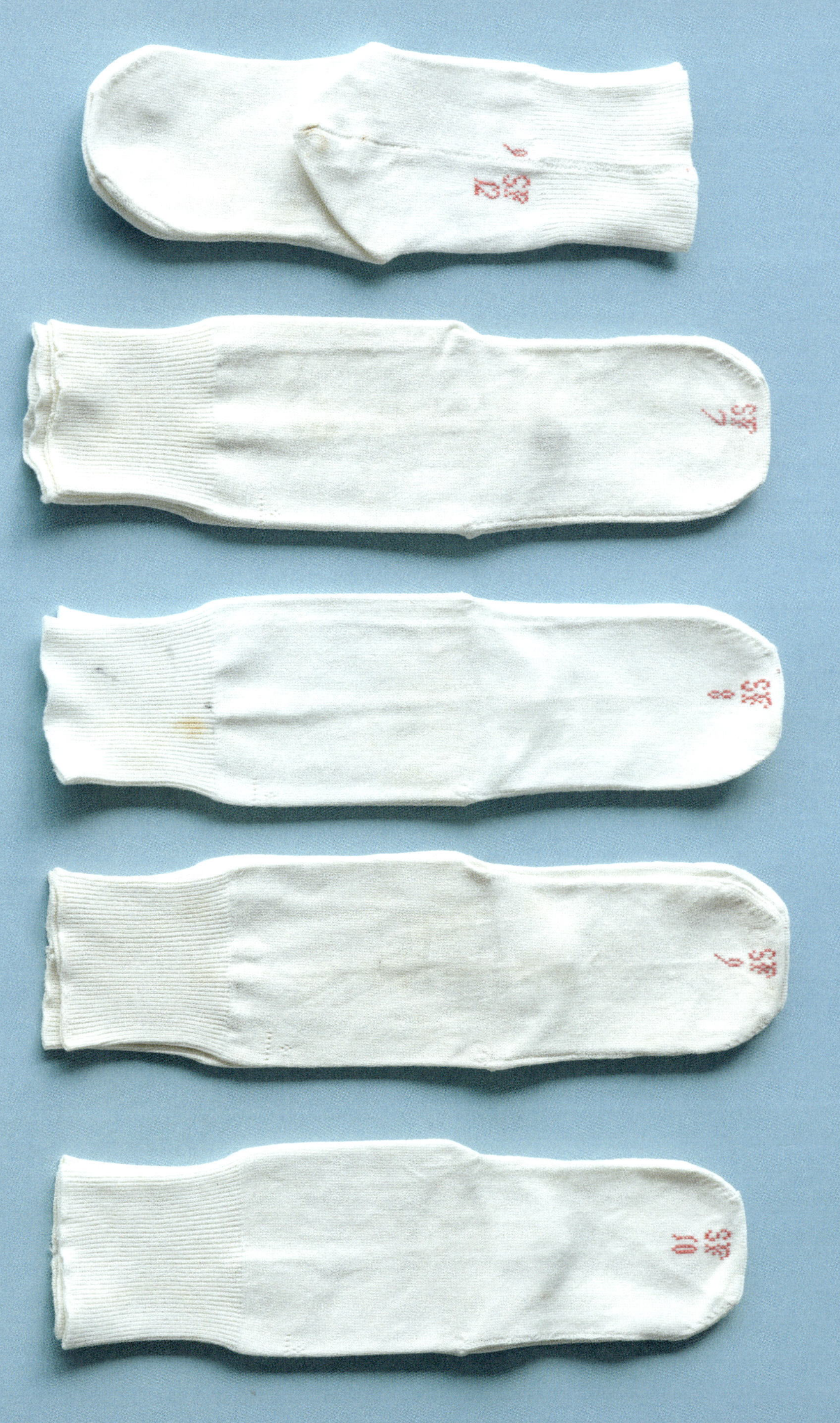

archetypes

Claire Marie Healy

white socks

In a certain vision of mid-century Americana, white socks feel as substantive of ideas of girlhood as a white T-shirt does of masculinity. Both items herald the birth of the teenager: bobby-soxers, so called for their preference for white ankle socks worn with loafers, were the first fangirls of the century (but when dancing with boys on linoleum gymnasium floors, it's *shoes off, please*). In fact, for an item that mothers have always pulled onto the feet of nice little girls well before their adolescence, white socks have always signalled the teenager's rebellious streak. It was only in the 1930s that young women even began to wear ankle socks rather than stockings, because to do so only became possible with the advent of women's trousers. As such, they were reserved for sports such as tennis and running, an association that still figures today.

From these early days of white socks as a tool for girls to move with more freedom, through to their use by the screaming girl-fans of artists such as Elvis and The Beatles, it's a *sock*-hop, skip and a jump to those girl-fuelled subcultures that went one step further, pulling on their white socks with subversive intention. In the UK in the 1960s, they were worn knitted and up to the knee by Mary Quant acolytes in miniskirts; on the alt-rock scene of the USA in the early-to-mid 1990s, white socks were seen paired with Mary Jane heels and babydoll nightdresses in a parodic interpretation of the ultra-childish. White socks, however, have probably been central to the look of one teen-girl subculture more than any other — for *kogyaru* in Tokyo in the 1990s, ribbed white cotton socks are worn oversized, white and loose around the ankles, thus easily picking up dirt from Shibuya pedestrian crossings. The moniker (meaning 'against *gyaru*') and schoolgirl-inspired look were a protest against the neat professional class that young women were increasingly expected to aspire to and join. Such uses of white socks demonstrate that while on the one foot the item is basic, on the other it is a tool in service of the contradictions of girlhood.

Children's socks, 1850–1880

hair slides

Despite its various names — hair clip, kirby grip, bobby pin, barrette — the humble hair slide is one of the most unchanging items of girl-coded dress in the last one hundred years. Yet it has rarely symbolised simply one thing, taking on contradictory ideas every time it is placed on, scraped through or clipped into our hair. Cheap, miniscule and yet highly visible, the origins of the 'bobby pin' are the hairstyle which gave the accessory its name and necessitated its usage: in the 1920s across Europe and America, parents despaired as their daughters cut their hair into sharp bobs, influenced by the flappers of the silent movie era whose image they were consuming. In this way, the hair slide is the first adornment that captures a certain dance that teenage girls will continue to perform throughout history: a balancing act of obedience and rule-breaking; self-control and self-adornment; innocence and sexuality. The style of short, uncovered hair with a slide fastened through it was an entry-point to flapper style, and an exit from daughterhood.

For Black 'daughters of' with Afro hair throughout the century, the colourful and vibrant barrette takes on another, more intimate meaning: here, it is attached to the intricate process of hair care between mothers and daughters, as well as public-facing notions of respectability in the context of white supremacy. Writer Emma Dabiri draws out such complexities of Black girlhoods and self-presentation in her book *Don't Touch My Hair*, writing that bold and colourful hair slides and baubles 'belong to a black aesthetic that is dismissed as "ghetto" until, of course, it becomes popularised by a white person and is reimagined as a trend'. The simple hair slide resonates with the politics already implicit in ideas of girlhood, especially Black girlhoods: all those projections of neatness, femininity and control that are historically entangled with the hair on girls' heads. Its simple shape and practical function are also why, as a fashion item, a hair slide is so archetypal that it can provide a jumping-off point for the experiments of designers: just look at the hair slides from designers such as Simone Rocha, Mei Kawajiri (Nails by Mei) in collaboration with D'heygere and Petra Collins, and Ashley Williams, who all take that archetypal straight line in strange new directions.

Micaiah Carter
***Adeline in Barrettes*, 2018**

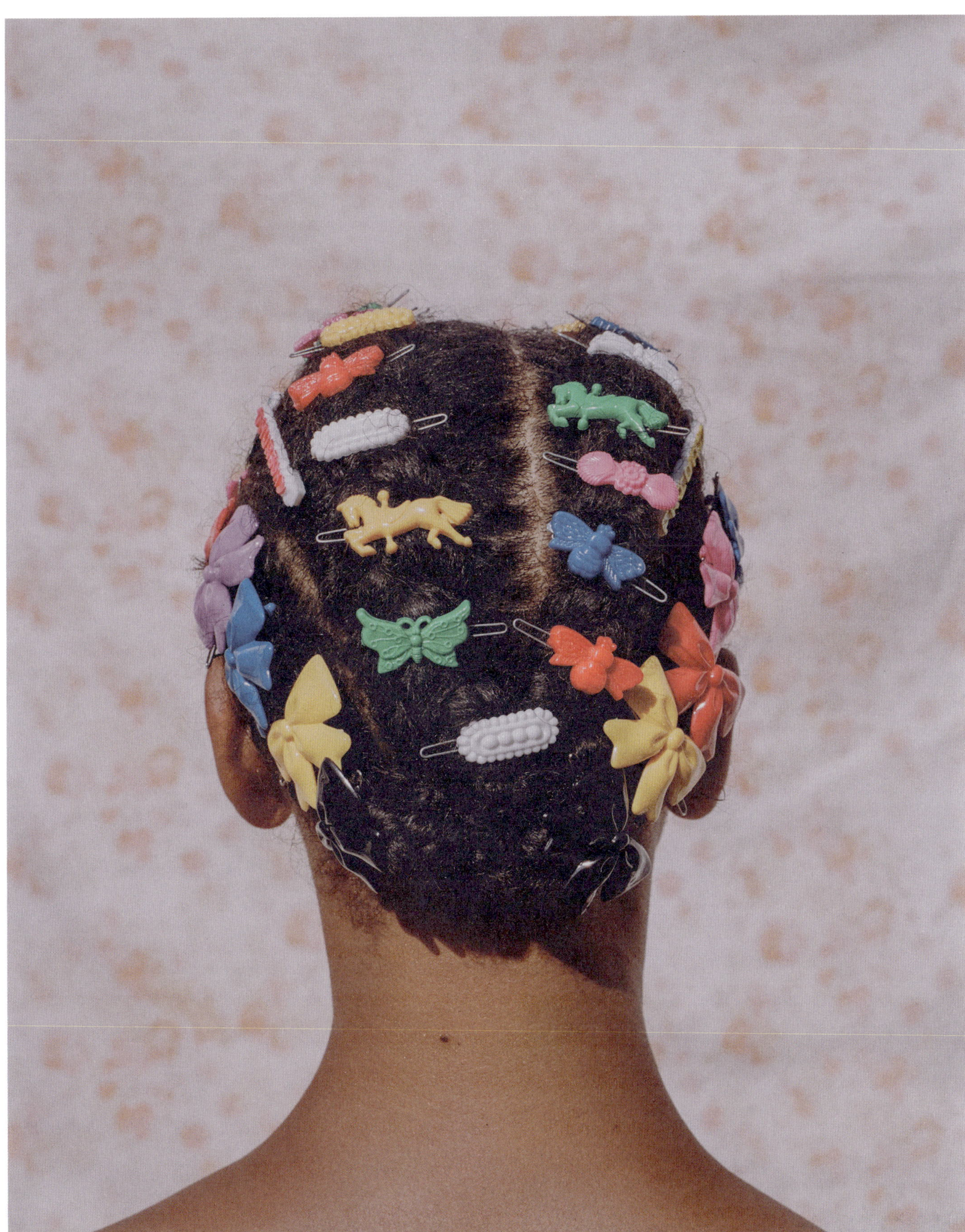

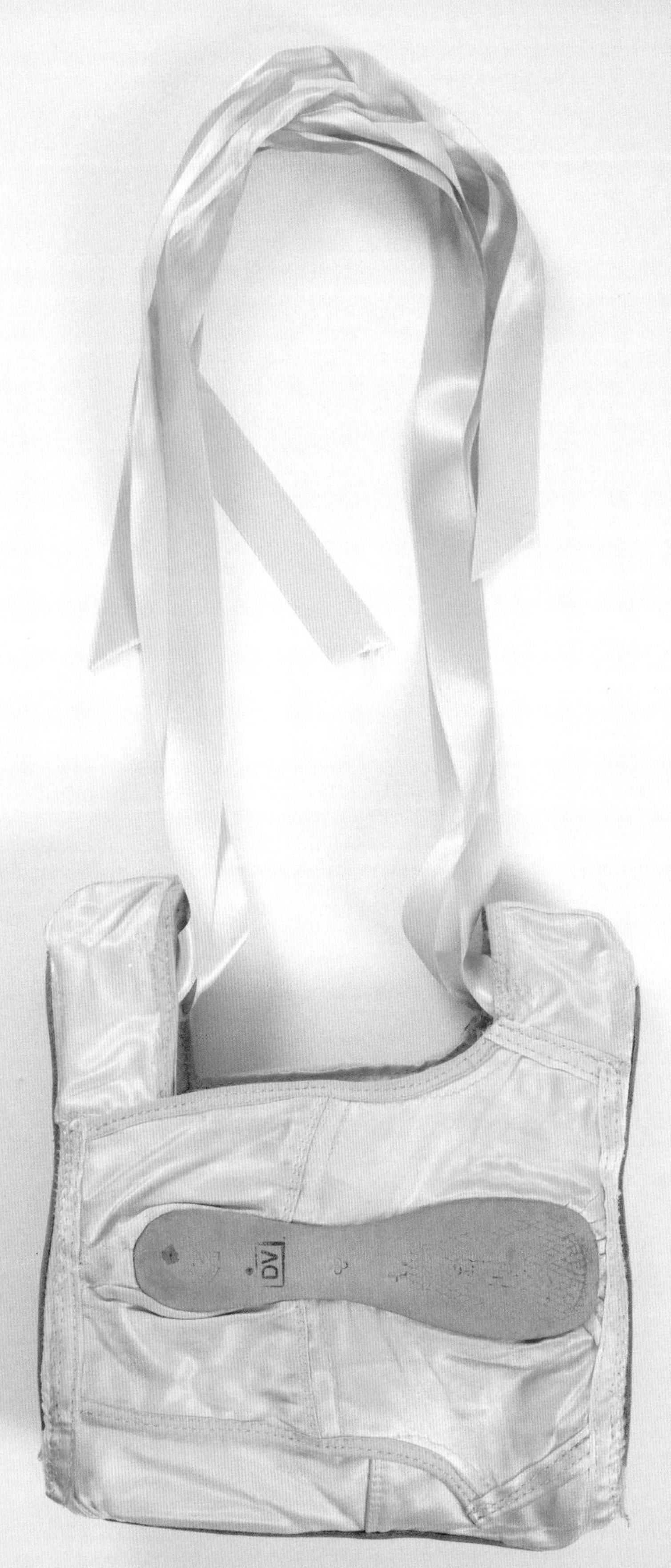
DV

ballet shoes

Picture a pair of ballet shoes. Are they on a foot: being worn? If so, are they flat on the floor, or vertical? Still, or pirouetting? (Even stamped in emoji-form, they are after all *en pointe*). Certainly, such a foot belongs to a girl — in fact, I would wager that the shoe and the ballerina's foot are one and the same in your mind, despite the fact that a ballet dancer will go through hundreds of individual pairs in her career, and several in the course of a mere week (some, such as prima ballerina Margot Fonteyn, have been known to clock up a pair a day). Think of a ballet shoe as a butterfly — their beauty is something to do with their short lifespans.

But when this shoe — also known as the pointe shoe, after its signature function in dance, or a toe shoe, after its signature pressure-point — is removed from the foot, we don't recognise it. After use in rehearsal or on stage, ballet shoes appear grubby, almost fleshy; their ribbons, if they remain laced into the shoes, unspool like entrails.

When it comes to a ballet shoe's anatomy, it is the shank — which forms the insole of the shoe — that provides the spine and the strength. The idea is that the bone of a girl's foot is one and the same with the bone of the shoe (which, of course, it isn't: young girls' bones *grow*). Such a shoe is intricately connected with girlhood, in part because to graduate to wearing them, the girl-ballerina has to be pubescent: like with the average age of first periods, girls go 'on point' at age twelve or thirteen. Despite contemporary physical therapists advising this age should be more like fifteen, the tradition remains.

The rituals between young girl and pointe shoe also abound with deeply held superstitions: a particular inscription becoming an article of faith, or a tradition. Little girls wait outside rehearsals and stage doors to take the used, signed shoes of their favourite ballerinas: they pin them to their bedroom walls like *ex-votos*. Ballet master George Balanchine's ingénue Suzanne Farrell always sewed the ribbons on her pointe shoes with twenty-nine stitches due to the fact she had counted twenty-nine steps the day she got into the School of American Ballet (this same day, as was standard, Balanchine had inspected her feet). But for dancers of colour, customisation rituals have long been connected with necessity as much as imagination: transforming the standard peachy tone to match their actual skin tone — hence maintaining a ballerina's ideal 'line' on stage — has required generations of young dancers to 'pancake' their shoes with brown foundation. As late as 2018, shoemakers such as Freed of London finally caught up: they now make shoes to match all skin tones.

Maison Martin Margiela
Autumn-Winter 2004–2005

hoodie

It's hard to tell who the first girl to wear a hoodie was. Perhaps it was Little Red Riding Hood who, coming up against the loss of innocence at the mercy of the Big Bad Wolf, might be one of the first bedtime story protagonists who feels teen-girl coded. Today, some of the greatest pressures enacted on teenage girls — and the quiet ways they resist those pressures — seem to crumple and coalesce around this item of clothing: usually jersey-cotton, soft, oversized. The story of the hoodie in the 2000s is a story of the everyday life of the girl, and contains certain rights in its folds: a girl's right to cover up, a girl's right to comfort, and (especially with the hood up) a girl's right to anonymity. To *not* be visible.

Like many garments symbolic of girlhood that are 'borrowed from the boys' — the androgyny of the leather jacket since the 1960s, or baggy jeans in the 1990s — the hoodie has been broadly associated with a moral panic around juvenile girl delinquency in our modern era. From 'chavs' in the UK, to B-girls in New York, such coverage says much about how the media disenfranchises girls through misrepresentation. But what really seems to threaten the patriarchy about this garment is the way it covers up the girl: offering ownership over her own body, it allows the girl to not partake in the usual expectations placed upon her. One need only consider the criticism provoked by Billie Eilish's propensity to wear baggy hoodies in her early career, swiftly followed by outrage when she took part in her first skin-revealing shoot, to understand that for teenage girls — who are always surveilled, famous or not — it is impossible to win. Another link to pop stardom is the rise of the hoodie as merch: the item is the perfect blank canvas to display all kinds of strongly felt associations.

Maybe the influence of the hoodie shows us that comfort, not rebellion, is the hidden desire that more profoundly shapes these contemporary girlhoods — in such a reading, its bagginess and softness become invested with a kind of potent longing. In a world hostile to girlhood(s) in ever-shifting ways, the desire to be comfortable outweighs the desire to display.

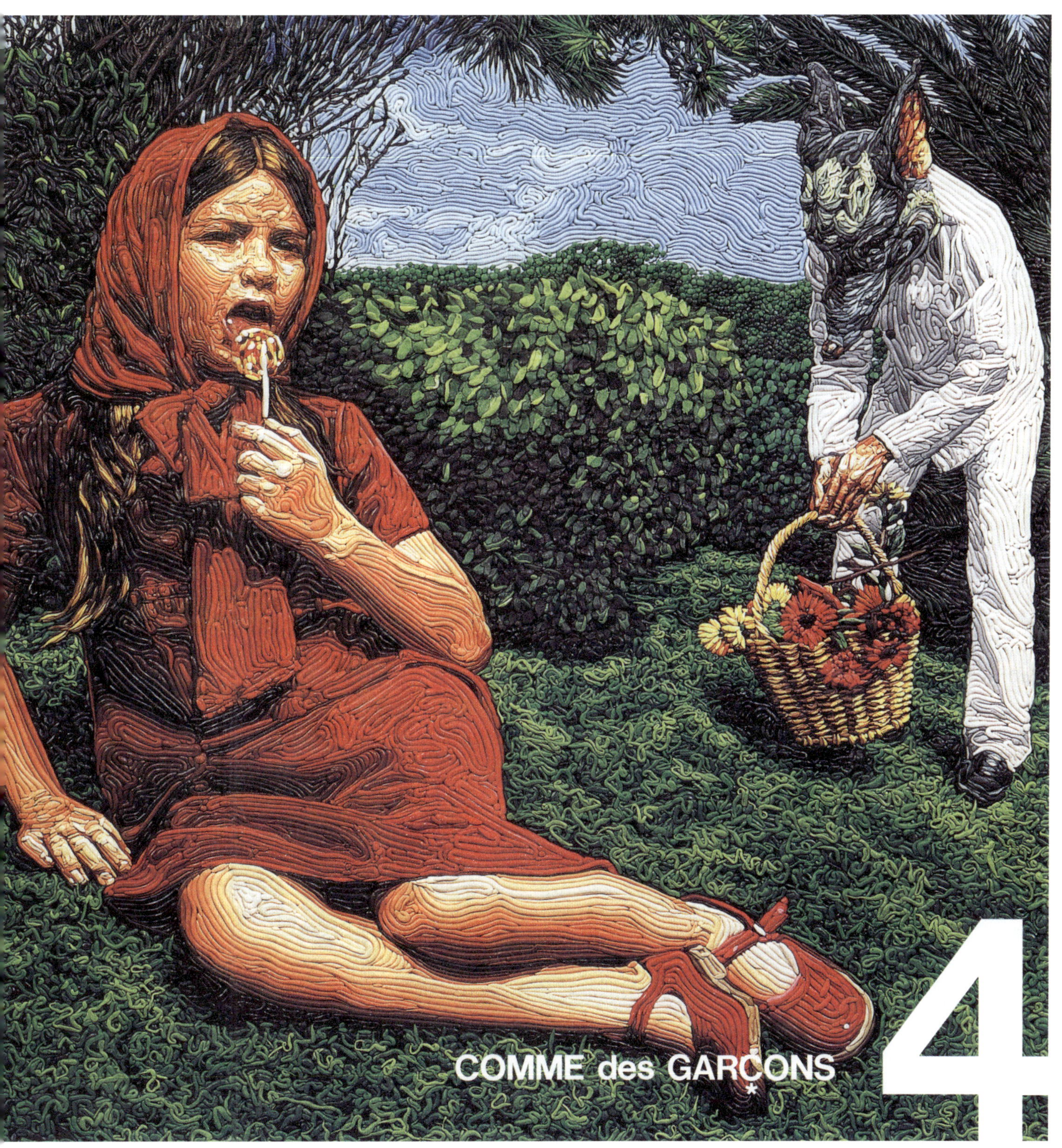

COMME des GARÇONS
Autumn-Winter 2008–2009 campaign by Mondongo

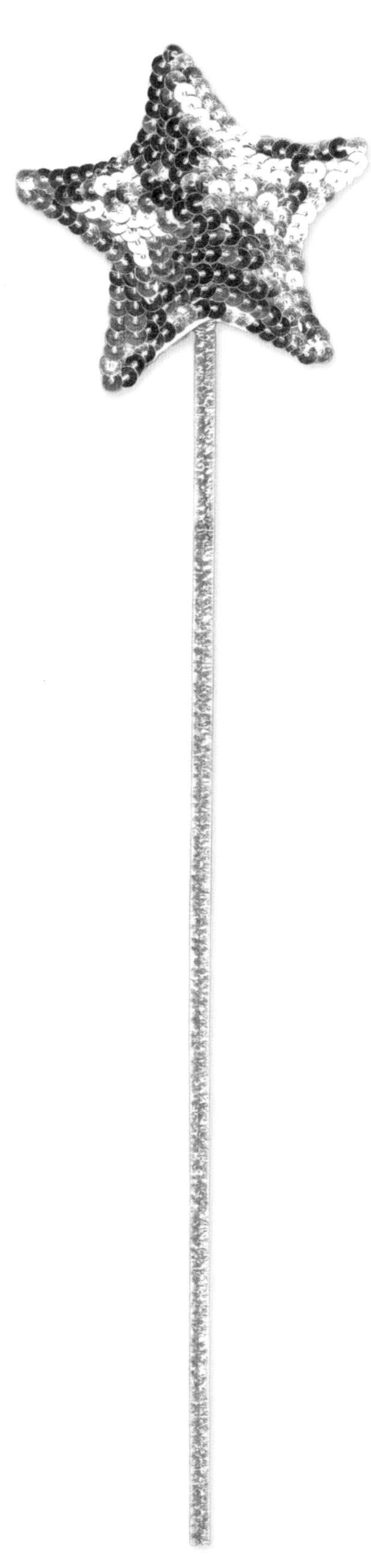

glitter

What is glitter? Intangible and physical, cosmetic and utilitarian, throwaway and sublime, and finite and forever, glitter reflects the many contradictions that stick to girlhood. Sparkling (for adolescents, on everything from clothes to nail polish to roll-ons to T-shirts) glitter — which doesn't degrade and is impossible to remove — feels so effervescent and unreal that it's hard to remember someone actually had to invent it (that person was an American machinist, Henry F. Ruschmann, who created it accidentally in the 1930s when he invented a machine originally designed to cut photo films and paper).

The cultural association of glitter with girls comes from its appeal to the magpie-eyed: glitter is school discos, Barry M pots, pencil-cases and hair stuck down on the skull. But the fact that glitter — a petroleum product made of particles of plastic — exists for aesthetic delight alone is a problem. Despite global activist movements fighting climate change in the public eye, such as the teenage girls of Fridays For Future or Just Stop Oil (many of whom spent time in prison for their underage protest actions), many young women display a disregard for sustainability. Just one glance at TikTok Christmas Haul clips — a time of year more glitter-covered than any other — will easily confirm this. But to pass judgement on these girls is to miss one of the prevailing issues with the way we conceptualise the fight against the climate crisis: as an issue that the youth are responsible for dealing with, rather than the adult lawmakers in charge.

But if glitter lacks definition, and can be widely found on any garment, accessory or make-up item, then it is a lack of definition that can feel like freedom. Cheap and widely available, glitter is often the first accessible tool that can be employed by trans and non-binary youths to experiment with the aesthetic pleasures of girlhood: experiments that shine a light on new forms of self-actualisation.

Taking us in with its shiny, sticky surfaces, glitter parallels an idea of girlhood as a state which, though bound to the physical in alarmingly non-biodegradable ways, transcends the actual years of adolescence to adhere to us forever. Such stickiness brings to mind those moments when, in our womanhood, we suddenly notice a single speck of glitter on our face in the mirror and wonder how on earth it got there.

Maison Martin Margiela
Autumn-Winter 2001–2002

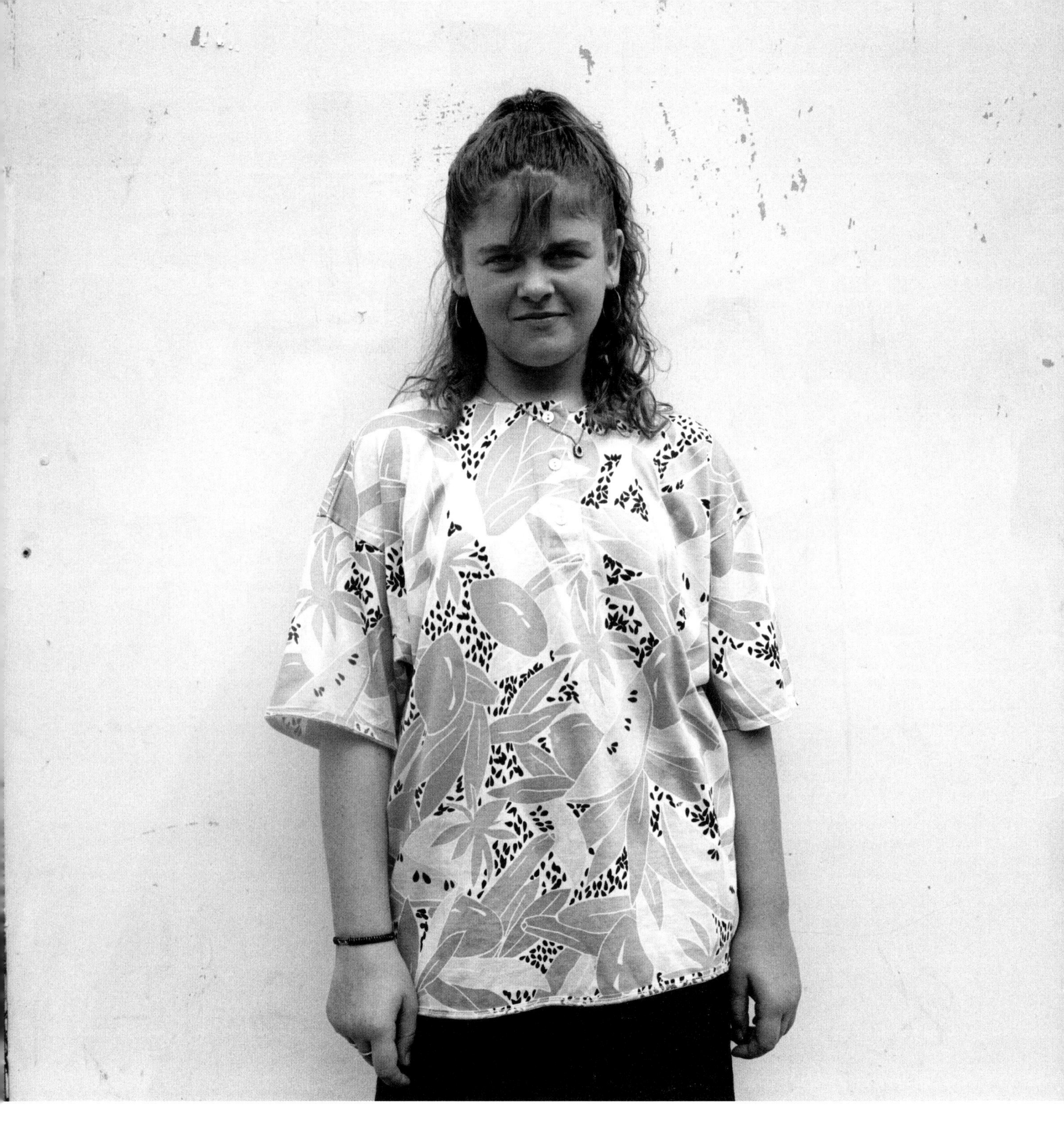

Nigel Shafran
Teenage Precinct Shoppers, 1990

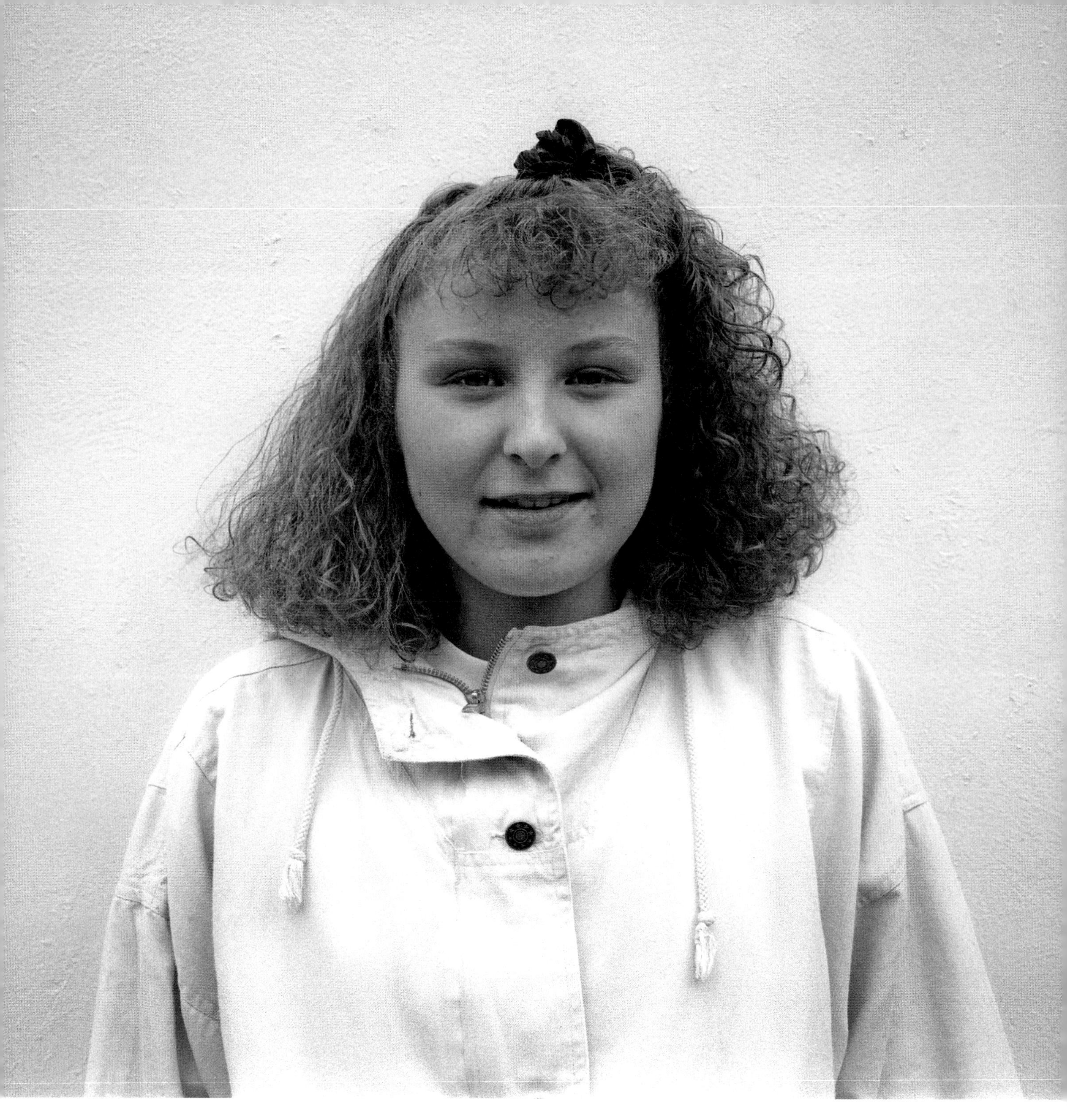

pp. 180–181

Jenny Watson
Cry / Neighbour, 2023
A4 coloured paper

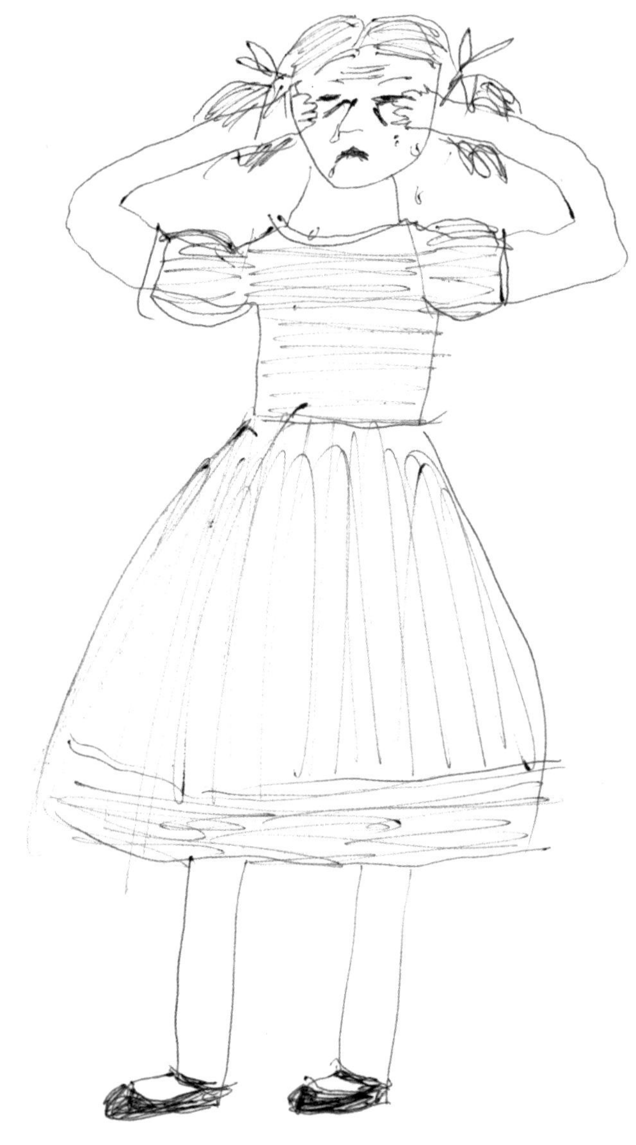

Cry

2003

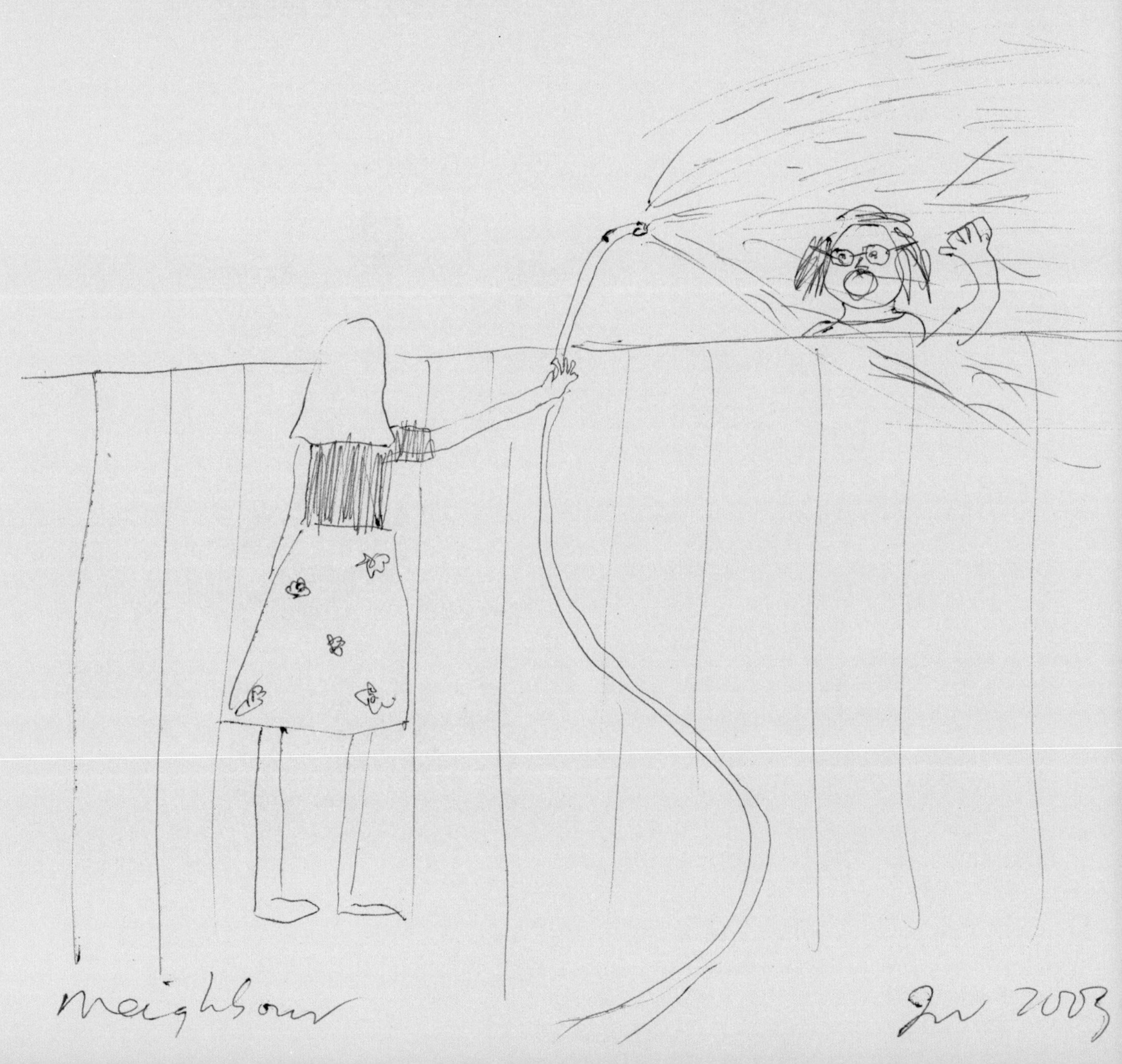
neighbour

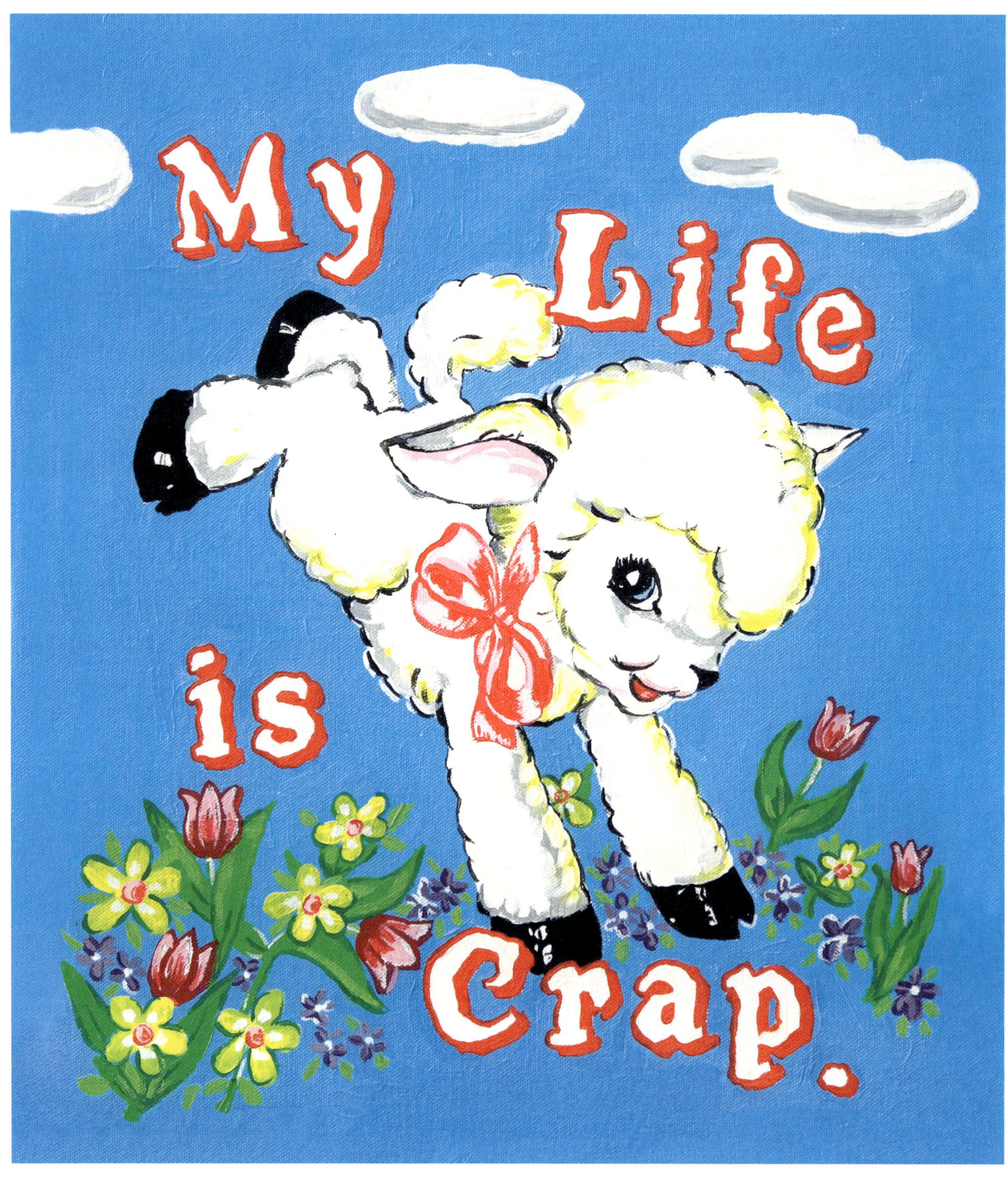

Magda Archer, *My Life is Crap*, as used in the
COMME des GARÇONS SHIRT Spring-Summer 2012 campaign

the teen brain

Peter Adriaenssens

boredom — the calm before the storm

'I'M BORED'

When puberty hits, boredom increases. Parents often worry that their teenager is caught up in a whirlwind of activities and that some calm and boredom would be more than welcome, or the teen feels that there is too much of the latter and continually complains: I'm bored.

FIRING ON ALL CYLINDERS

But this feeling can be very misleading. It gives the impression that life has ground to a standstill, while brain scans have revealed that the teen brain is firing on all cylinders. Lots of new connections are made, while networks that are not used are being eliminated or pruned. Below the waterline, a story of maturation and development is unfolding. In a sense, you could say it is like the calm before the storm — and for good reason. The adolescent is unravelling the threads of childhood. What remains, however, are loose threads that are still trying to find ways of weaving themselves into a fabric that connects to adulthood. Instead of the fun kid who used to love going to school and showed up punctually to football practice, parents are suddenly faced with a human who is seeking purpose and behaving erratically. The 'I'm bored' human dislikes anyone who says they know how to cure the boredom blues and rejects anyone who can't come up with a fun activity. What are your options, as a parent or as a friend? Bearing in mind all the signs of mental health concerns in teens, how can you be sure whether this behaviour is entirely normal or one on a long list of red flags? What do you call that? An annoying list, that's what.

LOOSE THREADS

Isn't it wonderful how a *desire for something* is inherent to boredom? That is also why it is so difficult to define the line between the bliss of doing nothing and dangerous silence. Slipping into daydreams, into games, into social media. Or into criminal behaviour 'out of boredom'. This is all very complex, but is society doing any better? Young people disparage adults who no longer know how to stop wars, enforce conventions, or resolve anything with dialogue despite their stellar school careers. Were they insufficiently bored perhaps? Did they spend too much time cherishing the wiring of their childhood, with lots of 'yes sir, no ma'am' copycat behaviour? Young people peer into the crack of time, so many layers, one rips the others to shreds, what is truth and what is fabrication, does it still have an identity, what is important? Is there any guidance?

THE CALM BEFORE THE STORM

Those who are bored are waiting for themselves. Educators are not there to provide continuous entertainment. Take your time, we tell them. We did.

BEHAVING ERRATICALLY

A DESIRE FOR SOMETHING

PEERING INTO THE CRACK OF TIME

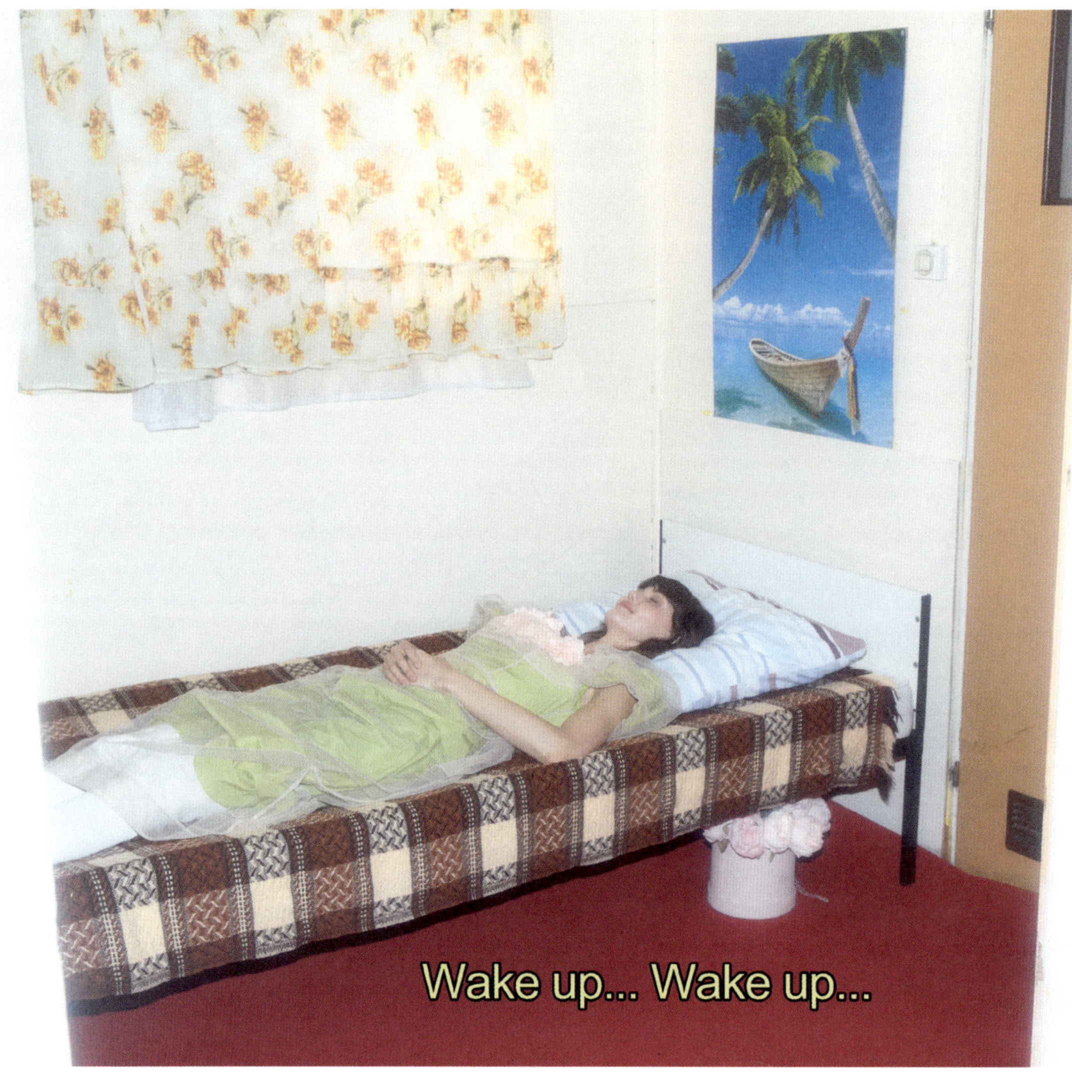

'I'd rather be asleep' editorial by Jumbo Tsui,
Lindsey Wixson wearing Simone Rocha Spring-Summer 2025

NIGHT OWLS

sleep — the clock is really ticking (in your head)

Teenagers are night owls. Their sleep-wake rhythm shifts. Sometimes melatonin, the hormone that makes us tired, plays a role in this. The signal that the brain sends that it is time to go to sleep is delayed, making it difficult to fall asleep. But there are all sorts of impediments that get in the way of sleep. In particular, stress and social media keep too many young people up well into the night.

STRESS

No big deal, you may think. But things are not that clear-cut. Without you knowing, the brain works hard while you sleep. Deep sleep, or non-REM sleep, is needed to process memories properly and store them in your memory. Some connections in your brain become stronger, allowing you to remember things. They sometimes refer to this sleep phase as the brain's washing machine. The cerebrospinal fluid drains waste products from the brain into your bloodstream, like a washing machine pumping out wastewater. In REM sleep, we dream, and brain activity increases again. Sleep can also help ease stress and regulate emotions. But that depends on how you feel when you go to bed. Young people tend to experience a lot of stress due to discussions on social media, conflicts, or the pressure of learning difficulties. Too much of this disrupts sleep, which becomes shorter and worse.

DEEP SLEEP

BRAIN ACTIVITY

So it is perfectly normal for teenagers to go to sleep a bit later, but the thing is, the world does not make that shift with them. So if you go to bed later after exercise, going out, or talking to friends, you still need to be at school at the same time every morning. The result? Sleep deprivation — and this has a wide range of consequences on several levels. Attention and concentration problems affect school performance; accessing memory also becomes more difficult. Unsurprisingly, adolescents' scores go up depending on whether they are given a test at 9 am or 11 am. Perhaps young people find the emotional ups and downs especially difficult. Impulsive reactions. Their self-control is weaker. If you are sleepy during the day you have less mental resilience. Making you more susceptible to negative thoughts. The reports of high rates of depression among young people are definitely related to this.

SOCIAL MEDIA

According to research, teens need 9 hours' sleep. 70% of teens don't get enough. Some understand the comparison with a gym workout better. You need rest and recovery after working your muscles or you will end up feeling sore. Self-control is that muscle. Looking for other solutions? There is a real fear that young people look for ways of concealing the effects of sleep deprivation and keep their pep by turning to stimulants or drugs. This marks a shift towards risky behaviour. You are less alert, will find it more difficult to assess situations adequately, and will become less adept at solving problems.

SLEEP DEPRIVATION

SELF-CONTROL

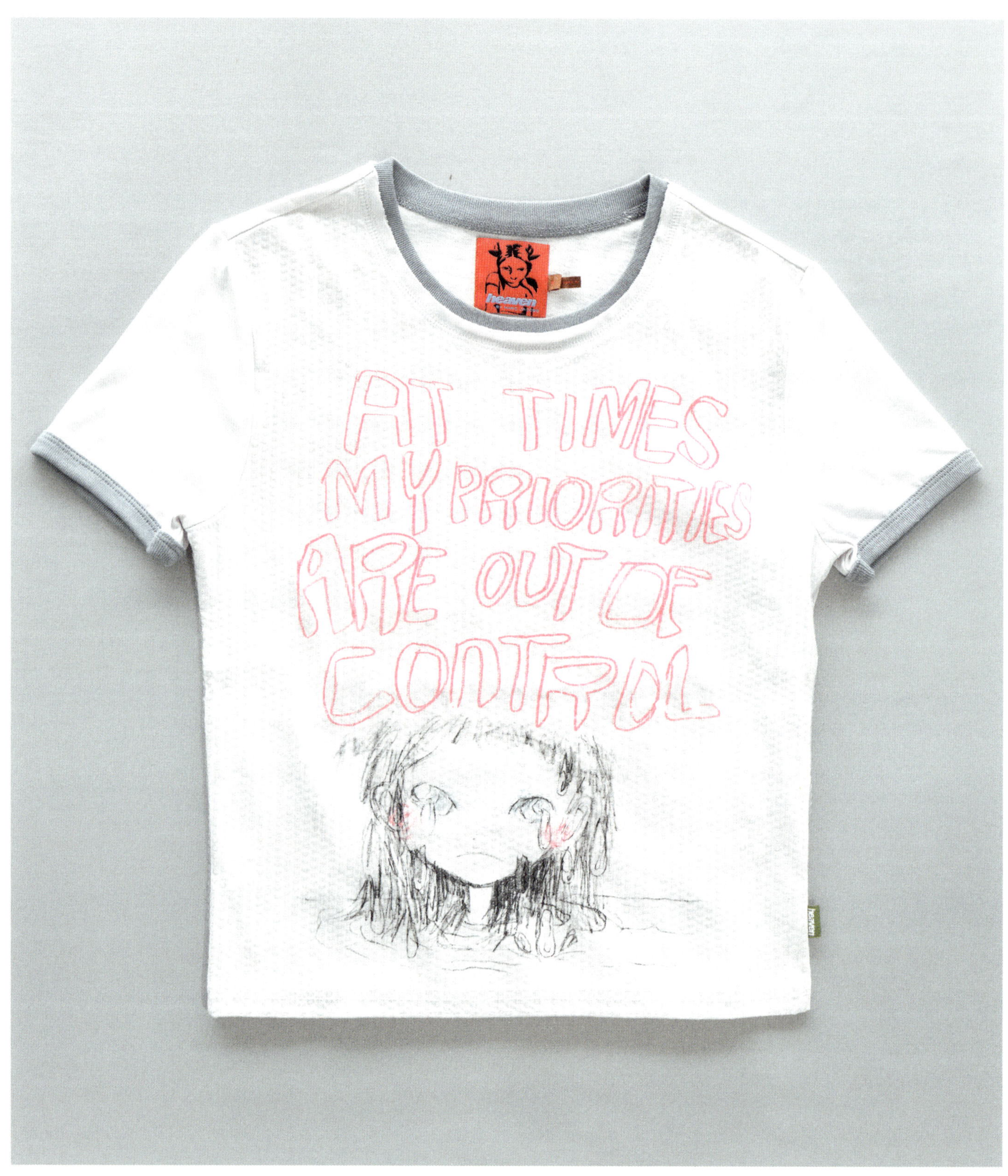

Heaven by Marc Jacobs Autumn-Winter 2023–2024,
'At Times My Priorities Are Out of Control' baby tee

MORE WORK, LESS FUN

Some teens move through adolescence effortlessly, without a hitch. But others kick up much more of a fuss while pulling away.

Research indicates that teens become more work and less fun to parent when adolescence sets in. Nice chats now seem a thing of the past as your child becomes less open, less willing to help, more self-centred, more impulsive. We now know the cause, thanks to brain scans. Adolescence — and to some extent hormones — triggers a structural reorganisation of the brain so as to optimise its function. This development takes time. Firstly, a lot changes because of the maturation of the emotion-focused regions in the brain that you have from before birth. Your rational, wise brain zones that think and develop solutions and later also rationalise your emotions only start to grow after birth. This renewal kicks into full force from adolescence. Big emotions can go either way because the wise part of your brain is still unable to override the emotional part. Sometime later, from the age of 14 onwards, this evolution becomes more visible as adolescents start to develop an identity. By 16, a real story of what you want to be, what you dream of becoming and doing in life is being woven, and this will continue to develop in the years to come, until the age of 25. What is noticeable is that this evolution is more difficult for boys than girls. Girls mature faster, which translates into being agreeable or reasonable, and more open in communication.

BIG EMOTIONS

GIRLS MATURE FASTER

BRAINS ARE INHIBITED

The risk of 'just for kicks', especially between the ages of 14 and 17, is a consequence of this gap in time between the emotional and smart brain regions, like an accelerator of impulsiveness that is being pressed. Breaking something for fun, bullying, dangerous driving, and criminal behaviour are some of the dangers that lurk.

SELF-CENTRED

That is why social media can have such a significant impact on a person's thoughts and behaviour. Another part of the teenage brain, the reward centre, amplifies the risks because it is so sensitive and even addicted to 'likes'. This also means that alcohol and drugs can act as a reward for this centre. However, because the brain is still developing and reorganising itself, the effect is stronger. Brains are inhibited, and must work even harder to keep up at school. Which puts teens at risk of reaching for alcohol and drugs again. If this behaviour continues over the years, the brain damage becomes more severe, and the highways of wiring become poorer and less qualitative.

From the age of 16 or 17, young people become more aware of the effect of their behaviour. They are less inclined to follow trends or groups. Their identity becomes clearer. As they grow older, the balance between thoughts, feelings and behaviour improves. This is not always an easy time for educators, parents or teachers. Sometimes, they think that all their efforts during the childhood years were in vain. But this is not the case. At the end of the journey, sometime during our twenties, everything is integrated.

'JUST FOR KICKS'

The adolescent brain really undergoes an important evolution, and our society should feel challenged in the process. The impact of influencers sucking others in with silly theories, the dangerous nutrition misinformation that all too often results in anorexia from a very young age, other harmful self-images... Often these are adults who are targeting a brain at an important but vulnerable stage. The fact that policy makers are saying that war is imminent, democracy is crumbling, there is no budget for climate action, and international conventions are of little use: it all has an impact on the choices teenagers make.

EVERYTHING IS INTEGRATED

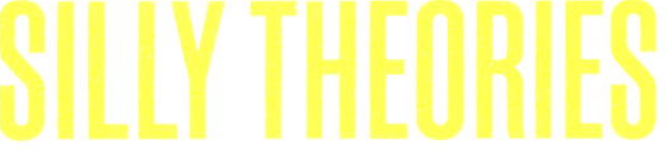

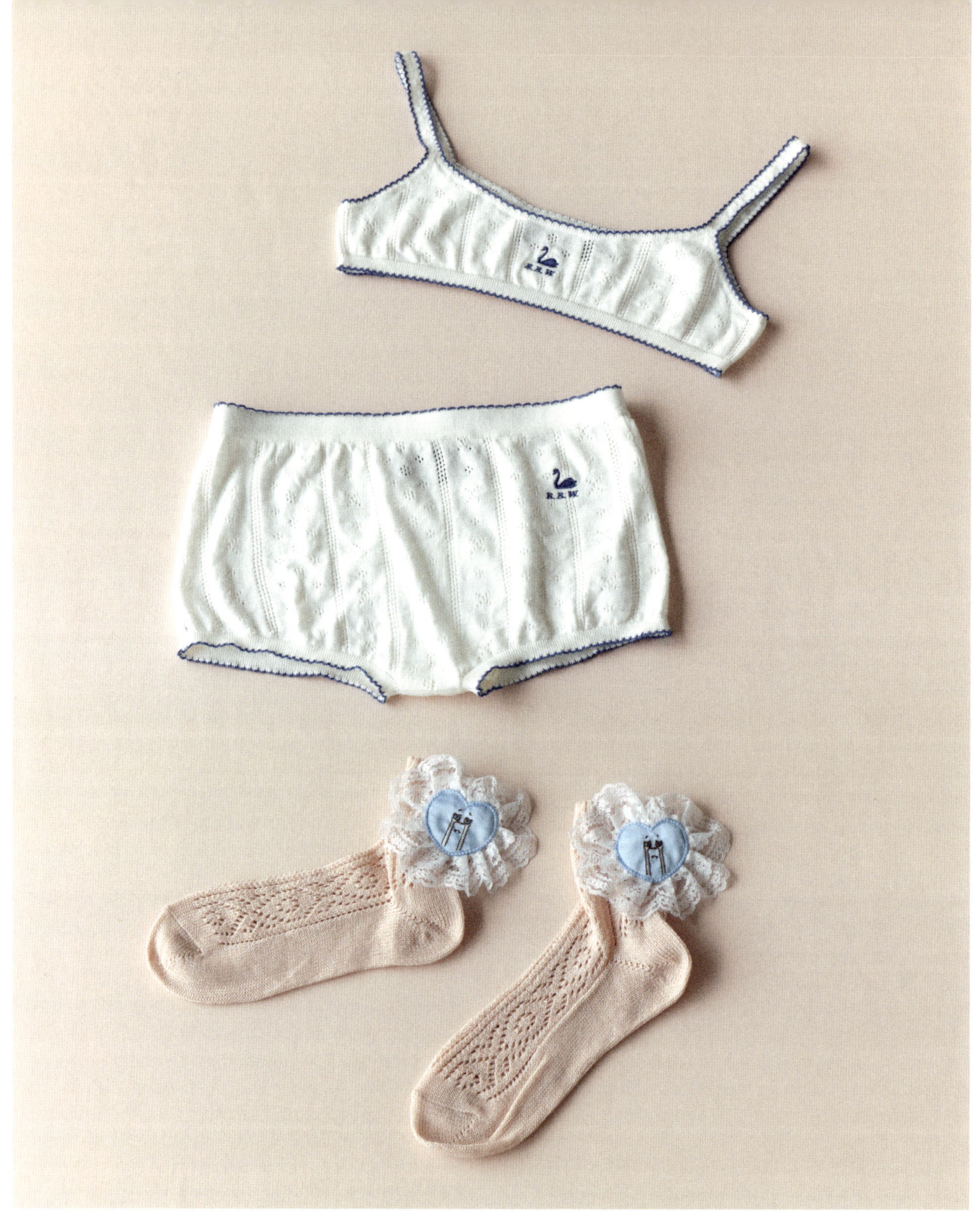

B.B. Wallace by Meryll Rogge Autumn-Winter 2025–2026, knitted underwear

Jenny Fax Spring-Summer 2024, crying heart socks

Ashley Williams (right)
Spring-Summer 2025

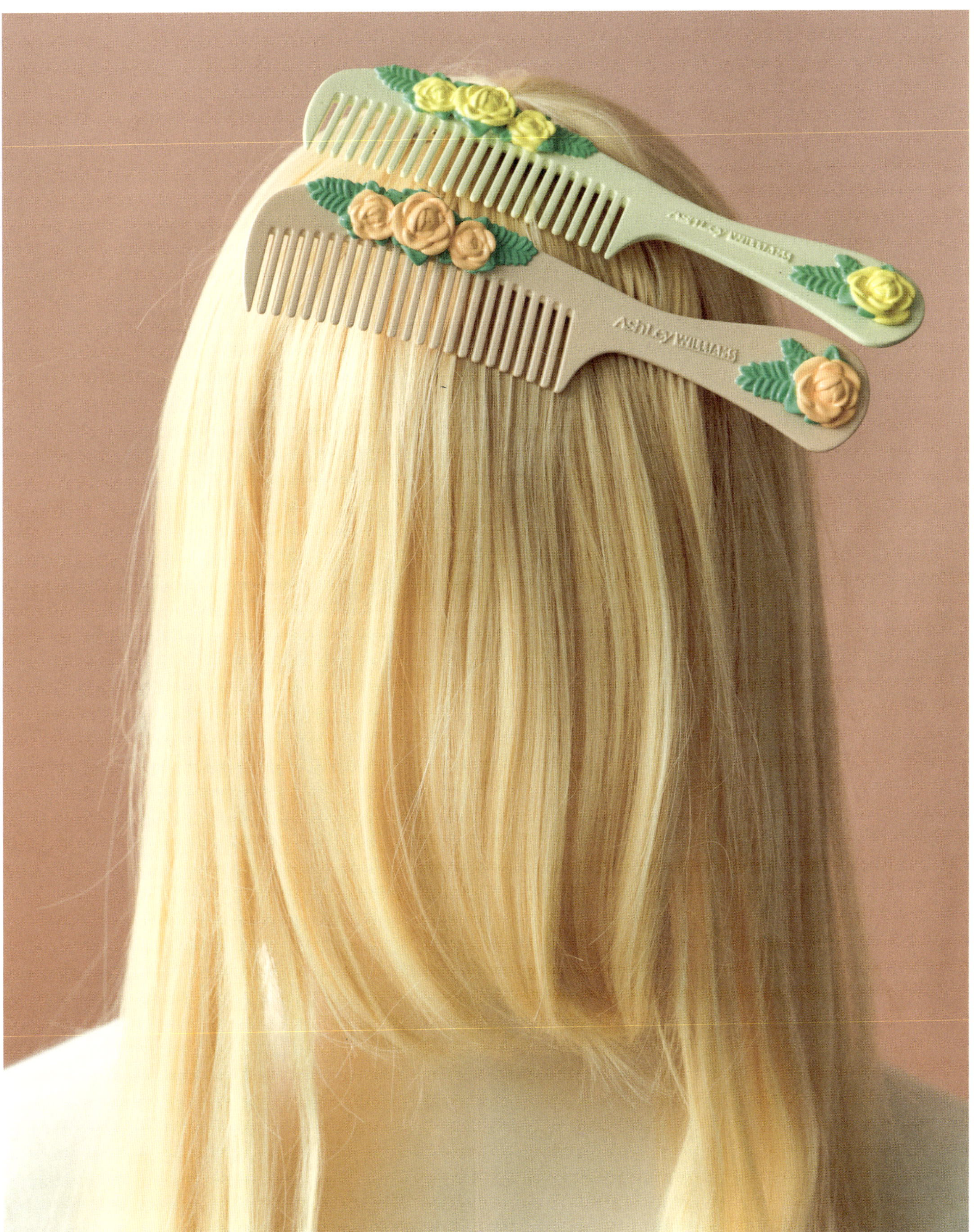
AshLey WILLIAMS
AshLey WILLIAMS

photo credits

P. 2 © Jim Britt
P. 4 © Mark Borthwick
P. 7 MSK Ghent, artinflanders.be.
Photo Dominique Provost,
© SABAM Belgium 2025
PP. 8–9 MoMu inv. T92/127,
© Frederik Vercruysse
PP. 10–11 © Frederik Vercruysse
P. 12 MoMu inv. T24/113/1-2,
© Frederik Vercruysse
P. 13 Design Museum Den Bosch Collection,
's-Hertogenbosch
P. 14 Courtesy of the artist and WeFolk
P. 16 © The Easton Foundation/SABAM,
Belgium 2025
P. 17 © The Easton Foundation/SABAM,
Belgium 2025
PP. 18–19 © The Easton Foundation/SABAM,
Belgium 2025
P. 20 Courtesy of The Fabric Workshop;
© The Easton Foundation/SABAM, Belgium
2025
P. 21 © The Easton Foundation/SABAM,
Belgium 2025. Photo Christopher Burke
P. 23 © Michella Bredahl
PP. 24–25 © Anuschka Blommers &
Niels Schumm
P. 26 Invitation MoMu Library inv. T18/510 and
dress MoMu inv. X4124 © Frederik Vercruysse
P. 29 © Frida Orupabo. Courtesy of the artist
and Stevenson, Cape Town, Johannesburg and
Amsterdam. Photo Michael Brzezinski
P. 30 © Courtesy of the artist and
Gladstone Gallery, New York
P. 31 © Courtesy of the artist and
Gladstone Gallery, New York
PP. 32–33 © Fish Zhang
PP. 34–35 Courtesy of the artist
P. 37 © Frederik Vercruysse
P. 39 Courtesy of the artist and
Xavier Hufkens, Brussels
PP. 40–41 © Jim Britt
PP. 42–43 Courtesy of the artist and
Xavier Hufkens, Brussels
P. 44 The Brand Family Collection.
Courtesy of the Estate of Alice Neel and
Xavier Hufkens, Brussels
P. 45 Courtesy of the Estate of Alice Neel and
Xavier Hufkens, Brussels
P. 46 Sainsbury Centre, University of East
Anglia. Photo © James Austin
P. 49 Museum Boijmans Van Beuningen
Collection, Rotterdam. Photo © Jannes Linders
PP. 50–51 Courtesy of the artist and
Daniel Faria Gallery, Toronto
PP. 52–53 Part of a series of 48 drawings.
Courtesy of the artist and Galerie Transit,
Mechelen
P. 54 © William Strobeck
P. 57 Photo 12/Alamy Stock Photo
P. 58 Pictorial Press Ltd/Alamy Stock Photo
P. 61 Moviestore Collection Ltd/
Alamy Stock Photo
P. 62 Collection Christophel/
Alamy Stock Photo, United Archives GmbH/
Alamy Stock Photo
P. 63 MoMu inv. T19/744,
© Frederik Vercruysse
P. 65 © AJ Pics/Alamy Stock Photo
PP. 67–69 © Sofia Coppola
P. 70 from left to right: Lady (Assa Sylla),
Adiatou (Lindsay Karamoh), Marieme/Vic
(Karidja Touré) and Fily (Mariétou Touré)
sing and dance to Rihanna's 'Diamonds' in
Céline Sciamma's *Girlhood* (2014)
P. 73 Top © Estelle Hanania,
bottom © Thaïs Despont
PP. 74–75 Part of a series of 48 drawings.
Courtesy of the artist and Galerie Transit,
Mechelen
P. 76 © Nancy Honey
PP. 78–79 Courtesy of the artist and
Kasmin Gallery, New York
PP. 80-87 Eimear Lynch/Institute
PP. 89–101 © Nancy Honey
PP. 102–107 © Sofia Coppola
PP. 108–112 American Zoetrope.
Photo © Frederik Vercruysse
P. 113 © Sofia Coppola
PP. 114–115 Lauren Greenfield/Institute
PP. 116–117 Lauren Greenfield/Institute
PP. 118–123 © Leticia Valverdes
P. 124 © Sofia Lai
P. 125 Photo © Luca Trevisani. The sculpture
is wearing: a Comme des Garçons mesh
corsage cupro collar, Comme des Garçons
see-through mesh leggings, vintage pink
silk and leather ballerina shoes, and vintage
stockings worn underneath.
P. 126 Photo © Luca Trevisani. The sculpture
is wearing: Junya Watanabe Comme des
Garçons rib-knit arm covers, Emilio Pucci
feather sandals, vintage silk underwear,
and a vintage bra.
PP. 127–128 © Sofia Lai
P. 129 Photo © Luca Trevisani. The sculpture
on the left is wearing: a dressing gown
by Comme des Garçons, a striped
scalloped T-shirt, a Comme des Garçons
poly cut-off design padded collar, vintage
stockings, and Comme des Garçons leather
switching-strap sandals. The sculpture on
the right is wearing: a dressing gown by
Comme des Garçons, a tulle-embellished
sleeveless vest, and vintage stockings.
PP. 130–131 © Sofia Lai
P. 132 © Nails by Mei
P. 134 © Petra Collins
P. 135 Petra Collins, *Red Selfie (Piper)*, 2014,
Green Selfie (Jackie), 2014, in: *Babe*, 2015
P. 136 Courtesy of Princess Gallery, New York
PP. 138 Part of a series of 48 drawings.
Courtesy of the artist and Galerie Transit,
Mechelen
P. 139 © Harley Weir. Courtesy of the artist
and Hannah Barry Gallery, London.
Photo © Damian Griffiths
P. 140 © Juergen Teller, all rights reserved
P. 143 Royal Museum of Fine Arts Antwerp
(KMSKA) – Flemish Community.
Photo Dominique Provost
P. 144 *The Age of Innocence*, c. 1788,
Sir Joshua Reynolds. Tate, London. Presented
by Robert Vernon, 1847. Photo © Tate
P. 147 © Jas Knight. Courtesy of the artist
Hannah Barry Gallery, London.
Photo © Damian Griffiths
PP. 148–149 © Juergen Teller, all rights reserved
P. 151 © Prada
P. 152 MoMu inv. T13/616/K47
© Frederik Vercruysse
P. 154 Rijksmuseum, Amsterdam, public domain
P. 157 Paris Musées/Palais Galliera,
Musée de la Mode de Paris, public domain
P. 159 La Bibliothèque des Arts Décoratifs,
Paris, public domain
P. 160 MoMu Library inv. 58.166
P. 161 La Bibliothèque des Arts Décoratifs,
Paris, public domain
P. 163 MoMu inv. T17/19, MoMu inv. T95/164 and
Private Collection © Frederik Vercruysse
P. 164 MoMu inv. X424, © Frederik Vercruysse
P. 165 MoMu inv. T13/742/K246,
© Frederik Vercruysse
P. 166 Collection Mu.ZEE, artsinflanders.be.
Photo © Cedric Verhelst
P. 167 © Frida Orupabo. Courtesy of the artist
and Stevenson, Cape Town, Johannesburg,
and Amsterdam. Photo Mario Todeschini
P. 168 MoMu inv. T13/821
© Frederik Vercruysse
P. 171 Micaiah Carter/International Art Advisory
LLC, New York
P. 172 © Maison Margiela
P. 175 MoMu Library inv. B18/1
P. 176 Archive Martin Margiela
PP. 178–179 © Nigel Shafran, assisted by
Melanie Ward
PP. 180-181 Part of a series of 48 drawings.
Courtesy of the artist and Galerie Transit,
Mechelen
P. 182 © Magda Archer
P. 184 © Jumbo Tsui, Styling Serafin Zielinski
PP. 186–189 © Frederik Vercruysse

This book is published in conjunction with the exhibition *GIRLS — On Boredom, Rebellion, and Being In-Between.* On view at MoMu — Fashion Museum Antwerp, from 27 September 2025 to 1 February 2026.

CURATOR
Elisa De Wyngaert

GUEST CURATOR FILM
Claire Marie Healy

EXHIBITION DESIGN
Janina Pedan

GRAPHIC DESIGN
Paul Boudens

MOMU — FASHION MUSEUM ANTWERP

DIRECTOR
Kaat Debo

BUSINESS MANAGEMENT
Sara Joukes

CURATORS
Romy Cockx
Elisa De Wyngaert

ASSISTANT CURATOR
Juliette de Waal

PRODUCTION MANAGEMENT
Marie Vandecasteele

ASSISTANT PRODUCTION
Kris Robbe

COLLECTION CURATOR
Wim Mertens

COLLECTION MANAGEMENT
Frédéric Boutié
Ellen Machiels
Pieter Pauwels
Wouter Pauwels
Belgiz Polat
Isabel Suengue
Kim Verkens
Danicia van Glanen-Weijgel

LIBRARY AND
DRIES VAN NOTEN STUDY CENTER
Birgit Ansoms
Hadewijch Bal
Ester Claes
Isabel Davis
Marguerite De Coster
Tobias Hendrickx
Dieter Suls
Stijn Van den Bulck
Eva Van den Ende
Ykje Wildenborg

PRESS AND COMMUNICATIONS
Michael Bex
David Flamée
Lies Verboven

EDUCATION AND EVENTS
Iris Adriaenssens
Leen Borgmans
Karl Kana
Shanti Ofori
Klaartje Patteet

PARTICIPATION
Jana Tricot

ADMINISTRATION
Diane Van Osta

MERCHANDISING MANAGER
Annik Pirotte

HOSPITALITY MANAGER
An Teyssen

WELCOME DESK
Lina Borgonjon
Aisja De Canne
Maaike Delsaerdt
Kristel Van den Wyngaert

FACILITY MANAGEMENT
Jan Maes

MAINTENANCE
Maria Sebastiao Viegas

SECURITY
In-house security provided by
AG Cultural Institutions Antwerp

LENDERS
American Zoetrope/Sofia Coppola
Ashley Williams
Chopova Lowena
Collection of Beth Rudin DeWoody
Daniel Faria Gallery, Toronto/Iris Häussler
Design Museum Den Bosch,
's-Hertogenbosch
D'heygere
Eimear Lynch
Fumiko Imano/WeFolk
Galerie Transit Mechelen
Hannah Barry Gallery/Harley Weir
Jenny Fax
Juergen Teller
Kasmin Gallery, New York/Tina Barney
Leticia Valverdes
Maison Margiela
Martin Margiela
Maya Man
Meryll Rogge
Micaiah Carter
Mu.ZEE, Ostend
Museum Boijmans van Beuningen,
Rotterdam
Museum of Fine Arts Ghent (MSK)
Nails by Mei
Nancy Honey
Nigel Shafran
Royal Museum of Fine Arts Antwerp
(KMSKA)
Sainsbury Centre, University of
East Anglia, Norwich
Senjan Jansen
Simone Rocha
Sofia Lai
The Easton Foundation, New York
Louise Bourgeois Archive, New York
Verbund Collection, Vienna

AND ALL LENDERS WHO WISH
TO REMAIN ANONYMOUS

WITH SPECIAL THANKS TO
Gladstone Gallery, New York
Xavier Hufkens, Brussels

COMPOSITION AND INTERVIEWS
Elisa De Wyngaert

AUTHORS
Peter Adriaenssens
Elisa De Wyngaert
Claire Marie Healy
Morna Laing
Wim Mertens
Alex Quicho

GRAPHIC DESIGN
Paul Boudens

IMAGE RIGHTS CLEARANCE
Birgit Ansoms
Marguerite De Coster
Juliette de Waal

LITHOGRAPHY
Pascal Van den Abbeele (Graphius)

PROJECT MANAGEMENT
Stephanie Van den bosch

TRANSLATION
Sandy Logan

COPY EDITING
Derek Scoins

PRINTING
Graphius, Ghent

BINDING
IBW, Oostkamp

PUBLISHER
Gautier Platteau

COVER IMAGES
Fumiko Imano, *Room 401/Paris/France*, 2018
Jim Britt, *Sisters*, 1976

ISBN 978 949 341 616 1
D/2025/11922/40
NUR 452

www.hannibalbooks.be
www.momu.be

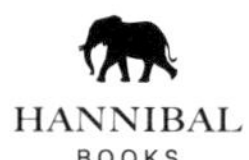

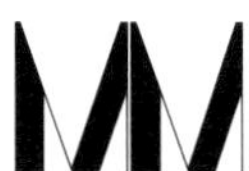
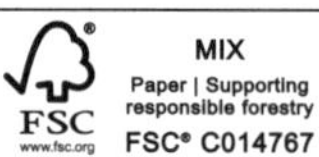